P9-BZV-549

THE
HANDY
ACCOUNTING
ANSWER
BOOK

About the Author

(photo by Darby Bullinger)

Amber K. Gray is a full-time accounting professor at Adrian College in Adrian, Michigan. She earned her bachelor's degree in business administration and master of science degree in accountancy from Western Michigan University. Gray currently serves on the Accounting Educators Task Force of the Michigan Association of Certified Public Accountants and is a member of the Institute of Management Accountants Educational Case Journal Editorial Advisory and Review Board. Prior to becoming a full-time accounting educator, Gray worked in public accounting and held various titles in corporate accounting such as accounting manager, assistant controller, and controller. During her time teaching at Adrian College, Gray earned the "Teacher of the Year" award and has been an honored guest at several leadership appreciation events. She has been published in the *International Journal of Business and Applied Social Science* and has presented at conferences and other events on behalf of the Michigan Association of Certified Public Accountants.

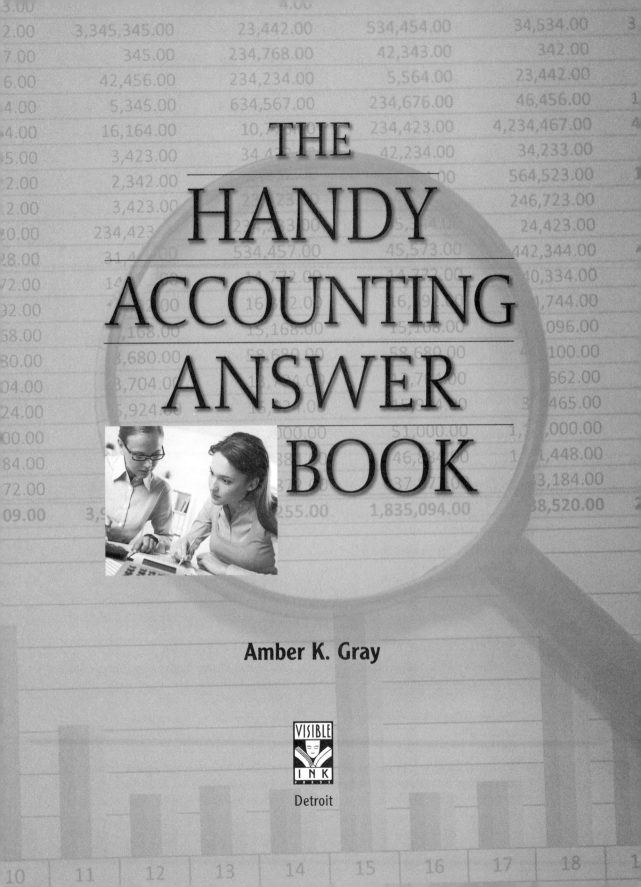

THE HANDY ACCOUNTING ANSWER BOOK

Amber K. Gray

VISIBLE INK PRESS

Detroit

Also from Visible Ink Press

The Handy African American History Answer Book
by Jessie Carnie Smith
ISBN: 978-1-57859-452-8

The Handy American Government Answer Book: How Washington, Politics, and Elections Work
by Gina Misiroglu
ISBN: 978-1-57859-639-3

The Handy American History Answer Book
by David L. Hudson Jr.
ISBN: 978-1-57859-471-9

The Handy Anatomy Answer Book, 2nd edition
by Patricia Barnes-Svarney and Thomas E. Svarney
ISBN: 978-1-57859-542-6

The Handy Answer Book for Kids (and Parents), 2nd edition
by Gina Misiroglu
ISBN: 978-1-57859-219-7

The Handy Art History Answer Book
by Madelynn Dickerson
ISBN: 978-1-57859-417-7

The Handy Astronomy Answer Book, 3rd edition
by Charles Liu
ISBN: 978-1-57859-419-1

The Handy Bible Answer Book
by Jennifer R. Prince
ISBN: 978-1-57859-478-8

The Handy Biology Answer Book, 2nd edition
by Patricia Barnes Svarney and Thomas E. Svarney
ISBN: 978-1-57859-490-0

The Handy Boston Answer Book
by Samuel Willard Crompton
ISBN: 978-1-57859-593-8

The Handy California Answer Book
by Kevin Hile
ISBN: 978-1-57859-591-4

The Handy Chemistry Answer Book
by Ian C. Stewart and Justin P. Lamont
ISBN: 978-1-57859-374-3

The Handy Christianity Answer Book
by Steve Werner
ISBN: 978-1-57859-686-7

The Handy Civil War Answer Book
by Samuel Willard Crompton
ISBN: 978-1-57859-476-4

The Handy Communication Answer Book
By Lauren Sergy
ISBN: 978-1-57859-587-7

The Handy Diabetes Answer Book
by Patricia Barnes-Svarney and Thomas E. Svarney
ISBN: 978-1-57859-597-6

The Handy Dinosaur Answer Book, 2nd edition
by Patricia Barnes-Svarney and Thomas E. Svarney
ISBN: 978-1-57859-218-0

The Handy English Grammar Answer Book
by Christine A. Hult, Ph.D.
ISBN: 978-1-57859-520-4

The Handy Forensic Science Answer Book: Reading Clues at the Crime Scene, Crime Lab, and in Court
by Patricia Barnes-Svarney and Thomas E. Svarney
ISBN: 978-1-57859-621-8

The Handy Geography Answer Book, 3rd edition
by Paul A. Tucci
ISBN: 978-1-57859-576-1

The Handy Geology Answer Book
by Patricia Barnes-Svarney and Thomas E. Svarney
ISBN: 978-1-57859-156-5

The Handy History Answer Book, 3rd edition
by David L. Hudson, Jr., J.D.
ISBN: 978-1-57859-372-9

The Handy Hockey Answer Book
by Stan Fischler
ISBN: 978-1-57859-513-6

The Handy Investing Answer Book
by Paul A. Tucci
ISBN: 978-1-57859-486-3

The Handy Islam Answer Book
by John Renard, Ph.D.
ISBN: 978-1-57859-510-5

The Handy Law Answer Book
by David L. Hudson, Jr., J.D.
ISBN: 978-1-57859-217-3

The Handy Literature Answer Book: An
Engaging Guide to Unraveling Symbols,
Signs, and Meanings in Great Works
By Daniel S. Burt, Ph.D., and Deborah G.
Felder
ISBN: 978-1-57859-635-5

The Handy Math Answer Book, 2nd edition
by Patricia Barnes-Svarney and Thomas E.
Svarney
ISBN: 978-1-57859-373-6

The Handy Military History Answer Book
by Samuel Willard Crompton
ISBN: 978-1-57859-509-9

The Handy Mythology Answer Book
by David A. Leeming, Ph.D.
ISBN: 978-1-57859-475-7

The Handy New York City Answer Book
by Chris Barsanti
ISBN: 978-1-57859-586-0

The Handy Nutrition Answer Book
by Patricia Barnes-Svarney and Thomas E.
Svarney
ISBN: 978-1-57859-484-9

The Handy Ocean Answer Book
by Patricia Barnes-Svarney and Thomas E.
Svarney
ISBN: 978-1-57859-063-6

The Handy Personal Finance Answer Book
by Paul A. Tucci
ISBN: 978-1-57859-322-4

The Handy Philosophy Answer Book
by Naomi Zack, Ph.D.
ISBN: 978-1-57859-226-5

The Handy Physics Answer Book,
2nd edition
by Paul W. Zitzewitz, Ph.D.
ISBN: 978-1-57859-305-7

The Handy Presidents Answer Book,
2nd edition
by David L. Hudson
ISB N: 978-1-57859-317-0

The Handy Psychology Answer Book,
2nd edition
by Lisa J. Cohen, Ph.D.
ISBN: 978-1-57859-508-2

The Handy Religion Answer Book,
2nd edition
by John Renard, Ph.D.
ISBN: 978-1-57859-379-8

The Handy Science Answer Book,
4th edition
by The Carnegie Library of Pittsburgh
ISBN: 978-1-57859-321-7

The Handy State-by-State Answer Book:
Faces, Places, and Famous Dates for All
Fifty States
by Samuel Willard Crompton
ISBN: 978-1-57859-565-5

The Handy Supreme Court Answer Book
by David L Hudson, Jr.
ISBN: 978-1-57859-196-1

The Handy Technology Answer Book
by Naomi E. Balaban and James Bobick
ISBN: 978-1-57859-563-1

The Handy Texas Answer Book
by James L. Haley
ISBN: 978-1-57859-634-8

The Handy Weather Answer Book,
2nd edition
by Kevin S. Hile
ISBN: 978-1-57859-221-0

The Handy Wisconsin Answer Book
by Terri Schlichenmeyer and Mark Meier
ISBN: 978-1-57859-661-4

PLEASE VISIT THE "HANDY ANSWERS" SERIES
WEBSITE AT WWW.HANDYANSWERS.COM.

THE HANDY ACCOUNTING ANSWER BOOK

Copyright © 2019 by Visible Ink Press®

This publication is a creative work fully protected by all applicable copyright laws, as well as by misappropriation, trade secret, unfair competition, and other applicable laws.

No part of this book may be reproduced in any form without permission in writing from the publisher, except by a reviewer who wishes to quote brief passages in connection with a review written for inclusion in a magazine, newspaper, or website.

All rights to this publication will be vigorously defended.

Visible Ink Press®
43311 Joy Rd., #414
Canton, MI 48187–2075
Visible Ink Press is a registered trademark of Visible Ink Press LLC.

Most Visible Ink Press books are available at special quantity discounts when purchased in bulk by corporations, organizations, or groups. Customized printings, special imprints, messages, and excerpts can be produced to meet your needs. For more information, contact Special Markets Director, Visible Ink Press, www.visibleink.com, or 734–667–3211.

Managing Editor: Kevin S. Hile
Art Director: Mary Claire Krzewinski
Typesetting: Marco DiVita
Proofreaders: Larry Baker and Shoshana Hurwitz
Indexer: Larry Baker

Cover images: Shutterstock.

Cataloging-in-Publication Data is on file at the Library of Congress.

ISBN: 978-1-57859-675-1

10 9 8 7 6 5 4 3 2 1

Printed in the United States of America.

Table of Contents

WHAT IS ACCOUNTING? ... 1

FASB'S CONCEPTUAL FRAMEWORK ... 11

FINANCIAL STATEMENT ELEMENTS ... 21

FOUR BASIC FINANCIAL STATEMENTS ... 35

FINANCIAL STATEMENT ANALYSIS ... 61

Dedication

This book is dedicated to Patrick, Lucas, and Olivia, whose patience, love, and support made writing this book possible. You guys are the best!

Acknowledgments

There are many people whose support and assistance made this book possible. I would like to thank Marsha Fielder for making me aware of this opportunity, Roger Jänecke and Kevin Hile for their support and brainstorming efforts, Patrick Quinlan for encouraging me to write, Keith Christy for motivating me to keep writing, and the rest of my colleagues at Adrian College for cheering me on in the process. Additionally, I'd like to thank Jack Ruhl of Western Michigan University for giving me my first teaching opportunity, and Jerry Kreuze, David Rozelle, and Chip Hines for helping me to see how cool accounting can be.

Photo Sources

Florida Times: p. 288.

Louvre Museum: p. 5.

Mblumber (Wikipedia): p. 7.

Museo Nazionale di Capodimonte: p. 6.

Shutterstock: pp. 3, 14, 16, 18, 20, 22, 25, 28, 36, 78, 82, 90, 107, 262, 269, 272, 276, 280, 284, 286.

U.S. Government: p. 283.

All line art by Amber K. Gray and Kevin Hile. Shutterstock images used in graphics created by Kevin Hile on pp. 164, 166, and 192.

Introduction

The study of accounting is often dreaded by business students. They seem to look at accounting as an unfortunate hurdle in the process of getting their business degree. My goal is to change their minds. A person cannot truly understand business without first understanding accounting. Most people know that profit is good and losses are bad, but they do not actually know what profit is or what transactions cause profit to increase or decrease. Accounting is the language of business. It is my hope that in reading this book, you will start to understand that language to make sense of business decisions that have been made and to understand the ramifications of those decisions.

Every item that shows up on a financial statement starts with a transaction. Accountants must analyze those transactions and record them in the accounting system. The accounting system summarizes the data and results in the preparation of financial reports. Those reports are consulted by both internal and external users to make decisions. Just as a good cook needs to understand how different ingredients and flavors work together in a recipe, a good business person needs to understand how various transactions impact the financial reports of the business.

This book touches on many aspects of accounting that are found in introductory accounting textbooks, such as how to prepare financial statements, how to calculate financial ratios, and how to budget. In addition, this book includes information that would be helpful to non-accountants who want to understand business better or perhaps start a small business one day. For them, it explains such important issues as business plans and employee payroll issues.

Many of the examples in this book are very simplistic so as to clearly illustrate basic accounting concepts. I have attempted to use examples that are relatable to most people. Not all accounting concepts are covered in this book, nor should they be. My hope is that this book will allow you to understand the language of business to be able to make better decisions, whether as an employee, owner, investor, or individual. Most importantly, I hope you enjoy it and find that you learn a little bit of something new and interesting.

—Amber K. Gray

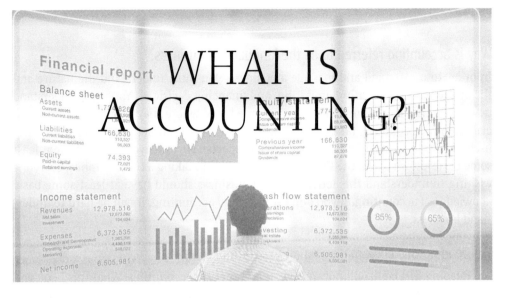

ACCOUNTING DEFINED

What is accounting?

Accounting is a system of record keeping designed to analyze, record, and summarize the activities of the business and report the results to users. The process of analyzing, recording, and summarizing these activities is discussed in detail in the chapter entitled "Bookkeeping and the Accounting Cycle."

What are the main activities of the business?

A business's activities can be divided into three main categories: operating, investing, and financing. Operating activities are those activities that involve running the business. For example, the operating activities of a Jimmy John's Sandwiches franchise would include buying ingredients and paying wages to employees. Investing activities are those activities that involve making an investment in your business or other business through the purchase of stock. For example, the investing activities of a Jimmy John's Sandwiches franchise could include buying the building for the restaurant and buying the furniture that goes in it. Financing activities are those activities that involve getting the funds necessary to cover the operating and investing activities of the business. A business can be financed with debt and/or equity. Debt involves borrowing money that must be paid back. Equity involves receiving investments from owners. For example, the financing activities for a Jimmy John's Sandwiches franchise could include any loans taken from the bank to finance the purchase of the building and any money contributed by the owners upon the start-up of the franchise. All of these activities must be recorded by the accounting system.

Why is accounting referred to as the language of business?

In order to understand and manage a business, you must understand the nature and the impacts of the operating, investing, and financing decisions. You must understand how transactions occur, how they are recorded, and where they show up in the financial reports. Accounting takes multitudes of data (daily transactions) and turns it into useful information (in the form of financial reports). Just like you would want at least some basic knowledge of the French language prior to taking a trip to France, everyone wishing to understand the activities of the business should have at least some basic knowledge of accounting. If you don't understand accounting, it will be hard to understand business.

Will reading this book make you an expert in accounting?

No. Reading this book will not make you an expert in accounting. What this book will do is give you some basic knowledge of both financial and managerial accounting so that you can better understand the business world and make more informed decisions. Think of it like taking a French/English dictionary with you on your trip to France. You won't be able to speak the language fluently, but you'll understand enough to have an enjoyable trip.

USERS OF ACCOUNTING INFORMATION

Who uses accounting information?

There are two basic types of users of financial information: external and internal. External users are those users who are outside the company. External users typically include creditors (people who loan the business money) and investors (stockholders). External users can also include other stakeholders, such as the government, customers, suppliers, etc. Internal users are those users who are inside the company. Internal users include executives, managers, supervisors, etc.

What type of financial information are external users most interested in?

External users are typically interested in evaluating the financial condition of the business to determine whether or not they will get a return on their investment or be paid back for any loans.

How is the accounting information reported to external users?

Information about the financial condition of the company is reported by the accounting system in the form of reports called financial statements. These reports provide information about the financial position, profitability, and cash flows of the business. Financial statements are covered in detail in the chapter entitled "Four Basic Financial Statements."

What type of financial information are internal users most interested in?

Internal users are typically interested in understanding the financial condition of the business so that they can make decisions to run the company. Decisions may range from day-to-day activities to the overall long-range strategy of the company.

How is the accounting information reported to internal users?

While internal users also rely on information provided in the financial statements, there are a large variety of other reports and information that are used by internal users. Examples of these reports include budgets, profitability by customer and by product analyses, and employee payroll data.

What is the difference between financial accounting and managerial accounting?

Financial accounting is directed toward preparing information for external users to evaluate the company. Financial accounting reports details about transactions that occurred in the past. Financial accounting places emphasis on precision and must follow the rules of accounting, called generally accepted accounting principles. Financial accounting is discussed in detail in the chapters entitled "FASB's Conceptual Framework," "Financial Statement Elements," Four Basic Financial Statements," "Bookkeeping and the Accounting Cycle," and "Specific Accounting Issues."

Internal users gain information about their business through financial statements provided by accountants. Various types of reports have to be reviewed to gain a complete picture of a company's financial health.

Conversely, managerial accounting is directed toward preparing information for internal users to use in running the business. Managerial accounting reports often emphasize a focus on decisions that will impact the future. Managerial accounting places an emphasis on having the data quickly in order to make decisions, and as such, many estimates are used. There are no prescribed formats for managerial accounting reports, and there are no rules that must be followed for managerial accounting. Managerial accountants work in the interest of the business and create whatever reporting formats they need to effectively run the business and make decisions. Managerial accounting is discussed in detail in the chapters entitled "Cost Accounting Basics," "Budgeting, Planning, and Controlling," and "Managerial Accounting Basics."

How are private accountants different from public accountants?

Private accountants are accountants who are employees of the business. Private accountants can be either financial or managerial accountants. As such, private accountants may focus their efforts on preparing financial information for external users or they may focus their efforts on preparing information for internal users. Public accountants are those accountants who work for an accounting firm and provide advice or perform tasks on behalf of their clients. Public accountants often provide tax advice, prepare tax returns, compile financial statements, or audit the financial statements of the business. Many businesses utilize both private and public accountants. For example, a Jimmy John's Sandwiches franchise may hire an employee as a bookkeeper to keep the day-to-day records of the business and also hire an accounting firm to compile quarterly financial statements and prepare tax returns.

How are accounting and finance different?

Finance is often described as the bridge between accounting and economics. Economics provides information about the environment in which businesses operate. Accounting provides detailed information about the results of the business. The field of finance utilizes accounting data and economic concepts to help make decisions affecting the financial results of the business. Finance and accounting roles and business functions often overlap. As such, it is a good idea for finance personnel to have a strong knowledge of accounting and for accounting personnel to have a strong knowledge of finance.

EARLY ACCOUNTING

What is the earliest known form of accounting?

The earliest known forms of accounting involved keeping track of inventory. Archaeologists have found accounting systems in Mesopotamia dating back to as early as 7000 B.C.E. These early accounting systems involved the utilization of clay tokens to keep track of items that were owned or exchanged. Different shapes of clay tokens related to different items. For example, a cylinder represented an animal. French archaeologist Denise Schmandt-Besserat first discovered that the token system was an early accounting system.

Did accountants really invent writing?

As discussed in the book *Double Entry* by Jane Gleeson-White, it does appear that accountants invented writing. The token system discussed above evolved through the ages. By 3500 B.C.E., there were more than three hundred token shapes used to record inventory. These tokens were stored in hollow, clay balls. Around 3300 B.C.E., the system evolved so that tokens were no longer stored in hollow, clay balls, but rather, the wet clay was flattened out, and the tokens were used to press an imprint of their shape onto the wet clay. This was essentially the creation of the world's first clay tablets. Eventually, this system evolved further. Rather than pressing the tokens onto the wet clay to record their shape, a stylus was used to draw the shape onto wet clay. Thus, as noted by Gleeson-White, writing was invented.

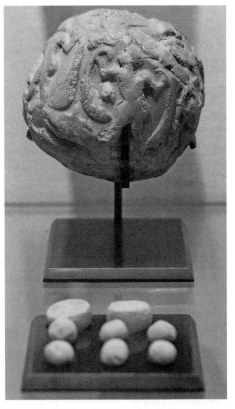

The ancient Mesopotamians used clay tokens like these (c. 3500 B.C.E.) on display at the Louvre Museum to keep track of items. Behind the tokens is a *Bulla,* a hollowed-out clay (or soft metal) envelope with a seal to contain smaller items such as these tokens.

When was modern accounting invented?

Our modern form of accounting, known as the double-entry system, dates back to around 1300.

Who invented modern accounting?

It is believed that modern accounting was first invented in Tuscany, Italy, by merchants. The earliest known records of double-entry accounting are from the Florentine merchants Rinieri Fini & Brothers and Giovanni Farolfi & Co., dating back to around 1300. By the 1430s, double-entry accounting had been perfected by the merchants of Venice.

Who is the father of modern accounting?

While not the inventor of modern accounting, Luca Bartolomeo de Pacioli is known as the father of accounting. He was an Italian mathematician, monk, and friend of Leonardo da Vinci. Pacioli was the first to codify and print the particulars of the double-entry account-

5

Franciscan friar and mathematician Luca Pacioli (at left) is considered to be the "Father of Accounting and Bookkeeping." He wrote the first book on double-entry bookkeeping (i.e., keeping track of both debits and credits by making entries in both the receiving and paying accounts).

ing system that is still in use today. Pacioli's publication on double-entry bookkeeping, entitled *Particularis de computis et scripturis,* was published in his mathematical encyclopedia in 1494. The title is translated to mean *Particulars of Reckonings and Writings.*

A VERY BRIEF HISTORY OF FINANCIAL ACCOUNTING IN THE UNITED STATES

How did the double-entry accounting system arrive in the United States?

The double-entry accounting system arrived in the United States with the European settlers. This was a trade passed down from master to apprentice.

When was the first American text on double-entry accounting written?

The first American double-entry accounting text was most likely the work of Thomas Sarjeant, entitled *An Introduction to the Counting House,* which was written in 1789.

How did the railroad industry impact accounting in the United States?

The boom of the railroad industry in the mid-1800s led to major advancements in accounting. Prior to the railroads, much of accounting was merely a function of bookkeeping. However, railroads were expensive and required a great deal of funds from investors. Additionally, the significant amount of assets required by the railroads led to a greater focus on accounting for depreciation. As these investors required greater details regarding their investments, accounting evolved to meet those needs. This helped lead to the emergence of published financial reports and the arrival in the 1880s of British chartered accountants to audit financial reports.

What was the first recognized professional accounting organization in the United States?

The first professional accounting organization recognized in the United States was the Institute of Accounts of New York, which was created in 1882 and had a focus on education of accountants and providing accounting literature. Similar organizations in other cities soon followed. The American Association of Public Accountants was formed in 1887 and has evolved into what is now the American Institute of Certified Public Accountants.

Deloitte Touche Tohmatsu Ltd. in Chicago is the modern version of Haskins & Sells, which was founded in America in 1895. It later merged with other auditing firms to become Deloitte.

Who formed the first major American auditing firm?

Two accountants, Charles Waldo Haskins and Elijah Watt Sells, both worked as book-keepers in the railroad industry and eventually for the government. They later got together and formed the first major auditing firm formed by Americans, Haskins & Sells, in 1895.

When was accounting first recognized as a profession in the United States?

The profession of accounting was first recognized in the United States in 1896 by the passing of a law in New York. The title of certified public accountant (CPA) was only given to people who had passed state examinations and had three years of experience in the field.

When did accounting practices in the United States become more standardized?

The stock market crash of 1929 led users of financial information to question the reliability of financial reports. Accordingly, Congress passed the Securities Acts of 1933 and 1934 to boost investor confidence. The Securities and Exchange Commission (SEC) was created by the 1934 Securities Act whereby Congress gave the SEC the authority to set accounting standards (rules) for publicly traded companies.

Does the SEC still have authority to set accounting standards?

Yes, it does, but it delegates that task to the private sector. Additionally, as a result of the large accounting frauds uncovered in the 1990s, Congress passed the Sarbanes–Oxley Act in 2002, which created the Public Company Accounting Oversight Board (PCAOB) to develop standards for the audits of public companies. The standards developed by the PCAOB are subject to the approval of the SEC.

What was the first private sector organization to set accounting rules under the authority of the SEC?

The first organization that was delegated the task of setting accounting standards was the Committee on Accounting Procedure (CAP). The CAP set accounting standards from 1938 to 1959. The CAP never created a theoretical framework for accounting but rather just issued rules addressing specific accounting issues. It was therefore criticized by the profession and later replaced.

What organization replaced the Committee on Accounting Procedure?

The second organization that was delegated the task of setting accounting standards was the Accounting Principles Board (APB), which was in operation from 1959 to 1973. Like the CAP, the APB was criticized for numerous reasons, including lack of creation of a conceptual framework, lack of efficiency, and lack of independence from the audit firms with which its members had relationships.

What organization replaced the Accounting Principles Board?

The third organization to be delegated the task of setting accounting standards was the Financial Accounting Standards Board (FASB), which was created in 1973. The FASB is still in place today as the standard setter for U.S. accounting. The FASB is discussed in more detail in the chapter entitled "FASB's Conceptual Framework."

How are the accounting standards organized?

As there are thousands of U.S. generally accepted accounting principle (GAAP) pronouncements (standards), the FASB implemented the Accounting Standards Codification in 2009 to help organize the multitude of pronouncements into approximately 90 topics, displayed using a consistent structure. The Codification can be accessed at www.fasb.org.

How did the development of modern technology impact the field of accounting?

Throughout the 1970s and 1980s, the inventions and utilization of personal computers, fax machines, and cell phones impacted the accounting profession in the ability to compute and share knowledge more efficiently and created the need for new accounting skills. The 1983 introduction of the spreadsheet software Lotus 1-2-3 was a first step into database accounting. Additionally, EDGAR, the electronic financial reporting filing system used by the SEC, was developed in the 1990s.

What other fields of accounting emerged in the United States?

Aside from financial accounting, the passage of the U.S. income tax law in 1913 created a demand for tax accounting practices. Additionally, cost accounting in the United States developed in the early 1800s (prior to financial accounting), as textile manufacturers used cost accounting techniques to estimate the labor and overhead costs required to turn materials into finished fabric.

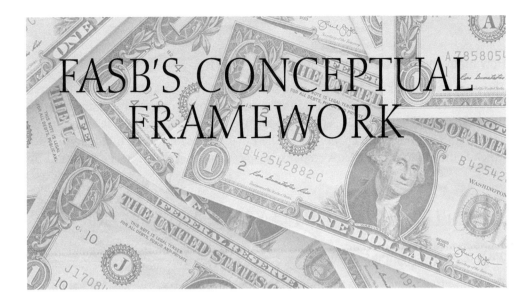

FASB'S CONCEPTUAL FRAMEWORK

THE FASB

What is the FASB?

The FASB (pronounced FAZ-bee) is the Financial Accounting Standards Board. The FASB is an independent, not-for-profit organization that establishes financial accounting and reporting standards for public companies, private companies, and not-for-profit organizations that follow generally accepted accounting principles (GAAP). The mission of the FASB is "to establish and improve financial accounting and reporting standards to provide useful information to investors and other users of financial reports and educate stakeholders on how to most effectively understand and implement those standards."

What is GAAP?

GAAP (pronounced gap) stands for generally accepted accounting principles. Put simply, generally accepted accounting principles are the rules that accountants must follow when recording and presenting accounting information. The FASB is responsible for setting those rules.

What authority does the FASB have?

The Securities and Exchange Commission (SEC) has designated the FASB as the accounting standard setter for public companies. Additionally, the American Institute of CPAs (AICPA) and state Boards of Accountancy also recognize the FASB as the authoritative standard setter for accounting in the United States.

When was the FASB created?

The FASB was established in 1973.

11

How many members are on the board of the FASB?

There are seven members on the board of the FASB who serve full-time and are required to cut all ties to the firms or institutions they worked for before serving on the board of the FASB. Board members are appointed for five-year terms and may serve up to ten years. FASB members are appointed by the Financial Accounting Foundation (FAF), which is the organization that is responsible for supporting and overseeing the FASB.

THE CONCEPTUAL FRAMEWORK

What is the conceptual framework?

The conceptual framework is the foundation that all accounting rules (GAAP) are based upon. The conceptual framework is to accounting what the U.S. Constitution is to the United States. The conceptual framework lays the groundwork for the rules of accounting much as the Constitution lays the framework for the laws of our country.

According to the FASB, "The Conceptual Framework is a coherent system of interrelated objectives and fundamental concepts that prescribes the nature, function, and limits of financial accounting and reporting and that is expected to lead to consistent guidance. It is intended to serve the public interest by providing structure and direction to financial accounting and reporting to facilitate the provision of unbiased financial and related information. That information helps capital and other markets to function efficiently in allocating scarce resources in the economy and society."

What are the Concepts Statements?

The conceptual framework is made up of several Concepts Statements issued by the FASB. Per the FASB, "Concepts Statements are intended to set forth objectives and fundamental concepts that will be the basis for development of financial accounting and reporting guidance." Concepts Statements Nos. 1, 2, and 3 have been superseded. Concepts Statement No. 4 relates to nonbusiness organizations. Concepts Statements Nos. 5, 6, 7, and 8 provide the key concepts for external financial reporting. These statements address the objective of financial reporting; the qualitative characteristics of financial reporting; the elements of financial reporting; recognition, measurement, and disclosure concepts; and the constraints of financial reporting, all of which are discussed in this chapter.

What is the objective of financial reporting?

The objective of financial reporting is to provide financial information that is useful to external users. External users are people outside the entity: namely, investors and creditors. Investors include both existing investors and potential investors. Creditors include both lenders and suppliers to the company.

QUALITATIVE CHARACTERISTICS

What are the qualitative characteristics of useful financial information?

The two fundamental characteristics of useful information according to the FASB are relevance and faithful representation. In addition to relevance and faithful representation, the FASB has also identified four enhancing characteristics of useful information: comparability, verifiability, timeliness, and understandability. These characteristics make information useful to external users.

What is relevance in the context of financial reporting?

In order for financial information to be relevant, it must make a difference in the decision process of the user. According to the FASB, information is relevant if it has predictive value and/or confirmatory value. If information has predictive value, that means it is useful to the user in predicting what future results might be. For example, looking at the net income from this year may help the user predict what next year's net income might be. Likewise, information has confirmatory value if it helps the user confirm or change prior assumptions about financial information. For example, if it is predicted that a company's net income will continue to increase over the next five years, the user can look at the net income each year to help confirm or change that prediction. In addition to predictive value and confirmatory value, materiality also impacts the usefulness of financial information.

What is materiality?

Financial information is considered material if its omission or misstatement would be significant enough to impact a user's decision. Materiality can be both quantitative and qualitative. For example, if McDonald's were to make a $10 revenue error on its financial statements, that would be considered quantitatively immaterial as compared to the total revenue of approximately $24.6 billion for 2016. As a matter of fact, the McDonald's Corp. financial statements are rounded to millions. So, really, errors or omissions between $1 and $49,000 wouldn't necessarily even change the appearance of the financial statements due to rounding. Essentially, a user wouldn't even notice the $10 if it were there, and as such, its omission or misstatement would not change the user's decision, and it would be quantitatively immaterial. However, if that $10 misstatement was enough to take McDonald's from having a net loss (negative) of $8 to a net income (positive) of $2, that would be considered qualitatively material, as it changes the overall financial information from a loss situation to a profit situation. Fortunately, for McDonald's, its 2016 net income was approximately $4.7 billion, so a potential $10 error in sales revenue would be both quantitatively and qualitatively immaterial, meaning that it wouldn't make a difference to the user whether it was there or not.

What is faithful representation?

Faithful representation means that the user can rely on the information as being presented truthfully. The technical definition of faithful representation means that there is

A successful company such as McDonald's has yearly earnings in the billions. Because of this, if there is an accounting error in the thousands, it will go pretty much unnoticed in financial statements because of rounding numbers to the millions. Therefore, such mistakes go unnoticed by shareholders.

agreement between a measure or description and the object that the measure is supposed to represent. For example, if a financial statement says "cash," the user will understand that this represents currency on hand and in checking and savings accounts, not a pile of beans kept in a drawer somewhere. The FASB breaks faithful representation down further into three components: completeness, neutrality, and freedom from errors.

Information is considered to be complete if it includes all the information necessary for faithful representation. This is similar in nature to materiality in that omitting a portion of information (being incomplete) can cause the information to be misleading and thus not represented faithfully.

Information is considered to be neutral if it is free from bias. The FASB is tasked with setting accounting rules that result in financial information that is free from bias and thus represents the true nature of each transaction. This can be a difficult challenge when political pressures arise, and interest groups argue for accounting rules that may be more advantageous to their institutions.

Finally, faithful representation is enhanced when information is free from error. While this sounds quite obvious, there are actually many estimates made in accounting and financial information. Those estimates can result in inaccuracies or errors in financial information. For example, accountants are required to estimate the amount of money that customers owe them that may eventually be uncollected (called bad debts). There is no way to know that information for sure, so accountants must rely on estimates and use their best judgment. Accordingly, estimates are considered to be faithfully represented when the user is made aware of the fact that the amount contains an estimate.

Why is conservatism not included in the conceptual framework?

Conservatism in the accounting sense generally refers to the idea that when in doubt, an accountant should err on the side of underestimating good news and overestimating bad news. However, this sentiment is rejected by the FASB in Concepts Statement No. 8, as conservatism is in direct contrast with neutrality, as described above. Conservatism adds bias, which is in opposition to being neutral. Regardless of the FASB's rejection of conservatism, many accountants employ conservatism in their estimates under the thought that users of financial information are typically less unhappy when results turn out better than expected versus when results turn out worse than expected, as common sense would tell you.

What is comparability?

Comparability enhances the usefulness of financial information by making financial information comparable across different companies and over time. For example, the financial statements of McDonald's Corp. can be compared to the financial statements of Wendy's Co. This comparison enhances the usefulness of the financial information contained in both companies' financial statements. For instance, McDonald's had total sales revenue in 2016 of approximately $24.6 billion, as compared to Wendy's total sales revenue of approximately $1.4 billion for the same period. Because users know that McDonald's and Wendy's are recording sales revenue according to the same rules, those two figures can be compared to each other to determine which company has more sales, etc.

Additionally, comparability means that you can compare information over time. For example, when looking at Wendy's Co. financial statements, you can see that sales revenues for 2014 were approximately $2 billion, sales revenues for 2015 were approximately $1.9 billion, and sales revenues for 2016 were approximately $1.4 billion. Knowing that Wendy's has followed the same rules for accounting for sales each year means that the user can determine that there was a downward trend in sales revenue for Wendy's over the three-year period noted. Likewise, when looking at McDonald's Corp. financial statements, you can see that sales revenues for 2014 were approximately $27.4 billion, sales revenues for 2015 were approximately $25.4 billion, and sales revenues for 2016 were approximately $24.6 billion. Users can note a similar downward trend over the three-year period. This information can be very useful to investors or creditors deciding to invest in the company or extend credit to the company.

It should be noted that accounting rules sometimes give the accountants a choice between several alternatives in how to record certain transactions. Accountants are required to disclose those choices to the users so that users are informed as they compare across companies and across time periods, as this would affect the comparability and consistency of the financial information.

What is verifiability?

Verifiability means that the financial information should be able to be independently verified, or audited. For example, if an entity says it has $1 million cash, an auditor should be able to verify that by obtaining a statement from the bank and performing a reconciliation. Obviously, verifiability enhances the usefulness of financial information, as users would be able to have more confidence in the reported information.

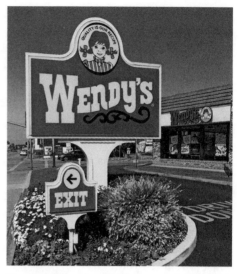

Comparability works well when comparing two similar companies. For example, if you are analyzing the profitability of the fast food chain Wendy's, a good comparison company would be McDonald's or, perhaps, Burger King.

What is timeliness?

Timeliness means that users have the financial information in enough time to use it in their decision-making process. Information that is not timely is not useful. For example, if a company were to issue 2016 financial statements in the year 2020, that would be very untimely and quite useless for making decisions about 2017. In order to make decisions about 2017 and beyond, users would require 2016 information as soon as reasonably possible after the end of the 2016 year. Accordingly, to enhance the usefulness of information, the SEC requires publicly traded companies to report financial information every quarter and every year, and it sets deadlines for when this information must be published.

What is understandability?

Information is considered to be understandable when a reasonably informed user can comprehend it. If a user cannot understand the information, then the information is not useful. Note that this definition of understandable includes the words "reasonably informed" user. As such, financial information may not be comprehensible to an elementary school student but should be comprehensible to a user with a reasonable understanding of business and economics.

What is the key constraint of financial reporting?

The overarching constraint of financial reporting is that the benefits of the information outweigh the costs of providing that information. This is known as the cost effectiveness constraint. The costs of providing the information are the burden of the preparer and involve collecting, processing, and distributing the financial information. The benefits of the financial information are in providing external users with better decision-making ability. When the FASB makes rules, it attempts to determine the cost effectiveness of the new rule. For example, a rule that enhances financial transparency in such a way that it only provides a slight benefit to the external users but will cost companies considerable time, money, and effort to implement would not meet the cost effectiveness constraint and would most likely not be implemented.

ELEMENTS OF FINANCIAL STATEMENTS

What are the elements of financial statements?

The FASB identifies ten elements of the financial statements. These elements are the building blocks that accountants can use to construct the financial statements. The ten elements are: assets, liabilities, equity, investments by owners, distributions to owners, revenues, expenses, gains, losses, and comprehensive income. The ten elements are discussed in detail in the chapter entitled "Financial Statement Elements."

What are the underlying assumptions of financial information?

There are four underlying assumptions of financial information that are not explicitly stated in the Concepts Statements. As these are assumptions, a reader can assume these four things when looking at financial information. The assumptions are: the separate entity assumption, the going-concern assumption, the time period assumption, and the monetary unit assumption.

What is the separate entity assumption?

The separate entity assumption is the assumption that the activities of the business are separate from the activities of the owner. Put another way, the activities recorded in the financial reports of a business reflect only the activities of that business. For example, the owner of a car wash business should not include his or her personal residence as part of the assets of the business.

What is the going-concern assumption?

The going-concern assumption is the assumption that the business will continue to operate into the foreseeable future. If a business does not believe that it will be able to meet its financial obligations through the next twelve months, it must disclose that information to users. Some common factors that could signal a decline in a company's ability to continue as a going concern are loss of a key customer, negative operating cash flows, and declining sales, among many others.

What is the time period assumption?

The time period assumption is the assumption that the long life of a business can be divided up and measured in shorter periods, such as a month, a quarter, or a year. It is common for small businesses to report results on a quarterly and annual basis and for larger companies to report results on a monthly, quarterly, and annual basis.

What is the monetary unit assumption?

The monetary unit assumption is the assumption that the activities of the business should be reported according to a common unit of measure, which is the U.S. dollar in the United States. For example, U.S. companies that do business internationally translate their foreign currency into U.S. dollars prior to issuing financial statements.

The common unit of measure in the United States is, of course, the U.S. dollar. Companies outside the United States convert their currency to dollars when issuing statements to American companies.

RECOGNITION, MEASUREMENT, AND DISCLOSURE CONCEPTS

What are the recognition, measurement, and disclosure concepts?

The recognition, measurement, and disclosure concepts tell accountants when to record a transaction, how much to record, and what additional details should be revealed to the users of financial statements regarding that transaction. Recognition deals with "when," measurement deals with "how much," and disclosure deals with "additional details." Each concept is discussed below.

What are the general recognition criteria?

Recognition deals with knowing when to record a transaction. In general, four criteria must be met in order to record a transaction in the accounting records. First, an item must meet the definition of a financial statement element, as discussed in the chapter entitled "Financial Statement Elements." Second, it must be measurable with sufficient reliability. Third, the information about the item must be relevant, in that it is capable of making a difference in a user's decision. Fourth, it must be reliable, in that the information is representationally faithful, verifiable, and neutral. In addition to these four criteria, recognition of any item in the financial statements is subject to the cost effectiveness constraint and the materiality threshold, as discussed earlier in this chapter.

Are all items subject to the same recognition criteria?

No. In addition to the four general criteria noted above, there are specific revenue and expense recognition rules that must be followed.

When is revenue recognized?

Revenue should be recognized (recorded in the financial statements) when goods or services are transferred to customers for the amount the company expects to be entitled to receive in exchange for those goods or services. Revenue may be recorded at a specific point in time or over time. For example, Pizza Hut recognizes revenue at a point in time when it sells a pizza. However, a landlord that rents a restaurant building to Pizza Hut recognizes revenue over time (each month) while Pizza Hut is its tenant.

It is important to note that revenue can be recognized before payment is received, at the same time payment is received, or after payment is received. Revenue is recognized when it is earned, not necessarily when payment is received. For example, Pizza Hut generally receives payment the same time it sells a pizza, thus it would record revenue in the same month as the cash payment. However, Pizza Hut may sell gift cards, thus receiving cash before it has actually earned any revenue by selling pizza. In that case, Pizza Hut would record the revenue after the month it received the cash. Likewise, a landlord that rents a restaurant building to Pizza Hut for the month of January may not receive payment from Pizza Hut until February. Accounting rules would tell the landlord to recognize the rent revenue in January, when it was earned, regardless of the fact that it won't be paid until the following month. Revenue is discussed further in the chapter entitled "Financial Statement Elements."

When are expenses recognized?

Expenses should be recognized in the period in which they are incurred to generate revenues. This is known as the matching principle. Expenses that have an exact cause-and-effect relationship or an associated relationship with sales revenue should be recorded in the same period as the revenue. For example, in the same month that Pizza Hut records the sale of a pizza, it should also record the expense of the dough for that pizza. Likewise, the monthly salary of the general manager of Pizza Hut should be recorded in the same month the manager performed the work. Even though the general manager did not make the pizzas that month, he or she had an indirect relationship to the sales of pizzas that month. Expenses that aren't directly related to sales should be allocated to the time period in which they were incurred. For example, if a Pizza Hut store spent $5,000 on coupon inserts for January, it should record the expense of those inserts in January, when it was incurred.

It is important to note that expenses can be recognized before payment is made, at the same time payment is made, or after payment is made. Expenses are recognized when they are incurred, not necessarily when payment is made. For example, Pizza Hut may pay for coupon inserts at the same time it receives them, thus recording the expense and the cash payment at the same time. However, it may pay rent in the month after it has used the building, thus recording the expense the month before it pays the cash. Likewise, it may pay for dough in the month before it uses it to make pizzas, thus recording the expense in the month after it pays the cash. Accounting rules would tell Pizza Hut to recognize the expenses when they are incurred, regardless of the fact that it may pay for it during a different month. Expenses are discussed further in the chapter entitled "Financial Statement Elements."

What is accrual basis accounting?

The revenue recognition principle and expense recognition principle make up the foundation for accrual basis accounting. Accordingly, accrual basis accounting means that revenues are recorded when earned and expenses are recorded when incurred, regardless of when cash is received or paid. Accrual basis accounting is required under generally acceptable accounting principles.

Expenses that are incurred during the same period as sales have an associated relationship with income. For example, the costs of delivering pizzas to customers need to be recorded concurrently with the sales from those pizzas, in arriving at net income.

What are the measurement attributes?

The measurement principle tells accountants what amount should be recognized for a particular financial item or transaction. There are five measurement attributes listed in Concepts Statement No. 5, which are: historical cost, net realizable value, current cost, present value of future cash flows, and fair value. Put simply, different items are measured different ways. For example, land is recorded at historical cost, which means land shows up in the financial statements at whatever amount was originally paid for it, regardless of its current market value. However, certain financial assets, such as investments in stocks held in an active trading account, are recorded at fair value, which may change over time. As this can get quite complex, these attributes are typically covered in intermediate to advanced accounting textbooks.

What is the full-disclosure principle?

The full-disclosure principle requires that any information that is not included in the primary financial statements that would affect the decisions of the users should be disclosed to the users. There are several ways in which these disclosures can be accomplished. Some disclosures are included right on the face of the financial statements, known as parenthetical disclosure. For example, companies report the number of shares of stock outstanding right on the face of the balance sheet in parentheses. Certain disclosures are made through the notes to the financial statements, in paragraph form, following the financial statements. Other disclosures are made by including supplemental schedules or tables that contain more detail than what is shown on the face of the financial statements. A copy of the annual report for Vera Bradley, Inc., is included in Appendix 2, showing examples of each of these types of disclosures. Additional discussion on disclosures is covered in the chapter entitled "Four Basic Financial Statements."

FINANCIAL STATEMENT ELEMENTS

ELEMENTS

What is a financial statement element?

According to the FASB, "elements of financial statements are the building blocks with which financial statements are constructed—the classes of items that financial statements comprise." These elements represent the major classifications of accounts shown on the financial statements.

What is an account?

An account is used to track the increases and decreases in specific financial statement elements. They are used to report the business activities of the entity. Each financial statement element may have many different accounts that roll up into that one classification. For example, cash is one typical account that is used in business. It rolls up in the "assets" element, as described later in this chapter.

How many financial statement elements are there?

The FASB identifies ten elements of the financial statements: assets, liabilities, equity, investments by owners, distributions to owners, comprehensive income, revenues, expenses, gains, and losses.

Why is it important to understand the definitions of the financial statement elements?

Each of the above mentioned elements are listed on the financial statements of a business. In order to understand the financial statements and make informed decisions, a reader must understand the building blocks that make up those financial statements.

For example, if a reader sees assets on a financial statement, the reader should have a general idea of whether assets are a good thing to have or a bad thing to have, etc. In addition, many financial statements use general headings with the element titles and don't list specific accounts. As such, having a good understanding of what types of accounts could be listed under that element is very helpful.

ASSETS

What is an asset?

According to the FASB, "assets are probable future economic benefits obtained or controlled by a particular entity as a result of past transactions or events." Assets are economic resources the business owns or controls. Put very simply, you can think of assets as the stuff the business owns.

What accounts fall under the asset element?

There are many accounts that fall under the asset category. One of the most common asset accounts is cash. Other common asset accounts are accounts receivable, inventory, and prepaid expenses.

How does an accountant determine which asset account titles to use?

While there are some very typical asset accounts that almost all companies use (cash, inventory, etc.), account titles can be tailored to the specific entity. Some account titles

Assets include things that a company owns. For example, the U-Haul moving truck company's fleet of trucks represent a significant asset for the business even when they are not in use.

have names that are not easily identifiable. As such, the classification under each element becomes very important. For example, if the financial statement user does not know what "television costs and advances" means, but he or she can see that this account is classified as an asset (as is done on the Walt Disney Co. financial statements), he or she can surmise that this is something the entity owns that should provide value in the future.

What does the cash account represent?

The cash account represents the entity's money. Cash can include funds in checking and savings accounts, petty cash on hand, or cash equivalents.

What is a cash equivalent?

Cash equivalents are those investments the company holds that will mature, and thus be turned into cash, within the next three months. As they will be realized in cash in the very near future, these investments are considered equivalent to cash and shown with cash on the financial statements.

What is accounts receivable?

Accounts receivable is the account that is used to record amounts owed to the business by its customers. Many businesses provide goods or services to other businesses and send an invoice for payment to the customer. The amounts unpaid by the customers are shown in the accounts receivable account. In essence, these are the amounts that are to be received from the customer. For example, if you go to the hospital and are later sent a bill for $500, the hospital records that $500 as an asset (accounts receivable). Because you owe the hospital $500, that I.O.U. has value for it. It will be able to use your $500 when it receives it to pay for other things. Thus, that $500 receivable should provide future economic benefits for the hospital, thereby meeting the definition of an asset.

What are "net" accounts receivable?

Accounts receivable are recorded as the amount owed, less an estimate for what won't be collected due to customer nonpayment. Financial statements show this amount as "net accounts receivable." This is covered in more detail in the chapter entitled "Specific Accounting Issues."

What are notes receivable?

Notes receivable are formal, documented loans to others (called promissory notes). These loans can be short term or long term and typically require payment of interest. In many cases when a customer is having difficulty paying an account receivable, the amount due may be negotiated into a formal loan, giving the customer longer payment terms in exchange for interest charges.

What is inventory?

Inventory is property the entity owns that is being held to sell to customers or that will be used to produce the goods to sell to customers. For example, Target Corp. has stores filled with clothing, food items, electronics, etc., waiting to be sold to customers. These items are considered inventory. Additionally, Ford Motor Company may have parts awaiting vehicle assembly, such as wheels, tires, and windshields. That inventory is intended to be used to make a product that will be sold to customers, thus generating an eventual cash payment from the customer.

What is a prepaid expense?

A prepaid expense represents a resource that an entity has paid for in advance. Common examples of prepaid expenses are prepaid rent and prepaid insurance. For example, if a business pays $2,000 for its 2018 liability insurance on December 31, 2017, it will record an asset called "prepaid insurance" for that amount. Just as an accounts receivable represents an I.O.U. from the customer, prepaid insurance represents an I.O.U. from the insurance agency. Rather than owing the business cash, the insurance agency owes the business liability coverage for the next twelve months. The same is true for "prepaid rent," where the landlord would owe the business occupancy for the prepaid time period.

Why is a prepaid expense an asset instead of an expense?

The prepaid expense name can be very misleading. These are items the company has prepaid for. Accordingly, the service provider (landlord, insurance agent, etc.) owes the company something. That I.O.U. represents a probable future economic benefit obtained or controlled by the entity as a result of a past transaction, meeting the definition of an asset. These prepaid expenses will be adjusted as they are used up and eventually recorded as an expense, as covered in the chapter "Bookkeeping and the Accounting Cycle."

What is a long-lived tangible asset?

Long-lived tangible assets are assets that have a physical, or tangible, substance that the entity intends to use in the business for at least one or more years. Long-lived tan-

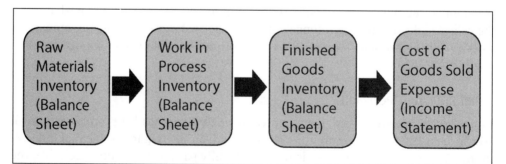

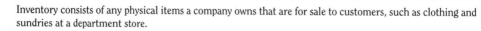
Inventory consists of any physical items a company owns that are for sale to customers, such as clothing and sundries at a department store.

gible assets are commonly referred to as "property, plant, and equipment" on the financial statements, "PP&E" for short, or "fixed assets." Examples of long-lived tangible assets include land, buildings, equipment, machinery, vehicles, and furniture.

What are intangible assets?

Intangible assets are long-lived assets that have no physical substance, such as trademarks, copyrights, and patents. You cannot touch these assets, aside from perhaps a legal document to prove their existence, hence the name intangibles. Additional examples of intangible assets are software and web development, licensing rights, franchises, and goodwill.

What is goodwill?

Goodwill is an intangible asset that represents what the entity paid to acquire another business over the amount the other business was worth on paper (net assets). For example, if you were to purchase an ice cream shop that had net assets (assets owned minus liabilities owed) worth $100,000 but had a purchase price of $150,000, you would record goodwill of $50,000 when purchasing the ice cream shop. Essentially, because the company was only worth $100,000 on paper but you were willing to pay an extra $50,000 to acquire it, you must be expecting future economic benefits from this "goodwill" that

An intangible asset is something that is worth money but you can't physically touch it. For example, Disney's large library of movies to which it owns copyrights are intangible assets. Owning the rights to a blockbuster film—even when not in the physical form of, say, a Blu-ray disc—commands considerable value.

you paid for. For example, the ice cream shop already has a loyal customer base and is well known for providing a quality product in the community. You don't have to start a marketing plan from scratch. That may be worth $50,000 to your business.

What is net property, plant, and equipment?

Both long-lived tangible and intangible assets are recorded at cost and then adjusted downward as the asset is used in the business. In general, long-lived tangible assets are adjusted downward with depreciation, and long-lived intangible assets are adjusted downward with amortization. Both long-lived tangible and intangible assets are shown on the financial statements at cost less depreciation or amortization, hence the term "net." This is covered in more detail in the chapter entitled "Specific Accounting Issues."

What are current assets?

Current assets are those assets that will be used up in the business (i.e., inventory) or turned into cash (i.e., accounts receivable) within one year, or within the company's operating cycle, whichever is longer. Operating cycles are discussed in the chapter entitled "Cost Accounting Basics." Current assets are shown on the financial statements before noncurrent assets and are typically preceded by a heading entitled "Current Assets." They are also listed in order of liquidity, meaning those closest to being used up and turned into cash are listed first. Typical examples of noncurrent assets include cash and cash equivalents, accounts receivable, inventory, and prepaid expenses.

What are noncurrent assets?

Noncurrent assets are those assets that will not be used up in the business or turned into cash within one year or the company's operating cycle. These assets are listed after the current assets in the financial statements and may or may not be preceded by a heading. Typical examples of noncurrent assets include property, plant, equipment, and intangible assets.

What are "other current assets" and "other assets"?

Financial statements will often show line items for "other current assets" or "other assets" to group together asset accounts that are not in the primary account titles such as cash, inventory, etc. If each account were listed separately, the financial statements would be quite long. These balances are usually small in comparison to the remaining assets listed separately on the financial statements.

Are assets recorded on the financial statements at the cost paid for the asset or at market value?

In general, accounting favors historical cost for assets, meaning that assets are recorded at the price paid for the asset. However, this is not the case for all assets in general. For example, certain investments can be recorded at market values. Inventory accounts are recorded at the lower of cost or market value. Additionally, certain assets, such as PP&E, are recorded net of depreciation. As mentioned previously, this is covered in more detail in the chapter entitled "Specific Accounting Issues."

LIABILITIES

What is a liability?

According to the FASB, "liabilities are probable future sacrifices of economic benefits arising from present obligations of a particular entity to transfer assets or provide services to other entities in the future as a result of past transactions or events." Put simply, liabilities are things or amounts owed to others. These things owed could be cash, some other asset, or services that need to be performed. For example, if you order a $25 subscription to *Time* magazine, the publisher will record a liability for $25 because it owes you $25 worth of magazines. Each time it sends you a magazine, it will reduce that liability by the appropriate amount.

What accounts fall under the liabilities element?

There are many accounts that fall under the liabilities category. Some of the more common liabilities are accounts payable, notes payable, and accrued expenses.

What are accounts payable?

Accounts payable are basically the opposite of accounts receivable. Whereas accounts receivable are amounts owed to the entity by its customers, accounts payable are amounts the entity owes to its vendors. When a business purchases something from a supplier or vendor, that supplier or vendor will typically send an invoice for payment. That invoice is entered as a liability because the business now owes something to someone else. In this case, cash is owed to a supplier.

What are notes payable?

Notes payable are basically the opposite of notes receivable. When an entity borrows money in the form of a formal, documented loan (called a promissory note), it records a liability for the amount due, called notes payable. Notes payable can be either short term or long term and typically require interest payments as well as repayment of the principal balance.

What are accrued expenses?

Accrued expenses, sometimes referred to as accrued liabilities, is the title given to amounts owed at the end of a reporting period that have not yet been recorded as an expense. A common accrued expense is accrued wages. For example, at the end of a reporting period (typically the end of every month), an employer may owe the employees for wages earned that month but not yet paid until payday, which occurs the first Friday the following month. The employer must record the amount owed to the employees but not yet paid at the end of the month. Other common examples of accrued expenses are accrued interest and accrued income taxes.

What are current liabilities?

Current liabilities are those liabilities that will be paid or fulfilled within one year, or within the company's operating cycle, whichever is longer. Operating cycles are discussed in the chapter entitled "Cost Accounting Basics." Current liabilities are shown on the financial statements before noncurrent liabilities and are typically preceded by a heading entitled "Current Lia-

Wages for employees is a common example of accrued expenses (accrued liabilities) for a business; they are something every company that hires people has to pay out during reporting periods.

bilities." Typical examples of current liabilities include accounts payable, short-term notes payable, accrued expenses, and the current portion of long-term debt.

What are noncurrent liabilities?

Noncurrent, or long-term liabilities are all liabilities other than those that are current liabilities. Put very simply, these are the amounts owed that are due in over one year's time frame. Typical examples of long-term liabilities are long-term notes payable (other than the current portion) and other liabilities.

What is meant by the term "current portion of long-term debt"?

When a business has long-term debt, it must be split between its current and noncurrent portions. For example, a business may have a $10,000 loan from the bank, in which pay-

What are "other liabilities"?

Similar to what was discussed in the "assets" section of this chapter, financial statements will often show line items for "other current liabilities" or "other liabilities" to group together liability accounts that are not in the primary account titles, such as accounts payable, accrued expenses, etc. If each account were listed separately, the financial statements would be quite long. These balances are usually small in comparison to the remaining liabilities listed separately on the financial statements.

ments of $1,000 are due at the end of each year. During the first year, the business would record $1,000 as a current liability and the remaining $9,000 as a long-term liability.

Is debt the same as liabilities?

Yes, you can use the term "debt" interchangeably with the term "liabilities." Many financial ratios use the terms "debt," or "long-term debt." Those are synonymous with "liabilities," or "long-term liabilities."

EQUITY, INVESTMENTS BY OWNERS, AND DISTRIBUTIONS TO OWNERS

What is equity?

According to the FASB, "equity is the residual interest in the assets of an entity that remains after deducting its liabilities." In essence, equity represents the owners' stake in the business. It can be computed mathematically by taking total assets minus total liabilities. For example, if a company has $100,000 in total assets and $70,000 in total liabilities, the owner's claim to the business is the $30,000 difference, called equity. If the business were to liquidate, it would sell all its assets, resulting in $100,000 cash. That cash would be used to pay the $70,000 in liabilities owed to others, leaving the owner with $30,000 cash left over.

What accounts fall under the equity element?

There are two basic categories of equity: contributed capital and retained earnings.

Contributed capital represents investments by owners, which the FASB defines as "increases in equity of a particular business enterprise resulting from transfers to it from other entities of something valuable to obtain or increase ownership interests (or equity) in it." Put simply, contributed capital represents the value of items or cash provided by an owner to the business. For example, if you were to start a small business and you put $3,000 of your own money into the business, you would have contributed capital of $3,000. Assuming all the business has at this point is the $3,000 cash and no liabilities to anyone, you could compute your ownership interest in the business as the $3,000 total assets minus $0 total liabilities, equaling $3,000 equity. For corporations, contributed capital is achieved by issuing stock to owners/investors. In this case, the contributed capital is referred to as common stock or preferred stock.

Retained earnings represents the profits earned by the business that have been kept in the business and not paid out to the owners as dividends or distributions. The FASB defines distributions to owners as "decreases in equity of a particular business enterprise resulting from transferring assets, rendering services, or incurring liabilities by the enterprise to owners." For example, if you start a business and in the first year the business earns profits of $10,000, you are entitled to those profits as the owner of the business. You can choose to pay those profits to yourself as a dividend, or you can choose to keep the profits in the business and use them to expand your business, such as buying a new machine, etc. You may choose to pay yourself a dividend of $2,000 and leave $8,000 in the business. In this case, you would have retained earnings of $8,000.

If you add the $3,000 contributed capital to the $8,000 retained earnings, you would then have total owner's equity of $11,000.

REVENUES AND EXPENSES

What is revenue?

According to the FASB, "revenues are inflows or other enhancements of assets of an entity or settlements of its liabilities (or a combination of both) from delivering or producing goods, rendering services, or other activities that constitute the entity's ongoing major or central operations." The key point is that revenue is what is recorded when a business delivers goods or provides services to customers. Put very simply, when a business does for the customer what it is in business to do, it earns revenue for the amount charged to the customer. For example, when Pizza Hut delivers a pizza to a customer, it earns revenue. When a cleaning company cleans a client's business suite, it earns revenue. When *People* magazine sends an issue to a subscriber, it earns revenue. When Target Corp. sells a toy to a customer, it earns revenue. Also note that the definition describes revenues as inflows of assets, etc. When an entity earns revenue, assets typically increase by either receiving a cash payment from the customer or recording accounts receivable (also an asset).

What accounts fall under the revenues element?

There can be many different types of revenue accounts. The more common account titles for revenue are service revenue and sales revenue. Many times, the financial statements will just show one line for revenue or net revenue. Sometimes revenue accounts can be very specific, as with General Motors Co., that lists "Automotive" and "GM Financial" as two separate revenue items on its financial statements.

What is net revenue?

Net revenue represents total revenues less any sales returns, sales allowances, and sales discounts. A company may either choose to show gross revenues first, then show separate line items subtracting sales returns, allowances, and discounts to arrive at a final net sales figure, or a company may simply list net sales as one line item on the financial statements.

What are expenses?

As defined by the FASB, "expenses are outflows or other using up of assets or incurrences of liabilities (or a combination of both) from delivering or producing goods, rendering services, or carrying out other activities that constitute the entity's ongoing major or central operations." Put simply, expenses are recorded when a business incurs costs in order to provide goods or services to the customers. These costs represent decreases of assets or increases in liabilities. For example, when Pizza Hut buys cheese, Pizza Hut will either have to pay cash for the cheese (reducing an asset) or will enter an invoice as accounts payable (increasing a liability).

What accounts fall under the expenses element?

There are many examples of expense accounts. Expenses usually fall into one of three categories: product or service costs; selling, general, and administrative costs; or nonoperating costs.

Product or service costs are referred to as the cost of goods sold or cost of sales. Cost of goods sold represents the cost of the goods that are sold to customers. For example, if you buy a $15.00 DVD from Target Corp. and Target paid its supplier $2.00 for that DVD, Target would record revenue for $15.00 and record an expense called cost of goods sold for $2.00.

Selling, general, and administrative costs, often referred to as SG&A for short, include expenses incurred to operate the business outside of the product costs mentioned above. SG&A expenses include items such as advertising expense, rent expense, utilities expense, wages and benefits expense, and many other account titles. Quite often, the accounts that make up SG&A expenses are not listed separately on the financial statements but are instead rolled up into just one line item called "selling, general, and administrative expenses."

Nonoperating costs are those other costs incurred by a business that are incidental to operating the business, such as interest expense and income tax expense.

GAINS, LOSSES,
AND COMPREHENSIVE INCOME

What is a gain?

The FASB defines gains as "increases in equity from peripheral or incidental transactions of an entity and from all other transactions and other events and circumstances affecting the entity except those that result from revenues or investments by owners." Put simply, if equity increases and it wasn't the result of earning revenue or an investment by the owners, then it is called a gain. There are specific circumstances in which gains are recorded. One of the more common forms of gains are gains on the sale of fixed assets. There are also more complicated gains, such as gains on foreign currency translation and pensions, which are outside the scope of this book. A good intermediate accounting textbook can provide further information on those more complicated gains.

How are gains different from revenue?

The key difference between a gain and a revenue is the nature of the transaction in relation to the nature of the business. Revenue arises from transactions that are part of the ongoing, central operations of the business. Gains arise from incidental or peripheral transactions, meaning they are not part of the ongoing, central operations of the business. For example, assume that you own a small bakery. You have a commercial oven that is recorded on your financial statements at $3,000. If you sell the oven for $4,000 to another bakery because you are going to purchase a bigger one, you would have a gain of $1,000. Basically, you made $1,000 on that sale, but you don't count it as revenue because you are not in the business of selling ovens. You are a bakery. However, a supplier of commercial ovens is in the business of selling ovens, so it would record revenue for each oven it sells at the selling price. This is covered in more detail in the chapter entitled "Specific Accounting Issues."

What is a loss?

The FASB defines losses as "decreases in equity from peripheral or incidental transactions of an entity and from all other transactions and other events and circumstances affecting the entity except those that result from expenses or distributions to owners." Just as with gains, there are specific circumstances in which losses are recorded. Losses are basically the opposite of gains. They are decreases in equity from something other than expenses or distributions to the owners. Anything that can cause a gain could potentially cause a loss. The difference is whether equity increased or decreased as a result of the transaction.

How are losses different from expenses?

Just as with revenues and gains, the key difference between a loss and an expense is the nature of the transaction in relation to the nature of the business. Expenses arise from transactions that are part of the ongoing, central operations of the business. Losses arise from incidental or peripheral transactions, meaning they are not part of the ongoing, central operations of the business. For example, assume you own a small bakery again. You have a commercial oven that is recorded on your financial statements at $3,000. This time, you sell the oven for $2,000 to another bakery because you are going to purchase a bigger one. In this case, you would have a loss of $1,000. Basically, you lost $1,000 on that sale, but you don't count it as an expense because you are not in the business of selling ovens. This is covered in more detail in the chapter entitled "Specific Accounting Issues."

What is net income?

Net income is the result of revenues and gains less all expenses and losses, and it is shown on the bottom line of the income statement. Basically, it is the good stuff less the bad stuff. Income statements will be discussed in detail in the chapter entitled "Four Basic Financial Statements." Net income is a key figure used in analyzing the performance of a business.

What is net loss?

If the calculation of net income results in a negative number, this is referred to as a net loss. A net loss means a company had more expenses and losses than it had revenues and gains. As such, the company had more bad stuff than good stuff.

What is comprehensive income?

At an introductory level and for the purposes of this book, an understanding of net income is sufficient. Typically, accounting students don't learn about comprehensive income until they are in upper-level accounting courses. The FASB defines comprehensive income as "the change in equity of a business enterprise during a period from transactions and other events and circumstances from nonowner sources. It includes all changes in equity during a period except those resulting from investments by owners and distributions to owners." Basically, comprehensive income equals net income plus or minus certain other changes in equity. Again, for the purposes of this book, an understanding of net income is quite sufficient.

How are net income and comprehensive income different?

Certain gains and losses that have not yet been realized (turned into cash) are able to be recorded on the financial statements. These unrealized gains or losses are calculated after net income, making up the total calculation of comprehensive income. For example, if a company has investments that it is willing to sell (for example, stocks it is hoping to buy at a low price and sell for a high price), it can record changes in the market value of those investments as gains and losses, even though it hasn't actually sold the investment. These types of gains and losses are not included in the traditional calculation of net income but are instead shown separately as other comprehensive income. Businesses may choose to show these gains and losses at the very bottom of the income statement, after net income, or they may show them on their very own financial statement.

A key point to remember is that net income includes those revenues, gains, losses, and expenses that have been realized. Comprehensive income includes everything that is in net income plus or minus gains and losses that have not yet been realized. As such, a company that has an investment in stocks that have increased in value by $10,000 during the period may be able to add that $10,000 gain to its financial statements but only *after* net income because it hasn't actually sold the stock yet and earned the $10,000. Remember that since it hasn't sold the stock yet, it could lose that $10,000 at any time if the market turns for the worse. Accordingly, this $10,000 gain is not comingled into net income, but rather, it is shown below net income so that readers of the financial statements are not misled.

FINANCIAL STATEMENTS

What are financial statements?

Financial statements are the financial reports of a business. They tell the readers about the financial condition of a company over a certain period of time.

How many different types of financial statements are there?

While there are four basic financial statements that will be covered in this book, there are also several other types of financial statements. The four basic financial statements that most businesses present are the income statement, statement of retained earnings, balance sheet, and statement of cash flows. Not-for-profit organizations have their own financial statements called statement of financial position (similar to a balance sheet), statement of activities (similar to an income statement), and statement of cash flows. In addition, some businesses prepare a statement of stockholders' equity and/or a statement of comprehensive income.

Who uses the financial statements, and what do they use them for?

Financial statements are used by both internal and external users. Internal users are those people who work for the company. An example of an internal user would be the CEO of a company. Internal users use financial statements to evaluate the past results of the business, to compare to budget or planned results, and to make decisions for the future.

External users are those people who don't work for the company but rely on the financial information from the business. Examples of external users are investors, creditors, directors, and the government. Investors rely on financial statements of an entity to determine whether or not they want to invest in a company or to determine what a company's stock is worth. Creditors lend the business money. Creditors can be banks that the company has borrowed money from or suppliers that send invoices to the company for repayment. Anyone that the business owes money to is a creditor. Accordingly, creditors rely on financial statements to determine whether or not they will be repaid. Members of the company's board of directors also rely on the financial statements to govern the business and ensure the management of the business is making good decisions. Finally, government agencies use financial statements for various reasons. For example, the IRS uses financial information to ensure that taxes are reported correctly.

Are there other names for the financial statements?

There are several names that financial statements may be called. For example, a balance sheet can also be called a statement of financial position. An income statement may also be called a statement of earnings or statement of comprehensive income. If the title of a financial statement is confusing to you, taking a look at the information portrayed on the financial statements should help you figure out which financial statement you are looking at.

How do you know which financial statement is which?

While the content on each financial statement is quite different to an informed reader, financial statements also provide headings at the top to help a reader identify which statement they are looking at. These headings identify three primary items: who, what, and when. The first line of a financial statement identifies the company that the finan-

The four basic financial statements include the Income Statement, Statement of Cash Flows, Balance Sheet, and Statement of Retained Earnings (or Equity).

cial statement represents. The second line lists the title of the financial statement, such as income statement or balance sheet. The third line identifies the time frame that the financial statement represents, such as the year or the month.

Who prepares the financial statements?

The financial statements are typically prepared by the accounting staff of a company. Depending on the size of the company, the statements may be prepared by a single bookkeeper or by an entire financial reporting department. Some small companies that don't have the accounting expertise on staff hire an accounting firm to prepare the financial statements for them.

How are the financial statements prepared?

The financial statements are typically generated automatically by computer software or prepared manually in Microsoft Excel or some other application. Whether the statements are generated automatically by software or prepared manually, the same rules apply. Using the basic equations and layouts for each financial statement, the different account balances are aggregated on the financial statement where they belong, and the appropriate math is computed. Each financial statement will be discussed in detail in this chapter.

How often are the financial statements prepared?

Financial statements are prepared for various reporting periods, depending on the size of the entity. Most large businesses prepare financial statements at the end of each month, each quarter, and each year. Some small businesses only prepare financial statements at the end of each year. Generally, the more often the financial statements are prepared, the better able internal users are of making business decisions. For example, companies that only prepare financial statements quarterly go through three months before having a solid idea of how the business performed compared to expectations.

Are financial statements required?

Public companies (those with their stock listed on the stock exchanges) are required to prepare and file financial statements with the government. Those statements are loaded onto the SEC website for anyone to view. You can view the financial statements of public companies by going to www.sec.gov and clicking on the "filings" menu option.

Private companies are not required to file financial statements with the government; however, many private companies are required to provide financial statements to their banks or other creditors and investors.

Who ensures the accuracy of the financial statements?

The management team of the business is responsible for the accuracy of the financial statements. In addition, public companies are required to have their financial statements audited by an accounting firm. It is important to note that auditors do not certify the ac-

Are there other financial reports that are used to make decisions?

External users have to rely on the financial statements. As external users don't work for the company, they are not privy to the day-to-day details of the business. However, there are many financial reports that are created and used by internal users. There are no prescribed formats for these reports, and each company may design or use whatever works best for them. For example, a company may prepare a report that tracks new customer growth in revenue over time. A company may prepare a report that tracks employee expense reimbursements for meals and entertainment by department. There is no end to the possibilities of internal reporting that can be created to help run the business.

curacy of financial statements. Audits are based on risk assessment and use sampling techniques. As such, auditors cannot provide absolute assurance that the financial statements are completely accurate. What auditors do is provide an opinion that lends credibility to the financial statements. This opinion provides reasonable assurance (not absolute) that the financial statements are free from material (i.e., big enough to make a difference to a user) misstatement. While not required by the government, many banks and creditors require audited financial statements of private companies they lend money to.

What are the four types of audit reports?

After auditing the financial statements, the auditors issue a report, also called an opinion. There are four types of audit reports: unmodified (or unqualified), qualified, adverse, and disclaimer of opinion. An unmodified report is the standard report. An unmodified report means that the auditor has obtained sufficient, appropriate evidence to conclude that the financial statements are free from material misstatement. This means the auditor is of the opinion that external users can rely on the financial information given to them as being free from errors or fraud that would be big enough to affect the overall view of the financial condition of the business. In other words, an unmodified report is the "clean" report that every business wants to have. The other three types of opinions are given as a result of the auditors finding misstatements (due to errors or fraud) that are large enough to affect the reader's view of the financial condition of the business or due to the auditors not being able to complete the necessary steps to perform the audit.

THE BASIC ACCOUNTING EQUATION

What is the basic accounting equation?

The most basic concept underlying the financial statements revolves around something called the basic accounting equation. Put simply, the basic accounting equation is:

Assets = Liabilities + Equity

The accounting equation tells us that everything the business owns comes from one of two sources. Either the business borrowed the money to buy it (liabilities), or it comes as a result of owners' equity in the business. Recall from the chapter entitled "Financial Statement Elements" that equity has two basic categories: contributed capital and retained earnings. Contributed capital represents the investments of the owners. Retained earnings represents the profits of the business that have been kept in the business and not paid out to the owners as distributions.

Accordingly, we can further state that the accounting equation tells us that everything that the business owns comes from either a) borrowing the money, b) owners investing money into the business, or c) using the profits that have been kept in the business. As such, we can start to expand on the basic accounting equation as follows:

Assets = Liabilities + Contributed Capital + Retained Earnings

For example, assume a small start-up business called Loretta's Lawn Care started out with the owner investing $10,000 of her personal funds into the business. The business now has assets of $10,000 (cash) and equity of $10,000 (contributed capital). The accounting equation is in balance:

$10,000 Assets (cash) = $0 Liabilities + $10,000 Contributed Capital + $0 Retained Earnings

What happens as the business enters into transactions during operations?

When a business enters into transactions, it must record those transactions in the accounting system. This will be discussed in detail in the chapter entitled "Bookkeeping and the Accounting Cycle." Each time a transaction is recorded, the accounting equation must still balance. For example, assume the same lawn care company noted above purchased a $3,000 lawn mower on credit from a small machinery supplier in town and received an invoice for the $3,000 due in sixty days. Recall from the chapter entitled "Financial Statement Elements" that this $3,000 due to the supplier represents a liability for the business, called accounts payable. The accounting equation now looks like this:

$13,000 Assets (cash and lawn mower) = $3,000 Liabilities + $10,000 Contributed Capital + $0 Retained Earnings.

What if the accounting equation doesn't balance?

The accounting equation must always balance. If it does not balance, the accountant has used an incorrect financial statement element in recording a transaction. If the accounting equation does not balance, an error has occurred and must be fixed.

How are retained earnings calculated?

Recall that retained earnings represent the profits of the business that are kept in the business and not paid out to the owners as distributions. Accordingly, retained earnings are calculated as:

Beginning Balance, Retained Earnings + Net Income − Distributions = Ending Balance, Retained Earnings

Assume the lawn care company had $9,000 in net income during the first month of operations that were all realized in cash. Retained earnings would have a beginning balance of $0, since it is the first month of operations, and there are no previous profits. Retained earnings would be calculated as:

$0 Beginning Balance + $9,000 Net Income − $0 Distributions = $9,000 Ending Balance

The new accounting equation would be:

$22,000 Assets (cash and lawn mower) = $3,000 Liabilities + $10,000 Contributed Capital + $9,000 Retained Earnings

What happens to retained earnings when dividends are paid to owners?

Dividends (or distributions) to owners reduce the retained earnings of a business. If the same lawn care company paid the owners a $4,000 cash dividend at the end of the first month, retained earnings would now be calculated as:

$0 Beginning Balance + $9,000 Net Income − $4,000 Distributions = $5,000 Ending Balance

Accordingly, the accounting equation would be recalculated as:

$18,000 Assets (cash and lawn mower) = $3,000 Liabilities + $10,000 Contributed Capital + $5,000 Retained Earnings

Notice that the accounting equation always stays in balance.

How is net income calculated?

In its most basic form, net income is a simple calculation. The formula for net income is:

Revenues − Expenses = Net Income

Remember the $9,000 net income that was used above for the lawn care company? Assume that in the first month of operations, the owner used the lawn mower to mow 250 lawns and collected $50 from each customer. That means the lawn care company earned $12,500 in revenue (and received $12,500 in cash) during the first month. Let's assume the company paid a few family members wages of $3,000 during the month and paid another $500 in various other operating expenses. (Assume these expenses were paid in cash, thus decreasing cash by $3,500 during the month.) We can compute net income as follows:

$12,500 Revenues − $3,500 Expenses = $9,000 Net Income

Can we write one expanded accounting equation?

Yes! Since all of the formulas are interrelated, we can expand on the basic accounting equation as follows:

Assets = Liabilities + Equity

Assets = Liabilities + Contributed Capital + Retained Earnings

Assets = Liabilities + Contributed Capital + Beginning Balance, Retained Earnings + Revenues − Expenses − Distributions

This equation contains all of the parts of the four basic financial statements.

Does it matter which financial statement is prepared first?

Since the financial statements are all derived from the basic accounting equation, they should be prepared in a particular order. For example, we have to calculate net income before we can calculate the retained earnings balance. We have to calculate the retained earnings balance before we can calculate total equity. The order of preparation for the four basic financial statements is as follows: 1) income statement, 2) statement of retained earnings, 3) balance sheet, 4) statement of cash flows.

THE INCOME STATEMENT

What is the purpose of the income statement?

The Income Statement shows the results of operations of the business. The final calculation of net income is an important figure used in evaluating the results of the business. In general, the higher the net income, the better the performance. Additionally, a net loss (negative income) generally signifies trouble.

What is a single-step income statement?

The single-step income statement is a simple income statement, like the example for Loretta's Lawn Care above. On a single-step income statement, all revenues are listed first, followed by all expenses (usually listed from largest to smallest), and then net income is calculated at the bottom.

What is the basic format for the income statement?

The basic format for the income statement is to show the calculation of net income. Thus, the income statement shows revenues and expenses. The income statement then comes to a final calculation of net income at the bottom, which is done by taking total revenues minus total expenses. An example of a simple income statement for the lawn care company is shown below.

41

Loretta's Lawn Care
Income Statement
For the year ended December 31, 2018

Revenues:		
Service Revenue	$	150,000
Expenses:		
Wages Expense		54,000
Utilties & Fuel Expense		12,000
Rent Expense		2,400
Insurance Expense		1,000
Advertising Expense		500
Depreciation Expense		100
Total Expenses		70,000
Net Income	$	80,000

What is a multiple-step income statement?

Businesses may choose to present a multiple-step income statement, where the revenues and expenses from the core operations of the business are listed separately from those that are nonoperating and not part of the core business activities. In addition, several important subtotals are calculated, such as gross profit and operating income. The figure below presents the financial information of Vera Bradley, Inc., "a leading designer of women's handbags, luggage, and travel items," in multiple-step form.

Vera Bradley, Inc.
Consolidated Statements of Income - USD ($), $ in Thousands
For the Fiscal Year Ended January 28, 2017

Net revenues	$ 485,937
Cost of sales	209,891
Gross profit	276,046
Selling, general, and administrative expenses	249,155
Other income	1,329
Operating income	28,220
Interest expense, net	178
Income before income taxes	28,042
Income tax expense	8,284
Net income	$ 19,758

Recall from the chapter entitled "Financial Statement Elements" that expenses usually fall into one of three categories: product or service costs; selling, general, and administrative costs; and nonoperating costs. Product or service costs are referred to as cost of goods sold or cost of sales and represent the cost of the goods that are sold to customers. Selling, general, and administrative costs include expenses incurred to operate the business outside of the product costs mentioned above. SG&A expenses include items such as advertising expense, rent expense, and utilities expense. Nonoperating costs are those other costs incurred by a business that are incidental to operating the business, such as interest expense and income tax expense.

Does a single-step income statement result in different net income than a multiple-step income statement?

A single-step income statement will result in the exact same net income as a multiple-step income statement. The information is not changed; it is just rearranged. The basic formula for net income is unchanged.

What is gross profit?

Gross profit is an important subtotal that calculates the difference between revenues earned and the costs of goods sold. You can think of it as the markup, or the amount the company charged the customer over what it paid for the goods. For example, if you buy a $15.00 DVD from Target Corp. and Target paid its supplier $2.00 for that DVD, Target would record revenue for $15.00 and record cost of goods sold for $2.00. That leaves Target with a $13.00 gross profit on that DVD. Gross profit can also be called gross margin or margin.

What is operating income?

Operating income is another important subtotal. It shows the income from operating the business before any nonoperating costs (those that are incidental to operating the business), such as interest expense and income tax expense. Operating income can be calculated by taking gross profit less selling, general, and administrative expenses.

How is operating income different from net income?

The difference between operating income and the bottom line of the income statement, net income, is due to nonoperating revenues and expenses, such as interest expense on loans and income taxes. Net income can be calculated by taking operating income plus or minus nonoperating revenues or expenses. Net income is the bottom-line-realized profitability measure for the business. It is a key figure in analyzing the financial strengths and weaknesses of the business, as discussed further in the chapter entitled "Financial Statement Analysis."

What is the time period that the income statement is recorded for?

The income statement is recorded for a period of time rather than at one point in time. For example, income statements are typically prepared for an entire month, a quarter, or a year. For instance, the sample company Loretta's Lawn Care referred to previously in this chapter may wish to compare revenues earned in January to those earned in February to see if the business is growing. It may also compare the first year of operations to the second year. Data is accumulated separately for each period.

What is a comparative income statement?

A comparative income statement is an income statement that lists the results of two or more time periods side by side in columns. Comparative income statements make it easier for users of financial statements to compare financial results from different time periods. For example, Loretta's Lawn Care may prepare a comparative income statement showing 2018 results next to 2019 results, as shown below. At a quick glance, you can see that revenues increased, as well as total costs, and that the bottom-line net income increased by $5,700. Without doing a lot of technical analysis, you can already start to identify some financial trends when you have a comparative income statement.

Loretta's Lawn Care
Comparative Income Statement
For the years ended December 31, 2019 and December 31, 2018

	2019	2018
Revenues:		
Service Revenue	$ 165,000	$ 150,000
Expenses:		
Wages Expense	62,100	54,000
Utilities & Fuel Expense	13,200	12,000
Rent Expense	2,400	2,400
Insurance Expense	1,000	1,000
Advertising Expense	500	500
Depreciation Expense	100	100
Total Expenses	79,300	70,000
Net Income	$ 85,700	$ 80,000

Does net income equal how much cash the company made during the period?

Net income does not equal the increase in cash during a particular period. Accounting rules require revenue to be recorded when earned, not necessarily when collected in cash. For example, if Loretta's Lawn Care mows lawns but leaves invoices for customer payment rather than collecting cash as the lawns are mowed, Loretta would still record the revenue she earned by mowing the lawns that month and record an asset, called accounts receivable, for the amount her customers owe her. Likewise, accounting rules require expenses to be recorded when they are incurred, not necessarily when they are paid in cash. For example, if Loretta ordered advertising materials and was given the materials along with an invoice to pay later, Loretta would record an expense for the materials and a liability, called accounts payable, for the amount owed to the vendor.

This is called the accrual basis of accounting. Accrual basis accounting is different from cash basis accounting. Accordingly, under accrual basis accounting, net income reflects the increase in profitability (how much better off the company is), not the increase in cash.

Can companies use the cash basis of accounting instead of the accrual basis?

Cash basis accounting is not allowed under the generally accepted accounting principles; however, some small companies that are not required to submit audited financial statements to the government or others can, and do, use cash basis accounting. As most businesses use credit, both in terms of letting customers pay later or in paying vendors later, the cash basis of accounting is not generally a good measure of the financial performance of the business, as it does not appropriately match revenues earned in a period with expenses incurred during that period.

Isn't the change in cash an important figure to track?

Yes! Cash is king! A business cannot survive without proper cash management. As the income statement is prepared on an accrual basis and does not describe the change in cash during a period, there is an entirely different financial statement devoted to describing the change in cash during the period, called the statement of cash flows, which will be discussed in detail in this chapter.

THE STATEMENT OF RETAINED EARNINGS

What is the purpose of the statement of retained earnings?

The statement of retained earnings shows the roll-forward of the net income that is kept in the business over time. Users can also see how much of the business's profits have been paid out to the owners as distributions.

Where does the beginning balance of retained earnings come from?

The beginning balance always comes from the ending balance of the last period. For example, where you ended with retained earnings on January 31 at 11:59 P.M., you will see the same number as where you start retained earnings on February 1 at 12:00 A.M. As such, January's ending balance becomes February's beginning balance, and so on. If a company is brand new, it will start with $0 as a beginning balance because at that time, it has no accumulated earnings.

What is the basic format for the statement of retained earnings?

The basic format for the statement of retained earnings follows the equation to calculate retained earnings. It starts with a row for the beginning balance in retained earnings. Then there are rows that follow to add net income and subtract dividends. The fourth and final row is the calculation of the ending balance of retained earnings. An example of a statement of retained earnings is shown below.

Loretta's Lawn Care
Statement of Retained Earnings
For the year ended December 31, 2019

Retained Earnings, January 1, 2019	$	50,000
Add: Net Income		85,700
Subtract: Dividends		(30,000)
Retained Earnings, December 31, 2019	$	105,700

Where does the net income figure on the statement of retained earnings come from?

The net income figure comes directly from the net income reported on the income statement. For this reason, the income statement must be completed before the statement of retained earnings.

How is the ending balance of retained earnings calculated?

The ending balance of retained earnings is calculated by taking the beginning balance plus the net income for the period less any distributions/dividends paid to owners during the period. The ending balance becomes the beginning balance for the next period.

For a visualization of this, imagine starting a small business. You get an old shoebox in which you intend to store your business's profits. The box is empty to start with because you have just started your business. At the end of the year, you put your profits in the box. Let's say you earned net income of $10,000. You look in the box and say to yourself, "I am the owner of this company. Aren't I entitled to these profits if I want them?" The answer is yes, assuming you actually have the cash to back it up. (Remember, due to the nature of accrual basis accounting, net income does not equal an increase in cash.) Assuming you have enough cash in the business, you decide to take a dividend of $6,000. That means you are taking $6,000 cash out of the business because you, as the owner, have decided you wish to take some of the profits for yourself, personally. That $6,000 comes out of your shoebox. That leaves you with $4,000 in your shoebox at the end of the year.

You are now starting year 2 of your business with $4,000 in your shoebox. That is your beginning balance of retained earnings. Assume you earn net income of $50,000 in year 2 and put it in the box. You decide to take a dividend of $20,000 out of the box. Your shoebox will now have $34,000 of accumulated profits that have been retained in the business. That is your retained earnings balance at the end of year 2.

What is the time period that the statement of retained earnings is recorded for?

Like the income statement, the statement of retained earnings is recorded for a period of time rather than at one point in time. For example, statements of retained earnings are typically prepared for an entire month, a quarter, or a year. Data is accumulated separately for each period.

THE BALANCE SHEET

What is the basic format for the balance sheet?

The basic format for the balance sheet is to present the basic accounting equation: assets equal liabilities plus equity. Balance sheets start by listing assets, which are then summed to compute total assets. Next, liabilities and equity are listed, which are also summed to compute total liabilities and equity. Once it has been double-checked that total assets equal total liabilities plus equity, the corresponding figures are marked with a double underline on the balance sheet, signifying that they match. A sample balance sheet is shown below.

Loretta's Lawn Care
Balance Sheet
As of December 31, 2019

Assets	
Cash	$ 119,000
Accounts Receivable	20,500
Supplies	3,000
Equipment	70,000
Total Assets	$ 212,500
Liabilities and Owner's Equity	
Liabilities	
Accounts Payable	$ 30,000
Notes Payable	66,800
Total Liabilities	96,800
Owner's Equity	
Contributed Capital	10,000
Retained Earnings	105,700
Total Owner's Equity	115,700
Total Liabilities and Owner's Equity	$ 212,500

What is the purpose of the balance sheet?

The balance sheet shows the financial position of the business. At any point in time, you can see the resources owned by the company as well as the resources owed by the company. Having more resources owned than owed is a good thing and will result in positive owner's equity.

What order are the assets listed in on the balance sheet?

Assets are listed on the balance sheet in order of liquidity, meaning the order in which they will be used up or turned into cash. Cash is listed first, followed by those assets that will be used up or turned into cash most quickly.

What order are the liabilities listed in?

Liabilities are also listed on the balance sheet in order of liquidity, meaning the order in which they will be paid. The liabilities that are due in the nearest time frame are listed first, followed by those that are due later.

What is a classified balance sheet?

A classified balance sheet is a balance sheet that includes subtotals for current assets and current liabilities. As covered in the chapter entitled "Financial Statement Elements," current assets are those assets that will be used up in the business or turned into cash within one year, or within the company's operating cycle, whichever is longer. Typical examples of noncurrent assets include cash and cash equivalents, accounts receivable, inventory, and prepaid expenses. Current assets are listed first on a classified balance sheet, in order of liquidity, and followed by a subtotal line item entitled current assets. Noncurrent assets are those assets that will not be used up in the business or turned into cash within one year or the company's operating cycle. These assets are listed after the current assets on the balance sheet and may or may not be preceded by a heading. Typical examples of noncurrent assets include property, plant, equipment, and intangible assets. Current assets are added to noncurrent assets to compute total assets on the balance sheet.

Current liabilities are those liabilities that will be paid or fulfilled within one year, or within the company's operating cycle, whichever is longer. Typical examples of noncurrent liabilities include accounts payable, short-term notes payable, accrued expenses, and the current portion of long-term debt. Current liabilities are shown on the balance sheet in order of liquidity and before noncurrent liabilities. Current liabilities are typically preceded by a heading of the same name. Noncurrent, or long-term, liabilities are all liabilities other than those that are classified as current liabilities. Typical examples of long-term liabilities are long-term notes payable (other than the current portion) and other liabilities. Current liabilities are added to long-term liabilities to compute total liabilities on the balance sheet.

An example of a classified balance sheet has been created using data from Vera Bradley, Inc., as shown below.

Vera Bradley, Inc.
Consolidated Balance Sheets - USD ($) $ in Thousands
As of January 28, 2017

Assets

Current assets:

Cash and cash equivalents	$	86,375
Short-term investments		30,152
Accounts receivable, net		23,313
Inventories		102,283
Income taxes receivable		3,217
Prepaid expenses and other current assets		10,237
Total current assets		255,577
Property, plant, and equipment, net		101,577
Deferred income taxes		13,539
Other assets		2,816
Total assets	$	373,509

Liabilities & Stockholder's Equity

Current liabilities:

Accounts payable	$	32,619
Accrued employment costs		12,474
Other accrued liabilities		16,906
Income taxes payable		508
Total current liabilities		62,507
Long-term liabilities		27,216
Total liabilities		89,723

Shareholders' equity:

Common Stock		-
Additional paid-in capital		88,739
Retained earnings		263,767
Accumulated other comprehensive loss		(50)
Treasury stock		(68,670)
Total shareholders' equity		283,786
Total liabilities and shareholders' equity	$	373,509

49

What is the difference between equity, owner's equity, shareholders' equity, and stockholders' equity?

Equity, owner's equity, shareholders' equity, and stockholders' equity are all names describing the same thing. They all describe the owner's stake in the business as represented by the two main categories of equity: contributed capital and retained earnings. Depending on the form of business organization, these different names are used. For example, when a sole proprietor invests money into the business, it is recorded as contributed capital and often referred to on the balance sheet as owner's equity when added to retained earnings. When a corporation issues stock to owners in return for the owners' investments, this contributed capital is recorded as common stock, preferred stock, and/or additional paid-in capital. When shown on the balance sheet, it will be called shareholders' or stockholders' equity when added to retained earnings. These different forms of organization will be covered in the chapter entitled "Starting a Small Business." While they may be called by different names, they are all referring to equity.

What is the time period that the balance sheet is recorded for?

Unlike the other financial statements, which are shown for a period of time, the balance sheet is shown at a point in time. For example, the income statement may show the operating results for the year 2018, whereas the balance sheet shows the financial position on December 31, 2018. The balance sheet is like a picture or snapshot of a company on a given day. The balance sheet represents real accounts with verifiable balances that change daily; as such, it is date specific. For example, the amount of cash in the bank on December 31, 2018, is most likely different from the amount of cash in the bank on January 5, 2019. Likewise, the amount of money customers owe the business—accounts receivable—changes daily based on customer payments coming in. As such, balance sheet headings include wording such as "At December 31, 2018" rather than "For the Year Ended December 31, 2018."

What is a comparative balance sheet?

A comparative balance sheet is a balance sheet that lists the results of two or more time periods side by side in columns. Comparative balance sheets make it easier for users of financial statements to compare financial positions from different time periods. For example, Loretta's Lawn Care may prepare a comparative balance sheet showing December 31, 2019, next to December 31, 2018, as shown below. At a quick glance, you can see that cash increased as well as total assets and total liabilities. Without doing a lot of technical analysis, you can already start to identify some financial trends and the like when you have a comparative balance sheet.

Loretta's Lawn Care
Comparative Balance Sheet
As of December 31, 2019 and December 31, 2018

	2019	2018
Assets		
Cash	$ 119,000	$ 70,000
Accounts Receivable	20,500	10,000
Supplies	3,000	2,000
Equipment	70,000	3,000
Total Assets	$ 212,500	$ 85,000
Liabilities and Owner's Equity		
Liabilities		
Accounts Payable	$ 30,000	$ 15,000
Notes Payable	66,800	10,000
Total Liabilities	96,800	25,000
Owner's Equity		
Contributed Capital	10,000	10,000
Retained Earnings	105,700	50,000
Total Owner's Equity	115,700	60,000
Total Liabilities and Owner's Equity	$ 212,500	$ 85,000

THE STATEMENT OF CASH FLOWS

What is the purpose of the statement of cash flows?

The statement of cash flows shows the changes in cash over a given period of time. It reconciles the beginning balance of cash for the period with the ending balance of cash for the period. For example, the Loretta's Lawn Care comparative balance sheet shows that cash at the end of 2018 was $70,000, and cash at the end of 2019 was $119,000. You can calculate that cash increased by $49,000 during 2019, but the balance sheet doesn't tell the reader why the cash increased. The statement of cash flows helps the reader understand why cash increased or decreased during the period.

What is the basic format of the statement of cash flows?

The statement of cash flows is divided into three main categories. The first category is cash flows from operating activities. The second category is cash flows from investing activities. The third category is cash flows from financing activities. The three categories are added together to form the change in cash during the period. Finally, the change in cash is added to the beginning cash balance to compute the ending cash balance. This ending cash balance matches the cash figure reported on the balance sheet. A simple formula is:

Cash flows from operating activities

+/- Cash flows from investing activities

+/- Cash flows from financing activities

= Change in cash

+ Cash balance at the beginning of the period

= Cash balance at the end of the period (matches cash reported on the balance sheet)

An example statement of cash flows for Loretta's Lawn Care is shown below. You can see that Loretta's Lawn Care increased cash by $89,300 from operations, decreased cash by $67,000 from investments, and increased cash by $26,800 from financing. Those three subtotals net together to form the increase in cash for the period of $49,000.

The beginning cash balance for the year ended December 31, 2019, comes from the prior year's ending cash balance (December 31, 2018). Essentially, your cash balance on December 31, 2018, at 11:59 P.M. is the same as your cash balance on January 1, 2019, at 12:00 A.M. As Loretta's Lawn Care started 2019 with $70,000 cash and increased cash by $49,000 during the year, the ending cash balance must be $119,000, which is the amount reported on the balance sheet.

Loretta's Lawn Care
Statement of Cash Flows (Direct Method)
For the year ended December 31, 2019

Cash Flows from Operating Activities:		
Cash collected from customers	$	154,500
Cash paid to suppliers		(3,100)
Cash paid to employees		(62,100)
Net cash provided by (used in) operating activities		89,300
Cash Flows from Investing Activities:		
Purchase of equipment		(67,100)
Net cash provided by (used in) investing activities		(67,100)
Cash Flows from Financing Activities:		
Cash dividends paid to stockholders		(30,000)
Cash borrowed from the bank		56,800
Net cash provided by (used in) financing activities		26,800
Change in Cash		49,000
Beginning Cash, December 31, 2018		70,000
Ending Cash, December 31, 2019	$	119,000

Why is the cash account so important that it has its own financial statement devoted to it?

As noted in the income statement section of this chapter, companies record revenues when earned, not necessarily when received in cash. Companies also record expenses when incurred, not necessarily when paid in cash. Thus, the reported net income or loss (revenues minus expenses) will not equal the increase or decrease in cash. A business could have ample sales revenue from customers, but if they can't get their customers to pay, the company will not have the cash required to pay its own bills. If the company cannot pay its bills, relationships with suppliers will be strained, and the company will have trouble securing the supplies needed to run the business. Accordingly, the company will have trouble operating, and this may eventually result in the downfall of the business. Thus, tracking cash is just as important as tracking profit, if not more so!

What types of activities are included in the operating activities section?

The cash flows from operating activities section includes the cash flows that are directly related to operating the business and earning a profit. These activities include items such as collecting cash from selling goods and services to customers and paying cash for inventory, supplies, wages, advertising, etc. Cash inflows (positive number) result from collecting cash, and cash outflows (negative numbers) result from payments of cash.

Should cash flows from operating activities be positive or negative?

A healthy company will have positive cash flows from operations, meaning that by running the business, the company is bringing in more cash than it is paying out. A business could be profitable, but if it is unable to collect on invoices sent to customers, it may still have negative cash flows from operations. The individual lines on the statement of cash flows can provide some detail into that matter. For example, Loretta's Lawn Care collected $154,500 cash from customers during 2019 and paid $3,100 to suppliers and $62,100 to employees. This resulted in a positive cash flow from operations of $89,300. As Loretta's Lawn Care was able to bring in more cash than it paid out for operations, Loretta's Lawn Care appears to be healthy from an operating cash flow standpoint.

It should be noted that healthy companies can, from month to month, experience negative cash flows from operations. It is important to understand the reasons why the cash flow turned negative and what is being done to correct the situation. For example, it could be a simple timing difference with customer collections that will correct itself in the following month, or it could be a sign of trouble with collections in general. In the long run, healthy companies will show positive cash flows from operating activities.

What types of activities are included in the investing activities section?

The investing activities section of the statement of cash flows represents the cash increase or decrease due to investing in your own company via the purchase of productive resources (such as a lawn mower for Loretta's Lawn Care), investing in others via the purchase of stocks, etc., and lending money to others via the issuance of a note receivable. Cash inflows (positive numbers) result from the sale of investments or collections on notes receivable, whereas cash outflows (negative numbers) result from the purchase of investments or issuance of notes receivable.

Are there different types of formats allowed for the statement of cash flows?

There are two different methods that may be used to prepare the statement of cash flows: the direct method and the indirect method. The difference between the two methods is in the formula for the calculation of operating cash flows only. There is no difference in the calculation of investing or financing cash flows between the two methods.

The direct method reports the cash flows from operating activities by showing each type of operating cash inflow and outflow separately, such as "cash collections from customers" and "cash payments to suppliers." The direct method is used above in the Loretta's Lawn Care example.

The indirect method computes operating cash flows by starting with net income and then adjusting net income for the items that do not involve cash. For example, a company may make sales to customers, thus increasing net income, but may not have received the cash payment yet for that sale. That lack of cash payment would need to be subtracted from net income in arriving at cash flows from operations.

The resulting subtotal for cash flows from operating activities will be the same amount regardless of which method is used to prepare the statement of cash flows. The method selected merely alters the route to get there, not the final destination. Again, there are no changes to the calculation of cash flows from investing or financing activities between the direct and indirect methods.

An example of a statement of cash flows prepared using the indirect method for Vera Bradley, Inc., is shown below.

Should cash flows from financing activities be positive or negative?

Cash flows from financing activities may either be positive or negative. Just like with the investing activities, whether or not this is good or bad depends on the nature of the transactions. If a company is growing and taking out a business loan, this will result in positive cash flows from investing and would be considered normal for a growing business. However, if a business is struggling and taking out a loan to help cover operating costs, this would result in positive cash flows but be considered a warning sign. Likewise, payments on loans result in negative cash flows from financing activities but are indicative of a company that can pay its debts. In summary, whether or not the direction of the cash flows from financing activities is a good thing or a bad thing depends on the nature of the transaction, not the direction of the cash flow.

Vera Bradley, Inc.
Consolidated Statements of Cash Flows - USD ($), $ in Thousands
For the Fiscal Year Ended January 28, 2017

Cash flows from operating activities

Net income	$ 19,758
Adjustments to reconcile net income to net cash provided by operating activities:	
Depreciation of property, plant, and equipment	19,516
Impairment charges	12,706
Provision for doubtful accounts	439
Loss on disposal of property, plant, and equipment	14
Stock-based compensation	4,032
Deferred income taxes	(2,176)
Discontinued operations	0
Gain on short-term investment	(152)
Changes in assets and liabilities:	
Accounts receivable	7,542
Inventories	11,307
Prepaid expenses and other assets	(798)
Accounts payable	9,001
Income taxes	(12,009)
Accrued and other liabilities	(3,994)
Net cash provided by operating activities	65,186

Cash flows from investing activities

Purchases of property, plant, and equipment	(20,778)
Purchase of short-term investment	(30,000)
Proceeds from disposal of property, plant, and equipment	8
Net cash used in investing activities	(50,770)

Cash flows from financing activities

Tax withholdings for equity compensation	(729)
Repurchase of common stock	(24,959)
Other financing activities, net	(27)
Net cash used in financing activities	(25,715)

Effect of exchange rate changes on cash and cash equivalents	(7)
Net (decrease) increase in cash and cash equivalents	(11,306)
Cash and cash equivalents, beginning of period	97,681
Cash and cash equivalents, end of period	86,375

Supplemental disclosure of cash-flow information

Cash paid for income taxes, net	24,824
Cash paid for interest	$ 248

Should cash flows from investing activities be positive or negative?

Cash flows from investing activities may either be positive or negative. Whether or not this is good or bad depends on the nature of the transactions. For example, a growing company will generally have negative cash flows from investing activities because it is investing in itself by purchasing new assets. In contrast, a mature company that is experiencing a decline in sales may be selling off assets, resulting in positive cash flows from investing activities. The Loretta's Lawn Care Statement of Cash Flows shows negative cash flows from investing activities of $67,100, which is entirely from the purchases of equipment. In this case, that is a result of Loretta's Lawn Care being in the second year of operations and growing, which is generally viewed as a positive thing.

What types of activities are included in the financing activities section?

The financing activities section of the statement of cash flows represents cash increased or decreased from transactions with lenders (such as borrowing from the bank or repaying loans) or from transactions with owners (issuing or repurchasing stock or payments of dividends). Cash inflows (positive numbers) result from obtaining loans from the bank or issuing stock to investors. Cash outflows (negative numbers) result from repayments of loans, repurchases of stock, or payment of dividends.

How is the statement of cash flows dated?

Like the income statement and the statement of retained earnings, the statement of cash flows is dated for a period of time rather than at a point in time like the balance sheet. The change in cash is measured over a period of time that is typically one month, one quarter, or one year.

Why are some amounts shown in parentheses?

In general, accountants use parentheses to indicate a negative number. In the case of the statement of cash flows, parentheses are used to indicate a cash outflow, or use of cash. Numbers not in parentheses indicate a cash inflow, or source of cash. Thus, positive numbers indicate cash coming in. Negative numbers indicate cash going out.

What are the supplemental disclosures required on the statement of cash flows?

In addition to the information shown on the statement of cash flows, companies are also required to disclose material investing and financing transactions that did not result in a change in cash. For example, if a company purchased a new building for $1,000,000 and signed a note payable for the purchase, this transaction would not affect cash and thus not be shown on the statement of cash flows. This information is typically shown in the notes to the financial statements (discussed below). In addition, if a company prepares the statement of cash flows using the indirect method, it is also required to report the amount of cash paid for interest and for income taxes. This can be seen in the statement of cash flows for Vera Bradley, Inc., shown above.

OTHER FINANCIAL REPORTING

What does financial reporting mean?

Financial reporting is the process of gathering and providing financial information to external users, such as investors and creditors. This useful information takes the form of the four basic financial statements along with the related financial statement disclosures.

What are the financial statement disclosures?

In addition to the four basic financial statements, companies are required to disclose any other information that could affect the decisions made by external users (investors, creditors, etc.). These disclosures can take the form of parenthetical amounts noted right on the face of the financial statement, in paragraph-style notes following the financial statements, and/or supplemental schedules and tables. In general, these items convey information regarding the nature of the business and its activities, additional information to explain financial statement line items, and information that might affect future cash flows. The financial statement disclosures frequently take up more pages than the financial statements themselves!

What is an example of a parenthetical disclosure?

A common parenthetical disclosure that is presented right on the face of the financial statements is stock information reported on the balance sheet. For example, the figure below is taken from the balance sheet of Vera Bradley, Inc., as of January 28, 2017. The balance sheet lets the reader know that Vera Bradley has 36,218 shares of common stock outstanding.

	Jan. 28, 2017	Jan. 30, 2016
Shareholders' equity:		
Preferred stock; 5,000 shares authorized, no shares issued or outstanding	0	0
Common stock, without par value; 200,000 shares authorized, 40,927 and 40,804 shares issued and 36,218 and 37,701 outstanding,	0	0
Additional paid-in capital	88,739	85,436
Retained earnings	263,767	244,009
Accumulated other comprehensive loss	(50)	(43)
Treasury stock	(68,670)	(44,147)
Total shareholders' equity	283,786	285,255
Total liabilities and shareholders' equity	$ 373,509	$ 380,679

What is an example of a disclosure presented in the notes to the financial statements?

Certain information that is useful to external users is presented after the financial statements in paragraph form. Examples of these notes include: description of the company, summary of significant accounting policies, and noteworthy events or transactions. The figure below shows the first note to the financial statements for Vera Bradley, Inc., for the period ending January 28, 2017.

Vera Bradley, Inc.
Notes to Consolidated Financial Statements

1. Description of the Company

Vera Bradley, Inc. ("Vera Bradley" or the "Company") is a leading designer of women's handbags, luggage and travel items, fashion and home accessories, and unique gifts. Founded in 1982 by friends Barbara Bradley Baekgaard and Patricia R. Miller, the brand's innovative designs, iconic patterns, and brilliant colors continue to inspire and connect women.

Vera Bradley offers a unique, multichannel sales model as well as a focus on service and a high level of customer engagement. The Company sells its products through two reportable segments: Direct and Indirect. The Direct business consists of sales of Vera Bradley products through the Company's full-line and factory outlet stores in the United States, verabradley.com, direct-to-consumer eBay sales, and the Company's annual outlet sale in Fort Wayne, Indiana. As of January 28, 2017 , the Company operated 113 full-line stores and 46 factory outlet stores. The Indirect business consists of sales of Vera Bradley products to approximately 2,600 specialty retail locations, substantially all of which are located in the United States, as well as department stores, national accounts, third-party e-commerce sites, the Company's wholesale customer in Japan, and third-party inventory liquidators.

Principles of Consolidation

The consolidated financial statements include the accounts of the Company and its wholly owned subsidiaries. The Company has eliminated intercompany balances and transactions in consolidation.

Fiscal Periods

The Company utilizes a 52–53 week fiscal year ended on the Saturday closest to January 31. As such, fiscal year 2017, 2016 and 2015 ending on January 28, 2017, January 30, 2016, and January 31, 2015, respectively, each reflected a 52–week period.

Does management have to prepare anything other than the four basic financial statements and the financial statement disclosures?

Public companies (those listed on the stock exchange) are required to file various other reports with the Securities and Exchange Commission. Two of the most common required filings are annual reports (also known as a Form 10-K) and quarterly reports (also known as Form 10-Q).

An annual report contains a wealth of information and is typically around one hundred pages. In addition to the financial statements and related disclosures, annual reports also contain a section entitled "management's discussion and analysis" (also known as MD&A), which details management's views on significant events, trends, and uncertainties. The MD&A section can provide the reader with a vast amount of knowledge about the company's operations, liquidity, and capital resources. Annual reports also include the report of financial statement auditors on the presentation of the financial statements (as discussed previously in this chapter). It should be noted that there are many other items included in an annual report besides those highlights mentioned here. A quarterly report is a somewhat watered-down version of an annual report, presenting unaudited financial statements for a given three-month period, along with the required disclosures, MD&A, etc.

What is an example of a supplemental schedule?

Additional information regarding line items on the financial statements is typically presented in a supplemental schedule in the notes to the financial statements. It is common to see supplemental schedules with details regarding leases, long-term debt, and property, plant, and equipment. For example, the figure below shows the note and supplemental schedule for Vera Bradley, Inc., regarding property, plant, and equipment for the period ending January 28, 2017.

Property, Plant, and Equipment

Property, plant, and equipment consisted of the following (in thousands):

	January 28, 2017	January 30, 2016
Land and land improvements	$ 5,981	$ 5,981
Building and building improvements	46,233	46,145
Furniture, fixtures, leasehold improvements, computer equipment and software	127,791	127,913
Equipment and vehicles	20,329	19,931
Construction in progress	7,885	8,034
	208,219	208,004
Less: Accumulated depreciation and amortization	(106,642)	(94,293)
Property, plant, and equipment, net	$ 101,577	$ 113,711

Property, plant, and equipment are reviewed for impairment whenever events or changes in circumstances indicate that the carrying amount of the assets may not be recoverable. The reviews are conducted at the lowest identifiable level of cash flows. If the estimated undiscounted future cash flows related to the property, plant, and equipment are less than the carrying value, the Company recognizes a loss equal to the difference between the carrying value and the fair value, as further defined in Note 2. An impairment charge of $12.7 million, $2.8 million and $0.4 million was recognized, using level 3 inputs, in the fiscal years ended January 28, 2017, January 30, 2016 and January 31, 2015, respectively, for assets related to underperforming stores and is included in selling, general, and administrative expenses in the Consolidated Statements of Income and in impairment charges in the Consolidated Statements of Cash Flows. The impairment charges are included in the Direct segment.

Depreciation and amortization expense associated with property, plant, and equipment, excluding impairment charges and discontinued operations (in thousands):

Fiscal year ended January 28, 2017	$ 19,516
Fiscal year ended January 30, 2016	19,418
Fiscal year ended January 31, 2015	14,425

Typically, upper-level accounting courses teach the details regarding which disclosures are required and how they are presented. For a user of financial statements, it is important to know where they are located (after the financial statements) and what type of information they convey (information that aids the external users in understanding the financial information of the entity).

FINANCIAL STATEMENT ANALYSIS

ANALYSIS BASICS

How do you know if a company is doing well?

In order to determine if a company is doing well, some detailed financial analysis is required. In its most basic form, financial analysis involves reviewing a company's performance over time and comparing a company's results to that of the industry, competitors, and expectations.

What types of information are users looking for?

The types of information users are looking for depends on the user. For example, creditors are generally interested in understanding if the company has the ability to repay loans and pay interest as it comes due. In addition, creditors are interested in the amount of collateral a company has in case the company runs into trouble paying its debts. Investors are generally interested in understanding what the return on their investment will be. This return on investment takes two forms. First, investors are interested in understanding if they will earn a short-term return on their investment through the form of dividends paid out by the company. Second, investors are interested in understanding if they will earn a long-term return on their investment through increased stock value. Managers, on the other hand, use financial analysis to make decisions for the company and evaluate the results of past decisions.

Where do you start when analyzing the financial statements?

A good place to start when analyzing financial statements is to read the financial statements themselves, the notes to the financial statements, and the accompanying annual report information, such as the MD&A (as discussed in the chapter entitled "Four Basic

Financial Statements"). After reading through the financial package of the company and getting a basic understanding, more detailed financial analysis can begin.

Can you just use the comparative financial statements to determine if a company is doing well?

Looking at comparative financial statements, those showing two years or more of data in columns, is a good start. However, most accountants and financial professionals prefer to add columns showing the dollar change from one year to the next and the percentage change. In this way, rather than just having columns that show revenue for Year 1 as $150,000 and revenue for Year 2 as $165,000, there would also be columns that show that revenue increased by $15,000, or 10%. An example is shown in the figure below.

Loretta's Lawn Care
Comparative Income Statement
For the years ending December 31, 2019, and December 31, 2018

	2019	2018	Increase/(Decrease) Amount	Percent
Revenues:				
Service Revenue	$ 165,000	$ 150,000	$ 15,000	10%
Expenses:				
Wages Expense	62,100	54,000	$ 8,100	15%
Utilities & Fuel Expense	13,200	12,000	$ 1,200	10%
Rent Expense	2,400	2,400	$ -	0%
Insurance Expense	1,000	1,000	$ -	0%
Advertising Expense	500	500	$ -	0%
Depreciation Expense	100	100	$ -	0%
Total Expenses	79,300	70,000	$ 9,300	13%
Net Income	$ 85,700	$ 80,000	$ 5,700	7%

How do you calculate a dollar change?

The dollar change is calculated by taking the current year amount and subtracting the base year amount. The base year is typically the prior year but can be any year that you are using to compare to. In the example above, the dollar change of revenue would be calculated as follows:

Current Year Amount − Base Year Amount = Dollar Change

$165,000 − $150,000 = $15,000

Since the result is a positive number, we know that revenue increased. If the result would have been a negative number, we would know that revenue decreased from Year 1 to Year 2.

How do you calculate a percent change?

The percent change is calculated as:

(Current Year Amount − Base Year Amount) / Base Year Amount

However, if you have already calculated the dollar change, you can simply calculate the percentage change as follows:

Dollar Change / Base Year Amount

Accordingly, the percent change in revenue from the previous example can be calculated as follows:

$15,000 / $150,000 = 0.1

As such, we would say that revenue increased 10% from Year 1 to Year 2.

How do you interpret the results of the dollar and percent changes?

When you calculate dollar and percent changes, you will know if a financial statement item increased or decreased and by how much. Whether or not this is good or bad depends on the financial statement item itself. In general, if the financial statement item is something that the company generally wants more of, like revenue, an increase would be looked at favorably. However, if the financial statement item is something that the company generally wants less of, like debt, an increase would be looked at unfavorably. It is important to note, however, that everything must be taken into context. For example, a growing company may be taking on debt in order to expand the business. So, while increasing debt may be looked at unfavorably, there is a very logical explanation for the increase. As such, one financial statement item should not be looked at in isolation. This is why a detailed and complete financial statement analysis should be performed.

In the example in the previous figure showing the comparative income statement for Loretta's Lawn Care, we can make some simple assumptions about the business. For example, we can see that revenue increased by 10%, but net income only increased by 7%. Additionally, we know that wages expense increased by 15%. We can assume that more hours were worked due to the increased sales revenue, causing the increase in the wages expense. However, since the wages expense increased by 15%, we might also guess that raises were given. A more detailed and thorough analysis can provide more insight into these assumptions.

HORIZONTAL ANALYSIS

What is horizontal analysis?

Horizontal analysis, also known as trend analysis, refers to financial statement analysis that looks at performance over time. The most basic form of horizontal analysis is computing dollar and percent changes on comparative financial statements, as discussed previously in this chapter. However, trend analysis can also take the form of a more comprehensive comparison of many years of financial data. This is typically achieved by computing trend percentages.

How is a trend percentage computed?

A trend percentage is computed by taking the current year value and dividing by the base year value of a financial statement item. As a result, each year is shown as a percentage of the base year. The formula for a trend percentage is:

Current Year Amount / Base Year Amount

In the case of a trend percentage, the base year refers to the first year of financial data shown on the analysis, and every year following is calculated as a percentage of that original year. The selected data in the figure below was taken from the Boston Beer Company, which, as noted in its annual report, is engaged in the business of producing and selling alcohol beverages primarily in the domestic market and, to a lesser extent, in selected international markets. The company's revenues are primarily derived by selling its beers, hard ciders, and hard seltzers to distributors, who in turn sell the products to retailers and drinkers. The company is perhaps best known for its Samuel Adams® beers. In this trend analysis, each year is divided by the first year presented, which is the base year. In this case, the base year is 2007.

Data selected from The Boston Beer Company, Inc.
($ in thousands)

	2007	2008	2009	2010	2011
Gross Revenue	$ 380,575	$ 436,332	$ 453,446	$ 505,870	$ 558,282
Trend Percent	*100%*	*115%*	*119%*	*133%*	*147%*
Net Income	$ 22,491	$ 8,088	$ 31,118	$ 50,142	$ 66,059
Trend Percent	100%	36%	138%	223%	294%

	2012	2013	2014	2015	2016
Gross Revenue	$ 628,580	$ 793,705	$ 966,478	$ 1,024,040	$ 968,994
Trend Percent	*165%*	*209%*	*254%*	*269%*	*255%*
Net Income	$ 59,467	$ 70,392	$ 90,743	$ 98,414	$ 87,349
Trend Percent	264%	313%	403%	438%	388%

By reviewing the data for gross revenue and net income over a ten-year period, the reader can see that 2016 revenues were 255% that of 2007 revenues. Stated another way, one can say that 2016 gross revenue was roughly two and a half times the size of 2007 gross revenue. One can also see that revenue increased each year in the ten-year period, with the exception of 2016, where the company reported a decrease in shipments to distributors. Net income in 2016 was 388% that of the 2007 net income or roughly four times the size of 2007 net income. One can also note that net income increased most years in the ten-year period, with decreases in 2008, 2012, and 2016. Further review of the company's annual report can provide some insight into these decreases. For example, in 2008, the company noted in its annual report that there had been a product recall.

Why is financial data sometimes shown "in thousands" or "in millions," etc.?

Financial data is often rounded on the financial statements for readability, that is, to make it easier for the reader to see the financial information. Companies that have billions of dollars in revenue, for example, would need columns on the financial statements wide enough to accommodate ten or more digits. Accordingly, it is preferable to keep the columns to a smaller number of digits. As such, companies round their financial information. If amounts are rounded to thousands, you can mentally add three zeros to the end of each number. If amounts are rounded to millions, you can mentally add six zeros to the end of each number, etc.

Is there only one way to perform horizontal analysis?

There are many ways to perform horizontal analysis. As noted previously in this chapter, one form of horizontal analysis is to compute dollar and percent changes on comparative financial statements. Another way to perform horizontal analysis is to calculate trend percentages. Additional methods include preparing charts and graphs that track amounts and trend percentages over time.

VERTICAL ANALYSIS

What is vertical analysis?

Vertical analysis, typically displayed as a common size financial statement, refers to financial statement analysis that looks at the relationships among financial statement amounts for a specific point in time. Analysts typically prepare statements called common size income statements and common size balance sheets to show these relationships.

How is vertical analysis different from horizontal analysis?

Horizontal analysis looks at results over time (side to side), while vertical analysis looks at how items on a financial statement are related to other items on the same statement (up and down). While vertical analysis specifically refers to the process of looking at the relationships of financial statement items at one specific time, it is common for analysts to compare trends in these relationships across multiple time periods, thus combining horizontal analysis with vertical analysis.

What is a common size income statement?

A common size income statement is a form of vertical analysis where the income statement line items are shown as a percentage of revenue. This is typically done by adding additional columns to the income statement showing the percentages. A sample common size income statement for Loretta's Lawn Care is shown in the figure below.

Loretta's Lawn Care
Common Size Comparative Income Statement
For the years ended December 31, 2019, and December 31, 2018

	2019	2018	Common Size % 2019	Common Size % 2018
Revenues:				
Service Revenue	$ 165,000	$ 150,000	100.0%	100.0%
Expenses:				
Wages Expense	62,100	54,000	37.6%	36.0%
Utilities & Fuel Expense	13,200	12,000	8.0%	8.0%
Rent Expense	2,400	2,400	1.5%	1.6%
Insurance Expense	1,000	1,000	0.6%	0.7%
Advertising Expense	500	500	0.3%	0.3%
Depreciation Expense	100	100	0.1%	0.1%
Total Expenses	79,300	70,000	48.1%	46.7%
Net Income	$ 85,700	$ 80,000	51.9%	53.3%

How do you compute the percentages on a common size income statement?

The common size percentages on the income statement are computed by taking each line of the income statement individually and dividing that amount by the revenue line of the income statement for that same period. If multiple periods are shown on the income statement, separate columns will be used to show the percentages for each year. It is important to note that each year is calculated independently; that is, each year's income statement items are divided by revenue for that particular year.

How do you analyze a common size income statement?

As each item on a common size income statement is shown as a percent of revenue, everything can be evaluated by saying "what portion of the revenue I earned from my customers went to this particular item." For Loretta's Lawn Care, 37.6% of revenues earned in 2019 went toward covering wages. Another 8% was spent on fuel. In total, 48.1% over every dollar earned from a customer was used to cover expenses. The remaining 51.9% stayed in the business as profit (net income). Stated another way, for every $1 earned by Loretta's Lawn Care, roughly 48 cents was used to cover expenses, resulting in roughly 52 cents left over for the company. The reader can also see that wages expense is by far the biggest expense for Loretta's Lawn Care and has been growing as a percent of total revenue from 2018 to 2019. It would be important to investigate whether this change was due to rising fuel prices that were not passed on to customers, or lower prices/discounts may have been given to customers when fuel prices remained consistent, etc.

It is important to note that when revenue increases, many costs are generally expected to increase as well. When reviewing the comparative income statement for Loretta's Lawn Care, a reader can see that revenues increased from 2018 to 2019, along with expenses. That seems reasonable. However, by preparing a common size income statement, the reader can see that expenses are increasing by more than the proportional share of revenue, making up 48.1% of revenue in 2019 as compared to only 46.7% in the prior year. This indicates shrinking profit margins. Even though net income increased by $5,700 from 2018 to 2019, the company did not make as much profit on each dollar of revenue that it earned. This may signal concerns over customer pricing and/or cost control.

When analyzing a common size income statement, it is useful to compare these percentages over time to find trends, to compare to budgeted expectations, and also to compare these percentages to competitors and/or the industry averages. This will give a clearer picture for evaluating whether the results are favorable or unfavorable.

Is there another way to perform vertical analysis on the income statement?

There are several ways to perform vertical analysis on the income statement. Aside from preparing a common size income statement, it can be very helpful to display the results in pie chart form, as well. An example for Loretta's Lawn Care is shown in the figure below.

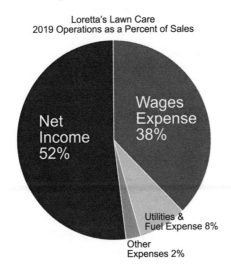

Loretta's Lawn Care
2019 Operations as a Percent of Sales

Net Income 52%

Wages Expense 38%

Utilities & Fuel Expense 8%

Other Expenses 2%

What is a common size balance sheet?

A common size balance sheet is a form of vertical analysis where the balance sheet line items are shown as a percentage of total assets. This is typically done by adding additional columns to the balance sheet showing the percentages. A sample common size balance sheet for Loretta's Lawn Care is shown in the figure below.

Loretta's Lawn Care
Common Size Comparative Balance Sheet
As of December 31, 2019 and December 31, 2018

	2019	2018	Common Size % 2019	Common Size % 2018
Assets				
Cash	$ 119,000	$ 70,000	56.0%	82.4%
Accounts Receivable	20,500	10,000	9.6%	11.8%
Supplies	3,000	2,000	1.4%	2.4%
Equipment	70,000	3,000	32.9%	3.5%
Total Assets	$ 212,500	$ 85,000	100.0%	100.0%
Liabilities and Owner's Equity				
Liabilities				
Accounts Payable	$ 30,000	$ 15,000	14.1%	17.6%
Notes Payable	66,800	10,000	31.4%	11.8%
Total Liabilities	96,800	25,000	45.6%	29.4%
Owner's Equity				
Contributed Capital	10,000	10,000	4.7%	11.8%
Retained Earnings	105,700	50,000	49.7%	58.8%
Total Owner's Equity	115,700	60,000	54.4%	70.6%
Total Liabilities and Owner's Equity	$ 212,500	$ 85,000	100.0%	100.0%

How do you compute the percentages on a common size balance sheet?

The common size percentages on the balance sheet are computed by taking each line of the balance sheet individually and dividing that amount by the total assets line of the balance sheet for that same period. If multiple periods are shown on the balance sheet, separate columns will be used to show the percentages for each year. It is important to note that each year is calculated independently; that is, each year's balance sheet items are divided by total assets for that particular year.

How do you analyze a common size balance sheet?

As each item on a common size balance sheet is shown as a percent of total assets, everything under the assets heading can be evaluated by saying "what portion of the total assets does this item make up." For each item under the liabilities or owner's equity headings, they can be evaluated by saying "what portion of the total assets were financed by this item." For Loretta's Lawn Care, cash made up 56% of total assets in 2019 as compared to 82% in 2018. Equipment made up 33% of total assets in 2019 as compared to only 4% in the prior year. The reader can also see that in 2018, roughly 29% of the total assets of Loretta's Lawn Care were financed with debt, whereas the other approximately 71% were financed with equity. This changed in 2019 when roughly 46% of total assets were financed with debt, leaving the remaining 54% financed with equity. In general, equity is a less risky method of financing than debt, so this increase would be viewed as a somewhat risky trend. However, given that Loretta's Lawn Care is in its second year of operations and has more than doubled in size (total assets) during the two years, it is understandable that additional debt would be taken on to finance that growth. As noted above, equipment increased during this same period, leading the reader to believe that the new equipment purchases were financed with loans (debt).

It is important to note that when total assets increase, total liabilities and equity will increase as well. (Remember, the basic accounting equation must always be in balance.) When reviewing the comparative balance sheet for Loretta's Lawn Care, a reader can see that total assets increased from 2018 to 2019, along with total liabilities and total owner's equity. However, by preparing a common size balance sheet, the reader can see that the proportion of financing is shifting more from equity to debt, while the overall balance still lies under the equity portion (making up 54.4% of total financing for 2019).

Just as with analyzing a common size income statement, when analyzing a common size balance sheet, it is useful to compare these percentages over time to find trends, to compare to budgeted expectations, and also to compare these percentages to competitors and/or the industry averages. This will give a clearer picture for evaluating whether the results are favorable or unfavorable.

RATIO ANALYSIS BASICS

What is ratio analysis?

Ratio analysis is another form of financial statement analysis that looks at the relationships between different financial statement items. These ratios compare financial statement items from the same time period. For example, it would be useful to compare the net income from 2019 to the revenue from 2019. It would not make sense to compare the net income from 2019 to the revenue from 2018. One of the main benefits of performing ratio analysis is that it can be used to compare companies of different sizes, as financial statement items are shown in relative proportion to other financial statement items.

Ratio analysis can also be conducted between financial statement items and nonfinancial data, such as revenue per square foot of a retail store. Revenue is financial statement data, whereas the square footage of a retail store is nonfinancial data. When divided by each other, the reader can compare the revenues of retail stores that are of different sizes, as revenue becomes proportional. If store A is twice the size of store B, you might expect store A to have twice the revenues of store B. Computing revenue per square foot would be a quick way of comparing the sales volume of the stores in proportion to their size. However useful these nonfinancial measures may be, the focus of the next section is on ratios that compare financial statement data to other financial statement data.

How is ratio analysis used?

Ratio analysis is used in tandem with horizontal and vertical analysis to complete a thorough financial analysis. Users of financial information are generally interested in certain types of information; as such, financial ratios are generally categorized as liquidity ratios, solvency ratios, profitability ratios, asset management ratios, or market performance ratios. Vendors who are going to send a company invoices are generally most concerned with whether or not their invoices will get paid and, as such, would be interested primarily in liquidity ratios. Bankers who lend the company money on a longer term would be most interested in liquidity and solvency ratios. Potential investors are typically interested in profitability and market performance ratios. No matter which category is of most interest to the user, a good financial statement analysis will include many, if not all, of the ratios discussed in the following sections in addition to many other possibilities.

It is important to note that ratios should be evaluated not only by looking at the result calculated in the formula but also by looking at trends over time, comparing to expected results, and comparing to industry and/or competitor data.

Where can I find industry data?

There are a variety of publications that report industry averages by SIC or NAICS codes. Many of these publications are listed in the references section of this book. There are also many Internet sources, such as Yahoo!Finance that publish industry data.

Does each ratio have a standard formula?

Most financial ratios have a standard formula. However, many companies tweak these formulas for use in internal reporting to better tailor them to the company's needs. It is common for accounting and finance personnel to have to learn how certain formulas are calculated by their company. In addition, different accounting and finance text-

---

Where can I find competitor financial information?

Publicly traded companies are required to file their 10-K annual reports with the SEC. Those statements are loaded on to the EDGAR company filings tool that can be found at https://www.sec.gov/edgar/searchedgar/companysearch.html. Unfortunately, if a competitor is not publicly traded, it is usually not possible to access their financial statements.

books do not always agree on the same formulas for ratios. For example, a particular finance textbook shows the calculation of inventory turnover as sales divided by average inventory, whereas most other accounting textbooks show this calculation as cost of goods sold divided by average inventory. A quick search of the Internet will give you different formulas for the same ratios as well. It is important to note that while the specific formulas may differ, the "spirit" of the ratio, or what the ratio is intended to convey to the user, is generally the same. Additionally, sometimes the ratio shown from different sources is actually the same formula but uses synonymous language. For example, one source may refer to the net profit margin formula as net income divided by sales, whereas another source may refer to the net profit margin formula as net income divided by revenues. These are two ways of saying the same thing but can be easily confusing to nonaccounting or finance individuals.

Are there more ratios than just those listed in this chapter?

This chapter covers a good selection of financial ratios that cover the main areas of financial analysis: liquidity, solvency, profitability, asset management, and market performance. There are many more standard financial ratios and even more nonfinancial ratios that companies and users of financial statement information may create to meet their needs. Nonfinancial measures are discussed at the end of this chapter in the section entitled "The Balanced Scorecard."

LIQUIDITY RATIOS

What do liquidity ratios measure?

Liquidity ratios measure a company's ability to pay its short-term obligations as they come due. In particular, liquidity ratios give an indication of the company's ability to use cash and other current assets to pay bills and other obligations that are due within the next twelve months.

Which users of financial statement information are most concerned about liquidity?

Short-term creditors are most concerned with liquidity. For example, vendors and suppliers want to be sure that their customers will pay the invoices they send them. As such, they want to make sure the customer has enough cash and other current assets to pay the bills that they send. If the customer doesn't have enough cash and current assets to cover their short-term obligations, they would be a credit risk, and the vendor would have to decide if it is worth it or not to extend credit to that customer. Additionally, banks and other long-term lenders are concerned with liquidity ratios because they want to ensure that whoever they lend money to has enough cash and current assets to pay the interest and principal payments on the loans as they come due.

What are some ratios that measure liquidity?

Three key ratios that measure liquidity that are covered in this chapter are working capital, current ratio, and quick ratio. These are all measures that evaluate a company's short-term survival and ability to pay its bills as they come due.

What is working capital?

Working capital is the difference between current assets and current liabilities. Recall that current assets include cash and other assets that will be used up or turned into cash within the next year (or operating cycle, whichever is longer). Current liabilities are the debts that are due within the next year (or operating cycle, whichever is longer). The formula for working capital is:

Current Assets − Current Liabilities = Working Capital

Working capital for Vera Bradley, Inc., for the fiscal year ending January 2017 (in thousands) would be calculated as:

$255,577 − $62,507 = $193,070

Essentially, working capital is good stuff minus bad stuff. A company needs more good stuff than bad stuff to survive. If a company does not have enough current assets to meet its current liabilities, the company may have to borrow money to pay its bills or sell off long-term productive assets, like machinery or buildings. You may be wondering, "If the company has to get a loan to pay its bills, how will the company have enough cash to be able to pay *that* loan back?" or "If the company has to sell its production equipment to pay its bills, how will the company be able to produce enough product to stay in business?" Both are important questions to consider and evaluate.

How is working capital evaluated?

When evaluating working capital, a positive balance is the desired result. In general, the higher the working capital, the better. The higher the working capital, the easier it is for a company to pay its short-term obligations. While a negative working capital balance may be cause for concern, it is important to note that companies have bad months, quarters, or years from time to time. This does not mean they will always have negative working capital or that the business will fail. It is important to complete a full financial analysis, including comparison to prior periods, the industry, and the economy.

In the Vera Bradley, Inc., example, working capital is $193,070,000. That means Vera Bradley, Inc., has $193 million more good stuff than bad stuff. This would be a positive indication of the company's ability to pay its bills within the next twelve months. It would also be interesting to note that the prior year's working capital was $187,090,000. Thus, working capital increased, which is another positive sign.

What is the current ratio?

The current ratio is a measure of a company's short-term ability to pay its debts as they come due and is the result of current assets divided by current liabilities. Like working capital, the current ratio compares cash and other current assets to current liabilities. However, instead of subtracting the two, division is used. In this way, it is possible to compare companies of different sizes, whereas with working capital, this would not be possible. The formula for the current ratio is:

Current Assets / Current Liabilities = Current Ratio

The current ratio for Vera Bradley, Inc., for the fiscal year ending January 2017 would be calculated as:

$255,577 / $62,507 = 4.09

How is the current ratio evaluated?

When evaluating the current ratio, a result greater than one is desired. A result that is less than one indicates that the company has fewer current assets than it has current liabilities, which may indicate trouble paying current obligations as they come due. The higher the result, the better a company is able to pay its short-term debts. While a current ratio that is less than one may be cause for concern, the analyst should also look at trends over time, the industry averages, and the economy. It is also important to note that just because a company has a quick ratio greater than one does not mean it is totally without risk. A large portion of the current assets could be tied up in inventory or accounts receivable. If the company cannot sell its inventory or cannot collect its accounts receivable from customers, then it will not have the cash to pay its bills, even though it may have a high current ratio. It is always important to look at the individual items making up each ratio when performing analysis.

Vera Bradley, Inc., has a current ratio for the fiscal year ending January 2017 of 4.09, which means that the company has approximately four times as many current assets as current liabilities. Stated another way, it appears that Vera Bradley, Inc., could pay its short-term obligations four times over if it had to! Vendors looking to sell supplies to Vera Bradley, Inc., would most likely determine that the company would not be a credit risk based on this ratio.

What is the quick ratio?

The quick ratio is a tougher version of the current ratio. Essentially, the quick ratio measures a company's ability to pay its short-term debts without having to rely on the sale of inventory to do so. Whereas the current ratio uses all current assets in the numerator, the quick ratio only includes "quick assets" in the numerator. Quick assets generally include only cash, marketable securities, accounts receivable, and short-term notes receivable. Essentially, quick assets are those current assets that are cash or can be turned into cash quickly without having to rely on additional sales to customers. Inventory is always excluded from quick assets because in order to turn inventory into

What is the acid test ratio?

The acid test ratio is just another name for the quick ratio. This name originated from the gold rush, where acid was used to test metals for the presence of gold. If acid was dropped on the metal and didn't corrode it, it was determined that gold was present and the metal had value. If acid corroded the metal, the metal was deemed worthless. Just like acid was used as a quick test for the value of a metal, the acid test is a quick test to help determine a company's short-term survival.

cash, the company must sell its inventory to customers, then send invoices to customers, then wait for the customers to pay the invoices. Thus, this wouldn't be considered "quick." Accounts receivable, on the other hand, are considered quick because the sale has already been made, and now the company is just waiting on final payment from the customer. The formula for the quick ratio is:

(Cash + Marketable Securities + Accounts Receivable + Short-term Notes Receivable) / Current Liabilities = Quick Ratio

Vera Bradley, Inc.'s quick ratio for the fiscal year ending January 2017 would be calculated as:

$139,840 / $62,507 = 2.24

How is the quick ratio evaluated?

The quick ratio is evaluated in a very similar manner to the current ratio in that a ratio greater than one is the ideal result. A quick ratio greater than one indicates a company's ability to pay its short-term obligations without having to rely on sales of inventory to customers. It is important to note that many healthy companies have quick ratios less than one. A trend analysis or comparison to competitors and the industry would be helpful in determining how much cause for concern there should be over a quick ratio less than one.

SOLVENCY RATIOS

What do solvency ratios measure?

Solvency ratios measure a company's ability to pay its long-term obligations as they come due. In particular, solvency ratios give an indication of the company's ability to repay loans over the long run and give an indication of how a company uses debt to acquire assets. Solvency ratios can also be called debt management ratios.

How is solvency different from liquidity?

The primary difference between solvency and liquidity is that liquidity looks at a company's short-term debt-paying capabilities, whereas solvency refers to a company's long-term debt-paying abilities. Accordingly, liquidity is a short-term survival measure, whereas solvency is a long-term survival measure.

Which users of financial statement information are most concerned about solvency?

Long-term creditors are most concerned with solvency. For example, bankers want to be sure that their clients will pay back the interest and principal owed on loans. As such, they want to make sure the client earns enough income to be able to pay the interest expense as it comes due. They also want to evaluate the risk involved with loaning a client money. This involves understanding what proportion of total financing is achieved through debt. Additionally, investors are concerned with solvency ratios because they want to ensure that the company is maintaining debt at an appropriate level given the industry and economic conditions.

What are some ratios that measure solvency?

Three key ratios that measure solvency that are covered in this chapter are the times interest earned ratio, debt-to-assets ratio, and debt-to-equity ratio. These are all measures that evaluate a company's long-term survival and utilization of debt.

What is the times interest earned ratio?

The times interest earned ratio is a measure of a company's ability to pay interest payments on loans. The formula for times interest earned is:

(Net Income + Interest Expense + Income Tax Expense) / Interest Expense = Times Interest Earned

Basically, times interest earned measures how many times a company could pay for its interest expense using earnings before interest and taxes, also known as operating income.

The times interest earned ratio for Vera Bradley, Inc., for the fiscal year ending January 2017 would be calculated as:

$28,220 / $178 = 158.5

What is the debt-to-assets ratio?

The debt-to-assets ratio is a measure of the proportion of total assets that are financed with debt (as opposed to equity). The formula for the debt-to-assets ratio is:

Total Liabilities / Total Assets = Debt-to-Assets

The debt-to-assets ratio for Vera Bradley, Inc. for the fiscal year ending January 2017 would be calculated as:

$89,723 / $373,509 = 0.24

How is the debt-to-assets ratio evaluated?

When evaluating the debt-to-assets ratio, a lower number is deemed to be less risky than a higher number. The greater the proportion of assets that are financed by debt, the

How is the times interest earned ratio evaluated?

When evaluating the times interest earned ratio, a result greater than one is desired, indicating that the company has enough operating income to cover its interest costs. A result that is less than one indicates that the company has less operating income than it has interest expense, which may indicate trouble paying interest expense as it comes due. The higher the result, the better able a company is to pay its interest expense. A negative result indicates a company that has operating losses, which means there is insufficient income to cover interest expense and would be cause for concern. While a times interest earned ratio that is less than one may be cause for concern, the analyst should also look at trends over time, the industry averages, and the economy.

Vera Bradley, Inc., has a times interest earned ratio for the fiscal year ending January 2017 of 158.5, which means that the company has approximately 159 times as much operating income as it has interest expense. Stated another way, it appears that Vera Bradley, Inc., could pay its interest expense 159 times over if it had to! Bankers looking to lend money to Vera Bradley, Inc., would most likely determine that the company would not be at risk of having insufficient funds to cover interest expense obligations based on this ratio.

more risky the entity is. Recall that assets can be financed through either debt or equity (borrowing money or owners' investments). Debt must be repaid, whereas the owners' investments do not. Thus, debt is a riskier form of financing than equity. This does not mean that debt is bad, however. Many companies intentionally finance their assets with debt in order to pay less income taxes, as the interest expense on the debt is tax deductible, whereas dividends distributed to owners are not.

The debt-to-assets ratio for Vera Bradley, Inc., for the fiscal year ending January 2017 was 0.24. This means that 24% of Vera Bradley, Inc.'s assets were financed with debt. One can then quickly determine that the remaining 76% of Vera Bradley, Inc.'s assets were financed with equity. It is interesting to note that Vera Bradley, Inc.'s prior year debt-to-assets ratio was 0.25. Accordingly, one could say that Vera Bradley, Inc., had a relatively steady debt-to-assets ratio over the two-year period, noting a slight reduction in risk. It would be important to compare this ratio to industry averages and economic trends to get a full picture of their performance in this area. One ratio should never be looked at in isolation.

What is the debt-to-equity ratio?

The debt-to-equity ratio is a solvency ratio that compares a company's debt balance to the equity balance. It is similar in nature to the debt-to-assets ratio and may be used by analysts in its place. Whereas the debt-to-assets ratio shows the percentage of assets financed with debt rather than equity, the debt-to-equity ratio compares the two financing options to each other. The formula for the debt-to-equity ratio is:

Total Liabilities / Total Owner's Equity = Debt-to-Equity

The debt-to-equity ratio for Vera Bradley, Inc., for the fiscal year ending January 2017 would be calculated as:

$89,723 / $283,786 = 0.31

How is the debt-to-equity ratio evaluated?

When evaluating the debt-to-equity ratio, a lower number is deemed to be less risky than a higher number. Again, this does not mean that debt is bad and that all companies should have a low debt-to-equity ratio. It simply means the higher the ratio, the more the company finances its assets with debt instead of equity. This represents the choices that management has made in financing the business.

The debt-to-equity ratio for Vera Bradley, Inc., for the fiscal year ending January 2017 was 0.31. This means that there were 31 cents borrowed from creditors for every one dollar invested by stockholders.

PROFITABILITY RATIOS

What do profitability ratios measure?

Profitability ratios measure a company's ability to generate income during a specific time period. These ratios measure the operating performance of the company.

Which users of financial statement information are most concerned about profitability?

Investors are concerned with the profitability of a company, as investors are looking to earn a return on investment. This return on investment can either come in the form of profits being shared with the investors through the payment of dividends or through increases in stock price over time. The profitability of the business will affect the company's ability to pay dividends and have an impact on the stock price. Additionally, managers inside the company are concerned with profitability ratios, as they are an indication of the success of the company's operations.

What are some ratios that measure profitability?

Four key ratios that measure profitability that are covered in this chapter are gross profit percentage, net profit margin, return on assets, and return on equity. These are all measures that evaluate a company's operating performance.

Investors in companies are, naturally, concerned about positive returns on their investments. Monitoring stock values is one way investors track their financial interests.

What is the gross profit percentage?

The gross profit percentage, often referred to as gross margin, is the percentage of sales remaining after deducting cost of goods sold. It is calculated by taking gross profit divided by sales. The formula for gross profit percentage is:

Gross Profit / Sales Revenue = Gross Profit Percentage

The gross profit percentage is similar to the markup on sales. For example, if a retailer bought a toy for $2 and sold it to a customer for $10, that means the retailer marked up the price by $8. The gross profit on the income statement would be that $8. (Recall that sales revenue − cost of goods sold = gross profit.) The gross profit percentage would be 80%. This means that the retailer was able to keep 80% of the revenue earned from customers after paying for the good that was sold. That 80% remaining is used to cover the operating expenses of the business. Anything left over is profit. Also, keep in mind that the gross profit percentage is actually calculated right on the common size income statement, where every line of the income statement is divided by sales revenue.

The gross profit percentage for Vera Bradley, Inc., for the fiscal year ending January 2017 would be calculated as:

78 $276,046 / $485,937 = 56.8%

How is the gross profit percentage evaluated?

When evaluating the gross profit percentage, the higher the result, the better. A higher gross profit percentage means the company is able to keep more of its revenues earned from customers to be used to cover operating costs and ultimately end up as net income. As with all ratios, gross profit percentages vary by industry. As such, it is important to evaluate the gross profit ratio in light of the industry averages and economic trends as well as looking at trends over time. Vera Bradley, Inc.'s gross profit percentage for the fiscal year ending January 2017 was 56.8%. The prior year gross profit percentage for Vera Bradley, Inc., was 55.9%. Accordingly, one can see that Vera Bradley's margin increased slightly over the two-year period, which would be looked at favorably. This increase in gross profit percentage could be due to increasing prices to customers, decreasing prices from suppliers, or some combination of factors. On average, for every dollar Vera Bradley, Inc., earns from making sales to customers, roughly 43 cents goes towards the cost of the goods that were sold, and the remaining 57 cents is used to cover operating expenses and ultimately make a profit.

What is net profit margin?

The net profit margin, often referred to as net margin, is the bottom-line measure of profitability as compared to sales. It is calculated by taking net income divided by sales. The formula for net profit margin is:

Net Income / Sales Revenue = Net Profit Margin

Just like the gross profit percentage, the net profit margin is shown right on the face of the common size income statement, as every line item is divided by sales revenue. The net profit margin shows what percentage of every dollar earned in revenue was able to be kept (not spent on costs) by the business as net income.

The net profit margin for Vera Bradley, Inc., for the fiscal year ending January 2017 would be calculated as:

$19,758 / $485,937 = 4.1%

What is return on assets?

The return on assets ratio measures a company's ability to utilize its total assets to generate net income. The return on assets shows the amount of profit generated for each dollar invested in assets. Companies invest in assets to use in operations. These assets are expected to be used to earn revenues and thus result in a profit. The return on assets ratio measures the effectiveness of using assets to gain a profit, thus the name "return on assets." The formula for return on assets is:

Net Income / Average Total Assets = Return on Assets

Notice that the denominator uses average total assets instead of just total assets. Because this ratio combines items from the balance sheet and the income statement, it would not be appropriate to divide net income earned over the entire year by a total

How is net profit margin evaluated?

When evaluating the net profit margin, the higher the result, the better. A higher net profit margin means the company is able to keep more of its revenues earned from customers as net income. As with all ratios, net profit margins vary by industry. As such, it is important to evaluate the net profit margin in light of the industry averages and economic trends as well as looking at trends over time. Vera Bradley, Inc.'s net profit margin for the fiscal year ending January 2017 was 4.1%. This means that for every dollar of revenue earned by Vera Bradley, Inc., roughly 4.1 cents was able to stay with the company as profit. The remaining 95.9 cents was spent on covering the operating costs of the business. It is interesting to note that the prior year net profit margin for Vera Bradley, Inc., was 5.5%. Accordingly, one can see that Vera Bradley's net margin decreased over the two-year period, which would generally be looked at unfavorably. A quick look at the comparative income statement for Vera Bradley will show you that while sales decreased over the two-year period, selling, general, and administrative expenses actually increased. This appears to be the primary cause for the decrease in net profit margin.

asset amount from just the last day of the year. As such, a simple average of total assets is used by taking the total assets at the beginning of the year (last year's total assets), adding to the total assets at the end of the year, and dividing by two.

The return on assets for Vera Bradley, Inc., for the fiscal year ending January 2017 would be calculated as:

$19,758 / (($373,509 + $380,679) / 2) = 5.2%

How is the return on assets evaluated?

When evaluating the return on assets, the higher the result, the better. The higher the return on assets, the better able a company is at utilizing its assets to earn a profit. The return on assets for Vera Bradley, Inc., for the fiscal year ending January 2017 was 5.2%. That means that for every dollar Vera Bradley, Inc., has invested in assets, it was able to generate 5.2 cents of profit.

What is return on equity?

The return on equity ratio compares the profits earned by a company to the dollar amount of owner's equity. This measure is similar to return on assets; however, return on assets compares net income to average total assets, whereas return on equity compares net income to average total stockholders' equity. The formula for return on equity is:

Net Income / Average Stockholders' Equity = Return on Equity

Note that average total stockholders' equity is used as the denominator because this ratio compares income statement data to balance sheet data. The average stockholders' equity can be calculated as a simple average of the prior year and the current year balances.

The return on equity for Vera Bradley, Inc., for the fiscal year ending January 2017 would be calculated as:

$19,758 / (($283,786 + $285,255) / 2) = 6.9%

How is return on equity evaluated?

When evaluating the return on equity, the higher the result, the better. The higher the return on equity, the better able a company is at generating profit in proportion to the owners' investment. The return on equity for Vera Bradley, Inc., for the fiscal year ending January 2017 was 6.9%. That means that for every dollar of investors' stake in Vera Bradley, Inc., they were able to generate 6.9 cents of profit.

ASSET MANAGEMENT RATIOS

What do asset management ratios measure?

Asset management ratios measure how efficient and effective a company is at managing their assets. Many of the asset management ratios are also included as part of a liquidity analysis in that they are typically measures of short-term survival.

Which users of financial statement information are most concerned about asset management?

Creditors and investors alike are concerned with how a company is managing its assets. The assets are financed by both creditors and investors. As such, each group has an interest in the efficient and effective deployment of those assets. Additionally, many asset management ratios are used regularly by members of the management team of a company to measure performance in managing those assets.

What are some ratios that measure asset management?

Six key ratios that measure asset management that are covered in this chapter are accounts receivable turnover, average collection period, inventory turnover, average sale period, operating cycle, and fixed asset turnover. These are all measures that evaluate a company's management of assets under its control.

What is accounts receivable turnover?

Accounts receivable turnover measures how quickly a company cycles through its accounts receivable. That is, it measures the times per year a company generates sales, sends invoices, and collects on those invoices, thus turning accounts receivable into cash. The formula for accounts receivable turnover is:

Sales on Account / Average Accounts Receivable = Accounts Receivable Turnover

It is important to note that only sales on account (credit sales) are included in the numerator, not total sales. It would not be appropriate to include cash sales, as they are never a part of accounts receivable and, thus, would distort the ratio. Additionally, as this ratio combines income statement data with balance sheet data, an average of accounts receivable must be used. This average is computed as a simple average of the prior year's accounts receivable balance and the current year's accounts receivable balance.

When you think of a creditor, you might think of a company pressuring you for overdue bill payments, but in the business world, creditors provide companies with debt capital while investors provide equity capital.

The accounts receivable turnover for Vera Bradley, Inc., for the fiscal year ending January 2017 would be calculated as follows (assuming all sales are on credit):

$485,937 / (($23,313 + $31,294) / 2) = 17.8

How is accounts receivable turnover evaluated?

When evaluating accounts receivable turnover, the higher the number, the more efficient and effective a company is at cycling through its accounts receivable and collecting on invoices sent to customers. In order to determine how well the company is doing at collecting from customers, this ratio should be compared to the payment terms noted on the invoices. For example, if a company sends invoices with terms due in thirty days, one would expect the company to collect every thirty days, or roughly twelve times per year. If that company has an accounts receivable turnover of ten times per year, one might think it is collecting more slowly than it should be. However, if that same company sends invoices with terms due in ninety days, having an accounts receivable turnover of ten would be impressive. Accounts receivable turnover rates vary by industry, as in some industries, it is common to send invoices with terms "due upon receipt" and in other industries, it is common to send invoices with terms "due in ninety days" or longer. Additionally, it is important to look at a company's accounts receivable turnover over time to see if collections are improving or worsening. The accounts receivable turnover for Vera Bradley, Inc., for the fiscal year ending January 2017 was calculated as 17.8. Accordingly, Vera Bradley, Inc., cycles through its accounts receivable roughly eighteen times per year.

What is the average collection period?

The average collection period, often referred to as days to collect, is another measure showing how quickly credit sales are turned into cash. The average collection period is simply another way of showing the accounts receivable turnover; however, the average collection period is stated in days to collect instead of times per year. The formula for the average collection period is:

365 Days / Accounts Receivable Turnover = Average Collection Period

Note that you are simply taking the number of days in the year divided by the accounts receivable turnover ratio to convert the accounts receivable turnover ratio from times per year to how many days it takes to collect.

The average collection period for Vera Bradley, Inc., for the fiscal year ending January 2017 can be calculated as follows:

365 / 17.8 = 20.5 days

How is the average collection period evaluated?

When evaluating the average collection period, the lower the number, the more efficient and effective a company is at converting its accounts receivable into cash. Basically, a lower number means the company is collecting faster (fewer days to collect). This ratio measures the exact same thing as accounts receivable turnover but is stated in a simpler fashion. In addition, it is somewhat easier to compare how well a company is collecting on receivables when using the average collection period as it is stated in days, which is the same way credit terms are stated on invoices. Thus, if you have a company that sends invoices out with terms due in thirty days and the average collection period is thirty days, you would most likely be satisfied. However, if the same company sends invoices with terms due in fifteen days, an average collection period of thirty days would most likely be unsatisfactory. The average collection period for Vera Bradley, Inc., for the fiscal year ending January 2017 was calculated as 20.5 days. This means it takes its customers an average of 20.5 days to pay invoices. This would need to be compared to credit terms on the invoices and company policy to determine if 20.5 is acceptable or not. Additionally, the average collection period should be compared to the average collection period for prior years to determine collection trends and get an understanding of whether or not collections are improving, worsening, or staying the same.

How is inventory turnover evaluated?

When evaluating inventory turnover, the higher the number, the more efficient and effective a company is at cycling through its inventory. Inventory turnover rates vary by industry. For example, you would expect a grocer that sells perishable food to cycle through its inventory much faster than a car dealership. Additionally, it is important to look at a company's inventory turnover over time to see if turnover is improving or worsening. The inventory turnover for Vera Bradley, Inc., for the fiscal year ending January 2017 was calculated as 1.9. Accordingly, Vera Bradley, Inc., cycles through its in-

> ## What is inventory turnover?
>
> Inventory turnover measures how quickly a company cycles through its inventory. That is, it measures the times per year a company purchases and sells its inventory. The formula for inventory turnover is:
>
> Cost of Goods Sold / Average Inventory = Inventory Turnover
>
> As this ratio combines income statement data with balance sheet data, an average of inventory must be used. This average is computed as a simple average of the prior year's inventory balance and the current year's inventory balance.
>
> The inventory turnover for Vera Bradley, Inc., for the fiscal year ending January 2017 would be calculated as follows:
>
> $209,891 / (($102,283 + $113,590) / 2) = 1.9

ventory roughly twice a year. It would be important to get an understanding of the industry averages to evaluate whether this result is adequate. If a company has an inventory ratio that is much lower than industry, it may indicate an overabundance of inventory or inventory that the company cannot sell. It could also indicate that management is trying to buy large quantities of inventory to receive discounts. These managerial decisions should be evaluated to determine if the cost of carrying the inventory is worth the benefits of ordering large quantities.

What is the average sale period?

The average sale period, often referred to as days to sell, is another measure showing how quickly inventory is bought and sold. The average sale period is simply another way of showing the inventory turnover; however, the average sale period is stated in the number of days to sell inventory instead of the times per year. The formula for the average sale period is:

365 Days / Inventory Turnover = Average Sale Period

Note that you are simply taking the number of days in the year divided by the inventory turnover ratio to convert the inventory turnover ratio from times per year to how many days it takes to sell the inventory.

The average sale period for Vera Bradley, Inc., for the fiscal year ending January 2017 can be calculated as follows:

365 / 1.9 = 192 days

How is the average sale period evaluated?

When evaluating the average sale period, the lower the number, the more efficient and effective a company is at cycling through its inventory. Basically, a lower number means the company is cycling faster (fewer days to sell). This ratio measures the exact same thing as inventory turnover but is stated in a simpler fashion. The average sale period for Vera Bradley, Inc., for the fiscal year ending January 2017 was calculated as 192 days. This means it takes Vera Bradley, Inc., approximately 192 days to sell its inventory. This would need to be compared to industry averages and economic trends in order to determine if this result is acceptable or not. Additionally, it should be compared to the average sale period for prior years to determine inventory trends and get an understanding of whether or not inventory management is improving, worsening, or staying the same.

What is the operating cycle?

The operating cycle measures the number of days it takes to turn inventory into cash. It is the combination of the average collection period and the average sale period. The operating cycle is the process of purchasing inventory, selling inventory, and collecting the cash from customers. The purchasing and selling of inventory is represented by the average sale period. The selling of inventory and collecting cash from customers is represented by the average collection period. The formula for the operating cycle time is:

Average Sale Period + Average Collection Period = Operating Cycle

The operating cycle for Vera Bradley, Inc., for the fiscal year ending January 2017 would be calculated as follows:

192 days + 20.5 days = 212.5 days

How is the operating cycle evaluated?

When evaluating the operating cycle, the lower the number of days, the more efficient and effective a company is at turning its inventory into cash. The operating cycle time for Vera Bradley, Inc., for the fiscal year ending January 2017 was calculated as 212.5 days. That means that 212.5 days pass, on average, between the time the company purchases the inventory and the time the company receives cash from the customer for that inventory. This result should be compared to the amount of time allowed before the company must pay its suppliers for the inventory and to industry averages and historical trends for the company in order to properly evaluate the efficiency and effectiveness of the operating cycle.

What is fixed asset turnover?

Fixed asset turnover measures a company's ability to utilize its fixed assets to generate sales revenue. This measure is similar to return on assets; however, the return on assets compares the bottom line of the income statement to average total assets, whereas fixed asset turnover compares the top line of the income statement to average fixed assets (long-lived tangible assets). The formula for fixed asset turnover is:

Net Revenue / Average Net Fixed Assets = Fixed Asset Turnover

Note that average net fixed assets are used as the denominator because this ratio compares income statement data to balance sheet data. The average net fixed assets can be calculated as a simple average of the prior year net fixed assets and the current year net fixed assets balances.

The fixed asset turnover for Vera Bradley, Inc., for the fiscal year ending January 2017 would be calculated as:

$485,937 / (($101,577 + $113,711) / 2) = 4.5

How is fixed asset turnover evaluated?

When evaluating fixed asset turnover, the higher the result, the better. The higher the fixed asset turnover, the better the company is at utilizing its fixed assets to earn sales revenue from customers. The fixed asset turnover for Vera Bradley, Inc., for the fiscal year ending January 2017 was 4.5, which means that for every dollar the company had invested in fixed assets, it was able to generate $4.50 in sales revenue.

MARKET PERFORMANCE RATIOS

What do market performance ratios measure?

Market performance ratios measure the overall financial performance of the company in the eyes of the stockholders.

Which users of financial statement information are most concerned about market performance?

Investors (stockholders) are concerned about the market performance ratios of the company, as they are the owners of the company. Many of the market performance ratios are key indicators of their return on investment.

What is earnings per share?

Earnings per share (EPS) is a ratio that measures the net income earned in the current year per share of common stock. Investors expect to earn a return on investment by either receiving dividends or through increases in stock prices. Since dividends are paid out of net income, and net income has an effect on the stock price, the earnings per share measure is of high interest to investors. Earnings per share shows how much income was earned for each common stock share outstanding. The formula for earnings per share is:

Net Income / Average Number of Common Shares Outstanding = Earnings per Share

Note that average number of common shares outstanding is used as the denominator because this ratio compares income statement data to balance sheet data. The av-

> ## What are some ratios that measure market performance?
>
> **F**ive key ratios that measure market performance that are covered in this chapter are earnings per share, price–earnings ratio, dividend payout, dividend yield, and book value per share. These are all measures that investors use to evaluate a company's overall performance.

erage number of common shares outstanding can be found in the notes to the financial statements as well as on the income statement. It is also important to note that earnings per share computes the earnings per share of common stock. It does not include shares of preferred stock. If a company also issues shares of preferred stock, the numerator is adjusted to be net income less preferred stock dividends divided by the average number of common shares outstanding.

The earnings per share for Vera Bradley, Inc., for the fiscal year ending January 2017 is calculated as:

$19,758 / 36,838 shares = $0.54

How is earnings per share evaluated?

When evaluating earnings per share, the higher the ratio, the higher the profitability. Vera Bradley, Inc., reported an earnings per share for the fiscal year ending January 2017 of $0.54. That means that the company earned 54 cents of net income for each share of common stock outstanding. It is important to review the trends over time as well as the industry averages and economic trends when evaluating earnings per share.

What is the price–earnings ratio?

The price–earnings ratio (P/E ratio) compares a company's stock price to its earnings per share. It measures investor expectations about a given company. The formula for the price–earnings ratio is:

Market Price per Share / Earnings per Share = Price–Earnings Ratio

Assuming a fiscal year end stock price of $11.60 for Vera Bradley, Inc., the P/E ratio for the fiscal year ending January 2017 can be calculated as:

$11.60 / $0.54 = 21.5

How is the price–earnings ratio evaluated?

When evaluating the price–earnings ratio, the higher the result, the higher the investor expectations are. If an investor is willing to pay a higher price per share of stock compared to the net income per share, then it can be said that the investor must be expecting something good from the company. The price–earnings ratio calculated above for Vera Bradley, Inc., of 21.5 means that investors are willing to pay 21.5 times the amount that the stock earns per share. As with all ratios, to properly evaluate this ratio, one must compare this ratio to industry averages, economic conditions, and trends over time.

What is the dividend payout ratio?

The dividend payout ratio measures the percentage of net income earned by the company that was returned to investors in the form of dividends paid. The formula for the dividend payout ratio is:

Dividends per Share / Earnings per Share = Dividend Payout Ratio

As Vera Bradley, Inc., did not pay dividends during the fiscal year ending January 2017, the dividend payout ratio is 0% and is calculated as follows:

$0 / $0.54 = 0%

How is the dividend payout evaluated?

When evaluating the dividend payout, the higher the result, the more of a company's earnings are returned to investors through the payment of dividends. A company that is looking to attract investors might pay more dividends and thus have a higher payout, whereas a company that has many growth opportunities and doesn't need to pay dividends to attract investors may have a lower payout. Accordingly, a high dividend payout is not necessarily good or bad. Again, it is important to compare to the industry, economy, and historical trends to get a better understanding of this ratio's significance. As Vera Bradley, Inc., does not historically pay dividends, this 0% for the fiscal year ending January 2017 is not surprising.

What is the dividend yield ratio?

The dividend yield ratio measures the investors' return on investment in stock through the payment of dividends. Basically, this ratio measures the immediate return on investment through payment of dividends as opposed to measuring the long-term return on investment through increases in the stock price. The formula to calculate the dividend yield ratio is:

Dividends per Share / Market Price per Share = Dividend Yield

As Vera Bradley, Inc., did not pay any dividends during the fiscal year ending January 2017, the dividend yield is 0%, calculated as follows:

$0 / $11.60 = 0%

How is the dividend yield evaluated?

In evaluating the dividend yield, the higher the result, the greater the return on investment through dividends is. The receipt of dividends is not the only way investors can earn a return on their investment. As such, a high dividend yield is not necessarily good or bad. It is merely a measure of one type of return on investment by the owners. Again, as Vera Bradley, Inc., does not historically pay dividends, this 0% for the fiscal year ending January 2017 is not surprising.

What is the book value per share?

The book value per share measures what each share of stock would receive if all of the company's assets were sold and all liabilities were paid. Recall that the basic accounting equation is assets = liabilities + owner's equity. It can be rewritten as assets − liabilities = owner's equity. As such, the difference between what the company owns and what it owes is equal to the owner's stake in the business. If the business were to close, the assets would be sold, and the resulting cash would be used to pay the debts of the business. Any cash left over would be distributed on a per-share basis to the stockholders. This resulting payment is the book value per share. It is important to note that the balance sheet reports most assets at historical cost (what was originally paid), not at market value. As such, the book value per share is based on historical cost, not market value. The formula for book value per share is:

Total Stockholders' Equity / Number of Common Shares Outstanding = Book Value per Share

The book value per share for Vera Bradley, Inc., as of the fiscal year ending January 2017 can be calculated as:

$283,786 / 36,218 = $7.84

How is the book value per share evaluated?

When evaluating the book value per share, the greater the result, the greater the amount of net assets exist to back the investment in stock. In general, the book value per share is typically lower than the market price of the share because the market price also reflects investor expectations. This is the case with Vera Bradley, Inc., as of the fiscal year ending January 2017 when the market price was $11.60 per share and the book value per share was $7.84.

THE BALANCED SCORECARD

What is the balanced scorecard?

The balanced scorecard is an approach to measuring a company's performance from both a financial and a nonfinancial standpoint. It is typically used by managers in measuring and reporting key indicators of the company's past and future performance.

Why is it important to evaluate nonfinancial measures as well as financial measures?

Financial measures generally indicate past performance. Recall that the balance sheet reports financial data at one point in time, and the income statement presents the results of the previous year. As such, they report on performance from the past (lagging indicators). Certain nonfinancial measures can be key indicators of a company's future performance (leading indicators). The balanced scorecard approach to evaluation utilizes a combination of financial and nonfinancial data to get a full picture of both past and future performance. Ideally, the measures selected for the balanced scorecard should come from and support the corporate strategy.

What is measured in the financial perspective?

The financial perspective includes measuring and reporting key financial ratios that the company has determined are most important indicators of its success. Items that may be measured under the financial perspective include: net income, earnings per share, cash flow from operations, etc. Measuring financial performance helps management evaluate the success of past decisions.

What is measured in the customer perspective?

The customer perspective of the balanced scorecard looks at the relationships with customers as an indicator of future sales. Items that may be measured under the customer perspective include: customer satisfaction survey results, number of complaints, percentage of market share, product returns as a percentage of sales, number of new customers, and number of repeat customers. Obviously, increases in customer complaints or decreases in the number of repeat customers might be cause for concern, as would declining market share or negative survey results, etc. If a company is regularly measuring and reporting on the customer perspective, it can solve problems before they get out of hand and cause a major impact on the financial performance of the company.

What is measured in the internal business process perspective?

The internal business process perspective measures the internal business processes that the company believes are most important in achieving its long-term financial goals. Items that may be measured from an internal business process perspective are: product quality/defect rates, number of vendors, operating cycle time, machine downtime, on-time deliveries as a percent of sales, delivery cycle time, etc. If a company is regularly measuring and reporting on the internal business process perspective, it can again work to solve problems before they get out of hand and cause a major impact on the financial performance of the company.

What is measured in the learning and growth perspective?

The learning and growth perspective measures a company's efforts to ensure that it can continuously improve. Items that may

One of the items measured to obtain customer perspective is the old-fashioned customer satisfaction survey, now mostly done online.

> ## What are the four perspectives of the balanced scorecard?
>
> The balanced scorecard evaluates a company's performance based on four perspectives: financial, customer, internal business process, and learning and growth. The financial perspective addresses the question, "How do we look to the owners?" The customer perspective addresses the question, "How do we look to our customers?" The internal business process perspective addresses the question, "What internal business processes are critical to our ability to provide value for the customer?" The learning and growth perspective addresses the question, "How do we continue to improve?"

be measured from a learning and growth perspective are: employee training hours, employee promotions, new products/services, employee turnover, etc. A company that can successfully train and keep employees should have more success adapting to changes.

How does a company know what items to measure on the balanced scorecard?

There is no one-size-fits-all approach to the balanced scorecard. The balanced scorecard should be linked to the company's organizational strategy. Once the organizational strategy is set, performance measures should be selected that provide either leading or lagging indicators about the success of that strategy.

BOOKKEEPING AND THE ACCOUNTING CYCLE

THE ACCOUNTING CYCLE

What is the accounting cycle?

The accounting cycle is the process by which business transactions are recorded in the accounting information system and reported in financial statements. During the accounting cycle, data is recorded and then summarized in a useful manner, thus converting that data into usable information for decision makers. The accounting cycle repeats itself every year.

What is an accounting information system?

An accounting information system is a system that is designed to track the transactions of the business and report the results. The accounting information system can take many forms. Accounting information systems used to use a manual, paper-based system of columnar paper and binders called journals. Some very small companies use spreadsheet programs, such as Microsoft Excel. However, now it is most common for large and small businesses alike, to purchase software programs designed to track and report accounting data. The software features and cost can vary dramatically. Small accounting software packages, such as QuickBooks™, can cost as little as $10 per month. Large companies running ERP packages can pay upwards of $10 million for implementation!

How is an ERP system different from an accounting information system?

ERP stands for enterprise resource planning. ERP systems are a type of information system that does more than the traditional accounting and financial packages. ERP systems integrate many aspects of the business processes into one system. For example, many ERP systems also have marketing and customer service modules. These are modules that are not ordinarily found in accounting information systems.

What is a transaction?

When a business enters into an exchange that affects the basic accounting equation (Assets = Liabilities + Equity), it is called a transaction. Sometimes, these exchanges are external and sometimes they are internal. External exchanges are those that occur between the company and an external party, such as the company getting a loan from the bank. Internal exchanges are those that occur only inside the company, such as using up supplies that were previously purchased. All transactions must be recorded in the accounting information system.

What are the steps in the accounting cycle?

The steps in the accounting cycle are listed below. Each step will be described in detail in this chapter.

Step 1: Analyze Transactions
Step 2: Record Journal Entries
Step 3: Post Journal Entries to the Ledger
Step 4: Prepare an Unadjusted Trial Balance
Step 5: Record Adjusting Journal Entries
Step 6: Post Adjusting Entries to the Ledger
Step 7: Prepare an Adjusted Trial Balance
Step 8: Prepare Financial Statements
Step 9: Record Closing Journal Entries
Step 10: Post Closing Journal Entries to the Ledger
Step 11: Prepare a Post-Closing Trial Balance

Steps one through three occur on a daily basis. Steps four through eight occur on a monthly basis and are typically referred to as the "month-end close" process. Steps nine through eleven occur annually and, when combined with steps four through eight of the last month of the year, are typically referred to as the "year-end close" process.

STEPS 1–3:
ANALYZE, RECORD, AND POST

How is a transaction analyzed?

When a business enters into a transaction, it needs to be documented. When analyzing transactions, it is important to identify what is being exchanged. Typically, the company gives something and receives something. As such, in order to analyze a transaction, you need to determine what is being exchanged and where it fits in the basic accounting equation. There are always at least two accounts being affected during a transaction. Also, the basic accounting equation (Assets = Liabilities + Equity) must always be in balance.

94

When analyzing a transaction, first picture the documents and/or what is being exchanged. This will help you determine which accounts are being affected. Next, determine where those accounts fit in the basic accounting equation and whether those accounts are increasing or decreasing. Finally, check your work by ensuring that the basic accounting equation is in balance.

What are some examples of transaction analysis?

Let's assume that a business bought office supplies worth $300 and received an invoice for them that it will pay next month. You can probably picture the box of office supplies and the paper invoice. Those are the two items being exchanged. The office supplies are an asset that is increasing, as the amount of office supplies the company has just went up. Additionally, that invoice is recorded in the account titled accounts payable, which represents amounts owed to vendors from invoices received. Accounts payable is a liability and it is increasing, as the amount of money the company owes someone just went up. When put into the accounting equation, you can see that it is in balance:

Assets (Supplies +300) = Liabilities (Accounts Payable +300) + Equity (+0)

300 = 300

Now let's assume that a business mowed a lawn for $50, collecting cash from the customer on-site. The company earned revenue by providing the services for the customer and received cash. Thus, service revenue is increasing by $50 and cash (an asset) is increasing by $50. As noted in the chapter entitled "Four Basic Financial Statements," the basic accounting equation can be expanded to:

Assets = Liabilities + Contributed Capital + Beginning Balance, Retained Earnings + Revenues − Expenses − Distributions

Accordingly, when put into the expanded accounting equation, you can see that it is in balance:

Assets (Cash +50) = Liabilities (+0) + Contributed Capital (+0) + Beginning Balance, Retained Earnings (+0) + Revenues (Service Revenue +50) − Expenses (+0) − Distributions (+0)

50 = 50

What is a chart of accounts?

Recall from the chapter entitled "Financial Statement Elements" that there can be numerous accounts under each type of financial statement element. For example, accounts under the assets element include items such as cash, accounts receivable, supplies, inventory, land, etc. In order for a company to keep track of all of its accounts, a listing called a chart of accounts is used. A chart of accounts lists both the names of the accounts and assigns an account number to each account. You can think of a chart of accounts like a drop-down list of choices you can make when recording transactions. An account has to be on the chart of accounts to be used.

Who determines the chart of accounts?

The accountant sets up the chart of accounts when a company is formed. There are many standard account titles that all companies use, such as cash and equipment. In addition, companies can create their own account titles that reflect their individualized needs. Very small companies may have a chart of accounts that uses between twenty to fifty accounts. Large companies may have a chart of accounts that is so long that when it is printed, it fills an entire binder!

How are accounts assigned with numbers?

Accounts are generally given a number to identify the account and help the user identify the type of account that it is. For example, most charts of accounts start asset account numbers with a one, liabilities with a two, equity with a three, revenues with a four, and expenses with a five. The numbering also typically follows financial statement order; that is, the numbering of accounts should match the presentation order on the financial statements. As the chart of accounts can be changed as needed, a gap is generally left in between numbers so that new accounts can be added later. A sample chart of accounts is shown below.

Loretta's Lawn Care Chart of Accounts

Account Number	Account Name
1000	Cash
1100	Accounts Receivable
1200	Supplies
1500	Equipment
2100	Accounts Payable
2500	Notes Payable
3000	Contributed Capital
3500	Retained Earnings
4000	Service Revenue
5110	Wages Expense
5120	Utilities & Fuel Expense
5310	Rent Expense
5320	Insurance Expense
5330	Advertising Expense
5400	Depreciation Expense

There is typically some additional strategy in developing a numbering scheme beyond that of the first digit. In the Loretta's Lawn Care example, the current assets are numbered below 1499. Noncurrent assets are numbered above 1500. The same strategy goes with the current and noncurrent liabilities. Expenses that are part of cost of sales are listed as 5100 accounts, whereas selling and administrative expenses are listed as 5300 accounts, etc.

How is a transaction recorded?

Once the transaction analysis has been completed and the correct accounts selected, a transaction is recorded within the accounting system. The standard form to record a transaction is through something called a journal entry. However, many accounting software packages allow the user to record transactions in a simpler fashion. For example, if you receive a cash payment from a customer in collection of an invoice, you may select a menu called "cash receipts." The cash receipts screen will ask you to record the customer who paid you, the amount of the payment, the invoice number that they paid, etc. The software package is smart enough to know that at least two accounts must be affected in every transaction, so it will automatically know that a cash receipt from a customer would be recorded as an increase to cash and a decrease to accounts receivable (the amount of money the customer owes the company is decreasing). When an accounting system lets the user enter a transaction, as above, without recording a journal entry in official form, the journal entry is actually recorded behind the screen the user sees in the system.

What does debit mean?

Debit means left. That's it. Nothing more. Accordingly, since assets increase on the left side, we can say that assets increase with debits. Since liabilities decrease on the left side, we can say that liabilities decrease with debits. The common abbreviation for debit is "dr." Also note that there is a history behind the word "debit," which is Latin for "what is due," but in modern accounting, it simply means "left."

What does credit mean?

Credit means right. That's it. Nothing more. Accordingly, since assets decrease on the right side, we can say that assets decrease with credits. Since liabilities increase on the right side, we can say that liabilities increase with credits. The common abbreviation for credit is "cr." Again, note that there is a history behind the word "credit," which is Latin for "something entrusted to another," but in modern accounting, it simply means "right."

What is a journal entry?

A journal entry is the standard form for recording a transaction. Journal entries show the accounts affected by the transaction as well as the amounts increased or decreased. Journal entries use the debit/credit framework to record increases or decreases in an account.

What is the debit/credit framework?

The debit/credit framework is the framework that modern accounting was built on. As discussed in the chapter entitled "What Is Accounting?", this double-entry accounting system was established over 500 years ago by Italian merchants. The double-entry accounting system revolves around the basic accounting equation and the notion that it must be in balance. It is helpful to picture the accounting equation (Assets = Liabilities + Equity) as a scale that must always be in balance.

If you add something to the left side of the scale, you must add something to the right side to keep it in balance. Likewise, you could add something to the right side, then take something else off the right side to keep it in balance. This logic is used to keep the accounting equation in balance when recording journal entries. An easy way to remember how this works is to look at the basic accounting equation. Accounts increase on the side of the equal sign that they are on.

(left) Assets = Liabilities + Equity (right)

As such, since assets are on the left side of the equal sign, they increase on the left and decrease on the right. Since liabilities and equity are on the right side of the equal sign, they increase on the right side and decrease on the left. An illustration of the debit/credit framework is shown below.

Expanded Debit/Credit Framework

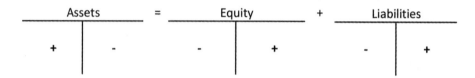

How do you expand the debit/credit framework to include revenues, expenses, and dividends?

Recall from the chapter entitled "Four Basic Financial Statements" that there are two main categories of equity accounts: contributed capital and retained earnings. Also recall that retained earnings is the accumulation of net income that is not paid out as dividends. As such, the formula for retained earnings is:

Beginning Balance, Retained Earnings + Net Income − Distributions = Ending Balance, Retained Earnings

Accordingly, net income increases the retained earnings balance. Net income equals revenues minus expenses. So, if you think it through, revenues increase net income, which in turn increases retained earnings. Since retained earnings increase with credits, revenue must also be recorded with credits.

Likewise, expenses decrease net income, which in turn decreases retained earnings. Retained earnings decrease with debits; therefore, expenses must also be recorded with debits.

Distributions (dividends) decrease retained earnings; therefore, distributions must be recorded with debits. The figure below presents an illustration of the expanded debit/ credit framework.

Expanded Debit/Credit Framework

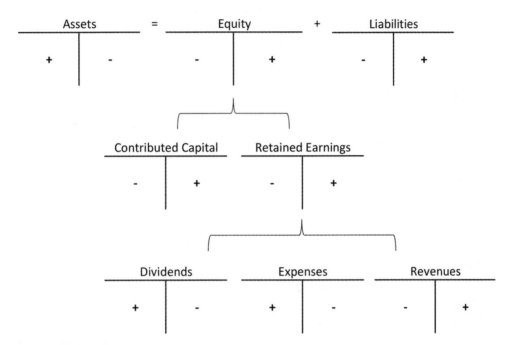

Note, this is a good page to mark for reference, as you will most likely want to consult this diagram as you analyze transactions later.

What is a normal balance?

The normal balance of an account is the side the account increases on. Assets have a normal debit balance, since they increase on the left/debit side. Liabilities and equity accounts have a normal credit balance, since they increase on the right/credit side. Revenues have a normal credit balance. Expenses have a normal debit balance. Distributions have a normal debit balance. The normal balance is the side you would expect to have the balance on. For example, it is not normal for a company to have negative cash; thus, a credit balance would be abnormal. It would be impossible for a company to have a negative value for land; thus, a credit balance would be impossible.

What does a journal entry look like?

A journal entry shows the date the transaction took place, the accounts affected by the transaction, and the debit and credit amounts. The standard form for a journal entry is to list the debits first, followed by the credits. Additionally, the credits are always indented to the right (remember, credit means right). For example, assume that Loretta's Lawn Care used $500 cash to purchase a lawn mower on January 10, 2019. You can determine the two accounts used are cash and machines. Both accounts are assets, so they both increase on the debit side and decrease on the credit side. In the example given, cash was paid; thus, cash is decreasing. This would result in a credit to cash, since assets decrease on the credit side. Machines are increasing in this example. Machines are also an asset, so they increase on the debit side. So far, the transaction analysis above resulted in the need to debit machines for $500 and credit cash for $500. The standard form for that journal entry looks like this:

Date	Account	Dr.	Cr.
1/10/2019	Machines	500	
	Cash		500

Note that it is also preferable to put a description under each journal entry to describe the nature of the transaction, such as "purchased lawn mower with cash." Most computerized accounting systems have an input field to record this description.

What are the two equalities that must be maintained when recording journal entries?

Just as the accounting equation must always be in balance, debits must also equal credits. These two equalities must be maintained at all times under the debit/credit framework. In the example above, one asset is increasing by $500 and another is decreasing by $500, thus netting to $0 and keeping the accounting equation in balance. Also, there is one debit for $500 and one credit for $500, maintaining the debits equal credits rule.

Do all journal entries have just one debit and one credit?

Journal entries can have any number of debits and credits necessary to record the transaction. There is no limit to the number of debits and credits. However, the two equalities must always be maintained. For example, assume Loretta's Lawn Care purchased a lawn mower for $500, paying $100 cash as a down payment and receiving an invoice for the remaining $400, due in sixty days. There are now three accounts affected: machines, cash, and accounts payable. In this case, machines (an asset) are still increasing by $500, but cash (an asset) is decreasing by $100 and accounts payable (a liability) is increasing by $400. The accounting equation remains in balance, as follows:

Assets (Machine +$500, Cash ?$100) = Liabilities (Accounts Payable +400) + Equity (+$0)

$400 = $400

Debits also equal credits, as machines are debited for $500 and cash and accounts payable are credited for $100 and $400, respectively. The journal entry for this transaction would look like the following:

Date	Account	Dr.	Cr.
1/10/2019	Machines	500	
	Cash		100
	Accounts Payable		400

Does it matter what order the accounts are listed in on a journal entry?

It does not matter what order the accounts are listed in as long as debits are recorded first, and credits are recorded second. In the journal entry above, accounts payable could be listed ahead of cash. Either way is acceptable.

Where are journal entries recorded?

Journal entries are recorded in the general journal. The general journal is merely a template for recording the journal entry. In paper-based accounting systems, the journal is a book of paper with columns for recording entries. In computerized systems, it is merely an online template that opens up and saves each journal entry.

How do you know how to record each journal entry?

In general, following the transaction analysis process by starting with identifying the accounts affected by the transaction, identifying the type of account it is, determining whether the account is increasing or decreasing, and then determining that the debit or credit will result in a correct journal entry. However, some transactions are complex, and other transactions have accounts with unfamiliar titles. As such, an appendix has been added to this book to give examples of common journal entries for reference.

What does it mean to "post" a journal entry?

A listing of journal entries by themselves would not provide useful information, as there would be way too much data. The posting process copies the information from the journal and puts it in an organized spot, called the general ledger. This process is known as posting. In computerized accounting systems, this process is completed automatically as soon as a journal entry is entered.

What is a general ledger?

The general ledger is the listing of all transactions that have been posted for each individual account. Each account has its own general ledger. For example, there is a cash general ledger, an accounts receivable general ledger, a supplies general ledger, and so on. The general ledger has rows for each transaction and columns to represent the debit or credit amounts. The general ledger is totaled up after each transaction to calculate the balance in each account. The general ledger takes all the journal entry data and turns it into useful information. Imagine if you wanted to know how much cash your company had. It would take you forever to go through each journal entry and track the increases and decreases in cash over time, not to mention that not every journal entry affects cash, so you would be looking through some journal entries that are irrelevant. If you have a cash ledger, you can just look at the entries that affected cash and easily find your answer. Again, in computerized systems, the process of finding the cash balance is as simple as touching a button to show the cash journal and looking at the balance.

The figures below provide a sample journal for January and the accompanying general ledger for the cash account. Note that the journal entries below include a description of each transaction in parentheses after the entry.

Journal

Date	Account	Dr.	Cr.
1/10/2019	Machines	500	
	Cash		100
	Accounts Payable		400
	(purchased lawnmower with $100 down payment)		
1/12/2019	Cash	1,000	
	Service Revenue		1,000
	(mowed lawns and collected cash)		
1/18/2019	Supplies	300	
	Cash		300
	(purchased fertilizer, paid cash)		
1/22/2019	Supplies	450	
	Accounts Payable		450
	(purchased fertilzer on account)		
1/30/2019	Cash	1,500	
	Service Revenue		1,500
	(mowed lawns and collected cash)		

General Ledger - Cash

Date	Description	Dr.	Cr.	Balance
1/1/2019	Beginning Balance	5,800		5,800
1/10/2019	Purchased lawnmower with $100 down payment		100	5,700
1/12/2019	Mowed lawns and collected cash	1,000		6,700
1/18/2019	Purchased fertilizer, paid cash		300	6,400
1/30/2019	Mowed lawns and collected cash	1,500		7,900

Note that the general ledger for cash only shows information that is relevant to cash. As such, the journal entry from January 22 does not show up on the cash general ledger, as cash was not affected by this transaction. Every account has its own general ledger, so each transaction is posted in at least two ledgers, as every journal entry affects at least two accounts. Thus, the journal entry from January 18 would show up as a credit in the cash journal and would also show up as a debit in the supplies journal. The final column includes a running total of the general ledger balance. Recall that cash is an asset; thus, it increases with debits and decreases with credits. Accordingly, the beginning balance is written on the normal side of the account (debit, since this is an asset) and any subsequent debits are added to the balance, while credits are subtracted.

What is a T account?

A T account is a simplified form of the general ledger. T accounts are useful learning tools and can also be helpful when trying to analyze complicated transactions. Most accounting textbooks have students post journal entries to T accounts rather than a general ledger. The figure below converts the cash general ledger in proper form into a cash T account.

General Ledger - Cash

Date	Description	Dr.	Cr.	Balance
1/1/2019	Beginning Balance	5,800		5,800
1/10/2019	Purchased lawnmower with $100 down payment		100	5,700
1/12/2019	Mowed lawns and collected cash	1,000		6,700
1/18/2019	Purchased fertilizer, paid cash		300	6,400
1/30/2019	Mowed lawns and collected cash	1,500		7,900

Cash

5,800	100
1,000	300
1,500	

T-Account

How do you calculate the total of a T account?

The T account in the figure above does not show the total cash balance. In order to total up a T account, you simply add up the positive side and subtract the negative side. If the answer is positive (which it should be since the normal balance is the positive side), write the balance on the positive side. If the answer is negative, write the answer on the negative side.

In the figure below of the totaled T account, the total for the cash balance would be calculated as follows:

$$5,800 + 1,000 + 1,500 - 100 - 300 = 7,900$$

Likewise, the total for the accounts payable balance would be calculated as follows:

$$2,000 + 450 + 600 - 450 = 2,600$$

(Asset)			(Liability)		
+	Cash	-	-	Accounts Payable	+
5,800		100		450	2,000
1,000		300			450
1,500					600
7,900					2,600

What is a subledger?

A subledger is a detailed listing of items in a general ledger. Not every account requires a subledger, but there are some very common accounts that require the use of subledgers. For example, the accounts receivable general ledger lists all invoices sent to customers and subsequent payments received. However, it is also useful to track this information separately by customer. Accordingly, most companies will also record accounts receivable transactions in a separate subledger that tracks the invoice and payment activity for each customer. That way, at any given time, they can determine the exact amount each customer owes them. This is also a way to generate customer statements showing balances owed. Again, computerized accounting systems track this automatically. When you add up the totals of all of the subledgers for a given account, they must equal the total of the general ledger for that account or else there is an error somewhere. For example, the total accounts receivable general ledger may show that, in total, customers owe the company $10,000. You should be able to add up each customer subledger and come up with $10,000. This might mean that customer A owes $5,000, customer B owes $3,000, and customer C owes $2,000. Other very common uses of subledgers are: accounts payable to track amounts owed to each specific vendor, inventory to track quantities and prices of individual inventory items, and fixed assets to track and depreciate each asset class such as computers, machinery, etc.

STEPS 4–8: THE MONTH–END CLOSE

What is a trial balance?

A trial balance is a listing of all accounts in a financial statement order showing the debit or credit balances. Trial balances list assets first, then liabilities, then equity, then revenues, and then expenses. The trial balance is used to prove that debits equal credits and to review account balances. There are three versions of the trial balance, all of which are discussed in this chapter. The first trial balance that is prepared is called the unadjusted trial balance. The unadjusted trial balance is followed by the adjusted trial balance and finally the post-closing trial balance. Note that if the chart of accounts is set up properly, the trial balance will show accounts in the same order as the chart of accounts. A sample unadjusted trial balance for Loretta's Lawn Care is provided in the figure below. The unadjusted trial balance serves as a starting point for calculating the necessary adjustments at month end.

Loretta's Lawn Care
Unadjusted Trial Balance
December 31, 2020

	Debit	Credit
Cash	130,000	
Accounts Receivable	30,000	
Supplies	4,000	
Prepaid Insurance	1,200	
Equipment	180,000	
Accounts Payable		40,000
Unearned Revenue		4,800
Notes Payable		62,000
Common Stock		10,000
Retained Earnings		100,900
Dividends	5,000	
Service Revenue		240,000
Wages Expense	80,000	
Utilities & Fuel Expense	18,250	
Rent Expense	5,000	
Insurance Expense	1,000	
Advertising Expense	2,000	
Depreciation Expense	1,250	
Total	457,700	457,700

Why are adjusting entries necessary?

At the end of each month, it is necessary to correct certain account balances that may be in need of adjustment. Generally accepted accounting principles require companies to record revenue when earned, regardless of when cash is received from customers. This is known as the revenue recognition principle. Additionally, companies are required to record expenses when incurred to generate revenues, regardless of when cash is paid.

This is known as the expense recognition principle. The revenue recognition principle and the expense recognition principle form the accrual basis of accounting.

How does the revenue recognition principle work?

Because generally accepted accounting principles require accrual basis accounting rather than cash basis accounting, the timing or recording revenues may not match the timing of when cash is received from customers. For example, a company can receive cash before it provides the good or service, at the same time it provides the good or service, or after it provides the good or service.

What happens when a company receives cash from a customer before it provides the good or service?

If a company receives cash before it provides the good or service, this creates a liability for the company because it now owes the customer something. This liability is called unearned revenue (because it hasn't earned anything yet, but it has the cash). Don't let the name unearned revenue fool you. It is actually a liability account, not a revenue account. For example, assume Loretta's Lawn Care received $250 from a customer on April 1 in advance for lawn mowing services for the season (five months at $50 per month). Loretta's Lawn Care would record a debit to cash for $250 and a credit to unearned revenue for $250. This journal entry shows that it received the cash but owes the customer $250 worth of services. (This is the same type of accounting that takes place when a store issues gift cards to customers.) At the end of each month, Loretta's Lawn Care would need to record an adjusting entry to show that $50 of service revenue has been earned. The journal entry to record this adjustment would be a debit to unearned revenue of $50 and a credit to service revenue of $50. This journal entry essentially says, "It isn't unearned anymore; now it is earned." After this journal entry is completed, Loretta's Lawn Care would only have $200 remaining in unearned revenue, representing the four months remaining.

What happens when a company receives cash from a customer at the same time it provides the good or service?

If a company receives cash at the same time it provides the good or the service, only a simple journal entry is needed at the time of the sale. Assume Loretta's Lawn Care mowed a lawn for a customer and collected $20 upon finishing the job. Loretta's Lawn Care would record a debit to cash for $20 and a credit to service revenue for $20. In this case, no adjusting entry is needed at month end since the revenue was earned at the same time the cash was received. Essentially, there is nothing left to do.

What happens when a company receives cash from a customer after it provides the good or service?

If a company receives cash after it provides the good or service, this creates an asset for the company because the customers owe it money. This asset is called accounts receivable. For example, if Loretta's Lawn Care mowed a lawn for $20 and left an invoice in the mailbox, Loretta's Lawn Care would record a debit to accounts receivable for $20 and a credit to service revenue for $20. This journal entry shows that it provided the service and, thus, earned the revenue, but the customer owes $20 in payment for the services. At the time of collection of the $20 customer payment, Loretta's Lawn Care would need to record an entry to show that $20 of cash has been collected, and the customer no longer owes the $20. The journal entry to record this adjustment would be a debit to cash of $20 and a credit to accounts receivable of $20.

How does the expense recognition principle work?

Just like with revenues, a company may incur an expense at a time other than when the cash payment took place. For example, a company can pay cash before it incurs the expense, at the same time it incurs the expense, or after it incurs the expense. The expense recognition principle can also be referred to as the matching principle, meaning that expenses should be matched to the same period they are incurred to earn the revenue. In this way, the income statement properly reflects the revenues and expenses of each period matched together. For example, Loretta's Lawn Care wouldn't want to record the revenue for mowing lawns in January but then record the wages paid to the lawn mowing crew when it distributes their paychecks in February. The wages for mowing the lawns in January should be recorded in January, when it provided the service to the customer, regardless of the date that paychecks are cut. This is the essence of the matching principle.

What happens if cash is paid to a vendor before an expense is incurred?

If a company pays cash before it incurs the expense, this creates an asset for the company because the vendor now owes it something. This asset is called a prepaid expense (because the company paid the cash before it has incurred the expense). Don't let the name "prepaid expense" fool you. It is actually an asset account, not an expense. Also, note that prepaid expense accounts are usually given a specific name depending on the type of expense that was prepaid. For example, if it was rent that was paid in advance, the company will typically use an account title called prepaid rent. Assume Loretta's Lawn Care paid $1,200 to its insurance carrier on January 1 for a twelve-month insurance policy (twelve months at $100 per month). Loretta's Lawn Care would record a debit

Cash for goods or services are often paid before such services are rendered or goods received. In that case, the money that has been spent is called a "prepaid expense."

to prepaid insurance for $1,200 and a credit to cash for $1,200. This journal entry shows that it paid the cash but the insurance carrier owes it twelve months of insurance coverage. At the end of each month, Loretta's Lawn Care would need to record an adjusting entry to show that $100 of insurance expense has been incurred. The journal entry to record this adjustment would be a debit to insurance expense of $100 and a credit to prepaid insurance of $100. This journal entry essentially says, "It isn't prepaid anymore; now the expense has been incurred." After this journal entry is completed, Loretta's Lawn Care would only have $1,100 remaining in prepaid insurance, representing the eleven months remaining.

What happens if cash is paid to a vendor at the same time the expense is incurred?

If a company pays cash at the same time it incurs the expense, only a simple journal entry is needed at the time of the payment. Assume Loretta's Lawn Care paid $40 cash to fuel the lawn mowers for the day. Loretta's Lawn Care would record a debit to fuel expense for $40 and a credit to cash for $40. In this case, no adjusting entry is needed at month end since the expense was incurred at the same time the cash was paid. Essentially, there is nothing left to do.

What happens if cash is paid to a vendor after the expense is incurred?

If a company pays cash after it incurs an expense, this creates a liability for the company because it owes money for the expense it has already incurred. For example, assume Loretta's Lawn Care employees worked the last two weeks in December, earning $3,000, but the payday for that period occurs the first Friday of January. On December 31, the company would be required to record the wages expense that had been incurred up to that date, even though the employees have not been paid yet. Loretta's Lawn Care would record a debit to wages expense for $3,000 and a credit to a liability called wages payable for $3,000. This journal entry shows that it incurred the labor cost but won't pay the employees until the following month. When the paychecks are cut, Loretta's Lawn Care would need to record an entry to show that $3,000 of cash has been paid, and it no longer owes the employees the $3,000. The journal entry to record this adjustment would be a debit to wages payable of $3,000 and a credit to cash of $3,000.

What are the two main types of adjusting entries?

The two main types of adjusting entries are deferral entries and accrual entries. Deferral entries are those where the cash transaction happens before the revenue is earned or the expense is incurred. Thus, the revenue or expense recognition is deferred to some point in the future. Accrual entries are those where the cash transaction happens after the revenue is earned or the expense is incurred. In this case, you need to accrue the revenue or expense, even though you haven't received or paid the cash yet. Recall that if cash is received at the same time revenue is earned or the expense is incurred, there is no adjusting entry that is needed.

Deferral entries are often easier to identify and record than accruals because with deferral entries, a cash exchange has already taken place, thus prompting the recording of an initial entry. Upon reviewing the trial balance, one can simply see which of those initial entries need adjusting. It is not so easy with accrual entries, however; since no cash exchange has taken place, there is no initial entry that was recorded in the books. As such, accountants have to think hard about revenues they may have earned without being paid for or expenses they may have incurred that they haven't paid yet.

What are some examples of accrual entries?

Accrued revenue entries are any of those where the goods or services have been provided to the customer but payment has not been received yet. Many businesses wait until month end to send out invoices to all customers. This accrual process records revenue during the month it was earned and records the accounts receivable due from customers.

Accrued expense entries are any of those where payment has not been paid yet but where the expense has been incurred. A very common accrued expense is employee wages, as most pay periods cross over the end of the month. Another common accrued expense is to record interest incurred on loans that may be paid in a subsequent period.

Do adjusting entries ever involve cash?

No. Adjusting entries never involve cash. If a cash exchange takes place at the same time the revenue is earned or the expense is incurred, then no adjusting entry is needed. Adjusting entries are needed for those transactions where the cash exchange took place before (deferrals) or after (accruals) the revenue was earned or the expense was incurred.

What are some examples of deferral entries?

Deferred revenue entries are any of those where customer payment is received before the good or service has been provided to the customer. Examples of deferred revenues include contractual arrangements where the customer pays in advance, down payments received, gift cards issued to customers, concert venues selling tickets in advance, and subscription service providers such as magazines, etc.

Deferred expense entries are any of those where payment is paid to the vendor before expense has been incurred. Examples of deferred expenses include rent paid in advance, insurance paid in advance, and depreciation on fixed assets.

Note that in the case of rent, the landlord receiving the cash in advance records a deferred revenue entry called unearned revenue. On the flip side, the tenant paying the rent in advance records a deferred expense entry called prepaid rent. The same is true with insurance carriers and the insured parties, magazine providers and subscription holders, etc.

What happens after adjusting entries are recorded?

After adjusting entries are recorded in the journal, they are posted to the general ledger in the same manner as any other journal entry. The accounts are retotaled and a new trial balance is prepared, called the adjusted trial balance (because the accounts have now been adjusted).

What is the adjusted trial balance used for?

The adjusted trial balance shows the corrected amounts for each account and is used to prepare the financial statements. Just as with the unadjusted trial balance, the adjusted trial balance is prepared automatically by computerized accounting systems.

How are the financial statements prepared from the adjusted trial balance?

The income statement is prepared first by taking the revenue and expense accounts from the bottom of the adjusted trial balance.

Next, the statement of retained earnings is prepared by taking the retained earnings figure from the adjusted trial balance as the *beginning* balance of retained earnings. Then, the net income figure from the income statement is added to retained earnings beginning balance and the dividends from the adjusted trial balance are subtracted in arriving at the retained earnings *ending balance*. Note that at this point, the retained earnings ending balance, is not what is listed on the adjusted trial balance. This will happen during the closing entry process, as described later in this chapter.

Finally, the assets, liabilities, and equity accounts (aside from retained earnings and dividends) are taken from the adjusted trial balance and listed on the balance sheet. Note that the retained earnings amount from the adjusted trial balance does not go on the balance sheet, as that represents the beginning balance. The ending balance in retained earnings, as shown on the statement of retained earnings, is the amount that goes on the balance sheet.

The figure on page 111 illustrates this process.

STEPS 9–11: THE YEAR-END CLOSE

Why are closing entries needed?

Imagine that you are the record keeper for a fitness competition. You are currently stationed at the quarter-mile run. Your job is to keep track of how long it takes competitors to run the quarter mile. When each competitor is ready, you start your stopwatch. When each competitor finishes, you stop your stopwatch. In between competitors, you must reset your stopwatch; otherwise, each consecutive runner's time will get higher and higher. The same is true for certain accounting records. In essence, closing entries are needed to reset the stopwatch on certain accounts and get them ready for the next year.

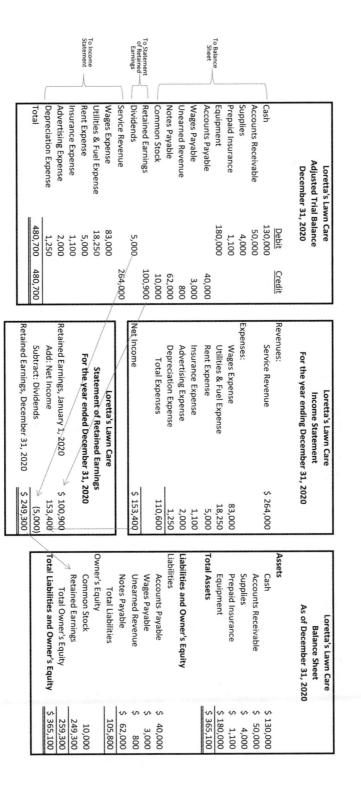

Loretta's Lawn Care
Adjusted Trial Balance
December 31, 2020

	Debit	Credit
Cash	130,000	
Accounts Receivable	50,000	
Supplies	4,000	
Prepaid Insurance	1,100	
Equipment	180,000	
Accounts Payable		40,000
Wages Payable		3,000
Unearned Revenue		800
Notes Payable		62,000
Common Stock		10,000
Retained Earnings		100,900
Dividends	5,000	
Service Revenue		264,000
Wages Expense	83,000	
Utilities & Fuel Expense	18,250	
Rent Expense	5,000	
Insurance Expense	1,100	
Advertising Expense	2,000	
Depreciation Expense	1,250	
Total	480,700	480,700

To Income Statement
To Statement of Retained Earnings
To Statement of Retained Earnings
To Balance Sheet

Loretta's Lawn Care
Income Statement
For the year ending December 31, 2020

Revenues:		
Service Revenue		$ 264,000
Expenses:		
Wages Expense	83,000	
Utilities & Fuel Expense	18,250	
Rent Expense	5,000	
Insurance Expense	1,100	
Advertising Expense	2,000	
Depreciation Expense	1,250	
Total Expenses		110,600
Net Income		$ 153,400

Loretta's Lawn Care
Statement of Retained Earnings
For the year ended December 31, 2020

Retained Earnings, January 1, 2020	$ 100,900
Add: Net Income	153,400
Subtract: Dividends	(5,000)
Retained Earnings, December 31, 2020	$ 249,300

Loretta's Lawn Care
Balance Sheet
As of December 31, 2020

Assets	
Cash	$ 130,000
Accounts Receivable	$ 50,000
Supplies	$ 4,000
Prepaid Insurance	$ 1,100
Equipment	$ 180,000
Total Assets	$ 365,100

Liabilities and Owner's Equity	
Liabilities	
Accounts Payable	$ 40,000
Wages Payable	$ 3,000
Unearned Revenue	$ 800
Notes Payable	$ 62,000
Total Liabilities	105,800
Owner's Equity	
Common Stock	10,000
Retained Earnings	249,300
Total Owner's Equity	259,300
Total Liabilities and Owner's Equity	$ 365,100

When are closing entries prepared?

Closing entries are prepared as part of the year-end close process. At the end of the twelve-month year, accountants will reset the stopwatch. Note that not all companies use a calendar year, opening on January 1 and closing on December 31. Some companies, especially those that operate on a seasonal basis, use what is called a "fiscal year," which can be any consecutive twelve-month period. Many retail organizations prefer to have a year end on January 31, after the close of the holiday shopping season. In that case, their year would start on February 1 and end each January 31.

Which accounts are closed?

Accounts can be divided into two groups: temporary and permanent. Only the temporary accounts are closed.

What are temporary accounts?

Temporary accounts are those that track activity over a certain period of time. Temporary accounts must be "reset" or "zeroed out" at the end of each year in order to start tracking activity for the following year. The temporary accounts are revenues, expenses, and dividends/distributions. We track revenues and expenses for a year, showing them on the income statement. At the end of the year, we must reset the stopwatch in order to start tracking the revenues and expenses for the new year. The same is true for dividends that show up on the statement of retained earnings. We just track the distributions to owners for each individual year. Recall that both the income statement and statement of retained earnings are dated "for a period of time" rather than "at a point in time." Once the period of time is completed, the accounts must be reset.

What are permanent accounts?

Permanent accounts are those that record real balances at a point in time. The permanent accounts are those that show up on the balance sheet: assets, liabilities, and equity accounts. Recall that the balance sheet is dated "at a point in time" rather than "for a period of time."

Why aren't permanent accounts closed?

Permanent accounts represent real balances that cannot just go away or be zeroed out at the end of the year. For example, the Loretta's Lawn Care balance sheet shows cash of $130,000 on December 31, 2020. Just because the year has ended doesn't mean the cash disappears. As such, it wouldn't make any sense to zero that out on January 1, 2021. Likewise, the balance sheet shows $50,000 of accounts receivable on December 31, 2020. Just because a new year is starting does not mean that Loretta's Lawn Care will forgive the debts of its customers and start them all with a clean slate. No, that $50,000 is a real amount that customers owe, no matter what day it is on the calendar. The same is true for buildings and equipment, etc. Those things are real and don't disappear at the end of the year. In summary, as permanent accounts represent real balances at a point in time, there is no need to close them and reset them for the next year.

What are the closing entries?

There are two main closing entries. Recall that the formula for the statement of retained earnings is:

Retained Earnings, Beginning Balance

+ Net Income

– Dividends

= Retained Earnings, Ending Balance

The first closing entry moves net income into retained earnings. The second journal entry takes dividends out of retained earnings. As a result of the two closing journal entries, the retained earnings balance will correctly match the ending balance on the statement of retained earnings.

How is the first closing entry recorded?

The first closing entry zeros out the revenue and expense accounts. Since revenues have a credit balance, they must be debited in order to zero them out. Since expenses have a debit balance, they must be credited in order to zero them out. Recall that revenue minus expenses equals net income. Once the revenue and expense accounts are closed out, the balance of the journal entry will be credited to retained earnings, thus moving net income into retained earnings. Note that if the company has a loss (negative net income), the balance will be debited to retained earnings. Using the Loretta's Lawn Care adjusted trial balance as of December 31, 2020, the first closing entry would look like the following:

Account	Dr.	Cr.
Service Revenue	264,000	
Wages Expense		83,000
Utilities		18,250
Rent Expense		5,000
Insurance Expense		1,100
Advertising Expense		2,000
Depreciation Expense		1,250
Retained Earnings		153,400

Note that the credit to retained earnings matches the net income on the income statement. Also note that debits equal credits, as they must.

How is the second closing entry recorded?

The second closing entry zeros out the dividends account. Since that account has a debit balance, it must be credited to be zeroed out. The matching debit for this journal entry goes to retained earnings. Accordingly, retained earnings will be reduced by the amount of dividends. Using the Loretta's Lawn Care adjusted trial balance as of December 31, 2020, the second closing entry would look like the following:

Account	Dr.	Cr.
Retained Earnings	5,000	
Dividends		5,000

What happens after the closing journal entries are prepared?

After the closing journal entries are prepared, they are posted to the general ledger just like with any other journal entry. At this point, the ending balance in retained earnings will match the ending balance on the statement of retained earnings. A T account for retained earnings is shown below to illustrate this process:

-	+

Retained Earnings

		100,900	Beg. Bal.
CE 2	5,000	153,400	CE 1
		249,300	End. Bal.

What is the post-closing trial balance used for?

After the closing entries have been posted, a final trial balance called the post-closing trial balance is prepared. This trial balance is used to confirm that all temporary accounts have been closed, double-check that the retained earnings balance matches what is on the statement of retained earnings, and to ensure that debits equal credits. The post-closing trial balance for Loretta's Lawn Care as of December 31, 2020, is shown below:

Loretta's Lawn Care
Post-Closing Trial Balance
December 31, 2020

	Debit	Credit
Cash	130,000	
Accounts Receivable	50,000	
Supplies	4,000	
Prepaid Insurance	1,100	
Equipment	180,000	
Accounts Payable		40,000
Wages Payable		3,000
Unearned Revenue		800
Notes Payable		62,000
Common Stock		10,000
Retained Earnings		249,300
Dividends	-	
Service Revenue		-
Wages Expense	-	
Utilities & Fuel Expense	-	
Rent Expense	-	
Insurance Expense	-	
Advertising Expense	-	
Depreciation Expense	-	
Total	365,100	365,100

What happens after the post-closing trial balance is prepared?

After the post-closing trial balance has been prepared and reviewed, the company is ready to start the new year.

SOURCE DOCUMENTS IN THE ACCOUNTING SYSTEM

What is a source document?

The activities and transactions of the business are documented on source documents. These documents provide evidence of the transaction and provide supporting details. There are many different types of source documents, depending on the nature of the transaction. Some common examples have been provided in this chapter.

What are the source documents in the sales and accounts receivables cycle?

Some documents that are commonly used when making sales to customers and billing customers for payment are: purchase orders, sales orders, bills of lading, sales invoices, and credit memos.

What is a purchase order?

The purchase order is a document initiated by the customer that specifies what the customer wants to purchase. Once the purchase order has been reviewed and approved by the company providing the goods, an internal sales order will be prepared.

What is a sales order?

The sales order takes the basic information from the customer purchase order and relays that information to various departments for approval. For example, the collections department may want to run a credit check on the customer to verify collectability of the account. The inventory management department will need to check to determine if sufficient quantities are on hand, etc.

What is a bill of lading?

Once the sales order and goods have reached the shipping department, another source document called a bill of lading is prepared and signed off by the carrier of the goods (the shipper). The bill of lading serves as evidence that the goods were shipped and represents a contractual agreement with the carrier of the goods.

What is a sales invoice?

A copy of the bill of lading, along with the sales order, is typically sent to the billing department to prepare the sales invoice. This invoice shows the quantity and price of goods sent to customers along with payment terms and total amount due.

What is a credit memo?

Occasionally, it is necessary to adjust the amount due from customers. This could be due to price allowances given for defective products, product returns, etc. Any reduction in the amount due from a customer is recorded on a credit memo. In essence, the accounts receivable subledger for that customer is being credited/reduced. All credit memos should be reviewed and approved by a supervisor to ensure they are legitimate reductions of a customer balance.

What are the source documents in the inventory cycle?

Some documents that are commonly used when purchasing, receiving, storing, issuing, processing, and shipping inventory are: purchase requisitions, purchase orders, receiving reports, materials requisitions, and shipping documents.

What is a purchase requisition?

When a department needs goods, that department fills out a purchase requisition. For example, a department that has hired a new employee may need a new laptop for that employee. In order to get the laptop purchased, a purchase requisition would need to be completed. The purchase requisition is the document used to request the goods and is typically approved by a supervisor to ensure the goods are requested for a legitimate purpose. The approved purchase requisition is then sent to the purchasing department to make the purchase.

What is a purchase order?

Once the purchasing department receives the purchase requisition, it will complete a purchase order that will be sent to the appropriate vendor. This purchase order authorizes the purchase of the goods or services. Most purchasing departments will go through a process of determining the need for the item, obtaining competitive pricing bids, and ensuring appropriate authorization for the purchase.

What is a receiving report?

Once purchased goods arrive, an independent receiving department should record the quantity and type of goods received. This information is detailed on a receiving report. This report will later be matched to the vendor invoice (among other things) to determine if the quantity of goods that is being billed for matches the quantity of goods received.

What is a materials requisition?

The materials requisition is similar to the purchase requisition in that the materials requisition is a request for materials that are needed. Unlike the purchase requisition, these items are already in the warehouse and thus do not need to be purchased. For example, a manufacturer of custom tables may store wood in the warehouse. The builder needing the wood to make a table for a customer would fill out a materials requisition for the wood. Typically, materials requisitions need to be approved by a supervisor, ensuring the request is legitimate. The materials requisition serves as permission for the warehouse to release the goods.

What is a shipping document?

Along with preparing a bill of lading for the carrier of the goods, companies will also prepare a shipping document. The shipping document indicates the quantity of goods being shipped. A copy is typically sent to the customer along with the goods, and another copy is sent to accounting to use in the billing process.

What are the source documents in the accounts payable cycle?

Some documents that are commonly used when making payments to vendors for purchases are: purchase requisitions, purchase orders, receiving reports, and vendor invoices. Upon receipt of an invoice from a vendor, quantities and prices should be matched to purchase requisitions, purchase orders, and receiving reports before issuing payment to the vendor. This ensures that the company only pays for goods that were approved for purchase and that the company only pays for the quantity of goods that were received.

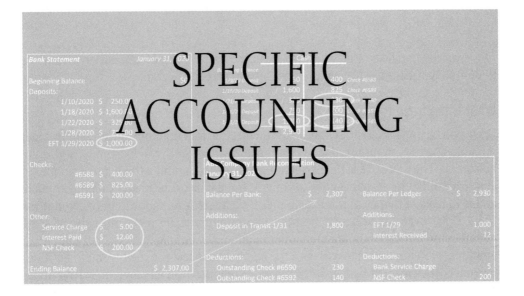

SPECIFIC ACCOUNTING ISSUES

FRAUD AND INTERNAL CONTROLS

What is fraud?

Fraud is an attempt to deceive others for personal or financial gain. There are two basic types of fraud: fraudulent financial statements and misappropriation of assets. Fraudulent financial statements is often referred to as "cooking the books" or "fudging the numbers." It involves misrepresenting the financial statements so that the amounts reported do not reflect the actual results of the business. Misappropriation of assets is often referred to as defalcation, embezzlement, or theft. It involves stealing the assets of the business.

Why would someone try to misrepresent the financial statements?

Financial statements are sometimes falsified to make the results look better than they actually are. Sometimes they are even falsified to make the results look worse than they actually are. A common reason for financial statements to be altered to look better than they actually are is to attract investors, fool creditors, or to meet organizational budgets and goals. For example, many managers have bonuses tied to meeting financial results. If a manager wants to ensure they receive their bonus, they may have an incentive to make the financial results look better than they are. A common reason for financial statements to be altered to look worse than they actually are is to avoid payment of taxes. For example, a company may try to skim cash receipts and not record them as sales in order to report less revenue and profit to the government and pay less in federal and state taxes.

Which is the asset most susceptible to theft?

Cash is typically the asset most susceptible to theft. Cash is portable and belongs to the person holding the cash, which makes it an easy target for thieves. In addition, companies typically handle a large volume of cash transactions, making it easier to hide the theft among the numerous day-to-day debits and credits to cash.

What is the fraud triangle?

The fraud triangle is a representation of the three factors that must be present in order for someone to commit fraud. The three factors are incentive, opportunity, and rationalization. The incentive is the reason for someone to commit a fraud. For example, an employee might have an incentive to commit fraud if he or she has a gambling problem and is in need of money. If there is no incentive, there is no motivation to commit the fraud. Once an employee has an incentive to commit fraud, he or she must also have the opportunity to commit the fraud in order to physically be able to do it. For example, an employee who has access to cash and the ability to conceal the theft through fictitious journal entries may have an opportunity to steal. Finally, an employee may have an incentive to commit the fraud and have the opportunity to do so, but he or she must also be able to rationalize the fraud in order to actually commit the act. For example, an employee who has a weak moral character may think, "It's OK for me to steal the cash. I'm really underpaid, anyway!" If one of the three elements of the fraud triangle is missing, the fraud will not occur.

What is internal control?

Internal control is a process designed to promote the effectiveness and efficiency of operations, reliability of financial reporting, and compliance with laws and regulations. Basically, internal controls are the safeguards in place to meet the company's objectives. For example, most people have smoke detectors in their homes. This is a type of internal control over the operations of your house. If smoke is detected, the alarm will go off, notifying the homeowner of a problem. Additionally, many homes have fire extinguishers. If a fire is detected, a fire extinguisher can be used to correct the situation. Internal controls work the same way in business.

How do companies try to stop fraud?

In order to prevent fraud from occurring, companies try to counteract the incentives, opportunities, and rationalization. For example, to counteract incentives to commit fraud, companies will want to have a firm policy of prosecuting all employees who are caught committing fraud. This penalty is an attempt to counteract the incentive. To limit the opportunities, companies devise a system of internal controls to prevent and/or detect fraud. Finally, to counteract rationalization, companies try to encourage ethical behavior of employees through training, having a code of ethics that is reviewed regularly, and providing whistle-blower hotlines and protection.

What are the five components of internal control?

The five components of internal control are: control environment, risk assessment, control activities, information and communication, and monitoring. Control environment is known as the tone at the top. It is representative of the overall culture and attitude the organization and its leadership have regarding internal control. A company should have a strong control environment and build a culture of integrity. Risk assessment is the process of continually assessing risks to the company both in terms of meeting objectives and the potential for fraud. Control activities are the processes and procedures in place to mitigate risks. Controls can be designed to prevent, detect, and correct these issues. Information and communication refers to the process of collecting, generating, and communicating relevant information. The accounting information system is a key part of this component. Finally, monitoring activities are the continuous evaluation and improvement of the internal control system.

What are the principles of control activities?

In order to mitigate risks, an effective internal control system should cover the key principles of internal control. Those key principles include establishing responsibility, segregating duties, restricting access, documenting procedures, and independently verifying.

Establishing responsibility means that one person should be assigned to each task. Essentially, you should know whom to blame if something goes wrong. For example, it is common at grocery stores for one employee to be assigned to a cash register at a time. That way, if a cash drawer comes up short at the end of a shift, the store knows who is responsible for the shortage. If many employees share a cash register, it would not be as easy to know who is responsible. Thus, establishing responsibility can prevent an employee from committing fraud, as he or she knows he or she can be identified easily.

Segregating duties means that one employee should not be responsible for all aspects of a process. Essentially, duties need to be split up between various employees so that an employee cannot steal and conceal it. For example, an employee who handles cash should not also be able to record journal entries for cash. If an employee has access to cash and can make journal entries for cash, he or she could steal the cash and attempt to conceal it by booking a fictitious journal entry that makes the cash usage appear to be valid. In this case, it would be harder to detect that a theft had occurred.

Restricting access refers to the physical safeguards in place to prevent fraud. For example, most computer systems have passwords restricting access to the accounting software. Additionally, inventory is typically kept safe through various measures, including physical locks on warehouses and alarm systems. Many retail stores use a system of magnetic tags to prevent theft of inventory. These are all ways in which access can be restricted.

Documenting procedures is an important step in the internal control process, as documents can be reviewed and traced through the system. Companies should use documents to evidence transactions that have occurred and store them in an organized fashion. If possible, these documents should be prenumbered, or assigned numbers by the accounting system. For example, if a company uses check stock that is prenumbered, it would be possible to tell if a check was missing.

Independent verification is the process of checking or verifying the work of others. For example, many companies have supervisors review and sign off on certain transactions to prevent errors or fraud.

Will internal controls prevent or detect all fraudulent activities?

No. Internal controls are not perfect. They are subject to certain limitations. One type of limitation is human error. For example, an employee could accidentally type $1,000 instead of $100, and a supervisor may miss the extra zero when reviewing the entry. Another limitation is the fact that fraud is an intentional act of deceit, which makes it hard to prevent or detect. When someone is trying to get around the system, it can be hard to thwart. For example, duties could be properly segregated between multiple employees, but if those employees get together to beat the system (collusion), they can commit the fraud. Finally, internal controls are subject to the cost/benefit constraint, meaning that the cost of implementing the controls should not outweigh the benefit achieved. For example, a retail store could hire a security guard to stand at the entrance of the store and search everyone before they leave; however, the cost of the security guard and the cost of the potential lost sales by turning off customers would most likely be far greater than the cost of a few stolen articles.

What is a bank statement reconciliation?

A bank statement reconciliation involves reviewing transactions on the bank statement each month and comparing those transactions to the debits and credits in the cash gen-

How do companies protect their cash?

Due to the high risk of theft of cash, duties must be properly segregated over cash. An effective internal control system over cash receipts assigns a cashier to collect payments and document procedures; a supervisor to review the count of cash, store the cash in the vault, and prepare the bank slips; and an accounting department to record the cash receipt in the system. An effective internal control system over cash payments should follow a voucher system whereby purchases must be requested and authorized before being purchased, goods received should be handled by an independent receiving department, and payment checks should only be issued for goods that have been matched to the purchase request documentation, receiving records, and vendor invoices. The bank statement should also be reconciled monthly as part of the independent verification process.

eral ledger. Any items that do not match up should be researched and verified. Common items that are found when reconciling the bank statement occur in two categories: items that the bank is unaware of and items that the company is unaware of. The bank statement balance and the cash ledger balance should be adjusted for these reconciling items to arrive at a reconciled cash balance.

What are reconciling items to the bank statement balance?

Reconciling items to the bank statement balance are items that the bank is unaware of. These items are reflected in the cash general ledger but are not on the bank statement. They primarily include outstanding checks and deposits in transit. In addition, errors could be made on the bank statement that would be discovered during the reconciliation process. Outstanding checks are checks that the company has issued that have not yet been cleared by the bank. This could be because the check is in the mail or the vendor the check was sent to has not deposited the check yet. Outstanding checks should be subtracted from the bank statement balance when arriving at an adjusted cash balance. Deposits in transit are deposits that the company has made that the bank has not recorded yet. This could be because the company made a deposit in an overnight deposit slot on the weekend that the bank will not record until the following business day. Deposits in transit should be added to the bank statement balance when arriving at the adjusted cash balance. Errors on the bank statement could result in either additions to or subtractions from cash and must be investigated individually to determine the nature of the error and how to fix it.

What are reconciling items to the cash general ledger?

Reconciling items to the cash general ledger are items that the company is unaware of. These items are reflected on the bank statement but are not in the cash general ledger. They primarily include fees charged by the bank, interest paid by the bank, customer electronic payments, and bounced customer checks (non-sufficient funds, or NSF, checks). Additionally, errors could be made by the company that would be discovered during the reconciliation process. Bank fees or service charges are common on checking accounts. Those fees are automatically taken out of the checking account and should be subtracted from the general ledger balance when arriving at the adjusted cash balance. On the other hand, some bank accounts pay interest, which is deposited automatically into the bank account. Any interest received should be added to the general ledger balance when arriving at the adjusted cash balance. Sometimes customers pay electronically via EFT (electronic funds transfer). Companies might only receive notice of this when reviewing the bank statement. In this case, the EFT receipt should be added to the general ledger balance when arriving at the adjusted cash balance. On the other hand, if a customer sent a check that they don't actually have the funds to cover, the check will bounce. This is an NSF check. NSF checks need to be deducted from the general ledger balance in arriving at the adjusted cash balance. Errors in the cash general ledger could result in either additions to or subtractions from cash and must be investigated individually to determine the nature of the error and how to fix it.

How is a bank statement reconciled?

The bank statement is reconciled in a process that starts by adjusting the bank statement balance for reconciling items that the bank was unaware of and calculating an adjusted bank total. Next, the cash ledger balance is adjusted for reconciling the items that the company was unaware of, and an adjusted cash ledger total is calculated. In the end, the two adjusted balances are compared to each other. The two balances must match in order for the bank account to be considered reconciled.

An example of a bank reconciliation is shown in the figure below. The checks indicate items that match both the bank statement and the cash ledger. The circled items indicate reconciling items that must be shown as adjustments on the bank reconciliation. Note that the final adjusted balances for the bank statement and the general ledger match, as they should.

Are any journal entries necessary after reconciling the bank statement?

Yes. The items that are shown as adjustments to the cash ledger must be recorded with journal entries so that the cash ledger shows the true cash balance. In the example above, the cash ledger must be increased (debited) for the EFT deposit and the interest received. The cash ledger must be decreased (credited) for the bank service charge and the NSF check. No journal entries are needed for the reconciling items on the bank statement side, as those items are already reflected in the cash ledger. The journal entries for the bank reconciliation in this example are shown below. After the journal entries are posted to the cash ledger, the ending cash balance would be $3,737.

Account	Dr.	Cr.
Cash	1,000	
Accounts Receivable		1,000
Cash	12	
Interest Revenue		12
Bank Fees Expense	5	
Cash		5
Accounts Receivable	200	
Cash		200

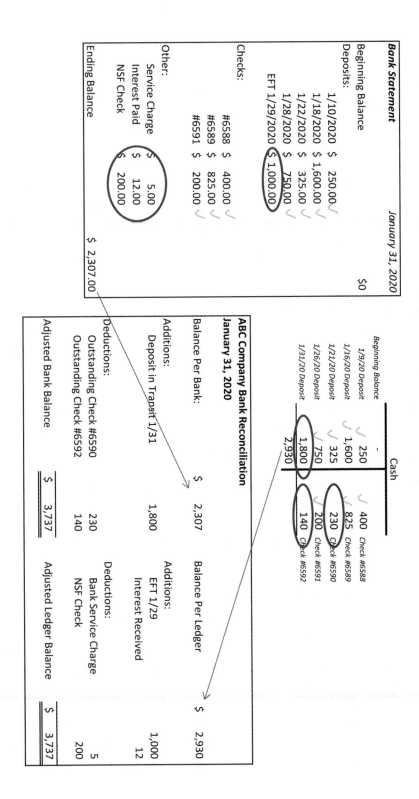

Bank Statement   January 31, 2020

Beginning Balance $0
Deposits:
       1/10/2020 $ 250.00 ✓
       1/18/2020 $ 1,600.00 ✓
       1/22/2020 $ 325.00 ✓
       1/28/2020 $ 750.00 ✓
       EFT 1/29/2020 $ 1,000.00

Checks:
       #6588 $ 400.00 ✓
       #6589 $ 825.00 ✓
       #6591 $ 200.00 ✓

Other:
       Service Charge $ 5.00
       Interest Paid $ 12.00
       NSF Check $ 200.00
Ending Balance $ 2,307.00

ABC Company Bank Reconciliation
January 31, 2020

Balance Per Bank: $ 2,307

Additions:
       Deposit in Transit 1/31   1,800

Deductions:
       Outstanding Check #6590   230
       Outstanding Check #6592   140
Adjusted Bank Balance $ 3,737

Balance Per Ledger $ 2,930

Additions:
       EFT 1/29   1,000
       Interest Received   12

Deductions:
       Bank Service Charge   5
       NSF Check   200
Adjusted Ledger Balance $ 3,737

Cash

Beginning Balance   -
1/9/20 Deposit   250 ✓
1/16/20 Deposit   1,600 ✓
1/21/20 Deposit   325 ✓
1/26/20 Deposit   750 ✓
1/31/20 Deposit   1,800
                       2,930

400   Check #6588 ✓
825   Check #6589 ✓
230   Check #6590
200   Check #6591 ✓
140   Check #6592

125

MERCHANDISERS

What is a merchandiser?

A merchandiser is an entity that purchases goods, called merchandise inventory, and sells those goods to their customers. For example, Wal-Mart and Target are both examples of merchandisers.

How does the accounting for a merchandiser differ from a service company?

Service companies purchase supplies and use those supplies in the business. Merchandisers purchase inventory and sell that inventory to customers. As service companies have no inventory, they do not have to account for it. Merchandisers must track and record all inventory purchases at the cost they paid for the inventory and record sales of inventory at the price charged to customers.

What is a periodic inventory system?

A periodic inventory system tracks and records inventory transactions at the end of the accounting period (typically the end of the month). This is usually accomplished through taking a physical count of inventory and using a formula to calculate the cost of the goods that were sold. The formula used in a periodic inventory system is:

Beginning Inventory Balance + Inventory Purchases = Goods Available for Sale

Goods Available for Sale − Ending Inventory Balance = Cost of Goods Sold

Basically, the company knows the beginning value of inventory from the physical count at the end of the previous month. It can then add the cost of the inventory it purchased that month to give it the value of the goods it had available for sale. If it counts inventory at the end of the month, it can back into the cost of the goods that were sold to customers. However, this formula assumes that all goods that are missing were sold. That might not be the case, as inventory could be missing due to theft or error. This is a major shortcoming of a periodic inventory system.

What is a perpetual inventory system?

A perpetual inventory system tracks and records inventory transactions in real time. It is typically accomplished by using a system of bar codes and scanning tools. Each time inventory is purchased, it is scanned and recorded in the accounting system. Each time inventory is sold, it is also scanned and recorded in the accounting system. Accordingly, the cost of the goods that were sold can be found at any time by checking the data on the inventory scans. At the end of the month, a physical count of inventory can be used to reconcile the system totals by rearranging the formula used for periodic inventory as:

Beginning Inventory Balance + Inventory Purchases = Goods Available for Sale

Goods Available for Sale − Cost of Goods Sold = Ending Inventory Balance

Note that as technology has become more readily available, periodic inventory systems are used by fewer and fewer companies, and perpetual inventory systems have become the norm for merchandisers.

What are the advantages of a perpetual inventory system?

Perpetual inventory systems have many advantages over periodic inventory systems in regard to the ability to track and record inventory data and produce financial analyses in real time. The primary advantage is in providing internal controls over inventory. As inventory is tracked with a system of bar codes and scanners, companies can determine the quantities and values of inventory at any time. When these quantities are compared to physical counts of inventory, it is possible to determine if any inventory is missing. For example, in the equation for perpetual inventory systems above, a company may determine that it should have $230,000 worth of inventory on hand. If the physical inventory count reveals that only $220,000 worth of inventory is in the warehouse, the company can determine that $10,000 of inventory is missing. This cannot be done with a periodic inventory system.

What is shrinkage?

Missing inventory is called shrinkage in the merchandising industry. Shrinkage is the loss of inventory through theft or error. According to the 2016 National Retail Security Survey prepared by the National Retail Federation, 39.3% of shrinkage was caused by shoplifting, 35.8% of shrinkage was caused by employee theft, and the remaining 24.9% of shrinkage was caused by administrative errors, vendor fraud/errors, or unknown reasons. The average loss per shoplifting incident was $377. The average loss from dishonest employees was $1,233.77 per incident.

How are inventory purchases recorded?

Inventory purchases are recorded at the cost paid for the inventory plus any transportation cost, less any discounts taken or returns made. For example, assume a small local toy store called Cabbage Kids purchased 200 fidget spinner toys from Spinz Company on January 15, 2020, for $1 each. The invoice stated terms 2/10, n/30. The goods were shipped FOB shipping point, and the freight charges were an additional $15 to be paid in cash upon delivery. Upon opening the package, the store manager found that forty of the fidget spinners were a larger size than expected and returned them to Spinz Company for a full discount. Additionally, another forty fidget spinners were the wrong color. Spinz Company agreed to a $0.25 allowance on each of those fidget spinners. On January 21, 2020, Cabbage Kids paid Spinz Company the amount due. These transactions must all be recorded as either increases (debits) or decreases (credits) to the inventory account.

How is the initial inventory purchase recorded?

The journal entry to record the initial receipt of the fidget spinner toys would be recorded as shown below. Note that the inventory account is debited (increased) for the purchase price (200 toys at $1 each), and accounts payable is credited (increased) for the amount owed to the vendor.

Account	Dr.	Cr.
Inventory	200	
Accounts Payable		200

What do purchase terms 2/10, n/30 mean?

Sometimes vendors will offer an incentive for their customers to pay invoices quickly. This is done through offering a purchase discount as part of the payment terms. In the case of 2/10, n/30 (spoken as two, ten, net, thirty), the customer will receive a 2% discount if they pay the invoice within ten days. Otherwise, the invoice is due in thirty days. Payment terms can be arranged in any fashion. For example, 5/15, n/45 means the customer will receive a 5% discount if they pay the invoice within fifteen days. Otherwise, the invoice is due in forty-five days. Additionally, if no purchase discount is offered and the invoice is due in thirty days, the terms may simply state "net 30." In the example above for Cabbage Kids, there is nothing that needs to be done with the purchase discount until the invoice is paid, as it is unknown at the time of purchase whether the invoice will be paid within the discount period (ten days) or not.

What do FOB shipping point and FOB destination mean?

Goods are typically shipped with sale terms FOB shipping point or FOB destination. FOB stands for "free on board." The words after FOB indicate where ownership transfers. In the case of FOB shipping point, the ownership transfers at the shipping point (when the goods are loaded onto the truck). In this case, the buyer owns the goods once they are on the truck and pays for the shipping. In the case of FOB destination, the ownership transfers at the final destination (when the goods arrive at the buyer's site). In this case, the seller owns the goods while they are in transit, and the seller pays for the shipping.

How is the freight charge recorded when purchasing inventory?

In the case of the Cabbage Kids example, the fidget spinner toys were purchased with sale terms FOB shipping point. That means Cabbage Kids owned the inventory while it was in transit, and Cabbage Kids must pay for the $15 shipping cost. This cost is necessary to obtain the inventory and thus is recorded as an increase in the value of the inventory. The journal entry for the shipping charges paid in cash by Cabbage Kids would be recorded as follows:

Account	Dr.	Cr.
Inventory	15	
Cash		15

How are purchase returns recorded?

If goods are sent back to the vendor, either because the goods are in unsatisfactory condition or because they are not needed, inventory and accounts payable are reduced by the amount returned. In the case of Cabbage Kids, forty of the fidget spinners arrived in unsatisfactory condition, as they were larger than anticipated. In this case, a journal entry must be made to reduce inventory (credit) by forty fidget spinners at $1 each and to reduce the accounts payable owed to the vendor (debit), as the $40 is no longer owed. The journal entry to record the return is shown below:

Account	Dr.	Cr.
Accounts Payable	40	
Inventory		40

How are purchase allowances recorded?

Sometimes goods that arrive in an unsatisfactory condition may be kept by the customer in exchange for a price reduction, called an allowance. You may have personally received a price allowance yourself if you've ever gone to a store and asked for a discount on an item that is slightly damaged. In the case of Cabbage Kids, forty of the fidget spinner toys arrived in the wrong color. Spinz Company agreed to a $0.25 per item allowance, resulting in a $10 total discount. In this case, a journal entry must be made to reduce (credit) the inventory value by $10 and to reduce (debit) the accounts payable owed to Spinz Company, as the $10 is no longer owed. This allowance would be recorded as follows:

Account	Dr.	Cr.
Accounts Payable	10	
Inventory		10

How is a payment for purchases recorded if a purchase discount is taken?

If Cabbage Kids pays Spinz Company within ten days, it is allowed to take a 2% purchase discount, as the terms were 2/10, n/30. In the example above, Cabbage Kids pays within the discount period. The amount owed to Spinz Company at the time of payment, before the purchase discount is computed, was $150. This is calculated as the $200 original purchase, less the $40 return and the $10 allowance. Note that the shipping charge of $15 was paid in cash and thus is not part of the calculation of the accounts payable balance. The 2% discount on $150 is $3. Accordingly, Cabbage Kids will only pay the vendor $147. The journal entry to record this payment is shown below. Note that the entire accounts payable balance of $150 must be eliminated, as Cabbage Kids does not owe Spinz Company anything anymore. However, since the cash paid was only $147, the journal entry would not balance. What is missing is the $3 purchase discount, which is recorded as a decrease in the inventory value (credit), as the inventory is valued at what was ultimately paid for it, and that $3 did not end up being paid. The journal entry to record the payment within the discount period would be as follows:

Account	Dr.	Cr.
Accounts Payable	150	
Inventory		3
Cash		147

How is a payment for purchases recorded if no purchase discount is taken?

If an invoice is not paid within the discount period, then the original amount due must be paid. Assuming Cabbage Kids did not pay within the ten days, the journal entry to record the payment would have resulted in a decrease (credit) to cash of $150 and a decrease (debit) to accounts payable for $150, as shown below:

Account	Dr.	Cr.
Accounts Payable	150	
Cash		150

How are sales of inventory recorded?

Sales of inventory are recorded with two journal entries. The first journal entry recognizes sales revenue earned and is recorded as a credit to sales revenue at the price charged to the customer. The offsetting debit to this journal entry is either to accounts receivable or cash, depending on the customer payment method. The second journal entry recognizes the reduction in inventory that is now out of the warehouse and in the hands of the customer at the price the vendor originally paid for the inventory and records the cost of the inventory as an expense called cost of goods sold on the income statement. This process is covered in depth in the chapter entitled "Cost Accounting Basics."

Using the example above for Cabbage Kids, assume that now that you are recording the entries for Spinz Company, who sold the toys to Cabbage Kids. Recall that Spinz Company sold 200 fidget spinner toys to Cabbage Kids on January 15, 2020, for $1 each. The invoice stated terms 2/10, n/30. These toys cost Spinz Company $0.10 each. Forty of the fidget spinners were returned to Spinz Company for a full discount. Additionally, another forty fidget spinners were the wrong color, so Spinz Company agreed to a $0.25 allowance on each of those fidget spinners. On January 21, 2020, Cabbage Kids paid Spinz Company the amount due.

In this case, the initial sale of inventory would be recorded with two journal entries. The first entry recognizes the sales revenue of $200 by increasing (debiting) accounts receivable and increasing (crediting) sales revenue by $200. The second journal entry recognized the fact that 200 fidget spinners are now gone, which cost Spinz Company $0.10 each. (Note that when Spinz bought the fidget spinners from the manufacturer, Spinz would have recorded those in the inventory account at that price.) Once the inventory is sold, the cost is reflected on the income statement as cost of goods sold expense. Note that inventory shows up on the balance sheet as an asset while the company holds the inventory. Once the inventory is sold, the cost of purchasing that inventory moves to the income statement, where it is properly matched against the revenues for the sale of that inventory. Again, this process is covered in depth in the chapter entitled "Cost Accounting Basics." The journal entries for Spinz Company would be recorded as follows:

Account	Dr.	Cr.
Accounts Receivable	200	
Sales Revenue		200
Cost of Goods Sold	20	
Inventory		20

Note that the gross profit on this sale is $180 (the difference between the selling price of the goods and what the goods cost Spinz Company).

How are sales returns recorded?

Sales returns are recorded with two journal entries that essentially serve to reverse the sales journal entries. The first journal entry reduces the account receivable owed by the customer and reduces the sales revenue by utilizing a contra-revenue account called sales returns and allowances. This contra-revenue account reduces sales revenue in arriving at net sales on the income statement (sales revenue − sales returns and allowances = net revenue). In the case of Spinz Company and Cabbage Kids, Cabbage Kids returned forty fidget spinners. Spinz must reverse the revenue recognition entry and record the return of inventory, as follows:

Account	Dr.	Cr.
Sales Returns and Allowances	40	
Accounts Receivable		40
Inventory	4	
Cost of Goods Sold		4

Note that this journal entry essentially says, "Oops, we didn't make the sale after all, so the customer doesn't owe us the money" and "I guess we have the inventory after all and didn't incur the cost of goods sold expense."

How are sales allowances recorded?

Sales allowances are also recorded using the sales returns and allowances contra revenue account. However, in the case of a sales allowance, the second journal entry is not needed because no inventory is being returned. In the case of Spinz Company, the $10 sales allowance given to Cabbage Kids would be recorded as follows:

Account	Dr.	Cr.
Sales Returns and Allowances	10	
Accounts Receivable		10

Why aren't sales returns and allowances recorded as debits (decreases) to the sales revenue account?

While using the sales returns and allowances contra revenue account ends up ultimately reducing net revenue on the income statement anyway, it is still useful to track this data separately by using a contra account. It is important for merchandisers to be able to track the amount of sales returns and allowances given, as that is a useful metric for determining quality, etc. If sales returns and allowances were recorded within the revenue account, it would be much harder to pick out that data. If it is recorded separately in its own contra account, it is very easy to track and monitor.

How is the collection of customer payment recorded if the sales discount is taken?

If a customer pays within the discount period, the entire accounts receivable balance must be reduced, as the customer no longer owes the invoiced amount. However, the cash collected will be less than the accounts receivable balance, as accounts receivable was originally recorded at the full invoice price. The difference between the accounts receivable balance and the cash received is recorded in a contra revenue account called sales discounts. Again, a contra revenue account is used so that sales discounts taken by customers can be easily tracked and monitored for effectiveness. Just like sales returns and allowances, sales discounts are also deducted from sales revenue in arriving at net sales on the income statement. The expanded calculation of net sales on the income statement is: sales revenue − sales returns and allowances − sales discounts = net sales. In the case of Cabbage Kids and Spinz Company, Cabbage Kids owed Spinz $150, calculated as the original invoice amount of $200 less the $40 return and the $10 allowance. Since the invoice was paid within the discount period, Cabbage Kids paid Spinz $147, taking the $3 sales discount. The journal entry to record this is shown below:

Account	Dr.	Cr.
Cash	147	
Sales Discounts	3	
Accounts Receivable		150

Note that a sales discount is the same thing as a purchase discount. The terminology changes based on whether you are talking about the buyer or the seller. Buyers refer to these discounts as purchase discounts because they are purchasing the goods. Sellers refer to these discounts as sales discounts because they are selling the goods.

How is the collection of customer payment recorded if the sales discount is not taken?

If Cabbage Kids had not paid Spinz Company within the discount period, the collection of payment would have been recorded as a debit to cash for the full amount paid and a credit to accounts receivable for the full amount owed. This entry is shown below.

Account	Dr.	Cr.
Cash	150	
Accounts Receivable		150

INVENTORY ACCOUNTING

When inventory is sold, how does the seller know what the cost of the inventory was?

Recall that when inventory is sold, two journal entries are recorded. The first journal entry records the revenue at the price charged to the customer. The second journal entry relieves the inventory and recognizes cost of goods sold at the price originally paid for the inventory. When the inventory was purchased, it was recorded at cost. The cost of each item would have been noted on the purchase invoice and most likely in the accounting system. The cost of inventory may change over time, as prices rise and fall. As such, a company has to determine which cost to use when recording the journal entry to relieve inventory and recognize cost of goods sold. Generally accepted accounting principles allow for a choice between four different inventory costing methods in order to make this determination.

What are the four inventory costing methods?

The four allowable inventory costing methods are: specific identification; first-in, first-out (FIFO); last-in, first-out (LIFO); and weighted average. Note that the inventory costing method does not need to match the physical flow of goods. For example, grocery stores typically sell food on a first-in, first-out basis, meaning the older food items are sold first. They do this by stocking the new items behind the older items. However, just because the flow of goods follows a FIFO pattern doesn't mean they must use FIFO for their accounting records. They are free to choose any of the four methods.

Why does it matter which inventory costing method is used?

As prices of inventory may change, the costing method used will determine the amount of inventory on the balance sheet and cost of goods sold expense on the income statement. Depending on whether costs are rising or falling, certain methods will result in higher net income than others, and certain methods will result in a higher valuation of

133

inventory than others. As such, the method used will affect the overall financial results of the business.

How is the specific identification method applied?

The specific identification method is used when items can be individually identified. This can be done with items that are unique and include some sort of identifier, such as a serial number. For example, when a car dealership sells a car, it will record the cost of that particular vehicle as cost of goods sold, as each vehicle has a different dealer invoice price due to the varying specifications of each vehicle. Assume a car dealership sold a truck for $40,000 that the dealership paid $28,000 for to the manufacturer. It would record the sale to the customer of $40,000 and then record the exact cost of goods sold of $28,000. In that way, specific identification is perhaps the most simple of the four inventory costing methods.

How is the FIFO method applied?

The FIFO method assumes that the first goods in are the first goods to be sold. For example, assume Spinz Company had no beginning inventory of fidget spinner toys at the start of January 2020 and bought fidget spinner toys from an overseas manufacturer as follows:

Purchase Date	Quantity	Item Cost	Total
1/10/2020	2,000	$ 0.10	$ 200.00
1/15/2020	1,800	$ 0.11	$ 198.00
1/22/2020	2,500	$ 0.13	$ 325.00
1/28/2020	600	$ 0.16	$ 96.00
Goods Available for Sale	6,900	$ 0.1187	$ 819.00

You can see that Spinz had 6,900 fidget spinners available for sale in January at a total cost of $819.00. Assume Spinz uses a periodic inventory system and sold 4,000 fidget spinner toys to toy stores during January for $1 each. Using the FIFO method, Spinz would assume the first fidget spinners it purchased were the first fidget spinners it sold. Accordingly, Spinz would start at the top of the list and work its way down. Spinz would assume it sold all 2,000 from the top row, plus all 1,800 from the second row, plus an additional 200 from the third row. Cost of goods sold would then be calculated as $424, as shown below:

Purchase Date	Quantity	Item Cost	Total
1/10/2020	2,000	$ 0.10	$ 200.00
1/15/2020	1,800	$ 0.11	$ 198.00
1/22/2020	200	$ 0.13	$ 26.00
Cost of Goods Sold	4,000		$ 424.00

The journal entries to record the sale would be as follows:

Account	Dr.	Cr.
Accounts Receivable	4,000	
Sales Revenue		4,000
Cost of Goods Sold	424	
Inventory		424

The 2,900 fidget spinners that were not sold would remain as ending inventory on the balance sheet at a value of $395, which can be illustrated as follows:

Purchase Date	Quantity	Item Cost	Total
1/22/2020	2,300	$ 0.13	$ 299.00
1/28/2020	600	$ 0.16	$ 96.00
Ending Inventory	2,900		$ 395.00

The calculations of cost of goods sold and ending inventory can be checked by using the formula for calculating cost of goods sold, as follows:

Formula:	Units	$
Beginning Inventory	-	$ -
+ Purchases	6,900	$ 819
= Goods Available for Sale	6,900	$ 819
- Ending Inventory	2,900	$ 395
= Cost of Goods Sold	4,000	$ 424

How is the LIFO method applied?

The LIFO method assumes that the last goods in are the first goods to be sold. Again, assume Spinz Company had no beginning inventory of fidget spinner toys at the start of January 2020 and bought fidget spinner toys from an overseas manufacturer as follows:

Purchase Date	Quantity	Item Cost	Total
1/10/2020	2,000	$ 0.10	$ 200.00
1/15/2020	1,800	$ 0.11	$ 198.00
1/22/2020	2,500	$ 0.13	$ 325.00
1/28/2020	600	$ 0.16	$ 96.00
Goods Available for Sale	6,900		$ 819.00

Assume Spinz uses a periodic inventory system and sold 4,000 fidget spinner toys to toy stores during January for $1 each. However, this time, using the LIFO method,

Spinz would assume the last fidget spinners it purchased were the first fidget spinners it sold. Accordingly, Spinz would start at the bottom of the list and work its way up. Spinz would assume it sold all 600 from the bottom row, plus all 2,500 from the third row, plus an additional 900 from the second row. Cost of goods sold would then be calculated as $520, as shown below:

Purchase Date	Quantity	Item Cost	Total
1/15/2020	900	$ 0.11	$ 99.00
1/22/2020	2,500	$ 0.13	$ 325.00
1/28/2020	600	$ 0.16	$ 96.00
Cost of Goods Sold	4,000		$ 520.00

The journal entries to record the sale would be as follows:

Account	Dr.	Cr.
Accounts Receivable	4,000	
Sales Revenue		4,000
Cost of Goods Sold	520	
Inventory		520

The 2,900 fidget spinners that were not sold would remain as ending inventory on the balance sheet valued at $299, which can be illustrated as follows:

Purchase Date	Quantity	Item Cost	Total
1/10/2020	2,000	$ 0.10	$ 200.00
1/15/2020	900	$ 0.11	$ 99.00
Ending Inventory	2,900		$ 299.00

The calculations of cost of goods sold and ending inventory can again be checked by using the formula for calculating cost of goods sold, as follows:

Formula:	Units	$
Beginning Inventory	-	$ -
+ Purchases	6,900	$ 819
= Goods Available for Sale	6,900	$ 819
- Ending Inventory	2,900	$ 299
= Cost of Goods Sold	4,000	$ 520

How is the weighted-average cost method applied?

The weighted-average method smooths the price changes by taking an average cost of inventory and using that to compute cost of goods sold and ending inventory. Once again, assume Spinz Company had no beginning inventory of fidget spinner toys at the start of January 2020 and bought fidget spinner toys from an overseas manufacturer as follows:

Purchase Date	Quantity	Item Cost	Total
1/10/2020	2,000	$ 0.10	$ 200.00
1/15/2020	1,800	$ 0.11	$ 198.00
1/22/2020	2,500	$ 0.13	$ 325.00
1/28/2020	600	$ 0.16	$ 96.00
Goods Available for Sale	6,900	$ 0.1187	$ 819.00

Note this time that a weighted-average cost of $0.1187 per unit has been calculated by taking a total cost of goods available for sale of $819 and dividing it by the 6,900 units available for sale. This is the cost that will be used to calculate cost of goods sold and ending inventory.

Again, assume Spinz uses a periodic inventory system and sold 4,000 fidget spinner toys to toy stores during January for $1 each. However, this time, using the weighted-average method, Spinz would use the weighted-average cost of $0.1187 to calculate the cost of the 4,000 units it sold. Cost of goods sold would then be calculated as $474.78, as shown below:

Purchase Date	Quantity	Item Cost	Total
Cost of Goods Sold	4,000	$ 0.1187	$ 474.78

The journal entries to record the sale would be as follows:

Account	Dr.	Cr.
Accounts Receivable	4,000.00	
Sales Revenue		4,000.00
Cost of Goods Sold	474.78	
Inventory		474.78

The 2,900 fidget spinners that were not sold would remain as ending inventory on the balance sheet valued at $344.22, which can be illustrated as follows:

Purchase Date	Quantity	Item Cost	Total
Ending Inventory	2,900	$ 0.1187	$ 344.22

The calculations of cost of goods sold and ending inventory can again be checked by using the formula for calculating cost of goods sold, as follows:

Formula:	Units	$
Beginning Inventory	-	$ -
+ Purchases	6,900	$ 819.00
= Goods Available for Sale	6,900	$ 819.00
- Ending Inventory	2,900	$ 344.22
= Cost of Goods Sold	4,000	$ 474.78

Does the calculation differ if a company uses a periodic versus perpetual inventory system?

Yes, if the LIFO or weighted-average methods are used! The examples above use a periodic inventory system, which therefore records all sales as if they'd happened on January 31, 2020. If a perpetual inventory system was used, the actual date of the sale would be taken into account. For example, assume Spinz company uses LIFO and sold 4,000 fidget spinners on January 23, 2020. At the time the sale was made, the purchase from January 28 had not occurred yet, and thus, the bottom row would be the January 22 purchase, not the January 28 purchase. This would result in different calculations of cost of goods sold and ending inventory, as shown below.

Purchase Date	Quantity	Item Cost	Total
1/10/2020	2,000	$ 0.10	$ 200.00
1/15/2020	1,800	$ 0.11	$ 198.00
1/22/2020	2,500	$ 0.13	$ 325.00
Goods Available for Sale	6,300		$ 723.00

Purchase Date	Quantity	Item Cost	Total
1/15/2020	1,500	$ 0.11	$ 165.00
1/22/2020	2,500	$ 0.13	$ 325.00
Cost of Goods Sold	4,000		$ 490.00

Purchase Date	Quantity	Item Cost	Total
1/10/2020	2,000	$ 0.10	$ 200.00
1/15/2020	300	$ 0.11	$ 33.00
Ending Inventory	2,300		$ 233.00

The same logic applies to the weighted-average method, as well, where the weighted average would be calculated without the January 28 purchase in it. If FIFO is used, the results will be the same under perpetual and periodic inventory, as the earliest date is always the same, no matter what the date of the sale is.

Which inventory costing method results in the highest inventory valuation?

When prices are increasing, FIFO will result in the highest inventory valuation, as the older, cheaper items will be recorded as sold, leaving the newer, more expensive items in ending inventory. The opposite is true when prices are decreasing, as LIFO will result in the highest inventory valuation, as the newer, cheaper items will be recorded as sold, leaving the older, more expensive items in ending inventory.

Which inventory costing method results in the highest cost of goods sold expense?

When prices are increasing, LIFO will result in the highest cost of goods sold expense, as the newer, more expensive items will be recorded as sold. The opposite is true when prices are decreasing, as FIFO will result in the highest cost of goods sold expense, as the older, more expensive items will be recorded as sold. Note that a higher cost of goods sold expense will result in a lower net income. Companies that wish to report a higher net income in order to attract investors may choose to use FIFO if prices are generally increasing. Likewise, companies that wish to report a lower net income in order to pay less in income taxes to the government may choose to use LIFO if prices are generally increasing.

Can companies change inventory costing methods?

In order to discourage companies from switching inventory valuation methods frequently to take advantage of the impacts of rising or falling inventory prices on the financial statements, generally accepted accounting principles only allow changes in inventory valuation methods when such a change improves the accuracy of the financial results. Companies can, however, use different inventory valuation methods for different classifications of inventory. For example, a superstore such as Wal-Mart could use FIFO to account for food products and LIFO to account for home goods, etc.

Additionally, tax rules state that if LIFO is used for tax purposes, it must also be used for the financial statements. This rule is called the LIFO conformity rule and is intended to discourage the use of LIFO during periods of increasing prices solely to avoid paying as much in taxes. Thus, the stance is that if you use LIFO to report lower income on your tax return, you must also use LIFO to report that lower income to your investors.

What is the lower of cost or market rule for inventory?

Sometimes inventory values can fall below the cost recorded on the balance sheet, primarily due to obsolescence or damage. For example, technology products often drop in value as soon as a newer model is released, sometimes rendering the old model obsolete. Likewise, a warehouse that has inventory damaged in a flood would find itself with useless inventory that is not worth what it is recorded at on the balance sheet. If the market value of inventory drops below the cost paid for the inventory, accounting rules require that the value of inventory be reduced on the balance sheet. This is known as a write-down of inventory.

For example, assume an electronics store has 100 graphing calculators that cost the store $20 each that it typically sells for $45. Now assume a newer model calculator has come out, and the old calculators can only be sold for $18 each. Since the market value of the calculators is lower than the cost, the electronics store would need to apply the lower of cost or market rule and write-down the calculators by $2 each (the difference between the cost of $20 and the market value of $18). This write-down would normally be recorded with a debit to cost of goods sold expense and a credit to inventory, as shown below.

Account	Dr.	Cr.
Cost of Goods Sold	200	
Inventory		200

However, if the market value of the calculators had dropped to $22, for example, no write-down would have been necessary because the $20 cost was still lower than the market value. Remember, the lower of cost of market rule means inventory should be recorded at the lower of the cost or the market value. If the cost is still lower than the market value, even though the market value may have decreased, there is no write-down necessary.

ACCOUNTS RECEIVABLE AND BAD DEBT

Why do companies extend credit to customers?

Companies extend credit to customers in an effort to make it easier for customers to make purchases, thus increasing the amount of sales made. Customers who are allowed to buy now and pay later will most likely end up buying more than if they had to pay cash on delivery. As such, most businesses extend credit to customers in the form of sending invoices and allowing customers to pay within thirty days or more. Many companies that extend credit to customers have a credit department that runs credit worthiness checks on customers prior to extending credit as a means of determining whether or not the bills will eventually be paid. Unfortunately, while extending credit to customers typically results in increased sales, there are also additional costs involved. Companies that extend credit to customers need a customer credit, accounts receivable, and/or collections department to handle the process of approving customer credit, sending invoices, processing customer payments, and calling past-due customers to collect. Additionally, there is a cost involved in waiting for the cash payment, as the company extending the credit will not have the cash in the bank as soon and, thus, will not earn as much interest or be able to use the cash for other obligations. Finally, there is always the potential for customers to neglect their obligations and not pay the amounts owed. Following the cost/benefit rule, the costs of extending credit to customers should not outweigh the benefits of extending credit. In most cases, businesses determine that the benefits outweigh the costs and therefore decide to extend credit to customers.

How do companies monitor the customer account balances and ensure they pay the amounts owed?

When invoices are sent to customers, journal entries are recorded to debit (increase) accounts receivable in the accounting system. Those journal entries are posted to the accounts receivable general ledger as well as a customer specific subledger. That subledger tracks all the invoices and payments to and from each individual customer. Customers should be sent monthly statements showing activity for the month along with the total amount owed. This is usually handled by the accounts receivable or collections department. In addition, an aging of accounts receivable is usually generated at least monthly to review customer balances and any amounts past due.

What is an aging of accounts receivable?

An aging of accounts receivable is an organized listing of all customers and their balances owed, with columns showing how old each amount is. Most accounting software packages can run this report automatically with the touch of a button. An example of an accounts receivable aging for Spinz Company is shown below.

Spinz Company
Accounts Receivable Aging
As of January 31, 2020

| Customer: | Total | Number of Days Unpaid | | | |
		0-30	31-60	61-90	91+
Antler Toys	$ 200	$ 200	$ -	$ -	$ -
Bugle Babies	$ 550	$ -	$ -	$ 550	$ -
Cabbage Kids	$ 600	$ 400	$ 200	$ -	$ -
Daisy Play, Inc.	$ 2,800	$ 1,000	$ 800	$ 1,000	$ -
Every Child Co.	$ 450	$ -	$ -	$ -	$ 450
Fun Enterprises	$ 9,500	$ 5,000	$ 4,500	$ -	$ -
Great Family Toys	$ 2,060	$ 600	$ 520	$ 740	$ 200
HMC Enterprises	$ 4,000	$ 4,000	$ -	$ -	$ -
Total	$ 20,160	$ 11,200	$ 6,020	$ 2,290	$ 650
x Estimated Uncollectible %:		1%	5%	10%	30%
Allowance Required	$ 837	$ 112	$ 301	$ 229	$ 195

You can see from the aging of accounts receivable that, in total, Spinz Company's customers owe $20,160 as of January 31, 2020. The largest customer balance is Fun Enterprises, which owes $9,500. Additionally, you can see that $11,200 is outstanding 30 days or less, $6,020 is outstanding between 31 and 60 days, $2,290 is outstanding between 61 and 90 days, and $650 is outstanding greater than 90 days. The older an accounts receivable is, the harder it is to collect it. As such, companies typically apply some measure of collection procedures once accounts start to get past due. Assuming Spinz Company usually sends invoices out with credit terms 2/10, n/30, you would expect most invoices to be paid within 30 days. Invoices outstanding greater than 30 days would be considered past due and would warrant the attention of the customer collections department.

What is bad debt expense?

Bad debt expense is the expense recorded on the income statement associated with the value of invoices that will ultimately end up not being paid by customers. It should be recorded in the same period that the sales are recorded in order to properly match revenues with expenses on the income statement. As companies do not have a crystal ball and cannot know, at the time of the sale, which invoices will ultimately be unpaid, companies estimate bad debt expense each period and record an adjusting journal entry for that estimate.

How is bad debt calculated?

Bad debt expense is calculated using estimates. The two methods of estimating bad debt expense are the percentage of credit sales method and the aging of accounts receivable method.

What is the process for estimating bad debt expense using the percentage of credit sales method?

When a company chooses to use the percentage of credit sales method, it must first determine the historical loss rate as a percentage of sales. This can simply be done by taking the amount of actual unpaid invoices each year divided by the credit sales of that year and coming up with an average, or normal, rate. Once the historical loss rate is determined, the company simply multiplies that loss rate by the amount of credit sales each period and records a journal entry to book the bad debt expense. This journal entry is done by debiting bad debt expense and crediting a contra-receivables account called allowance for doubtful accounts. The reason that the accounts receivable balance is not reduced (credited) is because this journal entry represents merely an estimate for bad debt. The specific customer invoices that may go unpaid are unknown at this time; thus, no particular customer's accounts receivable account can be credited. The allowance for doubtful accounts is subtracted from the accounts receivable balance in arriving at net accounts receivable on the balance sheet.

For example, assume that Spinz Company has historically noted that 1% of credit sales are ultimately unpaid. Also assume that total credit sales for Spinz Company for

January 2020 were $15,000. Spinz would simply multiply the $15,000 credit sales by 1% in estimating bad debt, thus recording $150 of bad debt expense as follows:

Account	Dr.	Cr.
Bad Debt Expense	150	
Allowance for Doubtful Accounts		150

This process would be repeated each month.

What are the advantages and disadvantages of the percentage of credit sales method?

The main advantage of this method is that it is simple. Additionally, this method is referred to as an "income statement" approach, as it is focused on calculating the bad debt expense on the income statement to achieve proper matching of revenues and expenses. A major flaw of this method, however, is that it neglects to review the allowance for doubtful accounts balance that is present on the balance sheet, which may end up resulting in under- or overstated net accounts receivable. To counteract this flaw, many companies use the percentage of credit sales method during the month-end process as a quick and easy approach and then use the more accurate aging of accounts receivable method at year end to finalize the financial statements.

What is the process for estimating bad debt expense using the aging of accounts receivable method?

The aging of accounts receivable method also utilizes historical loss rates, but instead of basing the historical loss rates on the credit sales, this method bases the historical loss rates on each aging category on the accounts receivable aging. As noted earlier in this chapter, the further past due an invoice gets, the harder it is to collect. As such, the loss rates typically increase as the invoices get older. These loss rates are multiplied by each aging category balance and then summed to calculate the total allowance for doubtful accounts needed. Accordingly, the balance in allowance for doubtful accounts will either be increased (credit) or decreased (debit) depending on this calculation, with the offsetting debit or credit going to the bad debt expense account. This method is considered a "balance sheet" approach, as it is focused on calculating the allowance for doubtful accounts in arriving at net accounts receivable presented on the balance sheet.

For example, assume Spinz Company has estimated that 1% of unpaid invoices between 0 and 30 days will be uncollectible, 5% of invoices unpaid between 31 and 60 days will be uncollectible, 10% of invoices unpaid between 61 and 90 days will be uncollectible, and 30% of invoices greater than 90 days unpaid will be uncollectible. Using the aging of accounts receivable, Spinz would multiply each aging category by the estimated percentage uncollectible to determine the estimated amount uncollectible for each aging category. Those amounts would be added together to form the total estimate of uncollectible invoices of $837. That represents the calculated balance in the allowance for doubtful accounts, as shown in the figure below:

Spinz Company
Accounts Receivable Aging
As of January 31, 2020

Customer:	Total	0-30	31-60	61-90	91+
		Number of Days Unpaid			
Antler Toys	$ 200	$ 200	$ -	$ -	$ -
Bugle Babies	$ 550	$ -	$ -	$ 550	$ -
Cabbage Kids	$ 600	$ 400	$ 200	$ -	$ -
Daisy Play, Inc.	$ 2,800	$ 1,000	$ 800	$ 1,000	$ -
Every Child Co.	$ 450	$ -	$ -	$ -	$ 450
Fun Enterprises	$ 9,500	$ 5,000	$ 4,500	$ -	$ -
Great Family Toys	$ 2,060	$ 600	$ 520	$ 740	$ 200
HMC Enterprises	$ 4,000	$ 4,000	$ -	$ -	$ -
Total	$ 20,160	$ 11,200	$ 6,020	$ 2,290	$ 650
x Estimated Uncollectible %:		1%	5%	10%	30%
Allowance Required	$ 837	$ 112	$ 301	$ 229	$ 195

Assuming the allowance for doubtful accounts currently had a credit balance of $600, the account would need to be credited by $237 in order to arrive at the calculated balance of $837, as shown in the figure below:

Account	Dr.	Cr.	- Allowance +
Bad Debt Expense	237		600*
Allowance for Doubtful Accounts		237	→ 237
			837

*Beginning Balance

However, if the allowance for doubtful accounts had a current balance of $1,000, the account would need to be debited by $163 in order to arrive at the calculated balance of $837, as shown in the figure below. Note that in this case, bad debt expense is actually reduced (credited) on the income statement, indicating an overestimate in previous periods that has been reversed.

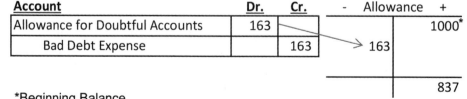

Account	Dr.	Cr.	- Allowance +
Allowance for Doubtful Accounts	163		1000*
Bad Debt Expense		163	→ 163
			837

*Beginning Balance

What is the primary difference in calculating bad debt using the percentage of credit sales method versus the aging of accounts receivable method?

The primary difference is that the percentage of credit sales method calculates the bad debt expense for the period. This amount is used for the journal entry to debit bad debt expense and credit allowance for doubtful accounts, with no concern for the eventual balance in the allowance for doubtful accounts. The aging of accounts receivable method calculates what the ending balance in the allowance for doubtful accounts should be. Then, the amount of the journal entry must be calculated by taking the current balance in the allowance for doubtful accounts and comparing it to the calculation. The resulting journal entry may be either a debit or credit to the allowance for doubtful accounts and an offsetting debit or credit to bad debt expense.

What happens if you determine that a customer will not pay?

If after attempting to collect on a past due receivable, it is determined that a customer will not pay, the unpaid invoice should be written off. Writing off an invoice essentially clears the accounts receivable recorded for that invoice and removes the estimate for uncollectible invoices by reducing the allowance for doubtful accounts. Essentially, you are saying, "This customer will not pay; as such, I don't need the estimate anymore because I know specifically which invoice it is."

Assume that Spinz Company has unsuccessfully been trying to collect the $450 invoice sent to Every Child, Co., and has recently learned that Every Child, Co., has filed for bankruptcy. Spinz would write off the invoice by debiting (decreasing) the allowance for doubtful accounts and crediting (decreasing) accounts receivable, as shown below:

Account	Dr.	Cr.
Allowance for Doubtful Accounts	450	
Accounts Receivable		450

This entry clears the receivable from the books and removes the estimate recorded, as it is no longer necessary.

What happens if an invoice that you've written off ends up ultimately being paid?

If a customer invoice that was previously written off ends up eventually being paid, that is considered an account recovery. In this case, the journal entry to write off the invoice must be reversed, and an entry to record the payment must be made. Assume that two months after Spinz Company wrote off the Every Child, Co., invoice, it received a check in the mail from Every Child, Co., for the $450 owed. Spinz Company would first reverse the write-off, as that journal entry was actually unnecessary. Then, Spinz Company would record the customer payment as it normally would with any other payment. The journal entries to record the account recovery are shown in the figure below:

145

Account	Dr.	Cr.
Accounts Receivable	450	
Allowance for Doubtful Accounts		450
Cash	450	
Accounts Receivable		450

Why is accounts receivable debited and credited during the account recovery process?

In the account recovery process, accounts receivable is debited in the first journal entry to reinstate the receivable and then immediately credited in the second journal entry once payment is applied. It may be tempting to, instead, combine the two journal entries into one journal entry that debits cash and credits the allowance for doubtful accounts without ever touching accounts receivable. While that shortcut would result in an identical impact on the financial statements, it would not result in an accurate record of what truly happened to that customer account. Remember that the account was actually paid by the customer; thus, it should be posted that way to reflect that the customer paid the account and that it wasn't actually a write-off. If a shortcut approach was taken, there would be no account history to reflect that the customer actually did end up paying the account.

FIXED ASSETS AND INTANGIBLES

What are fixed assets?

Fixed assets are assets with long lives that are tangible in substance. Accordingly, fixed assets are typically those assets that will be used in the company for a period greater than one year that can be touched and seen. Examples of fixed assets include: land, buildings, machinery, equipment, furniture, etc. These are all assets that the company intends to use for a long time that can be touched and seen. Fixed assets are commonly referred to as PP&E, or property, plant, and equipment. They are also called long-lived tangible assets.

How do you record purchases of fixed assets?

Fixed assets are capitalized, that is, they are recorded as assets when they are purchased rather than as an expense. All reasonable and necessary costs to acquire the asset and get it ready for its intended use should be included in the cost of the asset when recording the purchase. For example, land purchases may include the purchase cost plus any legal fees, survey fees, or title search fees paid. Building purchases may include the purchase or construction costs plus any legal fees, appraisal fees, and architecture fees paid.

Equipment purchases may include the purchase or construction costs plus any sales taxes, transportation costs, or installation fees paid.

When recording the journal entry, the appropriate asset account would be debited, and the payment method (cash, accounts payable, notes payable, etc.) would be credited. Assume that Spinz Company acquired a new, sixty-inch, flat-screen computer monitor to track shipments and deliveries in the warehouse. The cost of the monitor was $2,000 plus 6% sales tax of $120. The invoice also included delivery fees of $50. Additionally, Spinz had to pay $200 to have the monitor installed on the wall of the warehouse. Spinz would capitalize the monitor at the $2,370, as these costs were all reasonable and necessary to acquire the asset and get it ready for its intended use. Assuming Spinz Company received an invoice from the vendor for the $2,370, the journal entry to record this purchase would be as follows:

Account	Dr.	Cr.
Computer Equipment	2,370	
Accounts Payable		2,370

How do you record ordinary repairs and maintenance of fixed assets?

Ordinary repairs and maintenance are necessary for the general upkeep of fixed assets. Examples of ordinary repairs and maintenance include things like oil changes on vehicles, new paint on walls, and yearly cleaning of equipment. Ordinary repairs and maintenance are recorded as an expense when incurred. For example, assume that Spinz Company paid $300 to repair a broken window in its warehouse. Spinz would record this transaction as a debit to repairs and maintenance expense and a credit to cash, as shown below:

Account	Dr.	Cr.
Repairs and Maintenance Expense	300	
Cash		300

How do you record extraordinary repairs, replacements of, and additions to fixed assets?

Extraordinary repairs, replacements, and additions are those expenditures that occur infrequently and typically involve a large dollar amount. These expenditures actually increase the asset's value, as they either enhance efficiency, increase the capacity, or increase the useful life of the asset. Accordingly, these items are capitalized (recorded as an increase to the asset value) rather than being recorded as an expense because they actually enhance the asset rather than merely maintain its current condition. Extraordinary repairs can include things such as major overhauls, complete reconditioning of assets, and major improvements. Again, in order to be capitalized, these items must enhance the efficiency of the asset, increase the capacity, or increase the useful life. Assume that Spinz Company hired a contractor to build a 2,000-square-foot addition to the warehouse for $100,000. Spinz Company signed a note payable with the bank to finance the addition. This addition would be recorded as follows:

Account	Dr.	Cr.
Buildings	100,000	
Notes Payable		100,000

What is the purpose of recording depreciation on fixed assets?

Recall that when an asset is acquired, it is capitalized, meaning it is recorded as an asset. Also recall that the matching principle requires us to match expenses to the period in which they were incurred to earn the revenue. Accordingly, as a fixed asset is used up over the course of the business in order to generate revenues, the cost of that asset should be recorded as an expense. That is the purpose of recording depreciation expense, which is the systematic and rational allocation of an asset's cost over its useful life. Essentially, the cost of purchasing the asset is recorded as an expense over time as the asset is used.

Does depreciation equal the decline in market value of the fixed asset?

No. Depreciation does not equal the decline in market value of the fixed asset. Depreciation is merely an allocation of the cost of the asset over its useful life. Market value is never factored into the calculation. The cost principle requires us to record assets at historical cost, not market value.

Note, however, that if an asset becomes impaired, it should be written down to its market value. An asset may become impaired if the amount of cash generated by the asset is estimated to be less than the carrying value of that asset. (You can decrease a fixed asset to meet the market value but never increase it.) If an impairment loss is calculated (the difference between the book value of the asset and the market value), it is recorded as an impairment loss, which shows up under operating expenses on the income statement.

Are all fixed assets depreciated?

No. Land is not depreciated. As land is assumed to have an indefinite useful life, it would be impossible to allocate the cost of the land over that unlimited life. As such, land is not depreciated but rather subject to impairment, as discussed above.

How is depreciation expense calculated and recorded?

Depreciation expense is calculated using a systematic and rational method. Three of the most commonly used methods are the straight-line method, the units-of-production method, and the declining balance method. Once depreciation is calculated, it is recorded each period as a debit to depreciation expense and a credit to a contra-asset account called accumulated depreciation. Accumulated depreciation is subtracted from the fixed asset value on the balance sheet in arriving at net fixed assets.

What is book value?

Book value, also known as carrying value, is the cost of the asset less the accumulated depreciation. Basically, it is the remaining cost of the asset that has not been depreciated yet. The book value of all the assets is reported as net fixed assets on the balance sheet.

Why is the accumulated depreciation contra-account used instead of just crediting the asset itself?

The asset account (buildings, machinery, etc.) shows the historical record of the cost paid for each asset, while the accumulated depreciation expense shows the allocation for the cost of the asset that has been used up. It is important to keep those separate, as accumulated depreciation is an estimate and not an exact amount that can be verified. In fact, sometimes it is necessary to adjust the formula used to calculate depreciation, as changes may occur. As such, having a record of the historical cost of the asset versus the accumulated depreciation recorded becomes very important.

Which method of calculating depreciation expense is the most commonly used?

The straight-line method of depreciation is the most commonly used; as such, it is the only method discussed in detail in this chapter. It is the easiest method to calculate and, thus, is widely understood by users of financial information. Additionally, straight-line depreciation records the same amount of depreciation each period, which provides proper matching of expenses to revenues when the asset is used evenly over its useful life.

What is the formula for depreciation expense using the straight-line method?

In order to calculate depreciation expense using straight-line method, you must know three things: the cost of the asset, the useful life of the asset, and the residual value of the asset at the end of its useful life. The formula to calculate straight-line depreciation is:

(Cost − Residual Value) / Useful Life = Depreciation Expense

For example, assume the monitor that Spinz Company purchased for $2,370 is estimated to have a useful life of 7 years. At the end of the 7 years, management estimates that the monitor will be worth $200 (residual value). Spinz Company would need to decrease the book value of the asset from $2,370 to $200 over 7 years; that is, it needs to record depreciation of $2,170 over 7 years. Easy division would tell you that Spinz must then record depreciation of $310 each year. Note that as most companies prepare financial statements on a monthly basis, it is likely that instead of recording depreciation expense of $310 each year, Spinz would instead record depreciation expense of $25.83 each month ($310 / 12 months). Accordingly, the journal entry to record depreciation for one month for the monitor would be recorded as follows:

Account	Dr.	Cr.
Depreciation Expense	25.83	
Accumulated Depreciation		25.83

At the end of the 7 years, the asset will have been fully depreciated and have a book value of $200, which was the estimated residual value, calculated as follows:

$2,370 asset cost − $2,170 accumulated depreciation = $200 book value

No more depreciation would be recorded at that point for this particular asset.

Note that companies typically acquire assets at various dates during the month. As such, it is common for accountants to begin to depreciate the asset in the month closest to the purchase date. For example, an asset purchased on February 2 most likely would begin being depreciated in February. However, an asset purchased on February 27 would most likely begin being depreciated in March.

Do you have to use the same depreciation method for all fixed assets?

No, you do not have to use the same depreciation method for all fixed assets. However, you must use the same depreciation method across classes of assets. For example, you can use straight-line depreciation for all buildings but use units-of-production depreciation for all equipment and machinery.

Do companies have to use the same depreciation calculations on their tax returns as they do for the financial statements?

No. Companies may use a different method of calculating depreciation on their tax returns than they do for the financial statements. Many tax depreciation calculations involve accelerated methods that allow a much greater portion of depreciation expense to be recorded in the year the asset was purchased than in the later years. This is advantageous because less taxes will be paid in the year the asset was purchased; thus, the tax savings are recognized immediately and may help offset the cost of the asset purchase. This is one of the ways the government tries to encourage economic growth.

What happens when you sell or get rid of a fixed asset?

When a fixed asset is sold or disposed of, this must be recorded in the accounting system. First, you must ensure that all depreciation has been recorded up to the date of the disposal. Next, a journal entry is recorded to remove the asset and any accumulated depreciation on that asset and record the proceeds from the sale of the asset. The difference between the proceeds from the sale of the asset and the book value of the asset will be recorded as either a gain or a loss on the sale.

For example, assume Spinz Company sells the computer monitor for $1,000 cash 3 years after it was purchased. Spinz would have recorded 3 years of depreciation expense, totaling $930. As such, Spinz would have the following balances for the monitor:

+ Computer Equipment -	- Accumulated Depreciation +
2,370	930
2,370	930

Since the monitor has been sold, the cost of the asset needs to be removed by crediting the computer equipment account for $2,370. Likewise, since there is no monitor, there is no need for accumulated depreciation on the monitor. As such, accumulated depreciation would be debited for $930. Additionally, the $1,000 cash must be recorded as a debit to cash. The 3 journal entry items listed so far add up to total debits of $1,930 and total credits of $2,370. Debits must equal credits, so it is clear that an additional debit for $440 must be made. In this case, since the amount of cash received ($1,000) is less than the book value of the asset ($1,440), a loss of $440 must be recorded. The journal entry to record this disposal is shown below:

Account	**Dr.**	**Cr.**
Accumulated Depreciation	930	
Cash	1,000	
Loss on Disposal	440	
Computer Equipment		2,370

In the next example, assume that the monitor was instead sold for $1,500 after 3 years. Since the monitor has been sold, the cost of the asset needs to be removed by crediting the computer equipment account for $2,370. Likewise, since there is no monitor, there is no need for accumulated depreciation on the monitor. As such, accumulated depreciation would be debited for $930. Additionally, the $1,500 cash must be recorded as a debit to cash. The 3 journal entry items noted so far add up to total debits of $2,430 and credits of $2,370. Debits must equal credits, so it is clear that an additional credit for $60 must be made. In this case, since the amount of cash received ($1,500) is greater than the book value of the asset ($1,440), a gain of $60 must be recorded. The journal entry to record this disposal is shown below:

Account	**Dr.**	**Cr.**
Accumulated Depreciation	930	
Cash	1,500	
Gain on Disposal		60
Computer Equipment		2,370

Just like with impairment losses, gains and losses on disposal show up on the income statement under operating expenses.

What are intangible assets?

Intangible assets are assets with long lives that lack a tangible substance; that is, intangible assets are those assets that cannot be seen or touched. Examples of intangible assets include: trademarks, patents, copyrights, software, licensing rights, franchises, and goodwill.

What is a trademark?

A trademark is a name, slogan, or image that can be used to identify a company. Trademarks provide value to companies in the form of instant brand recognition and reputation. Apple's well-known logo is a trademark of the company. Trademarks can be registered with the U.S. Patent and Trademark Office. One of the many benefits of registering a trademark is that the U.S. Patent and Trademark Office will make sure that the proposed trademark is not already in use by another company, which could end up saving a company in legal fees later on if it has accidentally infringed on another company's trademark. Trademarks provide value to companies in the form of instant brand recognition and reputation.

What is a patent?

A patent is an exclusive right to use, manufacture, or sell an item. Patents are granted by the U.S. Patent and Trademark Office and provide rights to the item for 20 years. Many inventors seek to have their product patented in order to prevent being "knocked off" by other providers. For example, pharmaceutical companies often patent their drugs, which prevents generics from being offered at a much cheaper price, allowing the developer to recoup the costs of researching and developing the drug.

What is a copyright?

A copyright is the exclusive right to publish, use, and sell literary, musical, artistic, or dramatic work. Copyrights are good for 70 years following the death of the author. For example, most books you read are under copyright protection and cannot be duplicated without the permission of the author.

What is a licensing right?

A licensing right is a right to use a specified item for a specific purpose. For example, professional sports teams often sell licensing rights to certain vendors to use their logos on merchandise, such as shirts, hats, etc. In return, the sports team receives payment for the licensing rights, and the vendor can use those logos, etc. to sell merchandise. You may have noticed this personally, as there is typically a tag on the merchandise stating that it is an officially licensed product.

What is a franchise?

A franchise is the right to use products and services, trademarks, or perform activities within a specified geographic location. For example, Planet Fitness is an example of a

What is goodwill?

Goodwill is the most commonly reported intangible asset. Goodwill represents the amount that a company was willing to pay over the appraised value of the net assets for another company. For example, suppose a local car wash business went up for sale, and the appraised value of the net assets (assets − liabilities) for the company was $500,000. If you are willing to pay $700,000 for that company because you know there is value in the specific location, customer base, reputation, etc., then you will record $500,000 for the net assets of the business plus $200,000 in goodwill, equaling the $700,000 cash paid.

franchise that allows individuals to pay an up-front franchise fee along with an ongoing fee (typically a percentage of sales) in order to sell its products or provide services and use its branding. In return, franchisees get instant brand recognition, marketing, and support to open and run their business.

How do you record purchases of intangible assets?

Intangible assets are recorded at the purchase price in a similar fashion to fixed assets in that the amount recorded includes the costs necessary to get the asset to its desired condition and location. As such, many intangible asset purchase costs also include legal fees and filing fees.

What is the purpose of recording amortization on intangible assets?

Amortization is the fancy word used for depreciation when talking about intangible assets versus fixed assets. Amortization represents the allocation of the cost of the intangible asset over its useful life.

Are all intangible assets amortized?

No. Only intangible assets with limited lives are amortized. Intangible assets with unlimited lives (no legal ending point) are not amortized but are tested periodically for impairment, as discussed previously in this chapter. Trademarks and goodwill are the two most common intangible assets with unlimited lives and, thus, are not amortized.

How is amortization expense calculated and recorded?

Amortization expense is calculated using the straight-line method, as is discussed above under depreciation expense. However, most companies use a $0 residual value, as these assets most often have no value to the owner once the useful life of the intangible asset is up. Amortization is recorded as a debit to amortization expense and a credit to a contra-asset called accumulated amortization, much in the same manner as depreciation is recorded.

153

What happens when you sell or get rid of an intangible asset?

The sale or disposal of an intangible asset is handled in the same manner as a fixed asset, whereby a gain or loss is recorded based on the difference between the book value of the intangible asset at the time of disposal and the amount received in exchange.

PAYROLL ACCOUNTING

What are the costs of payroll other than the employee wages?

Employers incur many payroll-related costs in addition to employee wages and salaries. According to the U.S. Department of Labor's Bureau of Labor Statistics June 2017 report on Employer Costs for Employee Compensation, 68.3% of payroll-related costs are for wages and salaries, 8.7% of costs are for insurance (health, life, disability), 7.4% of costs are for taxes (Social Security, Medicare, unemployment, workers' compensation), 7% of costs are for paid leave (vacation, sick time, etc.), 5.4% of costs are for retirement benefits, and 3.1% of costs are for supplemental pay (overtime, bonuses, etc.).

What are employee withholdings?

Employee withholdings are amounts withheld from employees' gross pay to cover the costs of the employee share of any benefits, taxes, and other voluntary reductions. For example, it is common for employees to pay a share of health insurance and life insurance. Many employees voluntarily withhold for retirement benefits, such as 401(k) accounts. Federal and state governments that charge income taxes require withholdings of tax amounts. Additionally, Social Security and Medicare (together referred to as FICA) are shared taxes between the employer and employee; thus, the employee share must be withheld from the employee paycheck. These amounts are subtracted from the employees' gross pay in arriving at net pay on the paycheck. Any amounts withheld from the employee are recorded as a liability for the employer, as the employer must remit the funds to the various organizations. For example, assume Spinz Company has 100 employees. During the pay period, the employees earned $250,000 collectively. The federal income tax withheld from employees was $25,000, and the state income tax withheld was $5,000. The employee portion of FICA taxes was $19,125. Additionally, $6,000 was withheld for retirement benefits (401(k)). Accordingly, the net pay that the employees receive is $194,875. The journal entry to record the employee payroll would be recorded as follows:

Account	Dr.	Cr.
Salaries and Wages Expense	250,000	
Federal Income Tax Withholdings Payable		25,000
State Income Tax Withholdings Payable		5,000
FICA Tax Payable		19,125
Retirement Withholdings Payable		6,000
Cash		194,875

The various payable accounts will be relieved as they are paid to the government agencies or investment funds, etc.

What are the employer payroll taxes?

In addition to withholding payroll taxes from the employees, the employer must also pay certain payroll taxes out of their own pocket. The employer must match the FICA taxes paid by the employee. In addition, the employer also has to pay federal and state unemployment taxes (known as FUTA and SUTA). These taxes are recorded in a journal entry at the same time that the payroll journal entry is made. For the Spinz Company example above, assume that along with the employer portion of FICA taxes, Spinz Company also incurred $2,500 of FUTA and $1,000 of SUTA taxes. The journal entry to record the employer payroll taxes would be recorded as follows:

Account	Dr.	Cr.
Payroll Tax Expense	22,625	
FICA Tax Payable		19,125
Federal Unemployment Tax Payable		2,500
State Unemployment Tax Payable		1,000

Does every state have the same rules regarding payroll taxes?

No. Each state has different tax rates for employee income tax withholdings, unemployment tax, and workers' compensation. States also have different rules on the timing and method of paying the taxes. Federal payroll taxes can also be quite confusing for new employers. As such, new employers should always seek the advice of a professional in determining payroll requirements, as fines and penalties can be massive if these are not handled properly.

COST ACCOUNTING BASICS

THE OPERATING CYCLE

What is an operating cycle?

In general, an operating cycle represents the length of time it takes an entity to perform the activities required to generate sales and subsequently collect payment from the customer. Cash received from the customer payment will be used to pay for the operating costs of the business, and the cycle will then continue to repeat itself.

What are operating costs?

Operating costs represent the costs necessary to operate the business. These costs include the costs of goods provided to customers, labor, selling, and administrative costs. On a typical income statement, operating costs are deducted from sales revenue to arrive at operating income.

What type of costs are not considered operating costs?

In general, interest expense, income taxes, and other nonrecurring items, such as losses, are not included in operating costs and are shown after operating income on the income statement. These nonoperating costs are deducted from operating income in order to arrive at the final net income amount on the income statement.

What is the length of an operating cycle?

The operating cycle will vary by type of entity (service company, merchandiser, or manufacturer) and by industry. For example, a small pizzeria may purchase ingredients on a Monday, use those ingredients to prepare and bake a pizza on the following Tuesday, and deliver the pizza to the customer on Tuesday evening while simultaneously collecting the cash payment at the customer's door. In contrast, a residential home manufacturer may take over six months to buy the building supplies needed to construct a home, build the home, and subsequently collect payment from the customer.

What is a service company?

A service company is an entity that provides services, rather than goods, to the customer. Examples of service companies include law firms, accounting firms, fitness centers, hair salons, and lawn-care providers. Service companies perform a service for their clients, collect payment for that service, and use that payment to pay for their operating costs. This completes the operating cycle for a service company.

Can service companies also provide goods?

Some service companies operate in a hybrid fashion where their primary line of business is providing a service and their secondary line of business is to provide some type of merchandise. For example, many hair salons also sell hair products to their customers. In this case, the company would account for the sales and costs of providing the service separately from the sales and costs of providing the merchandise, using different general ledger accounts such as service revenue, merchandise revenue, etc.

What is a merchandiser?

A merchandiser is an entity that purchases goods, called merchandise inventory, and sells those goods to their customers. Merchandisers may either be retailers or wholesalers. Examples of merchandisers are grocery stores, clothing stores, and electronics stores. The operating cycle of a merchandiser includes purchasing the inventory from a supplier, selling the inventory at a mark-up to the customer, collecting payment from the customer, and using that payment to pay for their operating costs.

Are "club stores" like Costco and Sam's Club wholesalers or retailers?

Club stores can operate in both a wholesale and a retail fashion. When club stores sell goods to small businesses who will, in turn, sell those goods to their customers, they are operating as a wholesaler. When club stores sell goods to the individual consumer, they are operating as a retailer. In general, the accounting is the same for wholesalers and retailers.

What is a manufacturer?

A manufacturer is an entity that makes the goods that it sells. The operating cycle for a manufacturer is more complex than the operating cycles for service companies and merchandisers because the entity has to purchase raw materials and use those materials to manufacture a finished good. The finished good is then sold to the customer, and payment is subsequently collected. The customer payment will then be used to pay for the manufacturer's operating costs.

> ## What is the difference between a retailer and a wholesaler?
>
> **A** wholesaler buys goods from the manufacturer and sells them to a retailer, whereas a retailer typically buys goods from a wholesaler and sells those goods to the end consumer. Wholesalers are commonly referred to as "the middle man."

What are raw materials?

Raw materials are the materials used as inputs to the final product. Raw materials are recorded as an asset, called raw materials inventory, on the balance sheet. For example, the raw materials that go into making a pencil would include items like wood, graphite, and rubber.

How do we account for raw materials once we use them in production?

Once a raw material has entered the production process, it becomes a different asset called work-in-process inventory. Work-in-process inventory represents a partially completed product. Using the same pencil example above, a pencil may have the center column of graphite inserted into the wood, have the eraser banded to the top of the pencil, and be awaiting a final process of being wrapped with a colorfully painted pattern. This partially completed pencil would be included on the balance sheet as work-in-process inventory.

What costs are included in work-in-process inventory?

Work-in-process inventory includes all the costs necessary to manufacture the product. These manufacturing costs include the raw materials, noted above, as well as other manufacturing costs necessary to produce the final product. These other manufacturing costs include labor and overhead and will be discussed in detail in this chapter.

How are manufacturing costs added to work-in-process inventory?

The manner in which an entity assigns manufacturing costs to its work-in-process inventory varies. This is where cost accounting skills become necessary. There are three basic methods to accounting for manufacturing costs. Those methods are job-order costing, activity-based costing, and process costing. Each of these methods will be discussed later in this chapter. It is important to note, however, that there are many hybrid methods of cost accounting, and many entities use a combination of cost accounting approaches.

What is a finished good?

A finished good is a completed product that is packaged and ready for sale. When goods are completed, they are moved from work-in-process inventory to another asset account, **159**

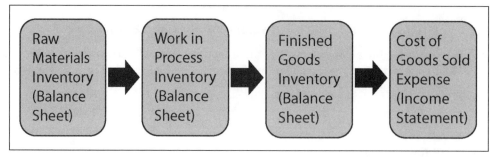

Figure: Inventory Accounts Cost Flows for Manufacturers

called finished goods inventory, on the balance sheet. For example, the completed pencil that is ready for shipment to the customer is a finished good. When finished goods are sold to the customer, the cost of those goods is expensed on the income statement using an account called cost of goods sold expense.

COST CLASSIFICATIONS

What is a cost?

A cost is a sacrifice of a business's resources. While there is a technical and important difference in the actual definitions of cost versus expense, accountants commonly use the terms interchangeably. For example, one may hear the term "selling and administrative costs" or "selling and administrative expenses."

What is the difference between a cost and an expense?

Recall that an earlier chapter in this book, entitled "Financial Statement Elements," presented the FASB definition of expenses as "outflows or other using up of assets or incurrences of liabilities (or a combination of both) from delivering or producing goods, rendering services, or carrying out other activities that constitute the entity's ongoing major or central operations." Thus, the term "expense" carries with it the idea that assets are used up in order to earn revenue. A cost does not carry that same criterion.

For example, when an entity purchases raw materials, those raw materials are recorded as an asset on the balance sheet. That purchase uses the company's resources (cash); however, the cost of purchasing those raw materials will not be recorded as an expense on the income statement until they are sold to the customer (revenue is earned). As such, a cost (sacrifice of resources) becomes an expense (on the income statement) as it is used to earn revenue.

Why is cost classification necessary?

In any entity, managers use cost data to make decisions that are necessary to run the business. Different costs, and different types of costs, are used to make various decisions. For example, in evaluating which department in department stores, such as JCPenney, is most profitable, you would use different cost classifications than if you were evaluating how many units of product JCPenney needs to sell to break even. These types of decisions are covered in the chapter entitled "Managerial Accounting Basics."

What are the different ways in which costs are classified?

Costs can be classified in several ways, including according to how they can be traced to a product or service (conveniently and easily or not), whether or not they relate to production in a manufacturing entity (manufacturing versus nonmanufacturing), and/or how the cost behaves when volume of the product changes (fixed or variable).

Can we assign costs to something other than a product or service?

Yes, we can assign costs to any "cost object." A cost object can be anything that the entity wishes to calculate costs for. These cost objects are frequently the products or services that the company offers but may also include specific customers, business departments, or specific jobs. When we assign costs to cost objects, we can classify them as direct or indirect.

What is a direct cost?

A direct cost is a cost that is conveniently and easily traceable to a particular cost object. For example, a residential home builder can easily trace the cost of the garage door installed in a house to that particular house. Other examples include wheels and tires installed on new vehicles by the manufacturer, the cost of wood used to make a table, and the time spent by a staff accountant (in the form of wages paid) on a particular client.

What is an indirect cost?

An indirect cost is a cost that is not conveniently or easily traceable to a particular cost object. For example, the same residential home builder discussed above cannot easily trace the cost of nails used to build a particular house. It would be a tedious process to track the exact count of nails used on each house, including the particular brand used and cost per nail.

Does it matter whether a cost is direct or indirect for accounting purposes?

Yes. Since direct costs can be conveniently and easily traced to cost objects, it is relatively easy to include them in assigning the costs to cost objects. For example, the residential home builder can very easily add the cost of a garage door to the total costs of a particular home. However, the very nature of indirect costs makes it harder to assign them to cost objects. Thus, some costing method is needed to allocate those costs to cost objects. For example, the residential home builder knows that nails were used in building the house but doesn't have an exact count. The builder must use some method to allocate the cost of the nails to each individual house if the builder wants a complete depiction of the cost of a particular house. These types of allocation will be discussed later in this chapter.

What is the difference between a manufacturing cost and a nonmanufacturing cost?

A manufacturing cost is a cost incurred to manufacture, or make, a product. A nonmanufacturing cost is a cost incurred by a manufacturer that was not part of making the product.

Do all companies incur manufacturing costs?

Not all companies incur manufacturing costs. Service companies do not manufacture or provide any goods. The primary cost incurred in order to earn revenue for a service company is typically labor. Service companies refer to those primary costs of earning revenue as "cost of sales" on the income statement. Additionally, merchandisers do not manufacture goods and, as such, incur no manufacturing costs. The primary cost in earning revenue for a merchandiser is typically the inventory purchased in order to re-sell to customers, and it is referred to as "cost of goods sold" on the income statement. Manufacturers make the products they sell. As such, the primary cost incurred in earning revenue is typically manufacturing costs, referred to as "cost of goods manufactured." Once these manufactured goods are sold, they are also expensed as "cost of goods sold" on the income statement, much like a merchandiser.

What is a product cost?

Product cost is synonymous with manufacturing cost. These are the costs incurred to manufacture the product. These can be direct (conveniently and easily traceable) or indirect. There are three categories of product cost: direct materials, direct labor, and manufacturing overhead.

What is a direct material?

A direct material is a raw material that is conveniently and easily traceable to the product. For example, a manufacturer of custom wood dining tables can easily trace the wood to each table. The type of wood used and the amount of wood used would be determined based on the selections made by the customer (size of table, choice of wood, etc.).

What is direct labor?

Direct labor is labor cost that is conveniently and easily traceable to the product. Using the example of the custom dining tables, this would be the labor of the worker who is building the table. Direct labor is typically tracked on a time card with some coding as to the product being worked on.

What is indirect labor?

Indirect labor is labor in the production facility that is not conveniently or easily traced to the product. Common examples of indirect labor are factory supervisors, custodians at the factory, and security guards at the factory. Notice that the word "factory" was used in each example. Indirect labor is a product/manufacturing cost. Indirect labor refers

> ## What is the difference between a direct material and an indirect material?
>
> Recall that raw materials are the materials used as inputs to the final product. Raw materials can either be direct or indirect. Raw materials that are not conveniently and easily traced to the product are called indirect materials. For example, the custom dining table manufacturer most likely uses some quantity of adhesive, staples, nails, and/or screws to build the table. The exact quantities of these items are not easily traceable to the individual table, nor would it be cost effective to do so, as it is probable that the builder has boxes and cartons of these items and just uses them as needed in the building process. Indirect materials are considered part of manufacturing overhead, to be discussed below.

only to labor in the production facility, manufacturing plant, or factory. Indirect labor does not refer to the labor of administrative employees. Labor of administrative employees will be covered below under "period costs."

Using the example of the custom dining tables, the custodian that sweeps the sawdust is a necessary part of the manufacturing process. However, the time spent sweeping is not conveniently or easily traceable to a particular unit of product. Additionally, it would not be cost effective to track the time spent sweeping under one table as compared to another product.

What is manufacturing overhead?

Manufacturing overhead represents the costs of manufacturing a product aside from direct materials and direct labor. As such, manufacturing overhead consists of indirect materials, indirect labor, and all other indirect costs of manufacturing. Common examples of other indirect manufacturing costs include rent on the factory, insurance on the factory, property taxes on the factory, and utilities for the factory. Again, notice the word "factory" was used in each example. Manufacturing overhead is a product/manufacturing cost; as such, it only refers to costs in the production facility, manufacturing plant, or factory. Rent on the corporate headquarters would be considered a "period cost," as discussed later in this chapter.

What is a prime cost?

Prime cost refers to direct materials plus direct labor. These are the primary, or direct, manufacturing costs in a business.

What is a conversion cost?

Conversion cost refers to direct labor plus manufacturing overhead. These are the costs necessary to convert the direct materials into a finished product. As manufacturing in

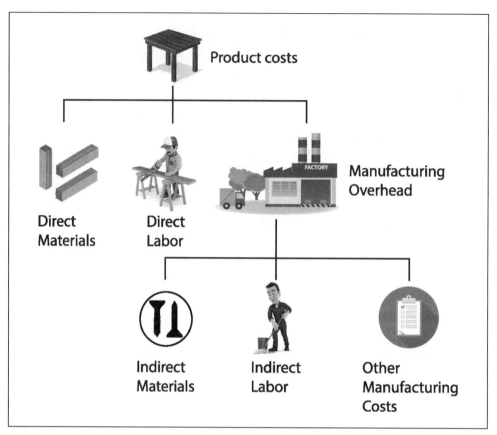

There are a number of expenses that go into converting direct materials into a final product ready for sale.

many industries has moved from a labor-intensive process to a machine-intensive process, direct labor has become a much smaller portion of the overall production cost. Accordingly, many companies only refer to two product costs, direct materials and conversion costs, rather than the three product costs: direct materials, direct labor, and manufacturing overhead.

What is a period cost?

Period cost is synonymous with nonmanufacturing cost. These are the costs of operating the business that are not included in product costs. Period costs are commonly grouped into two types: selling costs and administrative costs. Rather than being assigned to the product, these costs are assigned to a "time period." Typically, the time period is the month the cost was incurred. For example, the rent on the corporate headquarters of the custom dining table manufacturer would not be assigned to a particular table, but rather, it would be assigned to the month in which the rent was incurred and recorded as an expense on the income statement in that particular month.

What is a selling cost?

As the name implies, selling costs represent the costs of obtaining sales and delivering the finished product to the customer. Selling costs commonly include the costs of advertising the product, sales commissions paid to sales employees, wages paid to sales and marketing employees, the costs of warehousing and storing the finished product, and shipping costs to deliver the goods.

What is an administrative cost?

Administrative costs represent costs necessary to operate the business, with the exception of product costs and selling costs. These are the costs necessary to "manage" the business. Administrative costs commonly include rent on the corporate headquarters, insurance on the corporate headquarters, property tax on the corporate headquarters, utilities for the corporate headquarters, salaries of the executives, accounting, human resources, administrative support staff, etc.

What is SG&A?

SG&A stands for selling, general, and administrative costs. SG&A is a common term used in business to describe nonmanufacturing/period costs. The terms "SG&A" and "selling and administrative costs" can be used interchangeably.

How do you classify a combined product and period cost?

Not all costs can be clearly defined as product or period. For example, many companies have just one facility that houses both their production operations and their corporate headquarters. In that case, certain costs must be split between product and period in order to accurately calculate the cost of manufacturing overhead. The rent, insurance, and property tax on the factory may be split, or prorated, based on square footage occupied or some other measure deemed appropriate.

For example, consider the custom dining table manufacturer. If it has one facility that is 10,000 square feet, of which 7,500 square feet are occupied by the manufacturing process, and the other 2,500 square feet are occupied by executive and administrative staff, the manufacturer may allocate 75% of its rent to manufacturing overhead and 25% of its rent to administrative costs. If the monthly rent was $10,000, the company would allocate $7,500 to manufacturing overhead and $2,500 to administrative costs.

What does cost behavior mean?

Cost behavior refers to the way in which a cost changes with relation to changes in an activity, usually units sold. For example, what will happen to the cost of napkins when an ice cream parlor sells more ice cream cones? As an ice cream parlor sells more ice cream cones, the number of napkins handed out will also increase; thus, the cost of napkins will increase as the activity increases. The cost of napkins is variable with respect to the number of ice cream cones sold. However, as an ice cream parlor sells more ice cream

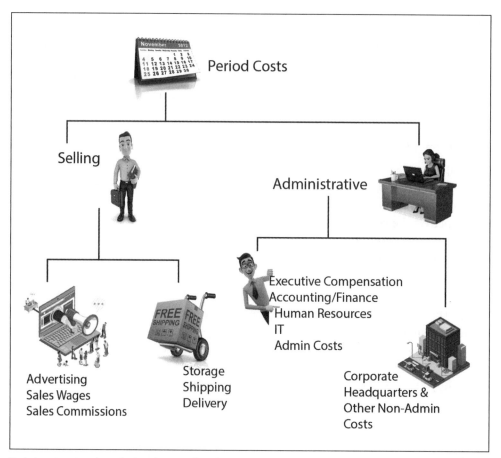

Period costs are used to calculate the cost of production when the expenses can't be clearly assigned to a specific product.

cones, the cost of lighting the store will not increase. The lights will be on from open to close regardless of how many customers enter the store and purchase ice cream cones. The cost of lighting is fixed with respect to the number of ice cream cones sold.

What is a variable cost?

A variable cost is a cost that changes in direct proportion to changes in an activity. For example, the more ice cream cones that are sold at an ice cream parlor, the more cones that are used up. Variable costs vary in total with the change in the activity. However, the cost per unit (per cone) remains constant.

For example, if the ice cream parlor purchases the cones for $0.05 each, the total cost of cones will be $5.00 if 100 ice cream cones are sold or $50.00 if 1,000 ice cream cones are sold. The total cost of ice cream cones varies in direct proportion to the number of ice cream cones sold. However, the cost per unit of the cone is constant at $0.05. These relationships are illustrated in the graphs below.

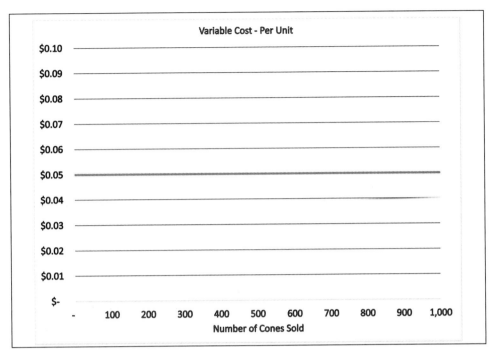

The cost per ice cream cone sold in his graph holds steady at $0.05 per cone.

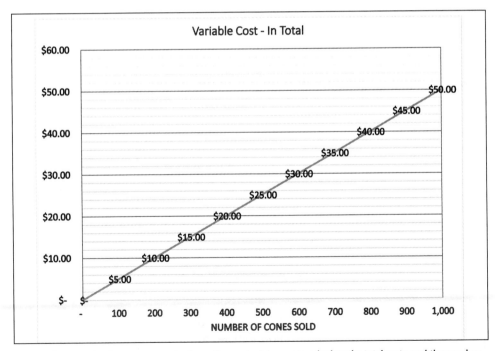

Because the cost of an ice cream cone is always five cents, it is easy to calculate the total costs, and the number of cones goes up.

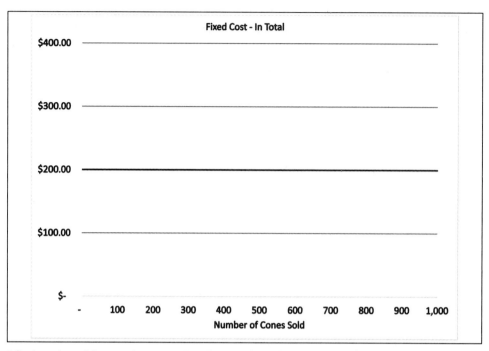

A fixed cost in total does not change over time. For example, in this graph, it costs $200 a month every month to provide lighting to a store.

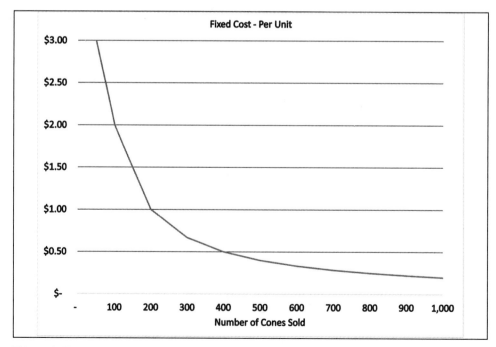

This graph illustrates that the more units produced, the lower the cost per unit.

What is a fixed cost?

A fixed cost is a cost that does not change with changes in an activity. For example, the cost of lighting (electricity) the ice cream parlor will not change if more ice cream cones are sold. Fixed costs are constant in total when an activity level changes. However, the cost per unit will decrease as the activity level increases.

For example, if the cost of having the lights on in the ice cream parlor from 11:00 A.M. to 10:00 P.M. seven days per week is $200 per month, the total cost of lighting the store will be $200 per month, regardless of the number of cones sold. However, if only one ice cream cone is sold that month, the cost of lighting the store was $200 for just one cone! If 1,000 cones were sold that month, the cost of lighting the store can be spread over the 1,000 cones, resulting in a cost of $0.20 per cone. These relationships are illustrated in the graphs on page 168 (see above).

Are all costs either variable or fixed?

No, there are many variations of cost behavior, including mixed costs and step costs. A mixed cost is a cost that includes both a fixed and a variable component. For example, a particular cell phone plan may include a flat fee of $40 for unlimited voice calling, plus a fee of $0.10 per text. In this case, the $40 represents a fixed cost, and the $0.10 represents a variable cost. At a minimum, the cell phone bill will be at least $40 each month and will increase from there depending on the number of texts sent. This graph is illustrated below.

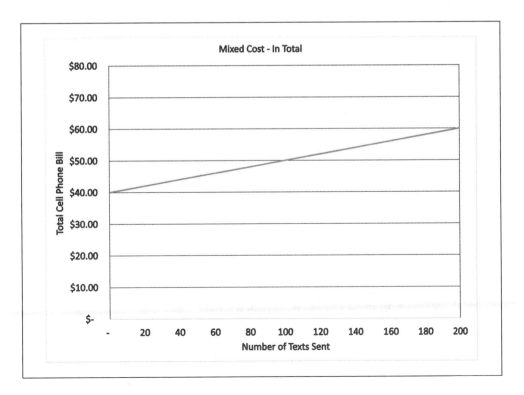

Are all costs linear in total?

Not all costs are linear in total. For example, a particular cell phone plan may be $60 per month for unlimited voice calling and texting and allow up to 3 GB of data. After 3 GB of data are used, the customer will be charged for the extra data. The phone bill will be mixed, however; it will not be linear. This graph is illustrated below.

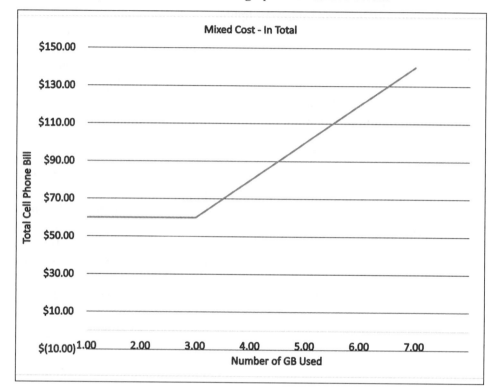

What is a step cost?

A step cost is a cost that increases in step increments. The cost is fixed in relation to a certain range of activity and increases in subsequent ranges. For example, the ice cream parlor may be able to run with only one associate behind the counter when the company is selling up to 100 cones per day. However, if the company sells between 100 and 200 cones per day, it will need a second associate working, etc. Assuming one employee works an 8-hour day and is paid $12.00 per hour, the cost of wages at the ice cream parlor would be $96 per day if the average cones sold per day was 100 or less. However, if the average number of cones sold per day was between 101 and 200, a second employee would be needed, increasing the cost of wages to $192. Thus, this cost would increase in step increments as illustrated in the graph below.

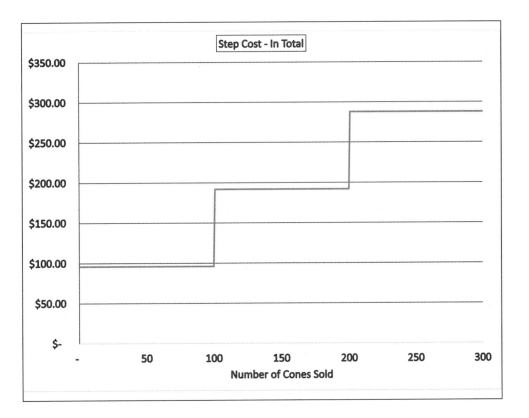

How do accountants identify fixed, variable, and mixed costs?

Accountants use a variety of methods to identify cost behavior. Many costs are obvious. For example, direct materials are always variable. The more tables we sell, the more wood we buy. Other costs, like salaries, are obviously fixed. It doesn't matter how many tables we sell, the rent on the factory stays the same. Mixed costs are harder to identify and break into their fixed and variable components.

Why do accountants need to break mixed costs into fixed and variable components?

Mixed costs should be split into fixed and variable components to help managers better understand their corporate cost structure and to plan for the future. For example, if a small, fifty-room hotel was trying to budget the electricity expense for the following year, it would need to understand how the cost of electricity changes in relation to guest occupancy. There is a certain amount of electricity that will be used whether the hotel is empty or fully occupied. This would include things like the parking lot lighting, the lighting in the lobby, electricity to run front-desk computers, etc. This represents the fixed portion of electricity. There is an additional amount of electricity that will increase due to guest occupancy. For example, guests will use the lighting in the rooms, hair dryers, televisions, coffee pots, and air conditioning. These represent the variable portion of electricity.

171

How is a mixed cost separated into its fixed and variable components?

There are several ways a mixed cost can be separated into its fixed and variable components. Some of the more basic methods are scatterplot and the high-low method. Both of these methods rely on historical data to arrive at the fixed and variable components of a mixed cost.

What is the scatterplot method?

The scatterplot method plots data points for cost on a graph, with the cost object on the x-axis (independent variable) and cost in dollars on the y-axis (dependent variable). In the hotel example, the hotel could track occupancy days and electricity cost per month for the past year. It could then graph the data plotting occupancy days on the x-axis and electricity cost on the y-axis.

The next step would be to draw a line of best fit. This is easily done in Microsoft Excel by adding a trend line to the scatterplot graph. The equation of the line, $y = mx + b$, can be used to compute the fixed and variable components. In this case, y = total electricity cost, m = variable cost per occupancy day, x = occupancy days, and b = fixed cost of electricity per month. Accordingly, the slope of the line, m, is equivalent to the variable cost per unit. The y intercept, b, is equivalent to the fixed cost per month. (Note that an occupancy day is a room booked for one night. As there are 50 rooms in the hotel and approximately 30 days per month, the maximum capacity would be approximately 1,500 occupancy days per month.)

The following figures show an example of occupancy days versus electricity costs for the hotel, followed by a scatterplot with the equation of the line. You can see that the results of the scatterplot calculate the fixed portion of electricity as $443.63 per month and the variable portion as $2.64 per occupancy day. The cost equation can be rewritten as $y = \$2.64x + \$443.63$, or total monthly electricity cost = $2.64 per occupancy day + $443.63. The hotel can now budget electricity cost for the month based on forecasted occupancy days.

Month	Occupancy Days	Electricity Cost
January	465	$ 1,777
February	700	$ 2,200
March	310	$ 1,482
April	1,050	$ 2,585
May	775	$ 2,350
June	1,200	$ 3,800
July	1,395	$ 4,148
August	1,535	$ 4,945
September	1,500	$ 5,000
October	620	$ 2,350
November	1,200	$ 3,200
December	1,395	$ 3,590

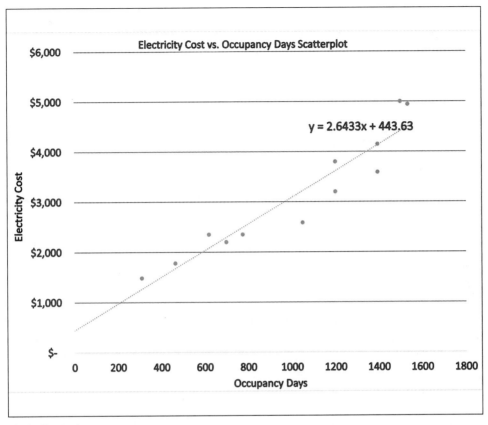

Figure: Scatterplot

What is the high-low method?

The high-low method is a method of splitting a mixed cost into its fixed and variable components that uses only two data points, the high activity level and the low activity level. Just like with the scatterplot method, the equation of the line, $y = mx + b$, can be used to compute the fixed and variable components. Again, y = total electricity cost, m = variable cost per occupancy day, x = occupancy days, and b = fixed cost of electricity per month. Accordingly, the slope of the line, m, is equivalent to the variable cost per unit. The y intercept, b, is equivalent to the fixed cost per month. However, with the high-low method, only two points are used to graph the line.

The first step is to identify the high and low data points. Using the previous figures on occupancy days versus electricity cost, we can see that the highest level of activity (occupancy days) occurred in August. The lowest level of activity occurred in March.

The second step is to calculate the variable cost per unit (slope) by using the algebraic formula for "rise over run," or $(y1 - y2) / (x1 - x2)$. In this case, it would be calculated as the change in electricity cost divided by the change in occupancy days, computed as follows:

	High	-	Low	=	Change
Electricity Cost	$ 4,945		$ 1,482		$ 3,463
Occupancy Days	1,535		310		1,225

Change in Electricity Cost	$ 3,463
/ Change in Occupancy Days	1,225
= Variable Cost per Day	$ 2.83

Figure: The High-Low Method

The third step is to calculate the fixed cost (y intercept) by plugging the high data into the cost equation $y = mx + b$. At the high activity level (August), total electricity cost is $4,945, and occupancy days are 1,535. We have already calculated the variable cost per unit as $2.83 per day. Accordingly, the cost formula $y = mx + b$ can be rewritten $4,945 = (\$2.83 \times 1,535) + b$. This can be solved algebraically to determine that $b = \$600.95$.

The final step in the high-low method is to rewrite the cost equation so that it can be used for planning purposes. In this case, the equation would be rewritten as $y = \$2.83x + \$600.95$, or total monthly electricity cost = $2.83 per occupancy day + $600.95. The hotel can now budget electricity cost for the month based on forecasted occupancy days.

What is the primary difference between the scatterplot method and the high-low method?

The scatterplot method uses all the data points that are available for the relevant period, whereas the high-low method uses only two data points. Accordingly, the results will vary between the two methods. As you can see from the hotel example, the scatterplot resulted in a variable cost of $2.64 per occupancy day and a fixed cost of $443.63 per month. The high-low method resulted in a variable cost of $2.83 per occupancy day and a fixed cost of $600.95 per month. If you were preparing a budget based on 1,000 occupancy days for a given month, the scatterplot would result in a budgeted electricity cost of $3,083.63, whereas the high-low method would result in a budgeted electricity cost of $3,430.95.

Which method is better?

The scatterplot with trend line method will generally provide more accurate results, as more data points are used. However, outliers (unusual data points that do not fit the pattern) in the data could distort the results. As such, when preparing a scatterplot, it is a good idea to look at the graph first and research and eliminate any outliers that could distort the results. The primary advantage of the high-low method is its relative ease of use. It is a "quick and dirty" method of splitting a mixed cost. In managerial accounting, estimates are commonly used, as timeliness of information is emphasized over absolute accuracy. As such, the high-low method provides a quick and easy method to analyze mixed costs when only a few data points are readily available.

JOB–ORDER COSTING

What is job-order costing?

Job-order costing is a method of assigning costs to cost objects (jobs) in companies that produce many different products or provide services, usually to customer specifications.

What types of businesses use job-order costing?

Any company that produces a variety of products or services that wishes to track costs by job can use job-order costing. For example, when The Walt Disney Company produces a particular film, it would want to track the costs for that particular film, or job, so that it can ultimately calculate profitability on that film. Different films require different resources; thus, tracking costs by film becomes an important part of the cost accounting process. Another example would be a custom home builder. Each house requires different materials (brick, siding, appliances, bath fixtures, etc.), differing amounts of labor, and manufacturing overhead. Job-order costing is the method used to track the costs per home. Service industries commonly use job-order costing. For example, lawyers and accounting firms track the costs per client, as clients are typically billed on a per-hour or per-service basis.

How are costs tracked in a job-order costing system?

Job costs are typically tracked on a "job cost sheet." The job cost sheet has heading information listing the job number and other specific order information. The job cost sheet tracks costs in three sections, one for each product cost: direct materials, direct labor, and manufacturing overhead. At the bottom, there is typically a section that adds up the three product costs and divides the total cost by the units produced, creating a cost-per-unit figure. For example, a caterer may take an order for 100 chocolate cupcakes for a graduation party. The caterer would have a separate job cost sheet for the particular graduation party. It would track the costs of the direct materials (ingredients and paper liners), direct labor (bakery labor), and overhead (rent on kitchen, utilities on kitchen, insurance, etc.) on a job cost sheet.

How are direct materials tracked and recorded?

When direct materials are needed for a job, they are typically requested on a document called a materials requisition form. This form lists the job number or name and the materials requested for the job. These documents are typically prenumbered and often require supervisor approval in the form of a signature at the bottom. The approved materials requisition form is given to the person in charge of storing and safeguarding materials in exchange for the requested materials. In a small company, such as the caterer mentioned above, this may be an informal document like a grocery shopping list accompanied by a shopping receipt.

However the materials are tracked, whether formally or informally, the information must be transferred to the job cost sheet. The job number on the materials requisition form is used to identify the appropriate job cost sheet and then the price of the materials is entered onto the job cost sheet. For bigger jobs, there may be multiple materials requisitions covering a span of time. In the case of the caterer, let's assume there was one materials requisition for the ingredients needed to bake 100 chocolate cupcakes, totaling $23.

What is a bill of materials?

A bill of materials is a listing of the quantities of each material that goes into making each particular product. For the caterer, the bill of materials for the chocolate cupcakes is essentially the recipe.

How is direct labor tracked and recorded?

Every company has some method of tracking employee time worked, as that is a necessary step in the payroll process. The methods of tracking employee time vary from simple paper forms to punch cards to computerized systems. In any case, a job-order costing system requires the employee to track hours by the job worked on. Time cards typically have sections for the hours worked on each particular job. A copy of the time card goes to payroll to process paychecks, and another copy goes to accounting, where the hours and labor cost are transferred to the corresponding job cost sheets. In the case of the caterer, let's assume a particular employee worked 3.5 hours baking the chocolate cupcakes for the graduation party (job #61008), as seen in the figure below.

How is manufacturing overhead tracked and recorded?

Manufacturing overhead costs are recorded in the accounting system as they are incurred. For example, the lease on the catering kitchen would be recorded in the general journal as the monthly fee is incurred. However, as manufacturing overhead costs are indirect, they are not conveniently and easily traced to the particular job. As such, they must be allocated to jobs using an estimate called the predetermined overhead rate, or POHR. This POHR is used on the job cost sheet to add the costs of manufacturing overhead to the job.

How is the POHR calculated?

The POHR is calculated at the beginning of the year by taking the total estimated overhead for the upcoming year and dividing it by an "allocation base." The allocation base

	Time Card					
	L & O Catering					

Time Card Number 111980   **Week Ending** 6/23/2018

Employee Kathryn Gawronski

Date	Started	Ended	Total Hour	Pay Rate	Amount	Job Number
6/19/2018	1:00pm	8:00pm	7	$ 13.00	$ 91.00	61006
6/20/2018	8:00am	2:00pm	6	$ 13.00	$ 78.00	61006
6/21/2018	8:00am	12:00pm	4	$ 13.00	$ 52.00	61007
6/21/2018	1:00pm	5:00pm	4	$ 13.00	$ 52.00	61007
6/22/2018	2:00pm	4:00pm	2	$ 13.00	$ 26.00	61008
6/23/2018	8:00am	9:30am	1.5	$ 13.00	$ 19.50	61008
6/23/2018	9:30am	12:00pm	2.5	$ 13.00	$ 32.50	61009
Totals			27		$ 351.00	

is the measurement the company will use to spread overhead to each job. As such, the allocation base should be carefully chosen and should be related to the incurrence of overhead costs. The allocation base can be referred to as a "cost driver," as it should be an activity that is driving the incurrence of overhead. The caterer in the example will allocate overhead on the basis of direct labor hours, with the assumption being the more hours are spent baking the cupcakes, the more overhead costs are being used up. The figure below shows an example of estimated overhead costs for the upcoming year, as well as the calculation of POHR, based on an estimate of 7,800 direct labor hours being worked in the upcoming year.

Estimated Overhead for 2018:

Lease on kitchen facility	$	18,000
Utilities on kitchen facility	$	2,400
Insurance	$	1,300
Catering Supervisor Salary	$	21,000
Indirect materials	$	3,600
Cleaning supplies	$	1,000
Total Estimated Overhead	$	47,300

Predetermined Overhead Rate:

Total Estimated Overhead	$	47,300
/ Total Estimated DL Hours		7,800
= POHR	$	6.06

Figure: POHR Calculation

How is an allocation base chosen?

If you can answer the phrase "the more I do _____, the more overhead I use" with an affirmative answer, that is an indication you have probably chosen an accurate allocation base. Many companies use direct labor hours or machine hours as an allocation base with the assumption that the more time people or machines spend working on a product, the more overhead resources are consumed. Additionally, direct labor hours and machine hours are an efficient measure, as those are amounts that are easily tracked. For example, direct labor hours are already being tracked on time cards in order to pay employees. In the case of the caterer, direct labor hours were chosen as the allocation base with the assumption being that the more time that was spent working on an order, the more time that was spent by the supervisor, the more indirect materials, such as cooking spray and plastic wrap, were used, the more electricity was used, etc.

How is manufacturing overhead allocated to jobs?

Manufacturing overhead is allocated to jobs by multiplying the POHR by the actual units of the allocation base incurred. For example, the caterer will allocate $6.06 of manufacturing overhead to a job for each hour of direct labor worked, as shown on the employee time card. The time card for our caterer shows a total of 3.5 hours worked on job #61008. The caterer would then multiply the 3.5 hours of actual direct labor (allocation base) by the POHR of $6.06 per hour and apply $21.22 of manufacturing overhead to that particular job.

How is the job cost sheet finalized?

Direct materials are added to the job cost sheet as materials requisition forms are processed by accounting. Direct labor costs are added to the job cost sheet as time cards are processed by accounting. Manufacturing overhead costs will be allocated on the job cost based on the appropriate POHR. In the case of the caterer, the allocation base chosen was direct labor hours. Accordingly, manufacturing overhead will be added to the job cost sheet on the basis of direct labor hours already recorded on the job cost sheet. Totals of the three product costs will be calculated at the bottom of the job cost sheet. The figure below of a completed job cost sheet illustrates this process.

How is the cost per unit of a job calculated?

The cost per unit is calculated by taking the total cost of a job (direct materials plus direct labor plus manufacturing overhead) and dividing by the total units produced. In the case of the caterer, the total cost of the chocolate cupcake order was $89.72 to prepare 100 cupcakes, arriving at a cost per cupcake of approximately $0.90.

How is gross profit of a job calculated?

The gross profit of a job can be calculated by taking the selling price of the job minus the cost of the job. For example, assuming the caterer sold the 100 chocolate cupcakes

Job Cost Sheet

L & O Catering

Job Number	61008			Date Initiated	6/22/2018
				Date Completed	6/23/2018
Job Description				Units Completed	100

Marcella Hansen's Graduation Party - 100 chocolate cupcakes

Direct Materials		Direct Labor			Manufacturing Overhead		
Req. #	Amount	Time Card	Hours	Amount	Hours	Rate	Amount
10911	$ 23.00	111980	3.5	$ 45.50	3.5	$ 6.06	$ 21.22

Cost Summary:

Direct Materials	$ 23.00
Direct Labor	$ 45.50
Manufacturing Overhead	$ 21.22
Total Cost of Job	$ 89.72
Cost Per Unit	$ 0.90

for $225, the gross profit on the job would be calculated as $225 selling price less $89.72 cost for a gross profit of $135.28, a 60% gross margin.

Is gross profit the same as net income?

Gross profit is not the same as net income. The caterer in the example above has other costs in addition to the three product costs: direct materials, direct labor, and overhead. Gross profit takes the selling price less only the three product costs. The caterer also has period costs, such as the salary of the owner, advertising expense, and office supplies. Those period costs are subtracted from total gross profit for the period (usually a month, quarter, or year) to arrive at operating income for the period, from which any interest expense on loans and income taxes are deducted before arriving at net income.

How are job order costs recorded in the accounting system?

Job order costs flow through the accounting system in much the same way as they do on the job cost sheet. Job order costs are accumulated and recorded as assets (raw materials inventory, work-in-process inventory, or finished goods inventory) until they are sold to customers, where the matching principle is applied and costs are finally expensed on the income statement as cost of goods sold expense. The following diagram illustrates the flow of costs in a job costing system using T accounts, as discussed in the chapter entitled "Bookkeeping and the Accounting Cycle." In addition, specific journal entries in proper form are covered in Appendix 1.

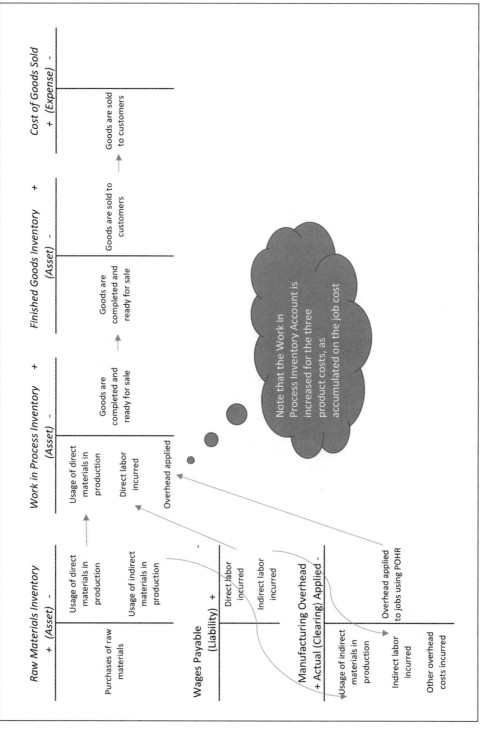

Figure: Job Order Cost Flows

How are period costs recorded in a job cost system?

Period costs are recorded as expenses when they are incurred. Unlike product costs, which are recorded as assets until sold, period costs are associated with a time period and are recorded when used in the month. For example, the cost of monthly advertising for the caterer in the church bulletin would be expensed as "advertising expense" on the income statement each month.

What is cost of goods manufactured?

Cost of goods manufactured is the accumulation of the three product costs (direct materials, direct labor, and overhead) that were used in the goods that were completed, or manufactured, during a particular period. As such, the name is also the definition: essentially, it represents the cost of the goods that were manufactured that month.

How is cost of goods manufactured different from cost of goods sold?

While the cost of goods manufactured represents the cost of the goods completed that particular period, it does not distinguish between whether the goods have been sold to the customer or whether they are sitting in finished goods inventory in a warehouse somewhere. Cost of goods sold represents the accumulation of the product costs (direct materials, direct labor, and overhead) for the goods that have been sold to customers that period. This is the cost that will be expensed on the income statement for that particular period and matched with the sales revenue earned from customers during that same period. Any cost of goods manufactured that have not yet been sold will remain in finished goods inventory as an asset account until they are sold. In the example of the caterer, since the product is food and is perishable, it is produced and sold within a one-day period. As such, the caterer would not have a sizeable balance of finished goods inventory at the end of a period, as most products are sold the same day they are produced. On the contrary, a home builder who builds "spec" homes may sit on those houses for months before they are sold. Thus, the cost of goods manufactured would not always be the same as the cost of goods sold.

What is a schedule of cost of goods manufactured and cost of goods sold?

The schedule of cost of goods manufactured and cost of goods sold is a schedule that shows the manufacturing cost flows for the period in schedule form rather than in T account form. In order to compute cost flows in and out of the manufacturing accounts, a simple equation is used:

Beginning balance + costs added = goods available.

Goods available − ending balance = costs transferred out.

This pattern repeats itself many times in accounting. For example, let's assume you like to snack on Twinkies while you study. You've opened up the box of Twinkies in your pantry and determined that you only have 2 Twinkies (beginning balance). Anticipating   **181**

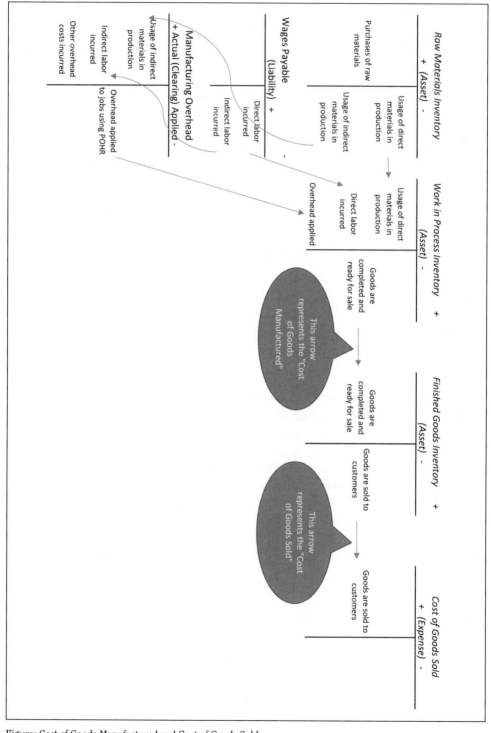

Figure: Cost of Goods Manufactured and Cost of Goods Sold

your hunger for more Twinkies, you go to the store and purchase a box of 10 Twinkies (costs added). You now have 12 Twinkies available.

2 + 10 = 12 Twinkies available

At the end of your study session, you have a slight stomachache from all the sugar you've just eaten, and you realize you've lost count of just how many Twinkies you ate. How can you figure out how many Twinkies you ate? Of course, you'll just look in the box and see how many Twinkies are left (ending balance). If you look in the box and find 4 Twinkies left, you can then determine that you have consumed 8 Twinkies that evening.

12 − 4 = 8 Twinkies consumed

This is the exact same logic for the schedule of cost of goods manufactured and cost of goods sold, except that we calculate the schedule in dollar amounts, not units. An example is provided in the figure below. In addition, a corresponding figure, using T accounts, follows.

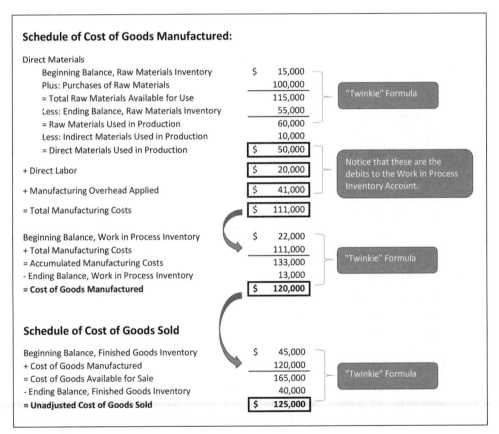

Figure: Schedule of Cost of Goods Manufactured and Cost of Goods Sold

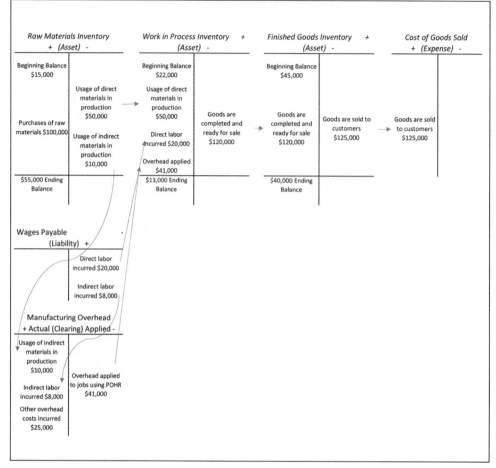

Figure: Cost Flows T Account Example

Why doesn't actual overhead equal applied overhead in the manufacturing overhead T account?

You may have noticed that the manufacturing overhead account is labeled as a "clearing account." This means the account should have a zero balance at the end of each period. However, in the example given in the figure above, this is not the case. The manufacturing overhead will not zero out on its own. This is because the debits to the manufacturing overhead account are based on the actual costs incurred, whereas the credits to the manufacturing overhead account are based on estimates using the POHR. Recall that the POHR is based off estimated overhead and the estimated allocation base. It is applied using the actual allocation base, but the POHR itself is based on estimates. Accountants do not have crystal balls and cannot predict the future with 100% accuracy. Accordingly, the likelihood of the actual and applied overhead being the same in any given period is slim.

How is the manufacturing overhead account balanced?

At the end of the period, an entry will be made to clear out (balance) the manufacturing overhead account. If the actual overhead incurred (debit) is greater than the overhead applied (credit), the manufacturing overhead is considered underapplied, meaning that not enough overhead was applied to production. In order to balance the account, an entry will be made to apply the difference with a credit to the manufacturing overhead and a corresponding debit to cost of goods sold expense. (Note: this entry can also be prorated between work-in-process inventory, finished goods inventory, and cost of goods sold expense.) In essence, the overhead that should have been applied earlier is "caught up" and moved to cost of goods sold, where it would have ultimately ended up had the POHR been an exact estimate. This scenario is what occurred in the previous example. The following diagram illustrates the "catch up" journal entry to balance the manufacturing overhead T account and zero it out. The actual overhead costs in the example were $43,000, whereas the applied overhead was $41,000. Accordingly, this company has $2,000 of underapplied overhead. In order to balance and zero out the manufacturing overhead T account, an entry must be made to apply an additional $2,000 of overhead. In this case, it will all be moved to cost of goods sold expense. The figure below illustrates this adjustment.

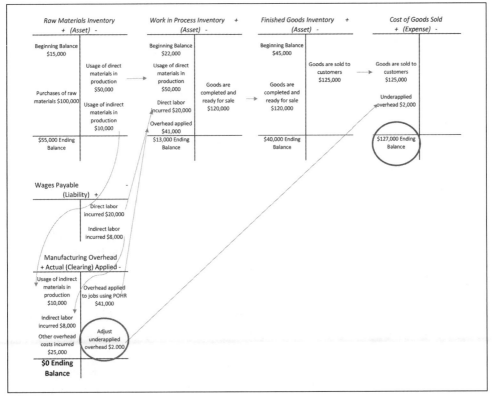

Figure: Adjusting Manufacturing Overhead for Underapplied Overhead

What if the manufacturing overhead is overapplied?

If the manufacturing overhead is overapplied, meaning the actual overhead costs incurred were less than the overhead applied, the adjustment to balance the manufacturing overhead account and zero it out is simply the opposite of underapplied. In this case, the manufacturing overhead account would be debited, and cost of goods sold expense would be credited. This journal entry essentially reduces cost of goods sold expense, which is appropriate because if you overapplied overhead, that means you applied too much to production. That overapplication would have flowed through the manufacturing T accounts and ended up in cost of goods sold expense, leaving you with overstated cost of goods sold expense. Thus, the entry to balance the manufacturing overhead T account will also correct the cost of goods sold expense account as well.

Does the schedule of cost of goods sold get updated for the underapplied or overapplied manufacturing overhead adjustment?

The cost of goods sold schedule will be updated to correct for any underapplied or overapplied overhead by adding to or subtracting from cost of goods sold expense as applicable. Underapplied overhead will be added to cost of goods sold expense, whereas overapplied overhead will be subtracted from cost of goods sold expense. The figure below provides an updated schedule of cost of goods sold.

Schedule of Cost of Goods Sold

Beginning Balance, Finished Goods Inventory	$ 45,000	⎤
+ Cost of Goods Manufactured	120,000	
= Cost of Goods Available for Sale	165,000	⎬ "Twinkie" Forumla
- Ending Balance, Finished Goods Inventory	40,000	
= Unadjusted Cost of Goods Sold	125,000	⎦
+ Underapplied Overhead	2,000	
= Adjusted Cost of Goods Sold	$ 127,000	

ACTIVITY–BASED COSTING

What is activity-based costing (ABC)?

Activity-based costing (ABC) is a method of assigning costs to cost objects in companies that produce many different products or provide services using multiple allocation bases.

How is ABC different from job-order costing?

ABC is quite similar to job-order costing. ABC is like job-order costing "on steroids." Whereas job-order costing applies overhead using one allocation base and one POHR,

ABC applies overhead using multiple allocation bases and multiple POHRs, called activity rates. Overhead costs are grouped into different "activity cost pools." Each activity cost pool will have its own allocation base, or "cost driver." For example, a restaurant may choose to group costs of serving customers into the following groups: costs of serving a party, costs of serving a customer, costs of serving drinks, and general restaurant overhead. In this case, there are different costs associated with each of those activities. The costs of serving a party would include setting the table, bussing the table, and the wages of the host/hostess. The costs of serving a customer would include the cost of washing the dishes and the wages of the wait staff and servers. The cost of serving drinks would include the wages of the bartender and the cost of washing the glasses. The general restaurant overhead might include the wages of the manager, the lease on the restaurant, insurance, and utilities.

What is the benefit to having more than one POHR?

The primary benefit to having more than one POHR is getting more accurate data. Using one single POHR is a good tool for estimation, but if a business engages in more complex processes, the overhead applied by one single POHR may not accurately apply overhead costs to products or jobs. For example, consider a company that makes tables and chairs. If the tables are processed mostly by hand and the chairs are processed mostly by machine, you will apply a far greater amount of overhead to the tables if your POHR is based on direct labor hours than you would to the chairs. This may not accurately reflect the actual consumption of resources. Accordingly, having multiple POHRs allows a company to more accurately apply manufacturing overhead and thus make better decisions.

How many activity cost pools does an ABC system use?

The number of allocation bases varies from company to company. In the previous example with the restaurant, 4 activity cost pools were used. A general rule of thumb is to use no more than 10 activity cost pools. If more than 10 are used, the likelihood is that the cost of managing that system far outweighs any incremental benefit achieved.

How are overhead costs grouped into activity cost pools?

Accountants and managers work together to identify overhead costs and determine the cost drivers (allocation bases) that relate to each of those groups. This is not an exact science but rather a best estimate. For example, in the previous restaurant example, one could argue that the wages of the waiter/waitress are really a cost of serving a party rather than a cost of serving an individual customer. After all, the waiter/waitress takes the entire table's order at one time whether there are 8 customers or just 1. On the flip side, one could argue that the more customers that are in a party, the more time the wait staff will need to take the orders, etc. This is just one simple example to illustrate the complexities of designing an ABC system. After all, there is no such thing as GAAP for managerial cost accounting.

What is an activity rate?

An activity rate is essentially a POHR with a fancy name. It is the rate at which manufacturing overhead will be applied for a given activity.

How is the activity rate calculated?

The first step in the ABC process is to split the estimated manufacturing overhead for the year into the various activity cost pools. Each activity cost pool should have a cost driver (allocation base). The second step is to calculate the activity rate by dividing the estimated overhead in each activity cost pool by the total expected activity for that cost pool. Note, this is the same formula used to calculate a POHR.

For example, assume a small boutique jewelry manufacturer makes 2 products, necklaces and earrings. The necklaces are started on a machine but finished by hand as the employees add different embellishments. The earrings are processed entirely by machine. The company typically produces 80,000 necklaces per year and 100,000 pairs of earrings per year. The jewelry manufacturer has estimated overhead for the upcoming year and assigned it to the following activities:

Activity Cost Pool	Estimated Overhead Cost
Maintaining parts inventory	$ 45,000
Processing customer orders	$ 30,000
Machine related costs	$ 150,000
Labor related costs	$ 65,000
General factory	$ 360,000
Total Estimated Overhead	$ 650,000

Activity Measure	Expected Activity Necklaces	Expected Activity Earrings	Total	Activity Rate
Number of Parts	25	5	30	$ 1,500
Number of Orders	170	190	360	$ 83
Machine Hours	800	900	1,700	$ 88
Direct Labor Hours	1,600	-	1,600	$ 41
Machine Hours	800	900	1,700	$ 212

Figure: ABC Overhead Assignments and Activity Rates

How is manufacturing overhead applied in an ABC system?

Manufacturing overhead is applied in the same manner as job-order costing. Each activity rate (POHR) is multiplied by the actual activity (allocation base) for each product during the period. For simplicity, let's assume the actual activity for the year was the same as what was expected. Using ABC, $356,667 of manufacturing overhead would be applied to the necklaces, and $293,333 of manufacturing overhead would be applied to the earrings. This is illustrated in the following figure.

Actual Activity

Activity Rate	Activity Measure	Necklaces	Earrings	Total
$ 1,500	Number of Parts	25	5	30
$ 83	Number of Orders	170	190	360
$ 88	Machine Hours	800	900	1,700
$ 41	Direct Labor Hours	1,600	-	1,600
$ 212	Machine Hours	800	900	1,700

Overhead Applied

Activity Measure	Necklaces	Earrings	Total
Number of Parts	$ 37,500	$ 7,500	$ 45,000
Number of Orders	$ 14,167	$ 15,833	$ 30,000
Machine Hours	$ 70,588	$ 79,412	$ 150,000
Direct Labor Hours	$ 65,000	$ -	$ 65,000
Machine Hours	$ 169,412	$ 190,588	$ 360,000
Total Overhead Applied	$ 356,667	$ 293,333	$ 650,000

Figure: Allocating Overhead to Products

How are the total product cost and per-unit product cost calculated using ABC?

The total product cost is calculated by adding up the direct materials cost, the direct labor cost, and the manufacturing overhead cost for each product. The cost per unit is calculated by dividing the total product cost by the units produced. This is illustrated in the following figure.

	Necklaces	Earrings
Direct Materials	$ 200,000	$ 90,000
Direct Labor	20,800	$ -
Manufacturing Overhead	$ 356,667	$ 293,333
Total Product Cost	$ 577,467	$ 383,333
/ Units Produced	80,000	100,000
Cost Per Unit	$ 7.22	$ 3.83

189

How do the results from using ABC compare to the results from using one POHR?

The results would be different if one single POHR was used. For example, if the jewelry manufacturer had used one single POHR based on machine hours, the end result would have been to apply $305,882 of manufacturing overhead to necklaces and $344,118 to earrings. This results in a per-unit cost of $6.58 for necklaces and $4.34 for earrings.

The figure below illustrates the product cost example using a single POHR. You can see that the single POHR applied more overhead cost to the earrings and less to the necklaces as compared to ABC. It is typical that a single POHR will apply more overhead to the high-volume products and less overhead to the low-volume products, which may not accurately reflect the true usage of overhead.

POHR:

Total Estimated Overhead	$	650,000
/ Total Estimated Machine Hours		1,700
= POHR	**$**	**382.35**

		Actual Activity		
POHR	Activity Measure	Necklaces	Earrings	**Total**
$ 382.35	Machine Hours	800	900	1,700

	Overhead Applied		
	Necklaces	Earrings	**Total**
	$ 305,882	$ 344,118	$ 650,000

	Necklaces	Earrings
Direct Materials	$ 200,000	$ 90,000
Direct Labor	20,800	$ -
Manufacturing Overhead	$ 305,882	$ 344,118
Total Product Cost	**$ 526,682**	**$ 434,118**
/ Units Produced	80,000	100,000
Cost Per Unit	**$ 6.58**	**$ 4.34**

Figure: Single Plant-wide POHR

How is gross profit per unit calculated using ABC?

Gross profit per unit is calculated by subtracting the product cost per unit from the selling price per unit. Assuming the jewelry manufacturer sells necklaces for $25 each and pairs of earrings for $15 each, the gross profit would be $17.78 per necklace and $11.17 per pair of earrings. That equates to a 71% gross margin for necklaces and a 74% gross margin for earrings. The figure below illustrates this.

ABC COSTING	Necklaces		Earrings	
Selling Price Per Unit	$	25.00	$	15.00
- Cost Per Unit	$	7.22	$	3.83
= **Gross Profit Per Unit**	$	**17.78**	$	**11.17**
Gross Margin		71%		74%

How does the gross profit per unit using ABC compare to the gross profit per unit using a single POHR?

As mentioned previously, using a single POHR will typically assign more costs per unit to the high-volume product—in this case, the earrings—thereby making the high-volume product look like it costs more to manufacturer than it actually does. Using the calculation for the jewelry manufacture, the single POHR results in a gross profit per necklace of $18.42 and a gross profit per pair of earrings of $10.66. That equates to a 74% gross margin for necklaces and a 71% gross margin for earrings. This figure below illustrates this.

SINGLE POHR	Necklaces		Earrings	
Selling Price Per Unit	$	25.00	$	15.00
- Cost Per Unit	$	6.58	$	4.34
= **Gross Profit Per Unit**	$	**18.42**	$	**10.66**
Gross Margin		74%		71%

Which method is better: ABC or a single POHR?

While ABC tends to give more accurate information, it is costly to gather data, set up, and run an ABC system. Managers must evaluate the costs versus the benefits of using ABC over a single POHR. As you can see from the jewelry manufacturer example, different cost calculations will be reached for each product depending on whether ABC or a single POHR is used. Accordingly, managers may make different decisions based on this cost information. The types of companies that are most likely to benefit from using ABC versus a single POHR are companies that have products that differ considerably in volume produced or those companies that have high and/or increasing manufacturing overhead costs and are unsure what is driving the overhead.

PROCESS COSTING

What is process costing?

Process costing is a method of assigning costs to products in companies that produce uniform products, usually on an assembly-line basis.

191

When should a company use process costing?

A company should use process costing if the products that it manufactures are uniform in nature; thus, the costs from one unit of product are the same as the next unit of product. Many products and industries, such as potato chips, ketchup, toilet paper, and pencils, are mass produced. It would be a tedious process to try to track the costs of every unit of product or every customer order, as with job-order costing.

How is process costing similar to job-order costing?

Both process costing and job-order costing are methods to assign the three product costs (direct materials, direct labor, and manufacturing overhead) to products. The flow of costs through the raw materials inventory, work-in-process inventory, and finished goods inventory is essentially the same; however, the calculations to arrive at the amounts follow a different process.

How is process costing different from job-order costing?

Recall that job-order costing is used when a company provides a unique product or service, typically to customer specifications. In job-order costing, costs are tracked by each job. Since process costing is used when products are homogeneous, costs are not tracked by job but rather by each processing department in the production process.

What is a processing department?

A processing department is a division of the business where direct materials, direct labor, and/or manufacturing overhead are added to the product. For example, a company similar to Jiffy Mix baking products may track costs in the following processing departments: wheat processing, mixing, and packaging, as illustrated in the following figure.

Processing Flour

Processing (wheat processed into flour) Mixing (ingredients added to make mix) Packaging (completed mix packaged for resale)

How are process costs recorded in the accounting system?

Process costs flow through the accounting system in much the same way as they do on the factory floor. Process costs are accumulated and recorded as assets (raw materials inventory, work-in-process inventory, or finished goods inventory) until they are sold to customers, where the matching principle is applied and costs are finally expensed on the income statement as cost of goods sold expense. The primary difference in cost flows between job-order costing and process costing is that process costing has a work-in-process inventory account for each processing department. The following diagram illustrates the flow of costs in a process costing system using T accounts, as discussed in the chapter entitled "Bookkeeping and the Accounting Cycle." In addition, specific journal entries in proper form are covered in Appendix 1.

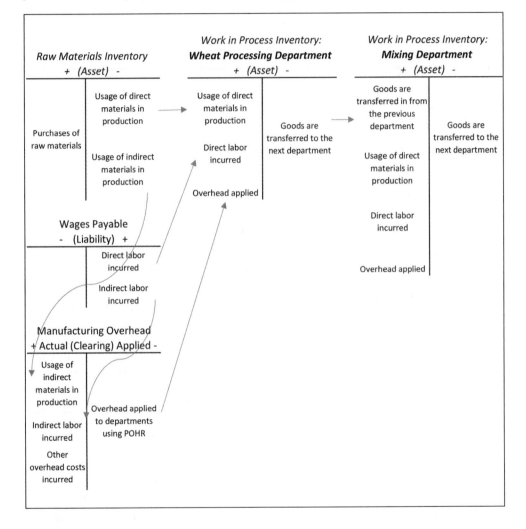

How are costs added to the first processing department?

Costs are added to processing departments as they are used in production. For example, our baking mix company will add raw materials (wheat) into the first processing department, wheat processing. There may also be direct labor added, as production employees are working in the factory in the wheat processing department. Additionally,

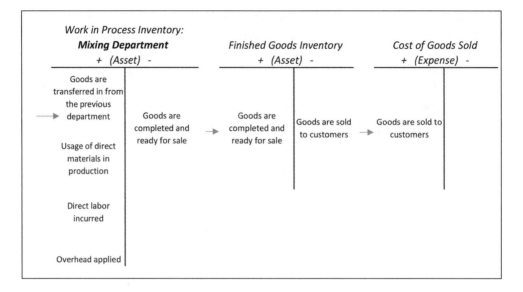

manufacturing overhead will be applied to the wheat processing department using a POHR in most cases.

How are costs added to subsequent processing departments?

In subsequent processing departments, as in the mixing department and/or the packaging department, the first step is to transfer in the costs of work completed from the previous department. For example, the accumulated costs of direct materials, direct labor, and manufacturing overhead for any wheat that has been completely processed and transferred out of the wheat processing department and into the mixing department must be transferred into the mixing department. Additional direct materials (baking powder, sugar, etc.), additional direct labor, and additional manufacturing overhead may be added to the mixing department as well. Once the product is completed in the mixing department, the accumulated costs of the completed mixture will be transferred out to the packaging department. In the packaging department, additional direct materials (package box and bag), direct labor, and manufacturing overhead may be added as well.

How are the costs of finished goods accounted for?

Once the product has been completed in the final processing department, the accumulated costs of the completed product are moved to finished goods inventory. When the product is sold, the costs will be expensed on the income statement as cost of goods sold expense.

How are costs tracked in the accounting system if one unit of product is indistinguishable from the next?

At the end of any given period, a particular processing department will most likely have some partially completed goods left. This makes it difficult to determine the value of the work-in-process inventory left in that processing department as well as the cost of goods transferred to the next department. In order to efficiently track costs in a process costing system, a method of estimation, called equivalent units of production, is used to calculate the value of work-in-process inventory in each department and the costs of goods completed and transferred to the next processing department. For example, if at the end of the month, the baking mix producer has some wheat in the wheat processing department that has not completed the sifting process to become the flour needed in the mixing department, the mixing company would need a method to account for the partially completed flour. The partially completed flour would be converted into something called an "equivalent unit."

What is an equivalent unit?

Put simply, an equivalent unit is an estimation of a completed unit.

How is an equivalent unit of production calculated?

An equivalent unit is calculated by multiplying the number of partially completed units by their percentage of completion. This is the same logic as saying two half cups of water equals one full cup of water ($2 \times 50\% = 1$). For example, assume the baking mix producer has 1,000 pounds of flour that are 60% completed through the sifting process. The baking mix producer would calculate $1,000 \times 60\% = 600$ equivalent units of production.

How are equivalent units used in the final determination of the value of ending work-in-process inventory and the value of units completed and transferred to the next department?

There are two primary methods used to calculate the values of ending work-in-process inventory and the value of units completed and transferred out using process costing. Those two methods are the weighted-average method and the FIFO method.

What is the difference between the weighed-average method and the FIFO method of process costing?

The weighted-average method combines the costs of the current period and the prior period together and, therefore, makes no distinction between the costs of the current and prior period. The FIFO method does not blend the costs of the current and prior periods together. As the weighted-average method is somewhat less complex, that is what will be covered in this text.

How are equivalent units of production calculated using the weighted-average method?

Equivalent units of production are equal to the number of units completed and transferred to the next department plus the equivalent units in ending work-in-process inventory. Using our baking mix example, assume the wheat processing department finished 10,000 pounds of flour during the month of February. At the end of February, the wheat processing department still had 1,000 pounds of flour that were 60% of the way through the sifting process. The processing department would calculate 600 equivalent units in ending work-in-process inventory. Thus, equivalent units of production would be 10,600 pounds. This is the unit value that would be used for the month of February to calculate cost per pound in the wheat processing department.

Are direct materials, direct labor, and manufacturing overhead tracked separately?

Yes, the costs of direct materials, direct labor, and manufacturing overhead are tracked separately. For example, the 1,000 pounds of flour that are 60% through the sifting process are actually 100% complete as far as direct materials are concerned, meaning that all the wheat has been added, but the wheat needs more time to process (consuming more direct labor and overhead). The direct labor and manufacturing overhead can be added together to form one category, called conversion cost, as discussed at the beginning of this chapter. As the flour sifting is done primarily by machine, with very little human effort involved, it is more efficient to combine the two categories together than to track them each separately. Accordingly, the 1,000 pounds of ending work-in-process inventory are 100% complete for direct materials but only 60% complete for conversion cost.

What is the first step in the weighted-average process costing method?

The first step is to compute the equivalent units of production for direct materials and for conversion costs. For example, assume that at the beginning of the month of February, the baking mix producer had 2,000 pounds of partially sifted flour in beginning work-in-process inventory. During the month of February, an additional 9,000 pounds of wheat were added to the sifter. This means that 11,000 pounds of flour were being

	Units (pounds)	Percentage Complete Direct Materials	Conversion Costs
Wheat Processing Department:			
Beginning work in process inventory	2,000		
+ Units started during February	9,000		
- Units completed and transferred to the mixing department	10,000	100%	100%
= Ending work in process inventory	1,000	100%	60%

Step 1: Calculate Equivalent Units of Production		
	Direct Materials	Conversion Costs
Units completed and transferred to the mixing department	10,000	10,000
+ Equivalent units in ending work in process inventory:		
Materials: 1,000 units at 100% complete	1,000	
Conversion: 1,000 units at 60% complete		600
= Equivalent units of production	11,000	10,600

"Twinkie" Formula

Figure: Calculation of Equivalent Units of Production

sifted during the month. If on February 28 there were still 1,000 pounds of flour in the sifter, you can calculate that 10,000 pounds of flour must have been finished and transferred to the mixing department (here is the "Twinkie" formula again).

The 10,000 pounds that were transferred out must have been 100% complete, or they couldn't have been transferred to the mixing department. The 1,000 pounds that are left are partially complete. Assuming again that they are 100% complete with respect to direct materials (all the wheat is included) but only 60% completed through the sifting process (conversion costs), we would calculate equivalent units of 11,000 pounds for materials and 10,600 pounds for conversion costs, as illustrated in the figure below.

What is the second step in the weighted-average process costing method?

The second step in the weighted-average process costing method is to calculate the cost per equivalent unit in the department. This is done by taking the cost of the beginning work-in-process inventory plus the costs added during the period and dividing by the equivalent units of production calculated in step one. For example, assume the baking mix producer started February with 2,000 pounds of beginning work in process in the wheat processing department that cost $500 for direct materials and $400 for conversion costs (note: these would come from the ending work-in-process inventory calculation from January). During the month of February, an additional $2,160 of wheat was added to the sifting process, and $1,850 of conversion costs were added. When dividing the total costs by the equivalent units calculated in step one, the cost per equivalent unit would be $0.24 for direct materials and $0.21 for conversion costs. In total, the cost of the whole unit would be $0.45 per unit. This means that the baking mix manufacturer has spent roughly $0.45 per pound of flour in the first processing department. This is illustrated in the figure below.

Wheat Processing Department:	Units (pounds)	Direct Materials Cost	Conversion Cost	Total
Beginning work in process inventory	2,000	$ 500	$ 400	$ 900
+ Units started during February	9,000	$ 2,160	$ 1,850	$ 4,010
- Units completed and transferred to the mixing department	10,000	?	?	
= Ending work in process inventory	1,000	?	?	

Step 2: Calculate Cost Per Equivalent Unit

	Direct Materials Cost	Conversion Cost	Total
Costs of beginning work in process inventory	$ 500	$ 400	
+ costs added during February	$ 2,160	$ 1,850	
= Total costs for February	$ 2,660	$ 2,250	
/ Equivalent units of production	11,000	10,600	
= Cost per equivalent unit	$ 0.2418	$ 0.2123	$ 0.4541

What is the third step in the weighted-average process costing method?

The third step is to assign the costs for the month to a) the units completed and transferred to the next department and b) the units in ending work-in-process inventory. Essentially, we are filling in the question marks in the diagram above. This is calculated by taking the cost per equivalent unit multiplied by either the units completed or the equivalent units in ending inventory. The baking mix manufacturer would calculate the cost of direct materials completed and transferred to the mixing department at $2,418 and conversion costs completed and transferred to the mixing department at $2,123. The value of the ending work-in-process inventory would be calculated at $242 for direct materials and $127 for conversion costs, as illustrated in the diagram below.

Step 3: Calculate Cost of Ending Work In Process and Costs of Units Completed and Transferred Out

		Direct Materials Cost		Conversion Cost	Total
Cost per equivalent unit	$	0.2418	$	0.2123	
x Units completed and transferred to the mixing department		10,000		10,000	
= Cost of units completed and transferred out	$	2,418	$	2,123	$ 4,541
Cost per equivalent unit	$	0.2418	$	0.2123	
x Equivalent units in ending work in process inventory		1,000		600	
= Cost of units in ending work in process inventory	$	242	$	127	$ 369

What is the final step in the weighted-average process costing method?

The final step in the weighted-average process costing method is to prepare a cost reconciliation. This cost reconciliation shows the roll forward of the costs incurred during the month. The reconciliation is divided into two sections. The first section is entitled "Costs to be Accounted For." These are the costs that have accumulated in the processing department for the month. We start with the cost of beginning work-in-process inventory and add to it any additional costs for the month. For the baking mix producer, this would be the costs of the 2,000 pounds of flour that were on hand at the start of February plus the additional costs that were added during February. They started with costs of $900 and added an additional $4,010 during the month. Added together, the baking mix manufacturer has $4,910 of accumulated cost in the wheat processing department during February.

The second section of the cost reconciliation is entitled "Costs Accounted For." This section answers the question, "Where did the $4,910 of costs spent in the wheat processing department during February go?" The flour has either been completed and moved to the mixing department, or it is still being processed and is in ending work-in-process inventory. The total costs to be accounted for must be equal to the costs accounted for. After all, that is what the reconciliation is for: to ensure that costs incurred during the month have been appropriately split between the ending work-in-process inventory and the costs of goods completed and transferred out.

Step 4: Prepare a Cost Reconciliation

Costs to Be Accounted For:

Cost of beginning work in process inventory	$	900
+ Costs added during February	$	4,010
= Total costs to account for	$	4,910

Costs Accounted For:

Cost of units in ending work in process inventory	$	369
+ Costs of units completed and transferred out	$	4,541
= Total costs accounted for	$	4,910

How does the cost assignment work in subsequent departments?

The cost assignment works in the same manner for subsequent departments, except that subsequent departments also have to account for the costs transferred in from the previous department. For example, in the mixing department, the costs to be accounted for would include costs of beginning work-in-process inventory, the costs added during the month (additional ingredients, labor, and overhead), and the costs of the flour completed in the processing department and transferred in.

OTHER COSTING SYSTEMS

Are there other methods of cost accounting?

There are many methods of cost accounting besides job-order costing, activity-based costing, and process costing. Many companies use hybrid methods that combine aspects from each of the various cost accounting systems.

What are some of the other costing methods?

Other costing methods that companies might use include standard costing, direct costing, throughput costing, and target costing. These costing methods are typically discussed in more advanced cost accounting textbooks.

How does a company know which cost accounting method to use?

Companies must carefully evaluate their business processes to determine which costing method is right for them. The goal is to develop a cost accounting method that accurately allocates costs to cost objects (products, services, customers, etc.). Accountants must keep in mind the cost of maintaining the cost accounting system versus the benefits obtained from the cost accounting system. In addition, it may be necessary to periodically evaluate the cost accounting system to ensure it is still meeting the needs of the users.

WHY BUDGET?

What is a budget?

A budget is a detailed plan for the financial transactions of the business for a specific time period. Budgets typically include schedules to calculate future transactions and account balances. Those schedules generally roll up into one complete budget that culminates in a set of budgeted financial statements.

Why do organizations need a budget?

The budget provides a road map for organizations for the future. If you were going to take a trip across the country for vacation, most likely, you would use some sort of mapping system. The mapping system can get you there in the shortest amount of time by providing a direct route and perhaps even help you avoid traffic jams and construction. You wouldn't normally try to drive from Los Angeles, California, to New York, New York, just by getting in your car and heading east. This could lead to you getting lost or taking a bad route that ends up taking very long to get you to New York. The same is true for business. The budget helps organizations plan for the future and make educated decisions on the best way to move forward. Just like a mapping system can help you avoid traffic jams, a budget can help organizations find and correct problems before they arise.

What are the advantages of budgeting?

One of the main advantages of budgeting is that the act of preparing a budget forces members of the organization to make a plan for the future and to communicate their plans with each other. This helps make sure everyone is on the same page. Additionally, as discussed above, many roadblocks or "bottlenecks" are found when preparing the budget. For example, a future shortage of production workers could be uncovered when preparing the direct labor budget. If an organization can see that it will not have enough workers to meet customer demand, it can begin the hiring and training process early or make plans for overtime needed. Finally, if an organization has a budget, it can use that budget as a benchmark and compare actual results to budgeted amounts as part of the controlling process (ensuring results were achieved and making corrections, if needed).

Who is responsible for the budget?

The overall approval for the budget rests with the CEO. However, the accounting staff typically compiles the budget. This involves communicating with and getting input from various departments and combining the results into one complete master budget. The budget process typically goes through a series of revisions before getting final approval from the CEO.

How is the budget prepared?

Most accounting software packages have a budgeting function included. However, it is common for companies to utilize Microsoft Excel to create many of the supporting schedules that calculate the data for the master budget. Many of the accounting software packages have limited means of calculating budget amounts, such as increasing everything from the previous year by 10% or keeping last year's data as the current year's budget. As such, budgets are commonly prepared in Microsoft Excel and uploaded into the accounting software package.

What is a top-down budget?

A top-down budget is a budget that originates from upper management and is then pushed down to levels of lower management and supervision. This limited participation

---

For what time frame is the budget prepared?

Most budgets are prepared for the upcoming year. The yearly budget is typically broken down by month and by quarter. In many companies, the budgeting process is started at the end of the third quarter or the start of the fourth quarter. As it takes some time to prepare all the budget schedules and go through appropriate levels of revision, this process can take months to be finalized. Accordingly, rather than wait to prepare a yearly budget all at once, some organizations take part in continuous budgeting whereby the budget is prepared on a twelve-month rolling basis, and as each month ends, a new month is added to the end of the budget.

It is important to note that in order to prepare a master budget, you will also need the ending balance sheet data from the previous year. This may be difficult if the previous year has not ended yet (which is usually the case). As such, you may also have to prepare an updated budget for the last few months of the current year to estimate these numbers.

from lower management and supervisors can sometimes result in budgets that are inaccurate and/or lead to reduced employee morale, as lower-level managers must work with budget data given to them rather than being able to provide input. Many managers prefer to have a hand in the budgeting process and work to develop a self-imposed budget.

What is a self-imposed budget?

A self-imposed budget is a budget that is calculated and prepared by all levels of management. These managers work with their staff to develop realistic budget estimates that are then used to roll up into one combined master budget. There are several advantages of utilizing self-imposed budgets as opposed to top-down budgets. First, utilizing self-imposed budgets means that the budget will generally be more accurate, as front-line managers usually have more knowledge of the day-to-day operations of the business. Second, motivation will generally be higher as all levels of management will feel like they are valued members of the team as they provide feedback and insight into the budgeting process. Third, it is easier to hold managers accountable for self-imposed budgets than for top-down budgets, as managers do not have the excuse that the budget was unrealistic or inaccurate since they had a hand in preparing it.

Even though self-imposed budgets are prepared by all levels of management, they must still roll up into a master budget that meets the approval of the CEO. As such, managers do not always get exactly what they want in a self-imposed budget. Additionally, as managers are often held to budget amounts and evaluated based on their ability to meet or beat the budget, managers may intentionally try to pad the budget and add additional costs to the budget to ensure they can meet these goals. As such, upper-level managers should be aware of this tendency toward padding the budget and try to clear that out during the review process.

THE MASTER BUDGET

What is the master budget?

The master budget is the preparation of the budgeted balance sheet and income statement and all necessary supporting schedules. The supporting schedules for a manufacturing company typically include the sales budget, the schedule of expected cash collections, the production budget, the direct materials budget, the schedule of expected cash disbursements for direct materials, the direct labor budget, the manufacturing overhead budget, the ending finished goods inventory budget, the selling and administrative expense budget, and the cash budget. The budget schedules are typically prepared in the order listed, as information from certain budgets is needed in the preparation of other budgets.

What is the sales budget?

The sales budget is the first budget that is prepared and shows both sales in units and sales revenue in dollars. The sales budget drives all other budgets. For example, you can't possibly figure out how many units need to be produced until you know how many you are going to sell. The sales budget is typically prepared with the assistance of the sales managers and staff. The main formula for the sales budget is:

Sales in Units × Selling Price per Unit = Budgeted Sales Revenue

For example, assume there is a firm called Spicy Pickle Company that is preparing its master budget for the first quarter of 2020 (January, February, and March). Also assume Spicy Pickle Company sells its pickles by the jar to specialty grocery stores across the Midwest for $4.00 per jar. Spicy Pickle Company's sales team predicts the following unit sales for January through April of the upcoming year:

January: 10,000 jars
February: 12,000 jars
March: 13,000 jars
April: 11,000 jars

The sales budget for the first quarter would be calculated as follows:

Sales Budget

	Jan	Feb	Mar	Total
Sales in units	10,000	12,000	13,000	35,000
x Selling price per unit	$ 4.00	$ 4.00	$ 4.00	$ 4.00
= Total Budgeted Sales	$ 40,000.00	$ 48,000.00	$ 52,000.00	$ 140,000.00

What is the schedule of expected cash collections?

The schedule of expected cash collections shows when the cash is expected to be collected for credit sales made during the budget period. Remember that most companies make sales on credit and send their customers invoices for the amounts owed. Depending on the payment terms and collection history, the cash may not be collected for one to three months (or more) following the date of the sale. Accordingly, if a company makes a credit sale in January, it cannot assume that it will receive all that cash in January. The schedule of cash collections takes the budgeted sales revenue and spreads it across the months it will be collected in using historical collection data.

For example, assume the Spicy Pickle Company makes all sales on credit. From past experience, the company has learned that 40% of a month's sales are collected in the month of the sale, and the remaining 60% are collected in the month following the sale. Assume the balance in accounts receivable is $20,000 as of December 31, 2019, and is expected to be collected in full in January.

Spicy Pickle Company would take the budgeted sales revenue from each month in the sales budget and assume 40% would be collected that same month, and 60% would be collected the following month. For example, the January budgeted sales are $40,000. If it collects 40% of that in January, that would result in $16,000 collected in January, with the remaining $24,000 being collected in February. When you add the $16,000 cash collected in January from the January credit sales plus the $20,000 accounts receivable from December that will be collected in January, you get total cash collections in January of $36,000, as shown below. This pattern is repeated for every month to determine the cash collected each month. The schedule of expected cash collections for the first quarter is shown below:

Cash Collections

	Jan	Feb	Mar	Total
Accounts Receivable	$ 20,000.00			
January Sales:				
	$ 16,000.00			
		$ 24,000.00		
February Sales:				
		$ 19,200.00		
			$ 28,800.00	
March Sales:				
			$ 20,800.00	
Total	$ 36,000.00	$ 43,200.00	$ 49,600.00	$ 128,800.00

It is important to note that the remaining 60% of March sales that will not be collected until April would be recorded as the accounts receivable balance of $31,200 on the budgeted balance sheet for the first quarter.

What is the production budget?

In a manufacturing company, a production budget shows the units that will need to be produced each month in order to meet the demand. The budgeted units to be produced are the key driver in the other manufacturing budgets, such as the direct materials budget and the direct labor budget. The production budget is typically prepared with the assistance of the production managers and supervisors. The general formula for the production budget is:

Budgeted Sales (in units) + Desired Ending Inventory − Beginning Inventory = Required Production

Why don't the units of required production in the production budget match the budgeted sales units in the sales budget?

In order to avoid stock-outs (running out of inventory), companies generally prefer to have a small amount of extra inventory, called safety stock, on hand at the end of every month. As such, this extra inventory must be accounted for in the production budget. For example, if you are going to sell 1,000 units in January and you know you want to end the month with an extra 100 units on hand (safety stock), then you can see that you will need 1,100 units in total for January. However, just because you need 1,100 units for January doesn't mean that is how many units you will actually have to produce. For example, if you plan to end December with 200 units of safety stock on hand, then you will start January with those 200 units already on the shelves. Accordingly, since you need 1,100 units for January but already have 200 of them produced, you will only need to produce an additional 900 units in January. These 900 units that will be produced in January will serve as your starting point for the rest of the production budgets (direct materials, direct labor, etc.).

Going back to the Spicy Pickle Company example, assume Spicy Pickle Company is now preparing its production budget. Spicy Pickle Company requires an amount of safety stock equal to 10% of the following month's sales. Assume the ending inventory on December 31, 2019, was 800 jars.

The required production for January would be calculated as 10,000 jars of budget sales in units for January plus 10% of February's budgeted sales in jars (12,000 jars × 10% = 1,200 jars of safety stock). Accordingly, 11,200 jars are needed for January. However, Spicy Pickle Company is starting January with 800 jars on hand; therefore, it only needs to produce 10,400 jars in January (11,200 jars needed, less 800 jars on hand). Remember, the ending inventory from the previous month becomes the beginning inventory for the current month. The production budget for the Spicy Pickle Company for the first quarter is shown below.

	Production Budget			
	Jan	Feb	Mar	Total
Budgeted Unit Sales	10,000	12,000	13,000	35,000
+ Desired Ending Inventory	1,200	1,300	1,100	1,100
= Total Needs	11,200	13,300	14,100	36,100
- Beginning Inventory	800	1,200	1,300	800
= Required Production (jars)	10,400	12,100	12,800	35,300

Note that the total column for the quarter is unique. The desired ending inventory for the quarter in total is the same as the desired ending inventory for the last month of the quarter (March). The month of March ends on March 31. The first quarter also ends on March 31. Accordingly, when we are talking about the desired ending inventory for March and for the first quarter, we are referring to the safety stock we want to have on March 31, which happens to be 10% of April budgeted sales of 11,000 jars.

Likewise, the beginning inventory for the quarter matches the beginning inventory for the first month of the quarter (January). The month of January begins on January 1. The first quarter also begins on January 1. Accordingly, when we are talking about the beginning inventory for January and for the first quarter, we are referring to the safety stock we will have on January 1, which happens to be the 800 units on hand as of December 31. (Recall that the previous month's ending inventory becomes the current month's beginning inventory. If we have 800 units on hand at 11:59 P.M. on December 31, we will likely still have those same 800 units on hand at 12:00 A.M. on January 1).

What is the direct materials budget?

Once a manufacturing company has prepared the production budget and determined how many units it must produce, the next step in the process is to calculate the amount of direct materials purchases required in order to produce the product. The direct materials budget is used to calculate the amount of direct materials that must be purchased to meet the required production needs. The direct materials budget is similar to the production budget in that beginning and ending inventory must be accounted for. Just as Spicy Pickle Company required safety stock of jars of pickles on hand at the end of each month, it will also require a safety stock of the direct materials (cucumbers, in this case), as it will not want to run out of cucumbers if there is a problem with a supplier, a late delivery, etc. The formula for the direct materials budget is:

Required Production in Units × Quantity of Direct Materials per Unit = Production Needs

Then:

Production Needs + Desired Ending Inventory − Beginning Inventory = Total Direct Materials to be Purchased

Then:

Total Direct Materials to be Purchased × Cost per Unit = Total Cost of Direct Materials

Recall that this is the direct materials budget, not a finished goods budget. As such, for Spicy Pickle Company, we are calculating the number and cost of cucumbers, not jars of pickles. Accordingly, the first step of the direct materials budget requires converting jars of pickles into quantity of cucumbers.

For example, assume six cucumbers are required for each jar of pickles. Management prefers to have 5% of the following month's cucumber needs on hand at the end of each month. Cucumbers cost $0.10 each. The company will have 4,000 cucumbers on hand at the end of December 2019 and expects to have 3,000 on hand as of March 31, 2020.

The cost of cucumbers for January would be calculated by converting the required production in January from the production budget of 10,400 jars of pickles into the amount of cucumbers needed for those jars. If each jar requires 6 cucumbers, then we can determine that 10,400 jars of pickles × 6 cucumbers each = 62,400 cucumbers needed for the January production. However, if Spicy Pickle Company also wants 5% of February's cucumber needs on hand in January, then the next step would be to calculate the number of cucumbers needed for February. February's required production is 12,100 jars of pickles, so 12,100 jars of pickles × 6 cucumbers each = 72,600 cucumbers needed for February production. Accordingly, at the end of January, the company will want 3,630 extra cucumbers on hand (72,600 × 5%). In total, it will need the 62,400 cucumbers necessary to meet the January production requirements plus the extra 3,630 cucumbers, which equals 66,030 cucumbers needed for January. However, just because it needs 66,030 cucumbers for January does not mean it will have to purchase 66,030 cucumbers in January because it is starting January with 4,000 cucumbers on hand. (Recall that December's ending inventory of cucumbers becomes January's beginning inventory of cucumbers.) Accordingly, it will only need to purchase 62,030 cucumbers in January (66,030 − 4,000 = 62,030). Since cucumbers cost $0.10 each, Spicy Pickle Company will need to spend $6,203 on cucumbers in January. The direct materials budget for the first quarter is shown below:

Direct Materials Budget

	Jan	Feb	Mar	Total
Required Production (jars)	10,400	12,100	12,800	35,300
x cucumbers per jar	6	6	6	6
Production needs	62,400	72,600	76,800	211,800
+ Desired Ending Inventory	3,630	3,840	3,000	3,000
= Total Needs	66,030	76,440	79,800	214,800
- Beginning Inventory	4,000	3,630	3,840	4,000
Total DM purchases (cucs)	62,030	72,810	75,960	210,800
x cost per cucumber	$ 0.10	$ 0.10	$ 0.10	$ 0.10
Total cost of DM	$ 6,203.00	$ 7,281.00	$ 7,596.00	$ 21,080.00

Just as with the production budget, notice that the total column for the quarter is unique. The desired ending inventory for the quarter is the same as the desired ending inventory for the last month of the quarter (March). The month of March ends on March 31. The first quarter also ends on March 31. Accordingly, when we are talking about the desired ending inventory for March and for the first quarter, we are referring to the extra cucumbers we want to have on March 31, which happens to be given in the example of 3,000 cucumbers.

Likewise, the beginning inventory for the quarter in total matches the beginning inventory for the first month of the quarter (January). The month of January begins on January 1. The first quarter also begins on January 1. Accordingly, when we are talking about the beginning inventory for January and for the first quarter, we are referring to the extra cucumbers we will have on January 1, which happens to be the 4,000 units on hand as of December 31.

What is the purpose of the schedule of expected cash disbursements for direct materials?

While the direct materials budget tells you the cost of direct materials purchased for each month, it does not tell you when you will actually pay the cash for those purchases. As such, in order to determine when the cash will be paid for direct materials, you must prepare a schedule of expected cash disbursements.

The schedule of expected cash disbursements for direct materials shows when cash is expected to be paid for direct materials purchases made during the budget period. Remember that most companies make sales on credit and send their customers invoices for the amounts owed. Depending on the payment terms, the cash may not be paid for one to three months (or more) following the date of the sale. Accordingly, if a company makes a purchase in January, it cannot assume it will pay all that cash in January. The schedule of cash disbursements takes the budgeted direct materials purchases and spreads it across the months it will be paid in using historical payment data. (Note that this process is identical to the schedule of cash collections.)

For example, assume that Spicy Pickle Company's direct material purchases are paid for in the following pattern: 50% paid in the month the purchases are made, with the remaining 50% paid in the following month. Also assume that the accounts payable balance on December 31, 2019, of $3,000 is expected to be paid in full in January 2020.

Spicy Pickle Company would then take the budgeted cost of direct materials from each month in the direct materials budget and assume 50% would be paid that same month, and 50% would be paid the following month. For example, the January budgeted direct materials costs are $6,203. If it pays 50% of that in January, that would result in $3,101.50 paid in January and the remaining $3,101.50 being paid in February. When you add the $3,101.50 cash paid in January from the January purchases plus the $3,000 accounts payable from December that should be paid in January, you get total cash paid for direct materials in January of $6,101.50, as shown below. This pattern is repeated for every month to determine the cash paid each month. The schedule of cash disbursements for direct materials for the first quarter is shown below:

	Jan	Feb	Mar	Total
		Cash Disbursements		
Accounts Payable	$ 3,000.00			
January Purchases:				
	$ 3,101.50			
		$ 3,101.50		
February Purchases:				
		$ 3,640.50		
			$ 3,640.50	
March Purchases:				
			$ 3,798.00	
Total	$ 6,101.50	$ 6,742.00	$ 7,438.50	$ 20,282.00

It is important to note that the remaining 50% of March purchases that will not be paid until April would be recorded as the accounts payable balance of $3,798 on the budgeted balance sheet for the first quarter.

What is the direct labor budget?

The direct labor budget calculates the cost of wages paid for direct labor during the budget period. The direct labor budget is based off of the required production budget. Once you know how many units you are going to produce, you can multiply the units to be produced by the amount of time it takes to produce each unit. That will tell you the total direct labor hours needed for each month. In order to calculate the cost of direct labor, you simply multiply the direct labor hours needed by the average hourly wage paid to direct labor workers. The formula for the direct labor budget is:

Required Production in Units × Direct Labor Hours per Unit × Direct Labor Wage per Hour = Total Direct Labor Cost

For example, assume that the Spicy Pickle Company pays direct labor workers $9 per hour and that each jar of pickles requires 0.05 hours (3 minutes) of direct labor. The January direct labor cost would be calculated by taking the required production of 10,400 jars × 0.05 hours per jar, totaling 520 direct labor hours for the month. At a wage rate of $9 per hour, that equals a total direct labor cost of $4,680 for January. The direct labor budget for the first quarter is shown below:

Direct Labor Budget

	Jan	Feb	Mar	Total
Required Production (jars)	10,400	12,100	12,800	35,300
x Direct Labor time per jar	0.05	0.05	0.05	0.05
= Total DL hours needed	520	605	640	1765
x DL cost per hour	$ 9.00	$ 9.00	$ 9.00	$ 9.00
Total Direct Labor cost	$ 4,680.00	$ 5,445.00	$ 5,760.00	$ 15,885.00

What is the manufacturing overhead budget?

The manufacturing overhead budget calculates the budgeted cost of both fixed and variable overhead during the budget period. Recall that manufacturing overhead includes things such as indirect labor (production supervisors, etc.), indirect materials (spices, etc.), and other manufacturing costs (rent on the production facility, etc.). The variable items are typically calculated based on a cost driver such as direct labor hours, etc. The fixed items are based on the typical monthly amount charged. Once the fixed and variable overheads are calculated, the two are added together to get total overhead cost. However, there are certain items included in overhead that do not result in an outflow of cash and, as such, should be subtracted from the total overhead cost in order to arrive at the cash payments for overhead each month that will be used on the cash budget. Specifically, depreciation on the manufacturing facility and manufacturing equipment would be charged to overhead. However, depreciation does not represent a cash outflow at that time, as discussed in the chapter entitled "Specific Accounting Issues." Accordingly, depreciation is subtracted from the total overhead cost in order to determine the cash payments for overhead that will show up on the cash budget.

For example, assume that Spicy Pickle Company uses a variable manufacturing overhead rate of $3.25 per direct labor hour to budget variable overhead. The fixed overhead rate is $4,000 per month, of which $500 is depreciation.

The variable overhead for January would be calculated by taking the $3.25 per direct labor hour times the 520 direct labor hours needed for January (as computed on the direct labor budget), resulting in total variable overhead of $1,690 for January. When added to the fixed overhead of $4,000, the resulting total budgeted overhead for January is $5,690. However, in order to arrive at the cash spent for overhead during January, the $500 of depreciation must be subtracted, resulting in cash disbursements for overhead of $5,190. The manufacturing overhead budget for the first quarter is shown below:

Manufacturing Overhead Budget

	Jan	Feb	Mar	Total
Budgeted DL hours	520	605	640	1765
x Variable OH rate	$ 3.25	$ 3.25	$ 3.25	$ 3.25
= Variable OH	$ 1,690.00	$ 1,966.25	$ 2,080.00	$ 5,736.25
+ Fixed OH	$ 4,000.00	$ 4,000.00	$ 4,000.00	$ 12,000.00
= Total OH	$ 5,690.00	$ 5,966.25	$ 6,080.00	$ 17,736.25
- Depreciation	$ 500.00	$ 500.00	$ 500.00	$ 1,500.00
= Cash disbursement for OH	$ 5,190.00	$ 5,466.25	$ 5,580.00	$ 16,236.25

What is the purpose of the ending finished goods inventory budget?

The ending finished goods inventory budget is used to compute the value of ending inventory shown on the budgeted balance sheet. In addition, the ending finished goods inventory budget also calculates the cost per unit of product, which is used in calculating cost of goods sold on the budgeted income statement. The unit product cost is calculated by adding up the three product costs: direct materials, direct labor, and overhead. The unit product cost is then multiplied by the units of ending inventory predicted in the production budget to determine the value of ending inventory shown on the budgeted balance sheet.

For example, recall that Spicy Pickle Company uses six cucumbers per jar of pickles and pays $0.10 per cucumber. The cost of direct materials per jar is then calculated as $0.60. Also recall that it takes 0.05 hours of direct labor to make one jar of pickles, and direct labor workers are paid $9.00 per hour. As such, the cost of direct labor per jar of pickles is $0.45. Calculating the overhead per jar requires a little more effort. By looking at the manufacturing overhead budget for the first quarter, you can see that the total overhead for the quarter was budgeted at $17,736.25. Since overhead is allocated based on direct labor hours and there are a total of 1,765 direct labor hours budgeted for the first quarter, you can divide the total overhead cost by the total direct labor hours to compute a budgeted total overhead rate (or POHR, as discussed in the chapter entitled "Cost Accounting Basics") of $10.05 per direct labor hour. Again, since each jar of pickles requires 0.05 direct labor hours, you can compute a total overhead per jar of pickles of roughly $0.50. You can then add the three product costs together to get a total product cost of approximately $1.55 per jar of pickles. The production budget shows

211

a desired ending inventory of 1,100 jars of pickles. As such, you can multiply 1,100 jars by a cost of $1.5524 per jar to compute the value of ending inventory as of March 31 of $1,707.69 for the budgeted balance sheet for the quarter. The ending finished goods inventory budget calculation is shown below:

Production Costs per Jar:	Qty	Cost	Total
DM (cucumbers)	6	$ 0.10	$ 0.6000
DL	0.05	$ 9.00	$ 0.4500
OH	0.05	$ 10.05	$ 0.5024
= Unit Product Cost			$ 1.5524

Budgeted finished goods inventory:	
Ending Inventory in Jars	1,100
x Unit Product Cost	$ 1.5524
= Ending finished goods inventory	$ 1,707.69

What is the selling and administrative expense budget?

The selling and administrative expense budget calculates the budgeted cost of both fixed and variable selling and administrative expenses to be incurred during the budget period. Recall that selling costs includes things such as sales wages, sales commissions, advertising, etc. Administrative expenses include things like rent on the corporate headquarters, wages of administrative employees, etc. The variable items are typically calculated based on units sold from the sales budget. The fixed items are based on the typical monthly amount charged. Once the fixed and variable selling and administrative expenses are calculated, the two are added together to get total cost. However, there are certain items included in the selling and administrative expense budget that do not result in an outflow of cash and, as such, should be subtracted from the total cost in order to arrive at the cash payments for selling and administrative expenses each month that will be used on the cash budget. Specifically, depreciation on the headquarters and administrative assets would be charged to administrative expenses. However, depreciation does not represent a cash outflow at that time, as discussed in the chapter entitled "Specific Accounting Issues." Accordingly, depreciation is subtracted from the total cost in order to determine the cash payments for selling and administrative expenses that will show up on the cash budget.

For example, assume that for Spicy Pickle Company, the variable selling and administrative cost is $0.10 per jar sold. The fixed selling and administrative cost is $8,000 per month, of which $800 is related to depreciation.

The variable selling and administrative cost for January would be calculated by taking the $0.10 per jar times the 10,000 jars of budgeted unit sales for January, resulting in total variable selling and administrative cost of $1,000 for January. When added to the fixed selling and administrative cost of $8,000, the resulting total budgeted selling and administrative cost for January is $9,000. However, in order to arrive at the cash spent for selling and administrative expenses during January, the $800 of depreciation must be subtracted, resulting in cash disbursements for selling and administrative expenses of $8,200. The selling and administrative expenses budget for the first quarter is shown below:

Selling & Administrative Expense Budget

	Jan	Feb	Mar	Total
Budgeted Sales (units)	10,000	12,000	13,000	35,000
x Variable rate	$ 0.10	$ 0.10	$ 0.10	$ 0.10
= Variable Selling & Admin	$ 1,000.00	$ 1,200.00	$ 1,300.00	$ 3,500.00
+ Fixed Selling & Admin	$ 8,000.00	$ 8,000.00	$ 8,000.00	$ 24,000.00
= Total Selling & Admin	$ 9,000.00	$ 9,200.00	$ 9,300.00	$ 27,500.00
- Depreciation	$ 800.00	$ 800.00	$ 800.00	$ 2,400.00
= Cash disbursement for S&A	$ 8,200.00	$ 8,400.00	$ 8,500.00	$ 25,100.00

How is the cash budget prepared?

After all of the budgeted schedules in the master budget have been completed, the cash budget can be prepared. There are four basic sections of the cash budget.

The first section is used to compute the total cash that will be available to spend during the period. This is computed by taking the beginning cash balance (from the prior period's ending balance) and adding in the expected cash collections for the period from the schedule of expected cash collections.

The second section is used to compute the total cash that will be paid out during the period. This is computed by taking the cash payments for direct materials from the schedule of expected cash disbursements for direct materials, plus the total direct labor cost from the direct labor budget, plus the cash cost for overhead from the manufacturing overhead budget, plus the cash cost for selling and administrative expenses from the selling and administrative expenses budget. Additionally, this section also includes any other cash outlays that may be included in other budget schedules not covered in this chapter, such as purchases of equipment, payment of dividends, etc.

The third section is used to compute a cash excess or deficiency and is merely the difference between the cash available and the cash disbursements. If the cash available is less than the cash disbursements for the period, a deficiency (negative balance) will result. This would signal potential trouble and alert the company to the need for possible financing arrangements.

The fourth section is used to compute any financing necessary for the period. Certainly, if section three computes a deficiency of cash, financing will be needed. Additionally, some companies require a minimum cash balance that can be used in case of emergencies or budget shortfalls. If there is an excess of cash that happens to be smaller than the required minimum cash balance, this would also signify a need for financing. Accordingly, this fourth section shows any loans that need to be taken, any repayments that can be made, and the corresponding interest payments to the bank for the loans.

The ending cash balance is then computed by taking the excess or deficiency of cash plus or minus any borrowings or repayments of loans. The ending cash balance from each period becomes the beginning cash balance for the next period.

For example, assume Spicy Pickle Company has a beginning cash balance on January 1, 2020, of $40,000. The company requires a minimum bank balance of $30,000 at the end of each month. The company maintains a $100,000 12% line of credit with the bank. The company borrows money on the first day of the month and repays on the last day of the month. Spicy Pickle Company intends to pay dividends of $17,161.60 in February. In addition, it intends to purchase a new labeling machine in January for $29,828.50 in cash.

The cash budget for the first quarter is shown below:

Cash Budget

	Jan	Feb	Mar	Total
Beginning Cash Balance	$ 40,000.00	$ 30,000.00	$ 30,000.00	$ 40,000.00
+ Cash Receipts	$ 36,000.00	$ 43,200.00	$ 49,600.00	$ 128,800.00
= Total Cash Available	$ 76,000.00	$ 73,200.00	$ 79,600.00	$ 168,800.00
Less Disbursements:				
Direct Materials	$ 6,101.50	$ 6,742.00	$ 7,438.50	$ 20,282.00
Direct Labor	$ 4,680.00	$ 5,445.00	$ 5,760.00	$ 15,885.00
Overhead	$ 5,190.00	$ 5,466.25	$ 5,580.00	$ 16,236.25
Selling & Admin	$ 8,200.00	$ 8,400.00	$ 8,500.00	$ 25,100.00
Dividends		$ 17,161.60		$ 17,161.60
Equipment Purchases	$ 29,828.50			$ 29,828.50
Total Disbursements	$ 54,000.00	$ 43,214.85	$ 27,278.50	$ 124,493.35
Excess or (Deficiency)	$ 22,000.00	$ 29,985.15	$ 52,321.50	$ 44,306.65
Financing:				
Borrowings	$ 8,000.00	$ 14.85		$ 8,014.85
Repayments			$ (8,014.85)	$ (8,014.85)
Interest			$ (240.30)	$ (240.30)
Total Financing	$ 8,000.00	$ 14.85	$ (8,255.15)	$ (240.30)
Ending Cash Balance	$ 30,000.00	$ 30,000.00	$ 44,066.35	$ 44,066.35

Note that in January, the excess of cash will be $22,000, which is less than the minimum cash balance required of $30,000. As such, Spicy Pickle Company can project that it will need to borrow $8,000 on January 1. Likewise, the February excess of cash of $29,985.15 is also below the minimum required balance, so another $14.85 will need to be borrowed. The March excess of cash of $52,321.50 is $22,321.50 greater than the minimum required balance. As such, Spicy Pickle Company can project that it will be able to pay the entire outstanding balance of its loans of $8,014.85 plus the interest owed of $240.30 on March 31 and still have more than enough cash to meet the requirement.

Also note that the formula for interest in this case is:

Amount Borrowed $\times$ Annual Interest Rate $\times$ Fraction of Year Outstanding $=$ Interest

In this case, $8,000 was borrowed for three months (January 1 through March 31) at an annual rate of 12%. Accordingly, the interest owed on the $8,000 would be calculated as follows:

$8,000 $\times$ .12 $\times$ 3/12 $=$ $240

Additionally, the interest on the $14.85 that was borrowed for two months (February 1 through March 31) would be calculated as follows:

$14.85 $\times$ .12 $\times$ 2/12 $=$ $0.30 (rounded)

As such, the total interest owed and paid on March 31 would be $240.30.

The ending cash balance on the cash budget is then used as the cash balance for the first quarter budgeted balance sheet.

How is the budgeted income statement prepared?

The budgeted income statement, like the cash budget, pulls information from the various schedules of the master budget. In general, the budgeted income statement starts with the budgeted sales dollars from the sales budget. Cost of goods sold is then subtracted from sales in arriving at gross profit. The cost of goods sold calculation comes from multiplying the cost per unit (as calculated in the ending finished goods inventory budget) by the units sold. Selling and administrative expenses are then deducted in arriving at operating income. Note that the selling and administrative expenses are pulled from the total selling and administrative expenses on the selling and administrative expenses budget, not the cash cost for selling and administrative expenses that is used on the cash budget. Finally, interest expense (as calculated in the cash budget) and any income tax expense calculated would be subtracted in order to arrive at net income for the budget period.

The budgeted income statement for the first quarter is shown below. (Note that, for simplicity, this example does not include income tax expense.)

How is the budgeted balance sheet prepared?

The budgeted balance sheet is the last budgeted financial statement that is prepared, as it pulls information from every other budget schedule and budgeted financial statement.

For example, assume that Spicy Pickle Company has the following balances on December 31, 2019:

Equipment: $300,000

Common Stock: $350,000

Retained Earnings: $12,541.95

The income statement and budgeted balance sheet for the first quarter of 2020 is shown below:

Spicy Pickle Company
Budgeted Income Statement
For the Quarter Ending Mar 31, 2020

Sales	$	140,000.00
- COGS	$	54,335.52
= Gross Profit	$	85,664.48
- Selling & Admin Expenses	$	27,500.00
= Operating Income	$	58,164.48
- Interest Expense	$	240.30
= Income before Tax	$	57,924.19

Spicy Pickle Company
Budgeted Balance Sheet
As of March 31, 2020

Current Assets:		
Cash	$	44,066.35
Accounts Receivable		31,200.00
Raw Materials Inventory		300.00
Finished Goods Inventory		1,707.69
Total Current Assets	$	77,274.04
Property and Equipment:		
Equipment	$	329,828.50
Total Assets	$	407,102.54
Liabilities & Equity:		
Accounts Payable	$	3,798.00
Common Stock		350,000.00
Retained Earnings		53,304.54
Total Liabilities & Equity	$	407,102.54

The cash balance comes from the ending cash balance on the cash budget. The accounts receivable balance was computed after preparing the schedule of expected cash collections. The raw materials inventory represents the cost of extra cucumbers on hand as of March 31 (3,000 cucumbers $\times$ $0.10 each). The finished goods inventory is pulled from the finished goods inventory budget. Each of those are added together to compute total current assets of $77,274.04.

The equipment balance of $329,828.50 is the sum of the beginning equipment balance from December 31, 2019, of $300,000 plus the $29,828.50 of new equipment purchases noted in the cash budget. (Note that, for simplicity, this example does not include depreciation on the new equipment purchase.) The equipment is added to the current assets in arriving at total assets of $407,102.54.

The accounts payable balance was computed after preparing the schedule of expected cash disbursements for direct materials. The common stock has not changed from the beginning balance, as there were no changes to common stock in this example. Finally, the ending balance in retained earnings can be computed using the formula given in the chapter entitled "Four Basic Financial Statements":

Beginning Balance, Retained Earnings + Net Income − Dividends = Ending Balance, Retained Earnings

In this case, the beginning balance in retained earnings was given as $12,541.95. Net income from the budgeted income statement was $57.924.19. Dividends as noted in the cash budget were $17,161.60. Accordingly, the ending balance in retained earnings as shown on the budgeted balance sheet would be $53,304.54.

Recall that total liabilities and equity of $407,102.54 must be equal to the total assets, or there has been an error somewhere that must be fixed.

FLEXIBLE BUDGETS

What does control mean in accounting?

Controlling is the regular and ongoing process of gathering information to ensure the plan is being achieved. It would not make sense to go through the planning process and

How is a flexible budget different from a static budget?

A flexible budget uses the same assumptions as a static budget. The only difference between the two is the quantity of units sold. Accordingly, Spicy Pickle Company would still use $4.00 per jar to calculate budgeted revenue and costs of $1.55 per jar to calculate cost of goods sold. However, instead of multiplying by the 10,000 jars budgeted for January, it would multiply by the 15,000 jars actually sold in January.

prepare a budget without also taking the time to see if the plans were accomplished. During the controlling process, actual results are compared to both the static (master) budget and flexible budget to determine favorable and unfavorable variances to the planned results. If variances are favorable, the controlling process will aim to determine what caused the variance and how those results can be repeated in the future. If variances are unfavorable, the controlling process will aim to determine what the root cause of the problem was in order to avoid that problem in the future.

What is a flexible budget?

A flexible budget is a budget that estimates revenues and costs based off of the actual quantity of goods sold. For example, in the master budget for Spicy Pickle Company, it budgeted January sales of 10,000 jars of pickles. Recall that the entire master budget was all calculated based upon that number, as every budget schedule builds upon the previous schedules. If January rolls around and Spicy Pickle Company actually sold 15,000 jars of pickles instead of the 10,000 jars budgeted, you would expect the actual results to be quite different from the budgeted results. Accordingly, a flexible budget can be prepared using the same assumptions as the original budget, but using the actual quantity of 15,000 jars sold instead of 10,000, to help identify variances due to nonvolume-related issues.

Is a flexible budget better than a static budget?

In many ways, a flexible budget is better than a static budget when used for controlling purposes. The flexible budget gives the reader an "apples to apples" comparison of data, whereas the static budget gives the reader an "apples to oranges" comparison of data. For example, if Spicy Pickle Company actually sold 15,000 jars in January, you would expect every item on the income statement to be larger than the static budget because it sold 50% more jars of pickles than expected. If it sells more pickles, revenue should be higher. Additionally, most costs (certainly the variable costs) should be higher as well. In this way, it is hard to compare a static budget to actual results without having the same answer of "Well, costs are higher because we sold more pickles" and "Revenue is higher because we sold more pickles." What if revenue for January was actually $52,500 versus the budgeted revenue of $40,000? A quick comparison of the actual revenue to the static budget would reveal that revenue was $12,500 higher than expected. It would be easy to say, "That seems right since we sold more jars of pickles than expected." However, if you dig a little deeper, you can see that revenue of $52,500 for selling 15,000 jars of pickles means that, on average, each jar was sold for $3.50. This may indicate a problem, as Spicy Pickle Company had budgeted each jar at $4.00. This is where the utilization of a flexible budget can be very helpful in identifying the variances that are unrelated to changes in the volume of sales.

How is a static budget used to control costs?

At the end of each accounting period, managers typically compare actual results to the static budget (master budget) to determine how well the company performed in comparison to what was expected. This is a useful benchmarking tool, even if it may not be as informative in determining the cause of the variances as a flexible budget is. For example, it would be useful information for Spicy Pickle Company to know that it had planned on revenue of $40,000 for January but actually came in at $52,500.

How is a flexible budget used to control costs?

A flexible budget is used in the same way as a static budget in that it is compared to the actual results of a period to determine how well a company performed. However, as mentioned previously, the flexible budget is recalculated based on the actual level of activity, giving a more useful comparison in determining cost control.

What does a flexible budget performance report look like?

An example of a flexible budget performance report is shown below. It is important to note that there isn't one set format that is required, as with managerial accounting, since reports can be tailored to meet the needs of users. As such, this is just one example of what one might look like. In the example provided below, you can see that the static budget data was provided as a reference for the users, but no variances were calculated based off the static budget. The flexible budget was prepared using the same formulas as the static budget; however, the actual volume of jars sold was used in the formulas instead of the budgeted volume of jars. The final column of the budget calculates the differences between the flexible budget and the actual results, known as revenue and spending variances.

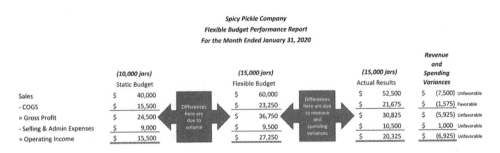

Spicy Pickle Company
Flexible Budget Performance Report
For the Month Ended January 31, 2020

	(10,000 jars) Static Budget		(15,000 jars) Flexible Budget		(15,000 jars) Actual Results	Revenue and Spending Variances
Sales	$ 40,000		$ 60,000		$ 52,500	$ (7,500) Unfavorable
- COGS	$ 15,500	Differences here are due to volume	$ 23,250	Differences here are due to revenue and spending variances	$ 21,675	$ (1,575) Favorable
= Gross Profit	$ 24,500		$ 36,750		$ 30,825	$ (5,925) Unfavorable
- Selling & Admin Expenses	$ 9,000		$ 9,500		$ 10,500	$ 1,000 Unfavorable
= Operating Income	$ 15,500		$ 27,250		$ 20,325	$ (6,925) Unfavorable

What is a revenue variance?

Revenue variances are variances that are caused by charging a different price for goods or services than what was budgeted. Revenue variances are favorable when revenue is higher than anticipated and unfavorable when revenue is lower than anticipated. In the case of Spicy Pickle Company, January resulted in an unfavorable revenue variance of $7,500, meaning that revenue was $7,500 less than what it should have been based upon the budget. Recall that a flexible budget adjusts for changes in volume, so the flexible budget revenue is based on selling the actual quantity of 15,000 jars. As such, the lower-than-anticipated revenue is not caused by selling fewer jars of pickles. Accordingly, it must mean jars were sold for less than the budgeted price of $4.00 per jar.

219

A good accountant would investigate this discrepancy by reviewing prices on invoices and/or questioning the sales team about pricing. If it is determined that the lower price will be charged going forward, then budget assumptions must be updated for the future and the reason for the variance should be noted in the management report. If it is determined that the lower price was due to something temporary, such as a special offer to customers or a sale of excess inventory at a discounted price, then this should be noted in the management report as the reason for the variance and include commentary that this is not expected to recur in the future.

It is also worth noting that the static budget planned for $40,000 of revenue in January, and the actual results were $52,500. This $12,500 favorable variance to the static budget can now be explained as an increase in sales revenue due to volume (selling 5,000 more jars than originally planned) that was partially offset by lower-than-anticipated prices charged to customers, as discussed above.

What is a spending variance?

Spending variances are variances that are caused by incurring expenses that are greater than or less than anticipated on the flexible budget. Spending variances are favorable when expenses are less than anticipated and unfavorable when expenses are greater than anticipated. In the case of Spicy Pickle Company, January resulted in a favorable spending variance for cost of goods sold expense, as cost of goods sold was $1,575 less than anticipated in the flexible budget. Recall that a flexible budget adjusts for changes in volume, so the flexible budget cost of goods sold is based on selling the actual quantity of 15,000 jars. As such, the lower-than-anticipated expense was not caused by selling fewer jars of pickles. Accordingly, it must mean the cost of manufacturing each jar was less than the budgeted cost of $1.55 per jar.

A good accountant would investigate this discrepancy by reviewing the manufacturing costs (direct materials, direct labor, and overhead) and preparing a standard cost variance analysis, as covered later in this chapter. If it is determined that the lower cost will be incurred going forward, then budget assumptions must be updated for the future, and the cause of the variance should be noted in the management report. If it is determined that the lower cost was due to something temporary, such as a one-time special offer on cucumber purchases, then this should be noted in the management report as the reason for the variance and include commentary that this is not expected to recur in the future.

It is also worth noting that the static budget planned for $15,500 of cost of goods sold expense in January, and the actual results were $21,675. This $6,175 unfavorable variance to the static budget can now be explained as being caused by an increase in volume (selling 5,000 more jars than originally planned) that was partially offset by a lower-than-anticipated cost per jar, as discussed above. It is obvious to an informed reader that if sales are higher than anticipated, most expenses should also be higher. However, in this case, the increased expense was partially offset by cost reductions per jar. The flexible budget helps highlight this good news that might otherwise be lost if only a static budget were prepared.

STANDARD COSTS AND VARIANCES

What is a standard cost?

A standard cost represents the benchmark for manufacturing costs per unit of product. Companies typically compute standard costs for direct materials, direct labor, and variable manufacturing overhead. These standards are used in the budgeting process to estimate total manufacturing costs as well as in the controlling process in the calculation of variances. Companies typically prepare a standard cost card for each product that shows both the quantity and dollar amount for each variable manufacturing cost. For example, assume Spicy Pickle Company has determined the following standard variable costs to manufacture one jar of pickles and has prepared a standard cost card, shown below. (Note that this data was used in the completion of the master budget.)

Standard Costs per Jar:	Qty	Cost	Total
DM (cucumbers)	6	$ 0.10	$ 0.6000
DL	0.05	$ 9.00	$ 0.4500
Variable OH	0.05	$ 3.25	$ 0.1625
= Standard Variable Product Cost per Jar			$ 1.2125

From the standard cost card, you can see that each jar of pickles should take 6 cucumbers, at a cost of $0.10 per cucumber, resulting in $0.60 of direct materials per jar. Each jar of pickles should require 0.05 hours of direct labor at an average pay rate of $9.00 per hour, resulting in $0.45 of direct labor per jar. Finally, Spicy Pickle Company uses a variable overhead rate of $3.25 per jar of pickles, using direct labor hours as a cost driver. Accordingly, the same 0.05 hours of direct labor is used as the standard quantity per jar for a total variable overhead of approximately $0.16 per jar. Note that the fixed overhead of $4,000 per month is not included on the standard cost card, as that is a fixed cost, which would not be expected to change based upon the number of jars of pickles manufactured.

How are standard costs determined?

Standard costs are determined in coordination with the various members of the engineering, development, production, and purchasing departments. Time and labor studies can be conducted to determine standard times and rates. It is important to note that the accountant cannot set the standard costs without data and assistance from other departments.

What is standard cost variance analysis?

A standard cost variance analysis breaks up the spending variance into two primary components: price and quantity. For example, the cost of goods sold favorable spending variance of $1,575 for Spicy Pickle Company can be researched further. Recall that cost of

221

goods sold is made up of total manufacturing costs, including direct materials, direct labor, and variable overhead. In order to better understand the reason for the variance (why the cost per jar of pickles was lower than anticipated), that spending variance can be analyzed by preparing a cost variance analysis on each manufacturing cost.

The direct materials variance analysis will tell Spicy Pickle Company if it used more or less direct materials (cucumbers) per jar of pickles than the standard and if it paid more or fewer per unit of direct materials (cucumbers) than the standard. The direct labor variance analysis will tell Spicy Pickle Company if the production workers worked more or fewer hours than anticipated and if they were paid more or less than the standard per hour. Likewise, the variable overhead variance analysis will tell Spicy Pickle Company if it spent more on indirect materials, indirect labor, and other variable overhead items.

This level of in-depth analysis helps provide much greater detail and insight into the spending variance, which can improve the operations of the business and provide better results in the future if corrections are made based upon findings.

What is the formula for standard cost variances?

The basic formula for standard cost variances is as follows:

$(AQ \times AP) - (AQ \times SP)$ = Price Variance

and

$(AQ \times SP) - (SQ \times SP)$ = Quantity Variance

These basic formulas can be illustrated using the basic model shown below:

Basic Model for Calculating Standard Cost Variances:

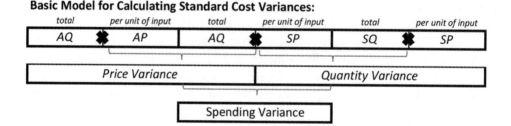

Note that when calculating variances for direct materials, the words "price" and "quantity" are used. However, when discussing variances for direct labor and variable overhead, the word "rate" is used instead of "price" (we pay a wage rate, not a price), and the word "efficiency" is used instead of "quantity." They mean the same things, but the vocabulary is adjusted.

What is AQ?

AQ represents the actual quantity of units of input in total. For example, the actual quantity for direct materials for Spicy Pickle Company is the number of cucumbers used for the month, not the number of jars of pickles. Remember, this is for direct materials, not finished goods. The actual quantity for direct labor is the actual number of hours worked in total for the month. Since variable overhead is based on direct labor hours in this example, the actual quantity for variable overhead would be the same as for direct labor, which is total direct labor hours worked for the month. Note that quantities are always in total for the month (total cucumbers, total hours worked).

What is AP?

AP represents the actual price paid per unit of input. For example, the actual price for direct materials for Spicy Pickle Company would be the amount paid per cucumber, not per jar of pickles. Again, remember that this variance is for direct materials, not finished goods. The actual price for direct labor is the actual wage paid per hour. The actual price for manufacturing overhead is the actual variable manufacturing overhead rate per direct labor hour (in this case). Note that prices are always per unit of input (per cucumber, per hour).

What is SQ?

SQ represents the standard quantity of units of input in total. For example, the standard quantity for direct materials for Spicy Pickle Company is the number of cucumbers that should have been used for the month, not the number of jars of pickles. Remember, this is for direct materials, not finished goods. The standard quantity for direct labor is the standard number of hours that should have been worked in total for the month. Since variable overhead is based on direct labor hours in this example, the standard quantity for variable overhead would be the same as for direct labor, which is total direct labor hours that should have been worked in the month. Note that quantities are always in total for the month (total cucumbers, total hours worked).

What is SP?

SP represents the standard price that should have been paid per unit of input. For example, the standard price for direct materials for Spicy Pickle Company would be the amount that should have been paid per cucumber, not per jar of pickles. Again, remember that this variance is for direct materials, not finished goods. The standard price for direct labor is the wage that should have been paid per hour. The standard price for manufacturing overhead is the standard variable manufacturing overhead rate per direct labor hour (in this case). Note that prices are always per unit of input (per cucumber, per hour).

How are direct materials variances calculated?

Assume that in January, Spicy Pickle Company purchased and used 97,500 cucumbers to make 15,000 jars of pickles. Also assume that Spicy Pickle Company paid $0.04 per cucumber ($3,900 in total). Utilizing this information and the data from the standard cost card, the direct materials variances can be calculated as follows:

Computing Direct Materials Variances

total cucumbers		per cucumber	total cucumbers		per cucumber	total cucumbers		per cucumber
AQ	✱	AP	AQ	✱	SP	SQ	✱	SP
97,500	$	0.04	97,500	$	0.10	90,000	$	0.10
$		3,900	$		9,750	$		9,000

$	5,850	$	750
Favorable		Unfavorable	
Materials Price Variance		Materials Quantity Variance	

$	5,100
Favorable	
Spending Variance	

Spicy Pickle Company actually used 97,500 cucumbers in January. The difference between the standard allowed price of $0.10 per cucumber and the actual price paid of $0.04 per cucumber resulted in a favorable materials price variance of $5,850. However, this favorable variance was partially offset by a $750 unfavorable materials quantity variance, as Spicy Pickle Company actually used 97,500 cucumbers to make 15,000 jars of pickles, whereas the standard allowed 90,000 cucumbers (6 cucumbers × 15,000 jars) for that same level of production. The two variances net together to equal the $5,100 favorable spending variance on direct materials. The spending variance is the difference between what was actually spent on cucumbers for the month ($3,900) versus what the standard allows for cucumbers at the actual level of production of 15,000 jars (6 cucumbers per jar × 15,000 jars × $0.10 per cucumber = $9,000).

Accordingly, this data can be summarized in the following way: Spicy Pickle Company spent $5,100 less on cucumbers in January than what was anticipated in the flexible budget. This variance is due to a favorable materials price variance of $5,850, which was partially offset by an unfavorable materials quantity variance of $750.

What does the direct materials price variance indicate?

The materials price variance indicates whether or not the price per unit of direct materials was greater than or less than the standard. A favorable variance indicates that the price was less than the standard. An unfavorable variance indicates that the price was greater than the standard. In the case of the Spicy Pickle Company, the favorable material price variance was the result of purchasing cucumbers for $0.04 each rather than the standard price of $0.10 each. This indicates that Spicy Pickle Company achieved better pricing from suppliers than anticipated.

Who is generally responsible for the direct materials price variance?

The purchasing manager is generally responsible for the materials price variances, as they are often the department that is negotiating prices with the suppliers. Assume, in this example, that Spicy Pickle Company was offered a special deal on some oddly shaped cucumbers that the supplier had unintentionally produced. As a result of this odd shape, they were given a considerable discount. The purchasing manager agreed to the deal in order to achieve considerable savings on the purchases of cucumbers. The purchasing manager will be held accountable for both positive and negative variances. The purchasing manager is often praised for favorable materials price variances and criticized for unfavorable materials price variances.

What does the direct materials quantity variance indicate?

The materials quantity variance indicates whether or not the quantity of direct materials was greater than or less than the standard allowed. A favorable variance indicates that the quantity was less than the standard. An unfavorable variance indicates that the quantity was greater than the standard. In the case of the Spicy Pickle Company, the unfavorable material quantity variance was the result of using 97,500 cucumbers to make 15,000 jars of pickles rather than the standard price of 90,000 cucumbers. This indicates that Spicy Pickle Company used more cucumbers than anticipated.

Note that when it comes to quantity variances, although using less than the standard is considered favorable, this could be an indication of a quality issue. For example, if the Spicy Pickle Company had used less than the standard of 6 cucumbers per jar, it may have produced jars of pickles that are not as full as they should be. Accordingly, both favorable and unfavorable materials quantity variances should be investigated.

Who is generally responsible for the direct materials quantity variance?

The production manager is generally responsible for the materials quantity variances. Recall in this example that Spicy Pickle Company was offered a special deal on some oddly shaped cucumbers that the supplier had unintentionally produced. Assume that as a result of investigating the cause of the unfavorable variance, it was determined that the oddly shaped cucumbers kept jamming the slicing machine, thereby creating waste and cucumbers that were mangled and had to be thrown away. The production manager will be held accountable for both positive and negative variances. The production manager is often praised for favorable materials quantity variances and criticized for unfavorable materials quantity variances. However, in this case, the production manager would most likely point the finger at the purchasing manager, as it was a decision made by the purchasing manager that ultimately led to the unfavorable quantity variance in the production department.

How are direct labor variances calculated?

Assume that in January, Spicy Pickle Company direct labor employees worked 1,050 hours to make 15,000 jars of pickles and were paid an average of $8.00 per hour. Utilizing this information and the data from the standard cost card, the direct labor variances can be calculated as follows:

225

Computing Direct Labor Variances

total hours		per hour	total hours		per hour	total hours		per hour
AQ	✳	AP	AQ	✳	SP	SQ	✳	SP
1,050	$	8.00	1,050	$	9.00	750	$	9.00
$		8,400	$		9,450	$		6,750

$		1,050	$		2,700
Favorable		Unfavorable
Labor Rate Variance		Labor Efficiency Variance

$	1,650
Unfavorable
Spending Variance

Spicy Pickle Company direct labor employees worked 1,050 hours in January. The difference between the standard pay rate of $9.00 per hour and the actual pay rate of $8.00 per hour resulted in a favorable labor rate variance of $1,050. However, this favorable variance was overshadowed by a $2,700 unfavorable labor efficiency variance, as direct labor workers actually worked 1,050 hours to make 15,000 jars of pickles, whereas the standard allowed 750 hours (0.05 hours × 15,000 jars) for that same level of production. The two variances net together to equal the $1,650 unfavorable spending variance on direct labor. The spending variance is the difference between what was actually spent on direct labor for the month ($8,400) versus what the standard allows for wages at the actual level of production of 15,000 jars (0.05 hours per jar × 15,000 jars × $9.00 per hour = $6,750).

Accordingly, this data can be summarized in the following way: Spicy Pickle Company spent $1,650 more on direct labor in January than what was anticipated in the flexible budget. This variance is due to a favorable labor rate variance of $1,050 that was more than offset by an unfavorable labor efficiency variance of $2,700.

What does the direct labor rate variance indicate?

The labor rate variance indicates whether or not the wage paid per hour was greater than or less than the standard. A favorable variance indicates that the rate was less than the standard. An unfavorable variance indicates that the rate was greater than the standard. In the case of the Spicy Pickle Company, the favorable labor rate variance was the result of paying workers $8.00 per hour rather than the standard rate of $9.00 per hour. This indicates that Spicy Pickle Company paid workers less per hour than anticipated.

Who is generally responsible for the direct labor rate variance?

The production manager is generally responsible for the labor rate variances, as the production manager is in control of staffing the department and assigning raises, etc. Assume, in this example, that Spicy Pickle Company utilized newer, less skilled workers than originally anticipated, thus resulting in the lower rate of pay. The production manager will be held accountable for both positive and negative variances. The production manager is often praised for favorable labor rate variances and criticized for unfavorable labor rate variances.

What does the direct labor efficiency variance indicate?

The labor efficiency variance indicates whether or not the number of hours worked was greater than or less than the standard allowed. A favorable variance indicates that the hours worked were less than the standard. An unfavorable variance indicates that the hours worked were greater than the standard. In the case of the Spicy Pickle Company, the unfavorable labor efficiency variance was the result of working 1,050 hours to make 15,000 jars of pickles rather than the standard of 750 hours. This indicates that Spicy Pickle Company direct labor employees worked more hours than anticipated.

Recall that when it comes to quantity and efficiency variances, although using less than the standard is considered favorable, this could be an indication of a quality issue. For example, if Spicy Pickle Company had worked less than the standard of 0.05 hours per jar, they may have produced jars of pickles haphazardly. Accordingly, both favorable and labor efficiency variances should be investigated.

Who is generally responsible for the direct labor efficiency variance?

The production manager is generally responsible for the labor efficiency variances. Recall in this example that Spicy Pickle Company utilized less-skilled workers. In addition, recall that the oddly shaped cucumbers kept jamming the slicing machine. Either of these conditions could lead to employees working more hours than the standard allowed. The production manager will be held accountable for both positive and negative variances. The production manager is often praised for favorable labor efficiency variances and criticized for unfavorable labor efficiency variances. In this case, the production manager would most likely point the finger at the purchasing manager, as it was a decision made by the purchasing manager that ultimately led to the machines jamming up and taking the workers more time than was planned. However, the purchasing manager would probably reply that it wasn't the oddly shaped cucumbers that jammed the machine, but rather, it was the less-skilled workers who didn't know how to run the machine that caused the unfavorable labor efficiency variance. In reality, it may be a bit of both.

How are variable manufacturing overhead variances calculated?

Assume that in January, Spicy Pickle Company applied variable overhead on the basis of direct labor hours worked and that direct labor employees worked 1,050 hours to make 15,000 jars of pickles. The actual variable overhead incurred for January was $5,375, amounting to $5.12 per direct labor hour. Utilizing this information and the data from the standard cost card, the variable overhead variances can be calculated as follows:

Computing Variable Overhead Variances

total hours		per hour	total hours		per hour	total hours		per hour
AQ	✹	AP	AQ	✹	SP	SQ	✹	SP
1,050 $		5.12	1,050 $		3.25	750 $		3.25
$		5,375 $			3,413 $			2,438

$	1,962	$	975
Unfavorable		Unfavorable
Variable Overhead Rate Variance		Variable Overhead Efficiency Variance

$	2,937
Unfavorable
Spending Variance

Because Spicy Pickle Company allocates overhead on the basis of direct labor hours, the quantities for the variable overhead variances are the same as for the direct labor variances (both using direct labor hours worked and standard direct labor hours allowed). Recall that Spicy Pickle Company direct labor employees worked 1,050 hours in January. The difference between the standard variable overhead rate of $3.25 per hour and the actual variable overhead rate of $5.12 per hour resulted in an unfavorable variable overhead rate variance of $1,962. Additionally, this unfavorable variance was paired with a $975 unfavorable variable overhead efficiency variance, as direct labor workers actually worked 1,050 hours to make 15,000 jars of pickles, whereas the standard allowed 750 hours (0.05 hours × 15,000 jars) for that same level of production. The two variances sum together to equal the $2,937 unfavorable spending variance on variable overhead. The spending variance is the difference between what was actually spent on variable overhead for the month ($5,375) versus what the standard allows for at the actual level of production of 15,000 jars (0.05 hours per jar × 15,000 jars × $3.25 per hour = $2,438).

Accordingly, this data can be summarized in the following way: Spicy Pickle Company spent $2,937 more on variable overhead in January than what was anticipated in the flexible budget. This variance is due to an unfavorable variable overhead rate variance of $1,962 combined with an unfavorable variable overhead efficiency variance of $975.

What does the variable overhead rate variance indicate?

The variable overhead rate variance indicates whether or not the actual variable overhead rate was greater than or less than the standard. A favorable variance indicates that the rate was less than the standard. An unfavorable variance indicates that the rate was greater than the standard. In the case of the Spicy Pickle Company, the unfavorable variable overhead rate variance was the result of incurring variable overhead at a rate of $5.12 per hour rather than the standard rate of $3.25 per hour. This indicates that Spicy Pickle Company paid more for variable overhead than anticipated.

Who is generally responsible for the variable overhead rate variance?

The production manager is generally responsible for the variable overhead rate variance, as the production manager is usually in control of the production facility and processes. Assume, in this example, that Spicy Pickle Company used more indirect labor for maintenance to clean up the machines after the mangled cucumbers, causing variable overhead to increase. The production manager will be held accountable for both positive and negative variances. The production manager is often praised for favorable variable overhead rate variances and criticized for unfavorable variable overhead rate variances. However, in this case, the production manager may point the finger back to the original root cause of the problem: the purchase of oddly shaped cucumbers.

What does the variable overhead efficiency variance indicate?

As the variable overhead in this example was based on direct labor hours, the variable overhead efficiency variance is merely caused by the number of direct labor hours used compared to the standard. Accordingly, the variable overhead efficiency variance does not actually tell the user anything about overhead but rather the cost driver that overhead was based on.

	Pickles	Carrots	Total
Sales	$ 880,000	$ 120,000	$ 1,000,000
- Variable Expenses:			
Variable Manufacturing	6,200	1,500	297,700
Variable Selling & Administrative	22,000	3,000	25,000
Total Variable Expenses	288,100	34,600	322,700
= Contribution Margin	591,800	85,500	677,300
- Fixed Expenses:			
Rent	47,52	6,480	54,000
Insurance	5,280	720	6,000
Production Supervisor Salary	52,800	7,200	60,000
Sales Salaries	70,000	40,000	110,000
Advertising	6,000	6,000	12,000
General Administrative	193,600	26,400	220,000
Total Fixed Expenses	375,200	86,800	462,000

THE CONTRIBUTION FORMAT INCOME STATEMENT

What is a contribution format income statement?

A contribution format income statement is an income statement that is presented with clear distinctions between fixed and variable costs. The contribution format income statement is a useful tool for managerial accountants when making decisions for the business. Recall that managerial accounting does not have to follow the rules of GAAP. Therefore, although the contribution format income statement does not follow the formatting required of the traditional format income statement, managerial accountants are free to present an internally used income statement following any other format they deem useful, such as the contribution format.

How does a contribution format income statement differ from a traditional income statement?

Unlike a traditional income statement, which reports costs in categories by product costs (cost of goods sold) or period costs (selling and administrative), the contribution format income statement reports costs in categories according to how the costs behave (fixed or variable).

What does a contribution format income statement look like?

The contribution format income statement starts with sales, just as the traditional format income statement does. However, on the next line, the contribution format income statement deducts variable expenses upon arriving at a subtotal called contribution margin. Finally, fixed costs are subtracted from contribution margin in arriving at net operating income. An example of a contribution format income statement compared to a traditional format income statement for Spicy Pickle Company is shown below:

Traditional Format	(10,000 jars)		Contribution Format		(10,000 jars)
Sales	$ 40,000		Sales		$ 40,000
- Cost of Goods Sold	15,500		- Variable Expenses:		
= Gross Profit	24,500		Variable Manufacturing	12,100	
- Selling & Administrative Expenses	9,000		Variable Selling & Administrative	1,000	
= Net Operating Income	$ 15,500		Total Variable Expenses		13,100
			= Contribution Margin		26,900
			- Fixed Expenses:		
			Fixed Manufacturing	3,400	
			Fixed Selling & Administrative	8,000	
			Total Fixed Expenses		11,400
			= Net Operating Income		$ 15,500

What is contribution margin?

Contribution margin is the excess of sales over variable costs. Basically, contribution margin is what is left over to pay for your fixed costs after covering your variable expenses. For Spicy Pickle Company, recall that each jar of pickles sells for $4.00. Variable manufacturing costs (direct materials, direct labor, and overhead) are $1.21 per jar, and variable selling and administrative costs are $0.10 per jar (assume that this is a commission paid to salespeople). That means that every time Spicy Pickle Company sells a jar of pickles, it earns $4.00 from the customer but has to pay $1.31 just to cover the costs of making that one jar of pickles and paying the sales commission on each jar. That leaves Spicy Pickle Company with a contribution margin of $2.69 per jar. That $2.69 is what Spicy Pickle Company gets to use to cover its fixed expenses, such as rent on the factory, rent on the corporate headquarters, salaries of administrative personnel, etc. The more jars of pickles it sells, the better it is able to cover its fixed costs. Once the fixed costs are covered, Spicy Pickle Company starts to earn a profit.

In the contribution format income statement example above, when Spicy Pickle Company sells 10,000 jars of pickles, it earns $40,000 in sales revenue, and it incurs $13,100 in variable costs. That leaves it with a contribution margin of $26,900, which is used to pay for the fixed costs that don't change whether or not it sells more or fewer jars of pickles. In this case, Spicy Pickle Company incurs $11,400 of fixed costs each month. Since Spicy Pickle Company had $26,900 in contribution margin to cover those costs, it ends up with $15,500 left over, which is its net operating income for the month.

How is contribution margin per unit different from contribution margin?

The contribution margin per unit is the selling price of one unit minus the variable costs of one unit. In the case of Spicy Pickle Company, the selling price of one jar is $4.00, and the variable costs of one jar are $1.31. As such, each jar contributes $2.69 toward covering fixed costs and ultimately earning a profit, which is known as the contribution margin per unit. The total contribution margin is the contribution margin in total for a given level of sales. In the example above, Spicy Pickle Company sold 10,000 jars of pickles; thus, the total contribution margin was $26,900.

Is the net operating income figure different on a contribution format income statement?

No. Net operating income does not differ between the two income statement formats. The data is just rearranged, not changed. Rather than sorting the expenses between product and period, the expenses are sorted between fixed and variable. This rearranged format allows users to easily calculate data needed for decision making, such as cost-volume-profit analysis.

What is the contribution margin ratio?

The contribution margin ratio expresses the contribution margin as a percent of total sales. This can be done by taking contribution margin per unit divided by selling price per unit or by taking the total contribution margin for the month divided by the sales revenue for the month. (Either way will give you the same result.) In the case of Spicy Pickle Company, the contribution margin ratio can be calculated as $2.69 contribution margin per unit divided by $4.00 selling price per unit, which equals 67.25%. Likewise, it can be calculated as $26,900 total contribution margin for the month divided by $40,000 sales revenue for the month.

The contribution margin ratio tells you what percentage of your sales revenue is available to cover your fixed costs. For Spicy Pickle Company, a contribution margin ration of 67.25% means that for every dollar it gets from a customer, it is able to keep roughly 67 cents in order to pay for its fixed costs and ultimately earn a profit. (Recall that the other 33 cents goes toward covering the variable costs of the pickles.)

COST–VOLUME–PROFIT ANALYSIS

What is cost-volume-profit analysis?

Cost-volume-profit analysis shows the relationships between cost (fixed and variable) and sales volume and how those two variables impact profit (net operating income). It is a type of analysis that lets managerial accountants make decisions such as which products to sell, what prices to charge customers, and whether to rely more on fixed costs or variable costs.

What is the cost-volume-profit equation?

The cost-volume-profit equation is basically the equation used for the contribution format income statement, as discussed earlier in this chapter. The basic equation can be shown as:

Sales − Variable Expenses − Fixed Expenses = Profit

We can further break this down as:

(Sales Price per Unit × Quantity) − (Variable Cost per Unit × Quantity) − Fixed Expenses = Profit

Using some basic algebra, this equation can be simplified as follows:

((Sales Price per Unit − Variable Cost per Unit) × Quantity) − Fixed Expenses = Profit

Recall that sales price per unit minus variable cost per unit equals contribution margin per unit. Thus, the equation can be simplified one last time as:

(Contribution Margin per Unit × Quantity) − Fixed Expenses = Profit

How can the cost-volume-profit equation be used?

The cost-volume-profit equation can be used to calculate profit at any given level of sales units. For example, assume Spicy Pickle Company wanted to know how much profit it would earn if it sold 20,000 jars of pickles in one month. It could simply use the equation and have the answer in a few seconds. It knows each unit has a contribution margin of $2.69, and fixed costs are $11,400 per month. As such, profit can be calculated as follows:

($2.69 × 20,000) − $11,400 = $42,400

Now assume Spicy Pickle Company wanted to know how much profit it would earn if it only sold 4,000 jars of pickles in one month. The profit would be calculated as follows:

($2.69 × 4,000) − $11,400 = ($640)

You can see that this equation results in a negative number, meaning that if Spicy Pickle Company only sells 4,000 jars of pickles in a month, it will actually have a loss of $640. Accordingly, you might be thinking that the next question Spicy Pickle Company might ask is, "How many jars of pickles must we sell in order to avoid having losses?" In this case, Spicy Pickle Company would want to compute its break-even point.

What is the break-even point?

The break-even point is the level of sales that provides $0 net income (no profit or loss). Essentially, at that level of sales, the company just covers its costs without earning a profit, known as breaking even. This is an important figure for managerial accountants to be aware of, as companies want to avoid having losses. While no company has an ultimate goal of just breaking even, it is still a very useful number to be aware of in trying to set sales goals and make sure goals are well above the break-even point.

What is a cost-volume-profit graph?

A cost-volume-profit graph is a graph that plots sales volume in units on the x axis and dollars on the y axis. Lines are then added to show sales revenue at each level of volume and total expenses at each level of volume. Where the total sales line crosses the total expenses line, that is the break-even point. Where the total sales line is lower than the total expenses line, losses will result. Where the total sales line is higher than the total expenses line, profits will result. (Note that it is common to also show a line for fixed costs on cost-volume-profit graphs.) Using the profit equation given earlier in this chapter, the following data can be used to prepare a cost-volume-profit graph for Spicy Pickle Company.

Units Sold	-	2,000	4,000	6,000	8,000	10,000	12,000	14,000	16,000	18,000	20,000
Sales Revenue	$ -	$ 8,000	$ 16,000	$ 24,000	$ 32,000	$ 40,000	$ 48,000	$ 56,000	$ 64,000	$ 72,000	$ 80,000
Variable Expenses	$ -	$ 2,620	$ 5,240	$ 7,860	$ 10,480	$ 13,100	$ 15,720	$ 18,340	$ 20,960	$ 23,580	$ 26,200
Fixed Expenses	$ 11,400	$ 11,400	$ 11,400	$ 11,400	$ 11,400	$ 11,400	$ 11,400	$ 11,400	$ 11,400	$ 11,400	$ 11,400
Total Expenses	$ 11,400	$ 14,020	$ 16,640	$ 19,260	$ 21,880	$ 24,500	$ 27,120	$ 29,740	$ 32,360	$ 34,980	$ 37,600
Profit / (Loss)	$ (11,400)	$ (6,020)	$ (640)	$ 4,740	$ 10,120	$ 15,500	$ 20,880	$ 26,260	$ 31,640	$ 37,020	$ 42,400

After the data has been calculated, a graph can be prepared plotting the units on the x axis and the dollars on the y axis. The graph below shows a line for total revenue and total expenses. Note the break-even point occurs somewhere between 4,000 and 6,000 jars of pickles sold. Also note that the further to the right you move on the graph, the bigger the profit area becomes. The opposite is also true; as you move left on the graph, the smaller the profit area becomes (or the larger the loss area becomes).

The cost-volume-profit graph is a useful visual to see cost structure, as the total expenses line intercepts the y axis at the fixed cost per month and goes up from there. The higher the y intercept (where the line crosses the y axis), the higher the fixed costs. Also, the slope of the line represents the variable cost per unit. Accordingly, the steeper the line, the higher the variable cost is per unit.

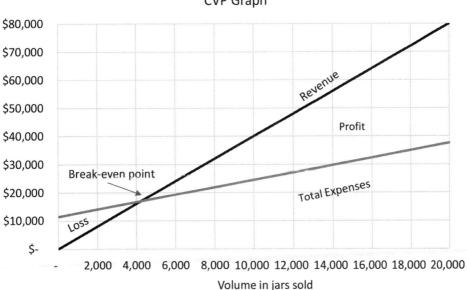

235

How does cost structure affect profitability?

Cost structure reflects management's choices regarding fixed and variable costs. Companies that choose to go with more fixed costs instead of variable costs will have a total cost line that starts higher on the graph but is less steep. This will result in larger shaded areas for profit and loss. Thus, the potential for reward is greater (more potential profit), but the risk is greater as well (more potential losses). These companies are considered to have higher operating leverage, as they are using (or leveraging) fixed costs in order to earn a greater profit.

What is the degree of operating leverage?

The degree of operating leverage is a ratio that measures how sensitive net operating income is to changes in sales. It is calculated as:

Contribution Margin / Net Operating Income = Operating Leverage

For Spicy Pickle Company, this could be calculated as:

$26,900 / $15,500 = 1.74

This means that a 1% increase in sales revenue would result in a 1.74% increase in net operating income. Likewise, a 10% increase in sales revenue would result in a 17.4% increase in net operating income. This can be proven in the contribution format income statement that follows:

	(10,000 jars)		(11,000 jars)	
Sales		$ 40,000		$ 44,000
- Variable Expenses:				
Variable Manufacturing	12,100		13,310	
Variable Selling & Administrative	1,000		1,100	
Total Variable Expenses		13,100		14,410
= Contribution Margin		26,900		29,590
- Fixed Expenses:				
Fixed Manufacturing	3,400		3,400	
Fixed Selling & Administrative	8,000		8,000	
Total Fixed Expenses		11,400		11,400
= Net Operating Income		$ 15,500		$ 18,190

Notice that a 10% increase in sales resulted in an increase in net operating income of $2,690, which is approximately 17.4% higher than $15,500. The greater the degree of operating leverage, the more sensitive net operating income will be to changes in sales.

How can a company change its cost structure?

A company can make decisions that change the mix of fixed and variable costs. These decisions change the cost structure and thus the degree of operating leverage. Consider the following two scenarios: Company A and Company B make the same product, which sells for $10 per unit. Company A decides to leverage fixed costs to its advantage by choosing to use leased machines (fixed cost) rather than labor (variable cost) to produce its product. Company A has fixed costs of $10,000 per month and variable costs of $2 per unit. On the other hand, Company B decides that it does not wish to risk having so many fixed costs and decides to produce its product by hand using direct labor (variable cost) with no machine usage. Company B has fixed costs of $2,000 per month and variable costs of $7 per unit. The cost-volume-profit graphs for the two companies are shown below:

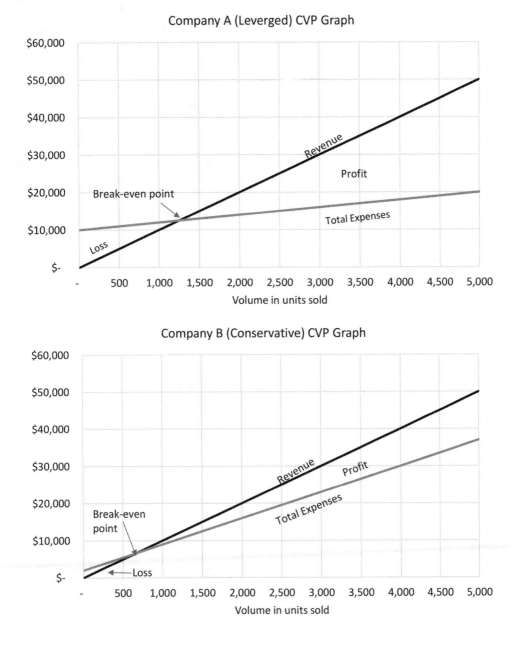

Company A (Leverged) CVP Graph

Company B (Conservative) CVP Graph

Notice that Company A will need to sell more units in order to break even than Company B. Also notice that both the risk and the potential reward are greater for Company A. If both companies are only able to sell 1,000 units, Company B, which made the conservative choice, will be better off, as it will have a slight profit, whereas Company A will have a loss. However, at 1,500 units or more, Company A, which made the leveraged choice, will be much better off, as the profit triangle is much wider than for Company B. Companies can change their cost structure over time. For example, Company B may have been conservative at the start of its business, but if it realizes it routinely sells 4,000 units per month, it may decide to buy a machine and use less direct labor in order to increase profitability. These types of managerial accounting decisions are addressed later in this chapter.

What is the formula to calculate the break-even point in units?

A precise break-even point can be calculated by using the following formula:

Fixed Cost / Contribution Margin per Unit = Break-even Point in Units

Recall that contribution margin per unit tells you how much is left per unit to cover the fixed costs. Thus, dividing fixed costs by the contribution margin per unit tells you how many units you need to sell to cover fixed costs and, thus, break even. Recall that Spicy Pickle Company has a contribution margin per unit of $2.69 and fixed costs per month of $11,400. As such, the break-even point in units can be calculated as:

$11,400 / $2.69 = 4,238 jars (rounded)

Accordingly, Spicy Pickle Company needs to sell 4,238 jars to break even. For each unit above the break-even point, Spicy Pickle Company will earn $2.69 in profit. For example, if Spicy Pickle Company sells 4,248 units (ten more than break-even), net operating income would be $26.90.

What is the formula to calculate the break-even point in sales dollars?

If you would rather calculate break-even in sales dollars rather than units, you can simply multiply the break-even units by the selling price per unit. Spicy Pickle Company has a break-even point of 4,238 units and sells each unit for $4.00, so the break-even point in sales dollars would be 4,238 × $4.00, or $16,952.

Likewise, the break-even point in sales dollars can also be calculated using the following formula:

Fixed Cost / Contribution Margin Ratio = Break-even Point in Dollars

Recall that Spicy Pickle Company has a contribution margin ratio of 67.25%. As such, the break-even point in sales dollars can be calculated as:

$11,400 / 67.25% = $16,952 (rounded)

What is the formula to calculate sales units needed to earn a target profit?

If a company wants to calculate how many units it needs to sell in order to earn a certain profit amount, it simply needs to add the desired profit to the numerator in the break-even equation. In this case, the company doesn't just want to cover fixed costs. It wants to cover fixed costs and earn some profit, so those items must both be covered by the contribution margin per unit. Accordingly, the formula for units needed to be sold in order to earn a desired profit is:

(Fixed Cost + Target Profit) / Contribution Margin Per Unit = Unit Sales to Earn a Target Profit

Recall that Spicy Pickle Company has a contribution margin per unit of $2.69 and fixed costs per month of $11,400. Also assume Spicy Pickle Company desires a profit of $30,000 per month. The unit sales needed to achieve this target profit can be calculated as:

($11,400 + $30,000) / $2.69 = 15,390 (rounded)

Accordingly, Spicy Pickle Company needs to sell 15,390 jars per month in order to have a profit of $30,000 per month.

What is the formula to calculate sales dollars needed to earn a target profit?

If you would rather calculate sales dollars needed to earn a target profit than units needed to earn a target profit, you can simply multiply the unit sales needed to earn the target profit by the selling price per unit. Recall that Spicy Pickle Company needs to sell 15,390 jars to achieve the target profit of $30,000 and sells each unit for $4.00, so the sales dollars necessary would be 15,390 × $4.00, or $61,560.

Likewise, the following formula can also be used:

(Fixed Cost + Target Profit) / Contribution Margin Ratio = Dollar Sales to Earn a Target Profit

Recall that Spicy Pickle Company has a contribution margin ratio of 67.25%. As such, the required sales dollars to earn a target profit of $30,000 can be calculated as:

($11,400 + $30,000) / 67.25% = $61,561 (rounded)

What is the margin of safety?

The margin of safety represents the amount of sales over the break-even sales. This can be computed in units or dollars or as a percentage. The larger the margin of safety, the further away a company is from incurring potential losses.

How is margin of safety in units computed?

The margin of safety in units is calculated as:

Actual Sales in Units − Break-even Sales in Units = Margin of Safety in Units

For example, Spicy Pickle Company actually sold 10,000 units and has a break-even point of 4,238 units. As such, Spicy Pickle Company currently has a margin of safety of 5,762 units. That means it has a 5,762-unit buffer from incurring losses.

How is margin of safety in dollars computed?

The margin of safety in dollars is calculated as:

Actual Sales in Dollars − Break-even Sales in Dollars = Margin of Safety in Dollars

For example, Spicy Pickle Company had actual sales revenue of $40,000 and has a break-even point of $16,952. As such, Spicy Pickle Company currently has a margin of safety of $23,048. That means it has a $23,048 revenue buffer.

How is margin of safety percentage computed?

The margin of safety percentage is calculated as:

Margin of Safety in Dollars / Actual Sales Revenue = Margin of Safety Percentage

For example, Spicy Pickle Company had actual sales revenue of $40,000 and a margin of safety in dollars of $23,048. As such, Spicy Pickle Company currently has a margin of safety of 57.6%. This means that sales would have to drop by 57.6% in order for Spicy Pickle Company to start incurring losses. The higher the percentage, the larger the buffer.

How do you calculate the break-even point if you sell multiple products?

The calculation of break-even becomes more complex if a company sells more than one product. If a company sells more than one product, break-even in sales dollars is computed using the overall combined contribution margin ratio and overall combined fixed costs. The resulting break-even sales level is then split between the products according to their sales mix. The sales mix is the relative proportion of each product sold. Note that in order to compute break-even under a multiproduct situation, you must make the assumption that the sales mix will not change.

According to data included in the annual report for the fiscal year ending September 2017 for Apple, Inc., 62% of its sales were from iPhone, 8% were from iPad, 11% were from Mac, 13% were from services, and the remaining 6% was classified as other. This was relatively consistent with the 2016 sales mix of 63% iPhone, 10% iPad, 11% Mac, 11% services, and 5% other.

Going back to the Spicy Pickle Company example, assume that in addition to selling pickles, Spicy Pickle Company also sells pickled carrots. An updated income statement example for Spicy Pickle Company is shown below:

Contribution Format Income Statement

	Pickles	Carrots	Total	
Sales				
- Variable Expenses:	$ 40,000	$ 8,000	$ 48,000	
= Contribution Margin	13,100	2,300	15,400	
- Fixed Expenses:	$ 26,900	$ 5,700	32,600	67.9% *Total*
= Net Operating Income			11,400	*CM Ratio*
			$ 21,200	

Break-even in sales dollars would be calculated using the combined contribution margin ratio of 67.9%, as follows:

Fixed Cost / Contribution Margin Ratio = Break-even in Sales Dollars

$11,400 / 67.9% = $16,789 (rounded)

That means that when total combined sales revenue is $16,789, Spicy Pickle Company will break even. This should then be split between pickles and carrots according to their sales mix. As pickle sales are $40,000 out of the $48,000 total sales, you can assume that pickles make up 83.3% of overall sales. Thus, carrots make up the remaining 16.7% of sales. As such, the combined break-even point of $16,789 should be split 83.3% to pickles and 16.7% to carrots. That means the break-even sales dollars for pickles would be $13,991 ($16,789 × 83.3%) and carrots would be $2,798 ($16,789 × 16.7%).

MANAGERIAL DECISION MAKING

What types of decisions are made with the help of managerial accounting data?

Managerial accounting data is useful in making a multitude of business decisions. Some of the more common decisions that managers make with the help of managerial accounting data are: whether to drop or retain a business segment, whether to make a component yourself or buy it from someone else, whether or not to accept a special order, and how best to utilize a constrained resource. In order to make these decisions, accountants must first identify the relevant costs and benefits to each decision.

What are relevant costs and relevant benefits?

Relevant costs and relevant benefits are those costs and benefits that differ between two alternatives. Relevant costs and relevant benefits are the only costs and benefits that should be considered when evaluating a decision. Incorrect decisions can be made if managers include irrelevant costs and benefits in the decision-making process. Accordingly, being able to identify which costs and benefits are relevant is an important skill for managerial accountants. The primary question that should be asked is, "Does this cost or benefit differ between the alternatives?" If the answer is yes, it is relevant. If the answer is no, it is irrelevant and should not be included in the decision-making process.

What is a differential cost?

A differential cost is a cost that differs between two alternatives and can be used synonymously with relevant costs. Differential costs are always relevant to a decision. For example, if you were deciding whether to drive or fly to Florida for vacation, the cost of the plane ticket is a differential cost. If you drive, you don't have to pay for the plane ticket. If you fly, you do. That is a cost that differs between the two alternatives. As such, it is relevant to the decision. Additionally, the cost of gasoline to drive would be relevant in this decision, as are many other costs. However, the cost of the theme park ticket won't differ whether you drive or fly and thus is not a differential cost in this decision and would be irrelevant.

What is differential revenue?

Differential revenue is a revenue that differs between two alternatives and can be used synonymously with relevant benefits. Differential revenues are always relevant to a decision. If you were deciding between two job offers that pay different amounts, obviously, the pay rate at each job would be relevant to the decision, as it differs between the two alternatives. Other differential benefits to consider might be the employer contribution to a retirement account, etc. If the two rates of pay were exactly the same, you would not include that in your decision, as it would be irrelevant. You would then base your decision on other factors.

What is an avoidable cost?

An avoidable cost is a cost that can be avoided if one alternative is selected over another. Avoidable costs are differential costs and thus are relevant to the decision. In the previous example of driving or flying to Florida, the cost of the plane ticket is an avoidable cost, as you won't purchase a ticket if you decide to drive. Likewise, the cost of gasoline to drive is an avoidable cost if you choose to fly. Again, the cost of the theme park ticket is not an avoidable cost in the decision to drive or fly to Florida and thus is irrelevant to this decision.

What is a sunk cost?

A sunk cost is a cost that has already been incurred. Sunk costs cannot change, since they already happened. As such, they are never differential costs and, therefore, never relevant in a decision. For example, in the decision to drive or fly to Florida, the cost that you paid for your car is a sunk cost. It happened in the past and does not change whether you drive or fly to Florida. As such, you would not include that in your decision.

If a cost is relevant to one decision, does that mean it is relevant to all decisions?

No. Each decision requires its own analysis of relevant costs and benefits. For example, the cost of the plane ticket is relevant in the decision whether to drive or fly to Florida. The cost of the plane ticket is not relevant in the decision of whether to visit the Magic Kingdom or Universal Studios. In the decision of which park to visit, the ticket prices of the two parks should be compared, etc. Most of this may sound like common sense in these simple examples, but in the business world, it can get more complicated.

What is an opportunity cost?

An opportunity cost is the benefit given up by selecting one alternative over the other. For example, in the decision to drive or fly to Florida, there is a benefit to flying in that you can relax, read, watch movies, etc. You cannot do that if you are driving. Therefore, if you choose to drive, you are giving up that benefit. That is an opportunity cost of driving. In this example, that opportunity cost would be hard to assign a dollar value to. However, in many business decisions, the dollar value of an opportunity cost is identifiable. For example, if you own a restaurant in a small downtown location with an upstairs unit and you can either rent the upstairs for $700 per month or use it for storage, the opportunity cost of using it for storage would be the $700 rental revenue you are giving up. Opportunity costs are relevant costs.

Why do managerial accountants try to segregate relevant costs and benefits?

When making business decisions, managers should isolate just the relevant costs and benefits related to the decision. The first reason is simply because it is rare that managers will have all of the data needed to prepare a full income statement showing multiple alternatives. As such, it is only necessary to gather data for the relevant costs and benefits, which will save time. The second reason is that using only the relevant costs and benefits keeps managers focused on the important aspects of the decision. If irrelevant costs and benefits are listed along with the relevant costs and benefits, it can be easy for someone to get lost in the details or focus on something that isn't relevant to the decision anyway. That may, in turn, lead a manager into making the wrong decision.

DROP OR RETAIN A SEGMENT

What is a drop or retain a segment decision?

A drop or retain a segment decision is a decision that involves evaluating the product lines and/or segments of the business to determine if the organization would be better off by eliminating seemingly unprofitable products or segments. For example, assume Spicy Pickle Company is evaluating the pickle and carrot product lines. Based on the year 2022 data, management has prepared the following income statement by product line: In this case, the loss of $1,300 shown on the carrot product line might cause managers to evaluate whether or not Spicy Pickle Company should continue to sell pickled carrots. In this case, a drop or retain a segment analysis should be prepared.

How do managers evaluate a drop or retain a segment decision?

The first step in a drop or retain a segment decision is to identify the relevant costs and benefits. Recall that only relevant costs and benefits should be included in the decision. After identifying the relevant costs and benefits, the revenues that would be lost by drop-

Spicy Pickle Company
Income Statement by Product Line
For the Year Ended December 31, 2022

	Pickles	Carrots	Total
Sales	$ 880,000	$ 120,000	$ 1,000,000
- Variable Expenses:			
Variable Manufacturing	266,200	31,500	297,700
Variable Selling & Administrative	22,000	3,000	25,000
Total Variable Expenses	288,200	34,500	322,700
= Contribution Margin	591,800	85,500	677,300
- Fixed Expenses:			
Rent	47,520	6,480	54,000
Insurance	5,280	720	6,000
Production Supervisor Salary	52,800	7,200	60,000
Sales Salaries	70,000	40,000	110,000
Advertising	6,000	6,000	12,000
General Administrative	193,600	26,400	220,000
Total Fixed Expenses	375,200	86,800	462,000
= Net Operating Income	$ 216,600	$ (1,300)	$ 215,300

ping the segment are compared to the expenses that would be avoided by dropping the segment. If it turns out that the company will avoid more expenses than it will lose in revenues by dropping the segment, then the segment should be dropped. A simple approach is to compare the contribution margin of the dropped segment (relevant benefits) to the fixed costs that can be avoided.

In the case of Spicy Pickle Company, if the carrot product line is dropped, it would lose all sales revenue for carrots (since it is not selling them anymore) and all variable costs for carrots (since it is not making them anymore or paying sales commissions on them). Recall that sales revenue minus variable costs equals contribution margin. Thus, if the carrot product line is dropped, all $85,500 of contribution margin would be gone.

Additionally, assume that management has determined that if it drops the carrots, it would be able to get rid of the carrot sales salaries and the advertising on the carrots. It would not be able to avoid any rent, insurance, production salaries, or general administrative expenses, as those are allocated shared costs for the company and not specific to any product line. Thus, only the $46,000 in sales salaries and advertising would go away.

Accordingly, Spicy Pickle Company can determine to following results of dropping the carrot product line:

Contribution margin lost by dropping the carrot line: ($85,500)

Fixed expenses avoided by dropping the carrot line: $46,000

Increase/(Decrease) in overall company net operating income: ($39,500)

From this analysis, you can see that if it drops the carrots, it will lose $85,500 of contribution margin. That is then compared to the $46,000 of expenses it can avoid. Put simply, it will lose $85,500 of good stuff but only $46,000 of bad stuff. Accordingly, it will actually be $39,500 worse off if it drops the carrots. A revised income statement showing the results if the carrot product line was dropped is shown below:

Spicy Pickle Company
Income Statement by Product Line
For the Year Ended December 31, 2022

	Pickles	Carrots	Total
Sales	$ 880,000	$ -	$ 880,000
- Variable Expenses:			
Variable Manufacturing	266,200	-	266,200
Variable Selling & Administrative	22,000	-	22,000
Total Variable Expenses	288,200	-	288,200
= Contribution Margin	591,800	-	591,800
- Fixed Expenses:			
Rent	47,520	6,480	54,000
Insurance	5,280	720	6,000
Production Supervisor Salary	52,800	7,200	60,000
Sales Salaries	70,000	-	70,000
Advertising	6,000	-	6,000
General Administrative	193,600	26,400	220,000
Total Fixed Expenses	375,200	40,800	416,000
= Net Operating Income	$ 216,600	$ (40,800)	$ 175,800

Notice that the total net operating income is $39,500 less than the original scenario.

How could a company actually be worse off by dropping a product line that is not profitable?

In this case, the answer lies in the shared fixed costs. Unavoidable costs, such as the rent on the building, are typically allocated to product lines using some type of arbitrary measure, such as percent of sales. In the case of Spicy Pickle Company, it allocated the rent between the two products based on the percentage of sales (88% to pickles and 12% to carrots). If it drops the carrot product line, it still has to pay the entire rent on the facility. That is unavoidable. Likewise, it still has to pay the insurance on the facility, the production supervisor's salary (assuming this individual supervised both products and will not be let go), and the general administrative costs, such as the accountant's salary, the CEO's salary, etc.

As such, the fixed costs that were allocated to the carrot product line made the product appear unprofitable when, in fact, it was profitable. Managers and accountants should take special care when making decisions where allocated costs are involved.

How should managers show shared fixed costs on the income statement if they can be so misleading?

One approach to fixing this problem on the income statement is to show shared costs separately from traceable costs and only in total. Essentially, this approach does not attempt to allocate shared costs among the product lines. An example for Spicy Pickle Company is shown below:

Spicy Pickle Company
Income Statement by Product Line
For the Year Ended December 31, 2022

	Pickles	Carrots	Total
Sales	$ 880,000	$ 120,000	$ 1,000,000
- Variable Expenses:			
Variable Manufacturing	266,200	31,500	297,700
Variable Selling & Administrative	22,000	3,000	25,000
Total Variable Expenses	288,200	34,500	322,700
= Contribution Margin	591,800	85,500	677,300
- Traceable Fixed Expenses:			
Sales Salaries	70,000	40,000	110,000
Advertising	6,000	6,000	12,000
Total Traceable Fixed Expenses	76,000	46,000	122,000
= Product Line Segment Margin	515,800	39,500	555,300
- Shared Fixed Expenses			
Rent			54,000
Insurance			6,000
Production Supervisor Salary			60,000
General Administrative			220,000
Total Shared Fixed Expenses			340,000
= Net Operating Income			$ 215,300

In this case, Spicy Pickle Company can now clearly see that it would be $39,500 worse off by dropping the carrot product line.

MAKE OR BUY

What is a make-or-buy decision?

Many manufacturing companies consider the choice of making the parts that go into a completed product or purchasing some or all of the parts and assembling the final product. The decision to either make the parts yourself or buy them from an outside supplier is a make-or-buy decision. For example, the Big Three U.S. automotive manufacturers purchase many of the components that go into their vehicles from Tier 1 automotive suppliers rather than making the component themselves. For example, Ford Motor Company purchases the seats for Super Duty pickup from Faurecia, a French auto supplier. At some point, it most likely engaged in a make-or-buy analysis to determine this.

How do managers evaluate a make-or-buy decision?

The first step in evaluating a make-or-buy decision is to identify the relevant costs of making the parts (those that differ between the alternatives) and comparing them to the cost of buying the parts. In general, a company should go with whatever option has fewer costs. Again, it is important to be aware of allocated costs and opportunity costs. Allocated costs may make a part appear to cost more to make than it actually does.

For example, assume that Spicy Pickle Company makes its own pickling solution out of vinegar and other spices. It currently makes 62,500 gallons of pickling solution per year. An outside supplier has contacted Spicy Pickle Company and offered to sell it a pickling solution for $3.00 per gallon. Assume Spicy Pickle Company gathered the following cost data for making its own pickling solution:

	Per gallon		62,500 gallons	
Ingredients	$	1.60	$	100,000
Direct Labor	$	0.40	$	25,000
Variable Overhead	$	0.20	$	12,500
Supervisor's Salary	$	0.48	$	30,000
Allocated General Overhead	$	2.24	$	140,000
Total Cost	$	4.92	$	307,500

At first glance, it appears that Spicy Pickle Company would be better off to buy the pickling solution from an outside supplier rather than make it itself. However, assume that upon further analysis, Spicy Pickle Company determined that the supervisor's salary is an allocated cost, as there is only one production supervisor for the entire facility, and this supervisor would not be let go or given a pay cut if Spicy Pickle Company stopped making its own pickling solution. In addition, it was also determined that the general overhead costs are allocated and would not be reduced by buying the solution from the outside supplier. As such, in this case, the only relevant costs to making the solution itself are the ingredients, the direct labor, and the variable overhead, which total $2.20. In this case, Spicy Pickle Company would be better off to continue making the pickling solution itself. As a matter of fact, if Spicy Pickle Company purchased the solution, it would actually be $50,000 worse off per year (as shown below):

	Make		Buy	
Ingredients	$	1.60		
Direct Labor	$	0.40		
Variable Overhead	$	0.20		
Outside Purchase Price			$	3.00
Total Cost	$	2.20	$	3.00
x 62,500 gallons per year		62,500		62,500
Total annual cost	$	137,500	$	187,500
Difference			$50,000	

By identifying only the relevant costs, Spicy Pickle Company can make an accurate determination of whether or not it will be better off by making or buying the pickling solution.

How do opportunity costs affect a make-or-buy decision?

If a company can utilize the space, machinery, etc., that it currently uses to make its own parts for some other profitable purpose if it buys the parts from someone else, that is an opportunity cost of making the parts and should then be added to the relevant costs of making the part. For example, assume that if Spicy Pickle Company purchased pickling solution from an outside vendor, it could use that space in the production facility to make a third product, pickled green beans. Spicy Pickle Company estimates that the segment margin (additional profit) on the pickled green beans would be $60,000 per year. In that case, the $60,000 is an opportunity cost of making the pickling solution and would need to be added to the analysis, as shown below:

	Make		Buy	
Total annual cost (from previous)	$	137,500	$	187,500
Opportunity cost	$	60,000		
Revised total annual cost	$	197,500	$	187,500
Difference			$10,000	

In this scenario, Spicy Pickle Company would actually be $10,000 worse off if it continues to make the pickling solution. Although an opportunity cost is not actually recorded in the accounting data, it is an important aspect of many business decisions and should not be neglected.

SPECIAL ORDER

What is a special order decision?

A special order decision is a decision on whether or not to accept a one-time order that would not be considered part of the company's regular, ongoing business. For example, assume Spicy Pickle Company was contacted by a local corporation that wanted to place a special order for 5,000 jars of pickles to be sent as a holiday gift to customers, with a special logo bow tied around the jar. The local corporation said it would be willing to pay $3.75 per jar. Also, assume Spicy Pickle Company has the excess capacity needed to complete the order, and completing this special order would not affect regular production. Spicy Pickle Company would need to prepare a special order analysis to determine the merits of this one-time special order.

How is a special order decision evaluated?

A special order decision is evaluated by calculating the incremental income from the special order by comparing the revenue from the special order to the relevant costs of making the special order. In general, special orders do not affect regular fixed costs, as they are one-time orders. Accordingly, variable costs are typically the only costs included in a special order analysis.

In this example, assume that Spicy Pickle Company has determined that the only costs in addition to normal variable costs for direct materials, direct labor, and variable overhead that are relevant to this special order would be the cost of the ribbons at $0.25 each and the cost of a machine that would be purchased to tie the bows on the jars. This machine would have no other use and would cost Spicy Pickle Company $2,000. Spicy Pickle Company has prepared the following analysis:

	Per Jar		Total 5,000 Jars
Incremental Revenue	$ 3.75	$	18,750
Less Incremental Costs:			
Variable Costs:			
Direct Materials	$ 0.60	$	3,000
Direct Labor	$ 0.45	$	2,250
Variable Overhead	$ 0.15	$	750
Ribbon	$ 0.25	$	1,250
Total Variable Cost	$ 1.45	$	7,250
Fixed Cost:			
Purchase of Machine		$	2,000
Total Incremental Cost		$	9,250
Incremental Income		$	9,500

As you can see from the analysis, Spicy Pickle Company would earn total revenue of $18,750 on this order. The costs to make the pickles would include the regular direct materials of $0.60 per jar, direct labor of $0.45 per jar, and variable overhead of $0.15 per jar, plus the $0.25 ribbon per jar. The variable costs on the order total $7,250 for 5,000 jars. In addition, Spicy Pickle Company will incur an additional $2,000 cost to purchase the ribbon machine, bringing the total costs on the order to $9,250. Subtracting the total costs from the revenues results in an incremental profit of $9,500 on this special order. As such, Spicy Pickle Company should accept the special order, as it will be $9,500 better off.

What is the lowest price possible that should be accepted on a special order?

In general, the lowest price that should be accepted on a special order would be the variable cost plus the cost of any additional fixed cost that would be necessary to complete the order, such as the purchase of the ribbon machine. For example, the special order for Spicy Pickle Company would cost $9,250 in total for 5,000 jars; as such, it should not accept a special order price of less than $1.85 per jar ($9,250 divided by 5,000 jars). The proof is shown below:

	Per Jar	Total 5,000 Jars
Incremental Revenue	$ 1.85	$ 9,250
Less Incremental Costs:		
Variable Costs:		
Direct Materials	$ 0.60	$ 3,000
Direct Labor	$ 0.45	$ 2,250
Variable Overhead	$ 0.15	$ 750
Ribbon	$ 0.25	$ 1,250
Total Variable Cost	$ 1.45	$ 7,250
Fixed Cost:		
Purchase of Machine		$ 2,000
Total Incremental Cost		$ 9,250
Incremental Income		$ -

It should be noted that sometimes, a special order can be priced below a product's "normal" cost per unit to make if the cost per unit includes fixed costs that would not actually increase as a result of accepting the special order. A special order is considered a short-run decision, meaning it only affects the short term, and, thus, does not affect fixed costs. However, if a long-run decision is being made, like accepting a new customer, pricing should include fixed costs, as those must be covered in the long run.

CONSTRAINED RESOURCES

What is a constrained resource?

A constrained resource is any resource in the business that limits the production output due to its capacity. Constrained resources are often referred to as bottlenecks. Examples of constrained resources can be time on a machine (the machine can only run for so many hours per day), scarce materials needed to make a product (shortages at the supplier for your materials), labor hours needed to make a product (not enough employees), etc. For example, the busiest cruise port in the world in 2016 was PortMiami in Miami, Florida, according to the Cruise Industry News Annual Report. The port and cruise ship terminals can only handle a certain number of cruise ships at one time; thus, the cruise ship terminals are a bottleneck, restricting the number of cruise ship passengers. As of 2017, PortMiami had capacity for approximately 750,000 Royal Caribbean passengers per year (representing about 15% of the port's total cruise ship traffic). In order to allow for more passengers, a new Royal Caribbean terminal is expected to be completed in 2018, which should increase Royal Caribbean passenger traffic by over one million passengers per year, thus increasing capacity.

What is an example of a constrained resource decision?

A constrained resource decision is any decision where management has a constrained resource such that it cannot meet customer demand for all of its products. In this case, management must determine which products it will produce. Of course, management should select the products that will maximize overall profitability. For example, assume Spicy Pickle Company now makes three products: pickles, pickled carrots, and pickled green beans. The machine that processes the vegetables before they are filled into the jars has a maximum run time of 14,400 minutes per month. In order to meet all of the customer demand, management has determined that it would need 18,500 minutes per month, which is not possible given the capacity of the machine. Accordingly, management must decide how many pickles, carrots, and green beans should be produced in order to maximize overall profitability.

What is the general rule with a constrained resource decision?

The general rule with a constrained resource decision is to produce the product that has the highest contribution margin *per unit of the constrained resource*. For example, if minutes of processing time on the machine are the bottleneck, you want to make the most money per minute.

What is the first step involved in evaluating a constrained resource decision?

The first step in evaluating a constrained resource decision is to calculate the contribution margin per unit of product. Assume Spicy Pickle Company has prepared the following calculations of contribution margin per jar for each of its three products:

	Pickles	Carrots	Green Beans
Selling Price per Unit	$ 4.00	$ 4.00	$ 3.50
Variable cost per unit	$ 1.31	$ 1.15	$ 1.00
Contribution margin per unit	$ 2.69	$ 2.85	$ 2.50

Note that based on the contribution margin per jar, Spicy Pickle Company makes the most money selling carrots, as carrots have a contribution margin of $2.85 per jar. However, as there is a constrained resource of time on the machine, this analysis must be taken a step further.

What is the second step involved in evaluating a constrained resource decision?

The second step in evaluating a constrained resource decision is to calculate contribution margin per unit of the constrained resource. This is done by dividing the contribution margin per unit of product by the units of the constrained resource needed for each unit of product. Since Spicy Pickle Company's constrained resource is time on the processing machine, it will need to divide the contribution margin per jar by the minutes used on the processing machine in order to arrive at the contribution margin per minute. Assume the pickles and carrots each take 1 minute of processing time per jar and that green beans only take 0.25 minutes per jar (since they don't need to be cut, peeled, or sliced). Spicy Pickle Company can calculate the contribution margin per minute as follows:

	Pickles	Carrots	Green Beans
Selling Price per Unit	$ 4.00	$ 4.00	$ 3.50
Variable cost per unit	$ 1.31	$ 1.15	$ 1.00
Contribution margin per unit	$ 2.69	$ 2.85	$ 2.50
Time on machine per unit (minutes)	1	1	0.25
Contribution margin per minute	$ 2.69	$ 2.85	$ 10.00

Note that although the green beans have the lowest contribution margin per jar, they actually have the highest contribution margin per minute. This is because four jars of green beans can be processed in the time it takes to process one jar of pickles or carrots. As such, for every minute the machine spends producing green beans, the company makes $10 of contribution margin. For every minute spent making carrots, the company makes $2.85 of contribution margin. For every minute spent making pickles, the company makes $2.69 of contribution margin.

What is the third step involved in evaluating a constrained resource decision?

The third step involved in evaluating a constrained resource decision is to rank the production priority of the products according to their contribution margins per unit of the constrained resource. In the Spicy Pickle Company example, it would prioritize the production of its products as: 1) green beans, 2) carrots, 3) pickles. In essence, it should meet all customer demand if it can for green beans. If there is still time left on the machine, it should work on carrots. Finally, if there is any time remaining, it should work on pickles.

What is the fourth step involved in evaluating a constrained resource decision?

The fourth step involved in evaluating a constrained resource decision is to calculate the most profitable product mix using the prioritization determined in step three. This is done by determining the customer demand for each product and multiplying that by the units of constrained resource needed to arrive at the demand for the constrained resource for each product. Assume Spicy Pickle Company has determined the demand for pickles is 15,000 jars per month, the demand for carrots is 3,000 jars per month, and the demand for green beans is 2,000 jars per month. Recall that jars of pickles and carrots take 1 minute each on the processing machine, and jars of green beans take 0.25 minutes each. Accordingly, the demand for time on the processing machine can be calculated as follows:

	Pickles	Carrots	Green Beans	Total
Monthly demand	15,000	3,000	2,000	
Time on machine per unit (minutes)	1	1	0.25	
Minutes needed to meet demand	15,000	3,000	500	18,500

As you can see, the total number of minutes needed to meet all of customer demand is 18,500 minutes per month, which exceeds the capacity of 14,400 minutes. Spicy Pickle Company will use those 14,400 minutes to make all of the demand for green beans, then work on carrots, and finally on pickles if there is any time left over. In preparing this calculation, Spicy Pickle Company has determined that it can make all 2,000 jars of green beans (using 500 minutes) and all 3,000 jars of carrots (using 3,000 minutes). That leaves 10,900 minutes left over to produce the final product, pickles.

Total capacity in minutes	14,400
Less: Minutes needed to fill green bean demand (2,000 jars)	500
Minutes available for carrots and pickles	13,900
Less: Minutes needed to fill carrot demand (3,000 jars)	3,000
Minutes available for pickles	10,900

Since pickles take 1 minute per jar on the processing machine, it can then be determined that with those 10,900 minutes, Spicy Pickle Company can produce 10,900 jars of pickles, as shown below:

Minutes available for pickles	10,900
/ minutes needed per jar of pickles	1
= Jars of pickles that can be produced	10,900

Accordingly, the most profitable product mix for Spicy Pickle Company is to produce 2,000 jars of green beans, 3,000 jars of carrots, and 10,900 jars of pickles per month. That will give it the highest profit possible with the capacity restraint it is under.

Are there ways to increase the capacity of a constrained resource?

Yes! Increasing the capacity of a constrained resource is known as relaxing or elevating the constraint. As noted earlier in this section with the cruise ship ports, PortMiami is planning to add an additional terminal for Royal Caribbean passengers that will more than double the Royal Caribbean capacity. As for Spicy Pickle Company, it could determine the costs and benefits of increasing capacity, such as adding another processing machine, running the machine for another shift, or outsourcing production, just to name a few.

RESPONSIBILITY ACCOUNTING

What is responsibility accounting?

Responsibility accounting is a system of tracking financial performance that holds managers accountable for their decisions. Responsibility accounting is necessary in decentralized organizations in order to appropriately track outcomes according to the manager who is responsible for them.

What is a decentralized organization?

A decentralized organization is one in which lower-level managers have responsibility for decision making, whereas in a centralized organization, decision making rests with a few key executives. In most organizations, it would not be efficient to leave all decision making to a few key executives. Accordingly, authority is delegated downward to lower-level managers.

What are the advantages of decentralization?

One of the primary advantages of decentralization is that companies can make decisions more quickly and operate more efficiently. Additionally, as lower-level managers have authority to make the day-to-day decisions, key executives are free to focus on the bigger operating strategy. Another advantage of decentralization is that the lower-level managers are empowered to make decisions about the day-to-day areas of the business that they are most familiar with and capable of making decisions for. This empowerment can also increase the motivation and job satisfaction of those managers.

What are the disadvantages of decentralization?

One of the primary disadvantages of decentralization is that there may be a lack of consistency between managers, as different managers may set different policies or make different decisions. Additionally, if the lower-level managers are not aware of or fully in support of the overall business strategy, they may make decisions that are in opposition to the strategy, thus thwarting the organization's ability to meet its objectives.

What is a responsibility center?

A responsibility center is any part of an organization where a manager has control over the cost, profit, or investment. Accordingly, responsibility centers are typically organized into cost centers, profit centers, or investment centers.

What is a cost center?

A cost center can be any area of the business where the manager has control over costs but not the revenues or investments. Most production departments of manufacturing firms are cost centers, as managers are evaluated on their ability to keep costs of making the product in check. This type of evaluation typically takes the form of variance analysis, as was discussed in the chapter entitled "Budgeting, Planning, and Controlling." Additionally, service departments such as accounting and human resources are organized as cost centers. Reports are typically prepared each month showing the departments' costs compared to budgeted or expected levels. Managers are held accountable for going over budget and are often praised for coming in under budget.

What is a profit center?

A profit center is an area of the business where the manager has control over both the revenues and costs but not investments. For example, the manager of a hotel chain location has control over the revenues and the costs of running the hotel but would probably not have control over major investments into the hotel property. Financial statements are typically prepared for each profit center showing revenues and costs compared to budget. Managers are held accountable for lower profits than budgeted and often praised for having higher profits than budgeted.

What is an investment center?

An investment center is an area of the business where the manager has control over revenues, costs, and making investments in fixed assets for the business. Using the hotel chain manager example above, now assume the manager also has the authority over investments for the hotel. Assume the manager decided that a hotel renovation was necessary in order to increase bookings and determined that all furniture and fixtures need to be replaced. The manager would be evaluated on some type of return on investment measure. Essentially, he or she would be evaluated by making sure the cost of the investment in hotel renovations provided an adequate increase in profits for the hotel. Investment centers are often evaluated using the return on investment formula.

How is the return on investment calculated?

The return on investment (ROI) is calculated as net operating income divided by average operating assets. The greater the ROI, the greater the profits are in comparison to the amount invested in operating assets. Recall that net operating income is income before interest and taxes. Operating assets are those assets that are used in the operations of the business, such as cash, accounts receivable, inventory, and property, plant, and equipment assets that are used in operating the business. Operating assets do not include assets that are not used in the operations of the business, such as an investment in another company or a building that is rented to someone else for use.

Is business performance evaluated using only financial measures?

Business performance should be evaluated using an integrated set of performance measures designed to determine whether the business is achieving its overall strategy. These integrated performance measures are typically referred to as the balanced scorecard, which divides the strategy of the business into four different perspectives, from which measurable goals can be determined. The balance scorecard is discussed in detail in the chapter entitled "Financial Statement Analysis."

CAPITAL BUDGETING

What is capital budgeting?

Capital budgeting refers to the process of planning for projects or investments that will have a long-term effect on the business. For example, if Target Corp. is evaluating putting in a new store location somewhere, that is a capital budgeting decision. In short, capital budgeting is the process of evaluating a potential investment for its return in the long run. Managers typically have many more options for investments than they do the funds for those projects. As such, each investment decision must be evaluated as part of the capital budgeting process.

How are capital budgeting decisions evaluated?

In general, capital budgeting decisions are evaluated by comparing the cash spent on the investment (cash outflows) to the increase in cash as a result of making the investment (cash inflows). There are several methods that can be used to evaluate a capital budgeting decision. Some of the more common methods are the payback method, simple rate of return, net present value method, and internal rate of return.

What is the difference between a screening decision and a preference decision?

There are two main types of capital budgeting decisions: screening decisions and preference decisions. A screening decision is a decision that determines whether a project is acceptable or not. For example, if Target had a policy of only putting in new stores in locations where there would be a 20% return, a new store investment would have to be evaluated to determine whether it meets that hurdle. If it was determined that a new store location would only provide a 15% return on investment, the project would not be undertaken. On the other hand, a preference decision involves selecting a project among several acceptable alternatives. For example, Target could evaluate 10 possible new store locations and choose the one that is expected to provide the greatest return on investment.

What are examples of typical cash outflows?

There are three basic types of cash outflows that should be considered when evaluating a capital budgeting decision. The first type is the initial cash outlay for the investment. Using the new Target store example, this would include things such as the cost of the land, the construction costs of the new store, etc. The second type of cash outflows would be any increase in working capital (current assets minus current liabilities) required for the new project. For example, in order to open a new location, Target would need to supply cash for the registers, inventory for the store, etc. The increase in working capital would be included as part of the initial cost of the investment. The third type of cash outflow to be considered in a capital budgeting decision would be any future cash outflows for operating costs and any potential repairs or maintenance. For example, it will cost Target money to operate the store (utilities, insurance, wages, etc.). These are netted against the cash inflows in each year.

What are examples of typical cash inflows?

There are three basic types of cash inflows that should be considered when evaluating a capital budgeting decision. The most common type of cash inflow to be considered is the increase in revenues as a result of the project (or decrease in costs, if applicable). For example, the projected sales revenue from the new Target store would be used as the primary cash inflow for the project. The second form of cash inflow that may be considered in a capital budgeting decision would be the cash received from selling the investment once it is at the end of its useful life. In the Target example, it would most likely not be planning a closure of the new store any time in the foreseeable future; thus, this would not be applicable to the company. However, in a capital budgeting decision for a new machine purchase that is only going to be used for 5 years, the cash received from selling the machine at the end of the 5 years would be applicable. Similarly, the third type of cash inflow that may be included would be the reduction in working capital at the end of the project. Again, Target would probably not include this, as it would not anticipate the store closing at any point in the foreseeable future.

How is the payback method used?

The payback method compares the initial cash outflows to the net cash inflows per year to determine how many years it takes for the company to recoup its initial investment. The time it takes is referred to as the payback period. When the cash inflows per year are the same amount every year, a simple formula for calculating the payback period is:

Investment Required / Annual Net Cash Inflows = Payback Period

For example, assume the cost of opening a new store location was $20 million, used as the initial cash outflow. Also assume that the new store location was projected to bring in cash of approximately $2 million per year. The payback period would be 10 years. In essence, it would take 10 years for the investment to pay for itself.

What is the time value of money?

The time value of money is the basic concept recognizing that a dollar today is worth more than a dollar in the future. For example, assume you had a dollar today that you could invest in your bank account and earn 10% interest. One year from now, you would have $1.10 in the bank. As such, you would rather someone give you one dollar today

What are the advantages and disadvantages of the payback method?

The primary advantage of using the payback method to evaluate capital budgeting decisions is that it is simple to understand and easy to use. It can be a simple prescreening tool to determine whether a capital investment decision warrants further evaluation. The primary disadvantage of using the payback method to evaluate investment decisions is that the payback method ignores all cash flows after the payback period. For example, assume that you were evaluating two different investment decisions that both have an initial cost of $10 million. Investment A provides net cash inflows of $2 million per year for 6 years, for a total of $12 million. The payback period on investment A is 5 years ($10 million / $2 million). Investment B provides net cash inflows of $1.8 million per year for 8 years, and a final cash inflow of $8 million in the ninth year, for a total of $22.4 million. The payback period on investment B is 5.6 years. Investment B provides a greater total overall return on investment. However, if the payback method was used to evaluate the investments, investment A would appear as the better choice, as it takes 5 years for the investment to pay for itself rather than 5.6. Accordingly, the payback method does not provide a true reflection of the profitability of an investment. Furthermore, the payback method does not consider the time value of money.

than give you one dollar one year from now because the dollar today could be investment and be worth more than a dollar in the future. Accordingly, you could say that the future value of $1.00 invested for one year at 10% is $1.10. Accountants use a technique called discounting cash flows to calculate the value of future cash flows using the time value of money concept. This is discussed in depth in accounting and finance textbooks due to its highly technical nature.

How is the simple rate of return method used?

The simple rate of return method compares the incremental net operating income of the project to the initial investment in the project to compute a return on investment. The formula for the simple rate of return is:

Annual Incremental Net Operating Income / Initial Investment = Simple Rate of Return

For example, assume you were evaluating two different investment decisions that both have an initial cost of $10 million. Investment A provides annual incremental net operating income of $2.5 million per year. The simple rate of return on Investment A is 25%. Investment B provides annual incremental net operating income of $1.5 million per year. The simple rate of return on Investment B is 15%. (Note that annual incremental net operating income is calculated as the annual incremental revenues for the project less the annual incremental expenses on the project.)

What is the net present value method?

The net present value method is a technically superior method of evaluating a capital budgeting decision. The net present value method discounts the future cash inflows of a project to the present date and nets the result against the initial investment. The interest rate used in discounting the future cash flows is equal to the required return on investment set by the company. For example, if the company requires a return of 15% on investments, 15% would be used as the discount rate when adjusting the future cash

---

What are the advantages and disadvantages of the simple rate of return method?

Similar to the payback method, the simple rate of return has the advantage of being simple to understand and easy to use. This makes the simple rate of return method a useful tool for prescreening projects. However, the simple rate of return method assumes a consistent stream of income each year, which is not always the case. Additionally, like the payback method, the simple rate of return does not consider the time value of money. In essence, $10 million of income received ten years from now is treated the same as having $10 million today. These are major limitations of the simple rate of return method.

flows to present date. This is discussed in detail in accounting and finance textbooks due to its highly technical nature.

In general, if the net present value is greater than zero, this means that the present value of the cash inflows is greater than the present value of the cash outflows. Put simply, a net present value that is greater than zero is acceptable because the project generates a greater return than what was required by the company (greater than 15%, in this example). A net present value of zero is acceptable because that means the project generated the exact same return as required by the company (15%, in this example). A net present value less than zero is unacceptable because that means the project generated a lower return than is acceptable (less than 15%, in this example). As this method considers the time value of money, it is considered superior to the payback method and simple rate of return method.

What is the internal rate of return?

The internal rate of return is the rate of return that sets the net present value equal to zero. In essence, this is a different alternative to using the net present value. The internal rate of return provides a time value adjusted return on investment rate, comparing the cash inflows to the initial cash outflow. Again, this is discussed in detail in accounting and finance textbooks due to its highly technical nature.

In general, if the internal rate of return is equal to or higher than the rate the company requires (equal to or higher than the 15% given in the previous example), the project should be accepted. If the internal rate of return is lower than the rate the company requires, the project should be rejected.

Which method is best to evaluate a capital budgeting decision?

While the net present value and internal rate of return methods are technically superior, there may be times when it is appropriate to use a simpler method. As discussed in this chapter, the payback method and the simple rate of return method can be useful tools to quickly compare project ideas before a more detailed analysis is completed. No matter which method is chosen, it is important to complete a post-audit of the investment by re-calculating the return on investment (using the same method that was initially used to evaluate the capital budgeting decision) based on actual results and compare the results to what was anticipated. This helps managers improve the capital budgeting process and should help identify ways managers may try to influence the outcomes of the capital budgeting decision by skewing the numbers in favor of or against a project idea.

STARTING A SMALL BUSINESS

CHOOSING A BUSINESS STRUCTURE

What is one of the first things that must be done when starting a small business?

Prior to starting up any small business, you must first decide what organizational form your business will take on. The organizational form will determine many things about the organization of your business, including ownership and how it is taxed.

What are the three primary forms of business organization?

The three primary forms of business organization are: sole proprietorship, partnership, and corporation. Additionally, there are several other hybrid forms of organization, such as S corporations and limited liability corporations, as discussed below. Before selecting any one of these forms of organization, small business owners should consult a tax accountant and/or attorney, as each business is unique, and there are no hard and fast rules about which form should be selected in any scenario.

Which form of business is the most common in the United States?

According to tax statistics showing the number of returns filed by form of business as reported by the Internal Revenue Service (IRS) as of 2013 (the latest figures available), the most common form of organization is the sole proprietorship, representing 72% of returns filed. The other forms of business represented the following percentages of returns filed: S corporations, 12.7%; limited liability corporations, 6.8%; C corporations, 4.8%; partnerships, 2.3%; and limited partnerships, 1.2%.

What is a sole proprietorship?

A sole proprietorship is a business owned by one individual.

261

What is the primary advantage of a sole proprietorship?

The primary advantage of a sole proprietorship is that it is simple to form. From a legal standpoint, a sole proprietorship is considered one with the owner. As such, the owner does not need to get a separate tax ID number or a DBA (doing business as) registration. The owner can essentially just start running the business. Profits or losses from the business are recorded on the owner's personal income tax return. Other advantages are the low cost of establishing the business and the high flexibility to switch to other organizational forms in the future.

What are some of the common disadvantages of a sole proprietorship?

As the business is not considered separate from the owner from a legal standpoint, the owner is personally liable for the debts of the business. Since the owner is not considered separate from the business from a legal standpoint, the owner risks losing his or her personal assets in the event of a lawsuit, etc. Additionally, depending on the profit level of the business, the income taxed at the personal tax rate and the self-employment taxes incurred may be more costly than taxes in other business forms.

What is a partnership?

A partnership is like a sole proprietorship; however, it is owned by two or more individuals.

Having one or more partners in your business has the advantage of making more resources available to your business.

What is the advantage in having a partnership over a sole proprietorship?

The main advantage of a partnership over a sole proprietorship is that, since there are more owners, there are typically more resources available to the partnership. For example, if you have $50,000 to invest in a business and you are able to bring a partner in with $50,000 more, the business now has double the funds available to it.

What is the disadvantage in having a partnership over a sole proprietorship?

One of the main disadvantages in setting up a partnership over a sole proprietorship is that the owners typically need a lawyer to draft a partnership agreement. The agreement states things like how profits will be shared and what happens if someone wants to leave the partnership. In addition to the increased start-up costs, there may also be increased liability, as both partners are personally liable for the debts of the business. If you have a partner who makes a decision, you may be held personally liable.

What is an LLP?

An LLP is a limited liability partnership. An LLP combines the organizational structure of a partnership with liability protection for the partners. In general, and depending on which state the LLP is in, partners in an LLP are not personally liable for the actions of the other partners. The LLP is generally the target of any lawsuits such that an owner could lose his or her share of company assets but wouldn't be at risk of losing his or her personal assets. A partner could be held personally liable if he or she were found to have done something wrong. In that sense, the liability is limited. Many accounting firms are set up as LLPs.

What is a corporation?

A corporation is a business that is a separate legal entity from its owners from both an accounting and a legal standpoint.

What are some of the primary advantages of a corporation?

Ownership in a corporation is divided up into individual shares, making it easy to raise large amounts of funds. These shares can be transferred from one owner to the next. Corporations can be private or public. Public corporations sell their stock to the public on

What is the primary disadvantage of a corporation?

A corporation files its own tax return and pays taxes on the profits of the business. Additionally, when the corporation shares those profits with the owners in the form of dividends, the owners are taxed on those dividends on their personal tax returns. This results in the profits of the corporation being taxed twice, commonly referred to as double taxation.

a stock exchange. For example, at the time of writing this publication, you can buy one share of Apple, Inc., stock for around $175. Private corporations do not sell their stock on a stock exchange and, thus, it is not available to the public. Mars, Inc., maker of chocolate candies, gum, pet food, and more, remains a privately held company. As such, as much as you may like M&Ms, you cannot be an owner of Mars, Inc.

An additional advantage of corporations is that the owners are not personally liable for the debts of the business since the corporation is a separate legal entity. As such, the corporation has the right to sue and be sued, not the individual owners.

What is an LLC?

An LLC is a limited liability company. LLCs are hybrid forms of business organization that blend the characteristics of partnerships with corporations. LLCs enjoy some of the limited liability characteristics of corporations while obtaining the tax benefits of partnerships. An LLC is a pass-through entity, which means that the business income is reported on the owner's personal income tax return. An LLC requires articles of organization to be filed with the state but is easier to set up than a corporation. A business continuation agreement is necessary to ensure the continuation of the business when one of the owners leaves or passes away.

What is an S corporation?

An S corporation is another hybrid form of business that blends the characteristics of partnerships with corporations. Like LLCs, S corporations enjoy some of the limited liability characteristics of corporations with the tax benefits of partnerships. In an S corporation, owners pay themselves salaries in addition to receiving dividends from the profits of the business.

Which form of organization is best for small business?

There is no answer to this question. Selecting a form of organization is a very important step in starting up a small business. It can have consequences in the future that small business owners are unaware of when starting up a business. Each form of organization has its own pros and cons. A good attorney and/or tax accountant can be very helpful in determining which form of organization would be most advantageous, depending on the particular business situation.

CREATING A BUSINESS PLAN

What is a business plan?

A business plan is a document that identifies the plan for the business. A business plan can take many forms (short, long, formal, informal), depending on the intended use and/or audience for the document.

Why do you need a business plan?

If you are starting a small business and intend to get a loan from the bank or attract investors, they will most likely request a business plan. After all, no one wants to loan money or invest money in something that they have no clue about. The business plan will give potential lenders and investors insight into your business idea, goals, and strategy for achieving those goals. Additionally, it is a good idea for existing businesses to regularly review and update their business plan as the business and the industry in which the business operates are continuously changing and evolving.

What are some of the key components of a business plan?

While business plans can be tailored to each business's individual needs, most business plans include an executive summary, a company overview, and sections that detail the management team, products and/or services offered, industry analysis, marketing strategy, financial plan, and key milestones and metrics used to evaluate the business. The Internet is full of resources on business plans and examples. Some basic information is provided below.

What is an executive summary?

An executive summary is a short (typically no more than one page) overview of the business plan. Think of it this way: If a busy executive only has time to read one page of your business plan, you need to tell them what you are going to tell them in the rest of the document in one simple, easy-to-read section. If they're interested or if they want more details, they can always read the entirety of the document. The executive summary is your sales pitch in one page or less. Make it count!

What is included in the company overview?

The company overview provides some of the basic information about your company. You should describe what your company will do, how it is unique, and what problem it solves. You can include a summary of the history of the business (if there is a history), the owners, the legal structure, the location, etc. You should also include a mission and/or vision statement.

What is included about the management team?

The management team section is optional but does give you a chance to show off your expertise. The management team section typically includes bios of the members of the management team, including a description of the role of each of the members. You can also point out any shortcomings that you see and how you plan to address those.

How detailed is the description of products and services?

The description of products and services should be very detailed. This is where you present your exact ideas about your product/service and why they are unique. Rather than simply saying, "We will sell pizza," you should say something like, "Our customers will build their own pizza from a buffet of toppings. Our pizza chefs will then place the pizzas into a stone-fired pizza oven that is visible to the customers from the dining room, creating a unique pizza creation and dining experience." You can also describe how you will obtain the supplies you need and what the perceived customer demand is for your product and/or service.

What is included in the industry summary?

Now that you have described your business, you need to focus on the industry that your business will operate in. You can start with a general overview of your industry and follow it up with details about how your business fits into that industry. This may be a good place to include a SWOT analysis or a Porter's five forces analysis.

What is a Porter's five forces analysis?

Porter's five forces is a framework to analyze the level of competition within an industry and analyze the business strategy in relation to that competition. This framework was developed by economist Michael E. Porter in order to help companies assess the nature of an industry's competitiveness and to develop an appropriate strategy.

What are Porter's five forces?

Porter's five forces are: competitive rivalry, bargaining power of suppliers, bargaining power of customers, threat of new entrants, and threat of substitutes.

Competitive rivalry analyzes how intense the existing competition is in the industry. It includes things like the number of competitors, quality differences, and customer loyalty.

What is a SWOT analysis?

A SWOT analysis is an analysis of your business in terms of its strengths, weaknesses, opportunities, and threats. It is usually shown in a matrix form. The strengths and weaknesses are internal in origin, meaning they contain the attributes of your business. The opportunities and threats are external in origin, meaning they contain the attributes of the environment your business operates in. Using the pizza restaurant example above, a strength may be that you have 30 years of pizzeria management experience. A weakness may be that since this is a start-up, you will be draining cash. An opportunity may be that there are no pizzerias with dine-in availability within 20 miles of your location. A threat may be the consumer trend to eat healthier, with whole wheat and gluten-free options. A good SWOT analysis should be well thought out, with several items in each area. Who knows, after completing your SWOT analysis, you may just decide you should offer gluten-free crust after all!

The bargaining power of suppliers determines how much power a business's supplier has and how much control it has over the potential to raise its prices. It includes things like the number of suppliers, size of suppliers, your ability to substitute, and the costs of changing suppliers.

The bargaining power of customers analyzes the customers' ability to affect prices and quality. It includes things like the number of customers, the size of orders, price sensitivity, and the cost of changing for the customer.

The threat of new entrants analyzes how easy it is for a competitor to enter your industry. This includes things like how much time or money it takes to start up a business in your industry, what special knowledge is required, economies of scale required, technology protection, and any barriers to entry.

The threat of substitutes analyzes the substitute products or services that could be offered in place of the products or services offered in your industry. Substitute products are products the consumer perceives as meeting the same need that can replace your product.

What goes into the marketing strategy section?

The marketing strategy explains how you will convince people to buy your product and/or service. The marketing strategy should identify your target market, including the geographic area, customer demographics, and customer lifestyle, values, and purchasing motivations. The marketing strategy should also identify what percentage of the market you will attempt to gain (market share). You should also include a description of the image you wish for your business to portray as well as any slogans or branding. Additionally, the marketing section should discuss the ways you will reach your customers through advertising and provide cost estimates for the advertising activities. The marketing section should identify your top competitors and their strengths and weaknesses, being sure to address how your business is superior. Finally, the marketing plan should address pricing of your products and/or services.

What is included in the financial plan?

The financial plan is a critical piece of the business plan. For a start-up business, the financial plan will project your financial results in the future and help you identify how much money you will need to start and run your business. A typical financial plan starts with a sales forecast. As discussed in the chapter entitled "Budgeting, Planning, and Controlling," the budgeting process starts with sales. Additionally, the financial plan includes budgeted financial statements (income statement, balance sheet, and cash flow statement). Existing companies will include actual financial statements and data as well.

What are the key milestones and metrics?

Key milestones represent specific tasks you plan to accomplish, including dates they should be accomplished by. In addition, a business plan should identify specific metrics

Do you need to hire a professional to draft a business plan?

No, you don't need to hire a professional to draft a business plan. As mentioned earlier, there are a wealth of resources that can help you draft a business plan. However, if you are new to business and are in need of finding investors or lenders, it couldn't hurt to get some professional advice or assistance.

that will be used to measure the success of the business. These can be referred to as KPIs, or key performance indicators. These metrics should cover financial and nonfinancial areas and can be aligned with the balanced scorecard approach, discussed in the chapter entitled "Financial Statement Analysis." In addition to identifying KPIs, goals should be set. For example, if you determine that current ratio is a KPI, you should determine what your target current ratio should be. When setting KPIs and goals, it is helpful to use the "smart" approach. The "smart" approach entails setting goals that are specific, measurable, attainable, relevant, and timely.

SETTING UP AN ACCOUNTING INFORMATION SYSTEM

Why do businesses need an accounting information system?

Upon starting up a business, one of the first things that needs to be done is to select an accounting information system. The accounting information system is what will be used to track the detailed, day-to-day events of the business and transform that data into internal and external reports, which will be used to evaluate the business and make decisions to run the business. Every transaction in the business, starting from the first day of operations, must be recorded. As such, a new business should have an accounting information system selected and implemented upon the start of the business.

What type of accounting information system is needed to run a small business?

Most small businesses can run quite well with smaller, prepackaged software systems, such as QuickBooks™. However, some companies require the sophistication of midsized accounting software packages, such as Microsoft Dynamics. Large companies typically run large enterprise resource planning (ERP) systems, such as SAP. These ERP systems are typically highly customizable and integrate many of the functions of the business, such as finance, sales and marketing, customer service, materials management, etc. There are many accounting firms that specialize in setting up and servicing accounting information systems. They can be very helpful in identifying which system best meets the business's needs. In addition, there are many accounting information systems that are industry specific and have modules tailored to the special needs of an industry.

How much does it cost to purchase an accounting information system?

Costs range quite a bit depending on the size of the system. Basic accounting software can be purchased for as little as $200. Costs go up from there depending on the level of sophistication and additional modules needed. Additionally, even with small accounting software packages, start-up businesses should budget in the cost of having an accountant assist with the setup of the accounting information system and providing ongoing technical support. Midsized ERP systems can cost over $100,000 to implement. The cost to implement a large ERP system can be over $10 million.

How much will a small business use spreadsheet software?

It is more likely than not that a small business will rely on spreadsheet software quite a bit. In fact, most accounting information systems have built-in links to export financial reports and information to Microsoft Excel. As sophisticated as accounting software packages may be, most accountants favor the ease of use and customizability of exporting information into these other tools.

The effectiveness and efficiency of accounting and finance's heavy reliance on spreadsheet programs has been debated for decades. However, the 2017 Benchmarking the Accounting & Finance Function report, put together by Robert Half and the Financial Executives Research Foundation (FERF), shows that 69% of U.S. executives surveyed said their company continues to use Microsoft Excel as their primary budgeting and planning tool. It is common to see Microsoft Excel experience listed among the required qualifications for accounting and finance job postings. Additionally, it is also common to see Excel tips and tricks courses among those offered as continuing education courses for accountants.

Spreadsheet software is inexpensive and very helpful to those owning small businesses. Microsoft Excel is an example of a popular program that is widely used.

PROFIT AND CASH FLOW

How do you know if a start-up business is successful?

There are several ways to determine if a start-up business is successful, but from a financial perspective, the two basic measures commonly used are profitability and cash flow.

Can a business be successful if it doesn't make a profit?

The goal of business is to make a profit. Profit is the excess of revenues over expenses. Put simply, it is what the business charged customers for providing goods and services minus the costs of providing those goods and services and administering the business. Of course, a successful business should charge its customers more than enough to cover its costs. Otherwise, what would the point of the business be? However, it may take a start-up several years to earn a profit as the customer base is growing, and early spending on infrastructure, employees, and advertising result in high expenses for the business. Accordingly, a start-up business can measure its success by other trends, such as increasing sales and decreasing losses. Additionally, results should be compared to the budgeted figures calculated as part of the business plan to determine congruence.

Can a business be profitable and still be unsuccessful?

A business can be profitable but still be unsuccessful if it is unable to manage its cash flow. For example, due to the accrual nature of accounting, a business may earn revenues and record profits but be unable to actually collect the cash from customers. Without the cash collection from customers, the business will be unable to pay its debts, which will create problems with the suppliers and lenders. Suppliers will stop supplying, and lenders will stop lending. Thus, the business will be unsuccessful. Accordingly, a strong cash-management plan is essential to the success of a small business.

What is the life cycle of a business in terms of cash flow?

The flow of cash varies throughout the life cycle of the business. Start-up businesses typically have negative operating cash flows and rely on investors and creditors to provide funding to get them through the growing pains of the business. These negative operating cash flows can last a few years. Once the start-up enters the growth phase of the business life cycle, operating cash flows should be positive and increasing. The growing business may still rely heavily on financing to fund the growth of the business, as it invests in itself. Stagnant operating cash flows with a decline in financing cash flows generally reflect a maturing business. Finally, a continual decline in operating cash flows along with repayments of debt and selling off of assets generally reflect a business at the end of its life cycle.

How often should financial results be reviewed?

There are certain results that should be reviewed daily and others monthly, quarterly, and annually. Based on the business plan and the KPIs identified, a small business owner should be able to determine what to review and how frequently to do it. Every industry is unique, and there is no one-size-fits-all approach. For example, a small ice cream shop owner could review the cash register sales totals daily and compare to the previous few days, the budget, and the similar period from the prior year. While this may be a simple and informal task, this is one where a small business owner can really put his or her finger on the pulse of the business with minimal effort. Another example of an item that could be reviewed daily is the cash deposits to the bank.

While some small businesses wait until the end of each quarter to prepare financial statements, a monthly review is preferable. For example, if profit was $10,000 in January compared to a budget of $20,000, and this information and trend was not reviewed until quarterly financials were prepared on April 10, months would have gone by before the business owner is made aware of this potential problem. If monthly financial statements were prepared, the problem could have been investigated and corrected much sooner.

Quarterly and annual financial packages can become more robust, including reviews or audits from accounting firms, formal ratio analyses, charts and graphs, etc.

EMPLOYEES AND PAYROLL

What is an employer?

Under the Fair Labor Standards Act (FLSA), commonly known as the Federal Wage and Hour Law, an employer can be any individual, partnership, association, business trust, legal representative, or any organized group of persons acting in the direct or indirect interest of the employer, such as an agent or manager. The characteristics of an employer include: the authority to hire and fire, supervision and control over the work, and the obligation to pay wages.

What are the obligations for reporting new hires to the government?

When hiring a new employee, the payroll processor must determine if an employer–employee relationship exists (versus independent contractor) and comply with the new hire reporting requirements required by federal law and the individual state, if applicable. If it is determined that the new hire is an employee and not an independent contractor, the new hire must fill out a Form W-4. The Form W-4 lists the employee's name, social security number, and selects their federal tax withholding status. Many states also have a similar form that must be filled out. In addition, an I-9 must be filled out, which verifies the employee's eligibility to work in the United States. Finally, each state has its own requirements for new hire reporting that must be complied with.

What is the difference between an employee and an independent contractor?

The rules for determining whether a new hire is an employee or independent contractor vary according to the FLSA (for determining minimum wage and overtime require-

Some companies might enjoy hiring independent contractors to keep down expenses and to have flexibility if the business is seasonal and doesn't need a full staff year round.

ments, etc.), the IRS (for determining payroll tax obligations), and the state (for determining state unemployment tax obligations). In general, the difference between an employee and an independent contractor is the degree of independence allowed to the individual. Independent contractors are typically not a permanent employee, operate with a greater degree of independence, may work for more than one firm, and have the opportunity for profit or loss. Independent contractors are not covered by the benefits of the FLSA. On the other hand, employees are generally those who are under the control of the employer. Employers must withhold for FICA and income taxes for employees and pay FUTA taxes on employees. It is wise to consult a human resources or payroll professional in making this determination if there is a gray area, especially since the rules are different for the different reporting entities.

Do all employees have to be paid the minimum wage and overtime rates?

The FLSA requires that all employees be paid the minimum wage of $7.25 per hour and overtime rates at one and one-half times the employees' regular pay rate for hours worked in excess of forty per workweek, unless specifically exempted. Exemptions vary; some exemptions are for both minimum wage and overtime, while others are specific to one or the other. A common example of employees who are exempt from the provisions of the minimum wage and overtime pay requirements are executives, professional employees, and teachers. Again, it is wise to consult a human resources or payroll professional if there is a question on whether an employee is exempt or not.

What records are required to be maintained and kept for employees under the FLSA?

The FLSA requires certain records to be kept for three years and other records to be kept for two years. Records that must be kept for three years include: payroll records, union contracts, employment contracts involving exclusions from the regular pay rate, negotiations to overtime pay, and sales and purchase records for the business. Records that must be kept for two years include: basic employment and earnings records; wage rate tables; work time schedules; order, shipping, and billing records; and records of additions to or deductions from wages.

How do you determine the payroll period?

A regular payroll period can be daily, weekly, biweekly, semimonthly, monthly, quarterly, semiannual, or annual. Specific states may have requirements regarding the frequency of the pay periods, the allowable time between the end of the pay period and the pay date, and the time in which a terminated employee should receive his or her final paycheck. Accordingly, it is wise to check with a human resources or payroll professional before selecting a pay period.

What are the basic types of payroll tax obligations?

The basic types of payroll tax obligations are employee federal income tax withholding, Federal Insurance Contributions Act (FICA) taxes, and Federal Unemployment Tax Act (FUTA) taxes.

What is a payroll withholding?

A payroll withholding is an amount withheld from an employee's gross earnings and paid to another entity on the employee's behalf. Common types of employee withholdings are federal income tax withholdings, FICA tax withholdings, medical insurance premiums, and retirement contributions. For example, assume an employee earned $1,000 for the pay period, known as the gross pay. The employee is not cut a check for that $1,000 because the employer is obligated to withhold federal income taxes and FICA taxes on the employee's behalf. Assume the federal income tax withholding was $150, and the FICA tax withholding was $77. Additionally, assume the employee selects the employer-sponsored health-care plan and has to pay $25 per paycheck. Finally, assume this employee elects to put 3% of his or her earnings in the company-sponsored retirement plan, totaling $30 for the pay period. The employee's gross pay of $1,000 would be reduced by the sum of these deductions ($282) in arriving at the amount of the paycheck, known as net pay, of $718. The employer still incurs wages expense of the total $1,000 in gross pay, but the amount is remitted to different parties. The $718 net pay is remitted to the employee. The $282 in withholdings is remitted to the federal government, health-care provider, and retirement account, all on behalf of the employee. This makes it very efficient for the employee; however, it is quite a tedious process for the employer.

What is FICA?

FICA taxes represent the taxes charged on employees and employers for Social Security and Medicare. The FICA tax is a shared tax, wherein the employer has to match the amount the employee pays. For 2017, the Social Security tax rate for individuals is 6.2% on the first $127,200 in wages paid. The 2017 Medicare tax rate for individuals is 1.45% on the first $200,000 and 2.35% for wages paid above $200,000. Those amounts are withheld from the employee paychecks. In addition to withholding these amounts from the employees, the employer must also match these payments for the employer portion of the tax. Accordingly, the Social Security Administration receives 12.4% in Social Security taxes for every $127,200 paid to each employee and so on. Independent contractors must pay all of these taxes themselves, known as self-employment income taxes, which are 15.3% as of 2017, of which 12.4% is for Social Security and 2.9% is for Medicare.

What is FUTA?

FUTA taxes represent the taxes charged to employers to cover benefits workers may receive during periods of unemployment. There is no employee portion of the FUTA tax and as such, it is only a burden to the employer. As of 2017, the FUTA tax rate is 6% on the first $7,000 of taxable wages paid to each employee.

What is SUTA?

SUTA taxes are the states' version of FUTA taxes. Each state has different rates. In most states, SUTA is a tax charged only to the employer, but some states also require employees to contribute. The tax rate is determined based on the utilization of unemployment benefits by qualified employees from that business. This is known as an experience rating. In essence, the more former employees you have who collect unemployment benefits, the higher your tax rate will be.

What type of software and hardware are needed to process payroll in-house?

Most accounting information systems have a payroll module available. Adequate payroll modules should include the ability to perform earnings and deductions calculations and compute all manners of payroll taxes. The software should be updated frequently to reflect changes in payroll tax rates, etc. Only basic hardware is needed, such as a computer to run the payroll software and a printer to print checks (if not using direct deposit).

What are the advantages and disadvantages of outsourcing payroll processing?

The primary advantage of outsourcing payroll is that a business can leave the complexities to the experts and therefore does not need to employ a payroll department, thus saving payroll department wages and the software costs of processing the payroll in-house. Additionally, a business that outsources payroll is free to focus its efforts on its core business and not be burdened with the administrative duties of processing payroll. One of the primary disadvantages of outsourcing payroll is the cost of the fees charged by the

> ## Should a small business outsource payroll processing?
>
> **P**ayroll is a complex process and is full of intricacies that, if not applied correctly, can be rather costly in fines and penalties. The fact that each state has its own payroll rules and rates further complicates the matter for multistate businesses. As such, a start-up business would be wise to seek the consultation of a payroll professional. It may be determined that the payroll is simple enough to be done in-house. In that case, a payroll professional can help with the setup of the payroll module in the accounting information system. However, it may also be determined that the payroll is rather complex and better outsourced to the experts.

service provider. Additionally, the business loses control of the payroll function and is at the mercy of the customer service provided by the service organization. Each business should consider its unique situation when determining whether or not to outsource payroll.

What types of benefits can be offered to employees?

Benefits that can be offered to employees include: retirement plans, health insurance plans, dependent care reimbursement, long-term care insurance, group term life insurance, educational expense reimbursement, automobile costs, meals, travel and lodging, and payment for dues for professional associations.

Should a small business provide benefits to employees?

Offering benefits to employees helps provide an attractive total compensation package. Many of the benefits are tax-free to the employees and serve as a tax deduction for the employers. Start-up businesses should consult a human resources professional and/or benefits provider to discuss options available to them.

TAX ISSUES

Should a small business hire a tax professional?

It is wise for a new small business to consult a tax professional to engage in tax planning strategies and, possibly, to prepare the tax returns. As the tax law and tax rates change, hiring a tax professional can help small businesses focus on the core aspects of their business and leave taxes to the experts. Accordingly, the remainder of this chapter doesn't explain the how-tos of business taxes but rather provides some basic terminology so that a small business owner can have an informed discussion with his or her tax professional.

275

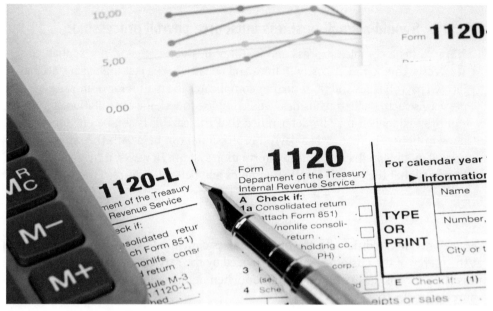

Corporations are required to file tax returns with the IRS just as individuals do. The form that is used is Form 1120.

Do businesses file a tax return?

The type of tax return filed is different depending on the form of business organization. For example, sole proprietorship income flows through onto the owner's personal tax return on Schedule C of the IRS Form 1040. Thus, the business itself does not file a separate tax return. However, as corporations are separate legal entities, they file their own tax return on IRS Form 1120. As over 70% of U.S. corporations are sole proprietorships, the remainder of this chapter will focus on tax issues for those entities.

What records are required to be maintained for tax purposes?

The tax law requires businesses to maintain an accurate and complete set of books. It does not specify any particular manner in which these books should be maintained. The need to maintain an accurate set of books for tax purposes further reflects the importance of selecting an appropriate accounting information system upon starting the business. Additionally, the utilization of a computerized accounting information system allows the business to easily forward business records to a tax professional, saving time and money in the preparation of tax returns, if applicable. In addition to general record-keeping requirements, the tax law requires additional substantiation for many things, including: travel and entertainment expenses, charitable contributions, depreciation, and basis.

What records must be kept for meal and entertainment expenses?

The tax law requires both written substantiation and documentary evidence. Written substantiation can be in the form of a diary, log book, or other system that notes specific information, such as the dates, locations, and the business purpose for the trip. Documentary evidence is typically in the form of the receipts, canceled checks, or bills for the expenses. Written substantiation is not needed if a standard per diem rate is used for meals and lodging.

What is a per diem rate?

A per diem rate is a flat rate set by the business to reimburse employees for travel and related expenses. This simplifies record keeping, as actual receipts are not needed. As long as the employer reimburses the employee at a rate that is equal to or below the federal per diem rates, the reimbursement is not reported on the employee's W-2. Federal per diem rates vary by geographic location. Per diem rates can be accessed online at www.gsa.gov.

What records must be kept for car expenses?

Evidence of car expenses can be documented in a log of odometer readings, showing the destination and the purpose of the trip. You do not need receipts or other proof of costs if you use a standard mileage rate.

What is a mileage rate?

A mileage rate is a flat rate per mile set by the business to reimburse employees for personal use of their automobile for business purposes. As long as the employer reimburses the employee at a rate that is equal to or below the federal standard mileage rate, the reimbursement is not reported on the employee's W-2. The standard mileage rate can be accessed online at www.irs.gov. The federal standard mileage rate for 2018 is 54.5 cents per mile.

What records must be kept for charitable donations?

Charitable donations must be documented by a written acknowledgment from the charity, a bank statement, or another permissible method. Generally, if the donation is property, rather than cash, and it is valued at over $5,000, it may also require a certificate of appraisal.

What records must be kept for depreciation?

In order to claim deductions for depreciation of assets, records must be kept indicating the cost of the asset, any capital improvements to depreciable assets, and depreciation deductions already claimed. Again, it is wise to invest in an accounting information system or tax software that will track all of this data for you.

What is basis?

In general, basis is the cost of the property being recorded for tax purposes. Depreciation deductions are based on this amount. Basis is also used to calculate a gain or loss on disposal of property.

What does the term taxable income mean?

Taxable business income includes income from service business, income from the sale of goods, investment-type income, and miscellaneous business income. Note that while the tax law uses the word "income," it is most similar to "gross profit" in financial accounting (sales revenue minus cost of goods sold), not "net income." The majority of business expenses are deducted from taxable income in arriving at the net profit or loss on the Schedule C form.

Additionally, taxable income is the amount of income the business actually pays taxes on, which is not necessarily equal to the total income of the business. For example, if a business invests in municipal bonds and earns interest income, that income is not taxable by the federal government. Thus, not all of the income from the business is taxable.

Where is business income reported on the tax return for sole proprietors?

Business income for sole proprietors is recorded on the Schedule C form and carried forward to the owner's personal income tax return on Form 1040. Note that for some small businesses, income can be reported on a Schedule C-EZ form.

What are capital gains and losses?

Capital gains and losses are an income classification used in the tax law that is generally provided with more favorable tax treatment than other types of income. Capital gains and losses generally arise from selling the capital assets of your business. Capital gains are calculated as the amount of proceeds received over the adjusted basis in the property. Conversely, capital losses result when the amount received is less than the adjusted basis. There are certain criteria that must be met to determine if an asset is treated as a capital asset, but in general, capital assets are property held for investment, such as the owner's interest in a partnership. The adjusted basis is the original basis in the property, adjusted upward or downward for things like improvements to the property (upward) and depreciation on the property (downward).

What are some common business deductions?

Some common business deductions that can be taken to offset business income are: employee compensation, business-related meal expenses, car and truck expenses, repairs and maintenance, bad debts, rent, taxes, interest, depreciation, advertising expense, retirement plans, home office deductions, and medical coverage.

Where are business deductions reported on the tax return for sole proprietors?

Business deductions are reported on the Schedule C form for sole proprietors.

ACCOUNTANTS AND THE FUTURE OF ACCOUNTING

ACCOUNTING CAREERS

What are the basic accounting career paths?

The basic accounting career paths are private and public accounting. Private accountants are employees of the business they provide accounting services for, while public accountants work for accounting firms and provide accounting services to their clients. Private accountants can work for public companies, private companies, or nonprofit organizations. Public accountants can work for local firms, regional firms, and international firms.

What are the different accounting functions and specializations for private accountants?

Private accountants can work in all sizes of business from very small organizations up to multinational organizations. The larger the organization, the greater the need for specialization among the accounting functions. Different areas of accounting include: general ledger accounting, budgeting, forecasting, cost accounting, taxation, internal audit, and many other areas, such as finance and information systems.

What are the different accounting functions and specializations for public accountants?

Public accountants can work in all sizes of accounting firms, from local proprietorships to regional firms, all the way up to the "Big Four" international firms. Most local firms specialize in taxation and bookkeeping services. Generally, the larger the firm, the more areas of specialization there are. The most common areas for specialization are audit, taxation, and consulting. Consulting services include forensic accounting, computer information systems security, and industry specialization.

What are the typical starting salaries for accountants?

Starting salaries for accountants vary across the type of function/specialization, size of the organization, and geographic location. However, typical starting salaries for accountants generally range from about $30,000 to $70,000.

What are typical salaries of senior-level accounting positions?

Again, salaries for senior-level accountants vary across the type of function/specialization, size of the organization, and geographic location. Per the 2018 Salary Guide published by Robert Half, typical chief financial officer compensation ranges from $119,000 to $497,000, and typical audit senior manager/director salary ranges from $108,250 to $206,500.

What are the typical senior-level accounting positions?

In private accounting, typical senior-level positions are chief financial officer (CFO), vice president of finance, director of accounting, director of financial reporting, controller, and treasurer. In public accounting, typical senior-level positions are senior manager, director, and partner.

CREDENTIALS

What are the different credentials relevant to the accounting profession?

Some of the most relevant credentials in the accounting profession are: CPA (certified public accountant), CMA (certified management accountant), CFE (certified fraud ex-

Of the several certifications available to accountants, one of the more familiar ones is certified public accountant (CPA). Not all accountants are CPAs, but the ones who are have to pass a vigorous examination for the honor.

aminer), CIA (certified internal auditor), MBA (master of business administration), MSA (master of science in accountancy), CFA (certified fraud examiner), CISA (certified information system auditor), and CPP (certified payroll professional).

What skills are in demand for accountants?

According to the 2018 Salary Guide published by Robert Half, some of the in-demand skills for accountants are: advanced Microsoft Excel expertise, general knowledge of ERP systems, experience with data analysis, QuickBooks™ experience, strong communication skills, leadership abilities, adaptability, and multilingualism.

Does CPA mean tax preparer?

No. Contrary to common thought, not all CPAs are tax preparers. Taxation is one of many areas of specialization that a CPA may engage in, so the next time you are introduced to a CPA at a dinner party, you might want to think twice about asking them your tax question.

What is a CPA?

CPA stands for certified public accountant. An individual who is a CPA has been licensed by his or her state to provide accounting services to the public. All CPAs are accountants, but not all accountants are CPAs. In order to become a CPA, an accountant must pass the CPA examination and meet the education and work requirements mandated by their state. According to the AICPA website, "A CPA is a trusted financial advisor who helps individuals, businesses, and other organizations plan and reach their financial goals."

What are the pass rates for the CPA exam?

The CPA exam is a national exam divided into four parts (each lasting four hours): financial accounting and reporting (FAR), auditing and attestation (AUD), regulation (REG), and business environment and concepts (BEC). Pass rates for the CPA exam for 2017 as reported by the AICPA were: FAR, 44.42%; AUD, 48.59%; REG, 47.24%; and BEC 52.99%.

MAJOR PLAYERS

Who are the major entities involved in setting financial accounting standards in the United States?

The major entities involved in setting financial accounting standards are the Financial Accounting Standards Board (FASB), International Accounting Standards Board (IASB), Governmental Accounting Standards Board (GASB), and Federal Accounting Standards Advisory Board (FASAB). The FASB, as discussed in detail in the chapter entitled "FASB's

Conceptual Framework," sets generally accepted accounting principles for U.S. entities other than federal, state, and local governments. The GASB sets financial accounting standards for state and local governments. The FASAB sets accounting standards for the federal government.

The IASB, founded in 2001, is the major standard-setting body for global financial accounting standards, known as International Financial Reporting Standards (IFRS). Per the IFRS website, www.ifrs.org, there are currently over 125 jurisdictions that require IFRS.

Does the United States follow IFRS?

No. As of the time of this publication, the United States still follows U.S. GAAP as set by the FASB.

What is the AICPA?

Per the AICPA website, "The American Institute of CPAs (AICPA) is the world's largest member association representing the accounting profession, with more than 418,000 members in 143 countries, and a history of serving the public interest since 1887. The AICPA sets ethical standards for the profession and U.S. auditing standards for private companies, nonprofit organizations, federal, state and local governments. It develops and grades the Uniform CPA Examination, and offers specialty credentials for CPAs who concentrate on personal financial planning, forensic accounting, business valuation, and information management and technology assurance."

What is the IMA?

Per the IMA website, the Institute of Management Accountants (IMA) "is the worldwide association of accountants and financial professionals in business." The IMA was founded in 1919 and is one of the largest and most respected associations focused exclusively on advancing the management accounting profession. The IMA is in 140 countries and is the organization that offers the Certified Management Accountant (CMA) credential.

What is the IIA?

Per the IIA website, "The Institute of Internal Auditors (IIA) is the internal audit profession's global voice, recognized authority, acknowledged leader, chief advocate, and principal educator. Generally, members work in internal auditing, risk management, governance, internal control, information technology audit, education, and security. Globally, the IIA has more than 185,000 members." The IIA was established in 1941.

What is the NASBA?

Per the NASBA website: "Founded in 1908, the National Association of State Boards of Accountancy (NASBA) has served as an association dedicated to enhancing the effectiveness of the country's 55 state boards of accountancy for more than 100 years. As a driving force within the accounting profession, NASBA accomplishes its mission by creating a forum for accounting regulators and practitioners to address issues relevant to the viability of the accounting profession. Together, state boards and NASBA provide the public with the assurance that only qualified licensees practice public accounting in accordance with state laws, rules and regulations and in accordance with professional standards."

What do the state boards of accountancy do?

State boards of accountancy assist state governments in the licensing and regulation of the public accounting profession. State boards evaluate an applicant's education and work requirements necessary for CPA licensure and verify the successful completion of the CPA exam. State boards also serve the role as disciplinarian, hearing cases brought against a licensee for substandard practice, violation of the state's code of ethics, etc.

What role does the SEC play in accounting?

As noted in the chapter entitled "What Is Accounting?", the SEC has the authority to set accounting standards; however, it delegates that task to the private sector, currently the FASB.

What is the PCAOB?

As noted in the chapter entitled "What Is Accounting?", the Sarbanes–Oxley Act of 2002 created the Public Company Accounting Oversight Board (PCAOB) to develop standards for the audits of public companies. The standards developed by the PCAOB are subject to the approval of the SEC.

What does the "Big Four" mean?

The Big Four refers to the four largest professional services firms globally. The Big Four firms are: PwC, Deloitte, EY, and KPMG. The Big Four firms emerged from the Big Eight firms of the twentieth century: Arthur Andersen, Arthur Young, Coopers and Lybrand, Ernst & Whinney, Deloitte Haskins & Sells, Peat Marwick Mitchell, Price Waterhouse, and Touche Ross. A series of mergers led to the Big Five, and the collapse of Arthur Andersen in 2002 led the Big Five to become the Big Four. The Big Four firms audit the vast majority of Fortune 100 companies.

According to its website, the U.S. Securities and Exchange Commission's mission is "to protect investors, maintain fair, orderly, and efficient markets, and facilitate capital formation." Part of that means it has the authority to set accounting standards.

NOTABLE ACCOUNTANTS

Who are some famous people who used to be accountants?

There are several notable famous people who studied and/or practiced accounting before going on to other things.

- Julia Sweeney, a *Saturday Night Live* cast member in the early 1990s, worked as an accountant for Columbia Pictures and United Artists.

- Bob Newhart, the comedy icon, worked as an accountant at the United States Gypsum Corporation.

- Kenny G, the well-known saxophone musician, holds a degree in accounting from the University of Washington.

- Peter Falk, best known for his role as the detective in the TV series *Columbo*, worked as an efficiency expert for the Budget Bureau of the State of Connecticut.

- Chuck Liddell, mixed martial artist and former UFC light heavyweight champion, earned a BA in business and accounting from California Polytechnic University.

- John Grisham, novelist, earned a bachelor of science in accounting from Mississippi State University.

- Walter Diemer, the inventor of bubble gum, was an accountant for a company called Fleer.

- Mick Jagger, Rolling Stones front man, studied accounting and finance in London.

- John Pierpont Morgan, founder of Wall Street firm JP Morgan, started his career as an accountant at a New York banking firm.

Who was the first CPA?

The first CPA was Frank Broaker, the person most instrumental in getting the New York law passed to recognize accounting as a profession. He established a school to prepare accountants for the CPA exam and was later criticized for publishing the questions and answers to the first CPA exam.

Who was the first female CPA?

The first female to become a CPA was Christine Ross in 1899. Among her clients were wealthy women and those working in the fashion industry.

A number of entertainers have accounting backgrounds, including former *Saturday Night Live* comedienne Julia Sweeney.

Who was the first African American CPA?

The first African American CPA was John Wesley Cromwell Jr. in 1921. He went on to become the controller of Harvard University in 1930.

Who is the patron saint of accountants?

Saint Matthew is the patron saint of accountants, bankers, bookkeepers, security guards, and tax collectors. Matthew was the author of one of the Gospels. He started out as a Jewish tax collector in the fishing village of Capernaum before becoming an apostle.

Do accountants control the ballots for the Academy Awards?

Yes. Big Four firm PwC has been the overseer of the Academy Awards (Oscars) voting since 1934. However, the reputation of the firm took a hit when, at the 2017 Oscars, PwC accountant Brian Cullinan gave the wrong envelope to the presenters, causing the presenters to announce the film *La La Land* as best picture rather than the firm *Moonlight*, which was the actual winner.

Is there an accounting hall of fame?

Yes. The Accounting Hall of Fame is located at Ohio State University and was founded in 1950. The Accounting Hall of Fame honors accountants who have made significant contributions to the advancement of accounting.

ACCOUNTING SCANDALS

What were some of the worst accounting scandals in recent history?

According to a publication on recent accounting scandals by CPA Canada, "Greed and misdeeds are major corporate themes defining the last 15 years—many notorious accounting scandals happened during that time." Some of the worst scandals involved: Waste Management (1998), Enron (2001), WorldCom (2002), Tyco (2002), HealthSouth (2003), Freddie Mac (2003), AIG (2005), Lehman Brothers (2008), Bernie Madoff (2008), and Satyam (2009).

What happened at Enron?

Enron, a Houston-based commodities, energy, and service corporation, under the direction of CEO Jeff Skilling and former CEO Kenneth Lay and audited by Arthur Andersen, misled shareholders by keeping huge amounts of debt off the balance sheet. Shareholders lost $74 billion when the scheme was uncovered. Skilling was sentenced to 24 years in prison, and Enron filed for bankruptcy. Arthur Andersen was found guilty of criminal charges relating to the audit of Enron. The Supreme Court later reversed that conviction in 2005; however, by then, it was too late for Arthur Andersen to recover from its demise.

This photo was taken in 2002 at the World Economic Forum in New York City shortly after the Enron accounting scandal that cost shareholders $74 billion.

What happened at Waste Management?

Waste Management, a Houston-based waste-management company founded by CEO and chairman Dean L. Buntrock and audited by Arthur Andersen Company, reported $1.7 billion in fake earnings by allegedly increasing the depreciation time length for its fixed assets. Waste Management settled a shareholder class-action suit for $457 million. In addition, the SEC fined Arthur Andersen $7 million.

What happened at WorldCom?

WorldCom, a telecommunications company (now MCI, Inc.) under the leadership of CEO Bernie Ebbers, inflated assets by approximately $11 billion by capitalizing costs rather than reporting them as expenses and inflated revenues by posting fictitious journal entries. The internal audit department at WorldCom discovered the fraud. Ebbers was sentenced to 25 years in prison for fraud, conspiracy, and filing false documents with regulators.

What happened at Tyco?

Tyco, a New Jersey-based security systems company, was under SEC investigation for questionable accounting practices, including loans made to the CEO that were forgiven. It turns out that the CEO, Dennis Kozlowski, and the former CFO, Mark Swartz, stole

$150 million and inflated Tyco's income by $500 million by siphoning money through unapproved loans and fraudulent stock sales that were subsequently taken out of the company as executive bonuses and benefits. The CEO and CFO were sentenced to eight to twenty-five years in prison, and Tyco was forced to pay $2.92 billion to investors as a result of a class-action lawsuit.

What happened at HealthSouth?

HealthSouth, a publicly traded health-care company under the leadership of CEO Richard Scrushy, allegedly inflated earnings by $1.4 billion to meet shareholder expectations. Scrushy sold $75 million in HealthSouth stock one day before the company recorded a huge loss. Scrushy was convicted of bribing the governor of Alabama and sentenced to seven years in prison.

What happened at Freddie Mac?

Freddie Mac, a federally backed mortgage and financing corporation, understated earnings by $5 billion in order to meet investor expectations and was caught as the result of an SEC investigation. Freddie Mac was forced to pay $125 million in fines and fired president and COO David Glenn, chairman and CEO Leland Brendsel, and CFO Vaughn Clarke.

What happened at AIG?

American Insurance Group (AIG), a multinational insurance corporation under the leadership of CEO Hank Greenberg, allegedly booked loans as revenue, persuaded clients to choose insurers that AIG had payoff agreements with, and manipulated its stock price, amounting to a $3.9 billion fraud. AIG settled with the SEC for a $10 million civil penalty in 2003. AIG later settled claims with federal and state securities and insurance regulators for $1.64 billion for deceiving the investing public and regulators. Greenberg was ultimately fired.

What happened at Lehman Brothers?

Lehman Brothers, a global financial services firm audited by Ernst & Young, disguised over $50 billion in loans as sales by selling toxic assets to Cayman Island banks under the agreement that they would eventually be repurchased. The scheme was discovered when Lehman Brothers was forced to file for bankruptcy, which was the largest bankruptcy in U.S. history.

What happened at Bernard L. Madoff Investment Securities LLC?

Bernie Madoff engaged in the largest Ponzi scheme ever as he tricked his investors out of $64.8 billion. Madoff was reported to the SEC by his sons after he informed them of his scheme. He was sentenced to 150 years in prison and fined $170 billion in restitution.

What is a Ponzi scheme?

A Ponzi scheme is a form of fraud in which investors in an entity are fraudulently paid a return on their investment out of newer investors' investments, not actually out of a return generated by the entity. Ponzi schemes get their name from Charles Ponzi, who came to the United States from Italy in 1903. Ponzi recruited investors into his postal voucher exchange system by promising 50% returns on investment in 90 days. However, the returns were merely payments of newer investors' money to old investors.

Italian immigrant Charles Ponzi (shown here in 1920) did not invent the investment swindle that now bears his name, but he was the first to make a colossal success out of it, cheating his clients out of $20 million.

What happened at Saytam?

Saytam, an Indian IT services and accounting firm founded by chairman Ramalinga Raju, fraudulently overstated revenue by $1.5 billion. Raju admitted to the fraud in a letter to the board of directors. He and his brother were charged with breach of trust, conspiracy, cheating, and falsification of records but were released as a result of India's Central Bureau of Investigation failing to file the charges on time.

THE FUTURE OF ACCOUNTING

What are some current trends in accounting?

Some of the many trends happening in accounting right now involve changes to the profession, the effect of IT advancements on accounting, sustainability accounting, and globalization of financial accounting standards.

What changes are expected to happen to the accounting profession?

According to a 2015 survey of accounting study conducted by Henry and Hicks, in the future, accountants will be expected to participate more in decision making and less on transactional work, accountants will seek more education and specialization, competition to provide accounting services will increase from nontraditional providers, and performance measures will include more nonfinancial measures.

How might IT advancements impact the accounting profession?

According to a *Forbes* article by Bernard Marr (2017), "The profession is going to become more interesting as repetitive tasks shift to machines. There will be changes, but those changes won't completely eliminate the need for human accountants, they will just alter their contributions. Machine learning is the leading edge of artificial intelligence (AI). It's a subset of AI where machines can learn by using algorithms to interpret data from the world around us to predict outcomes and learn from successes and failures. As machines infiltrate accounting tasks to take over the more mundane and repetitive tasks, it will free up accountants and bookkeepers to spend more time using their professional knowledge to analyze and interpret the data to provide recommendations for their clients." Marr further suggests, "When accounting software companies eliminated desktop support in favor of cloud-based services, accounting firms were forced to adapt to life in the cloud. Similarly, accounting departments and firms will be forced to adopt machine learning to remain competitive since machines can deliver real-time insights, enhance decision making and catapult efficiency."

What is sustainability accounting?

According to Jean Rogers (2016), founder of the Sustainability Accounting Standards Board (SASB), sustainability accounting is a complement to financial accounting that helps provide a more complete view of a corporation's performance and its ability to create long-term value by defining qualitative and quantitative nonfinancial metrics on industry-specific sustainability topics likely to be of interest to investors and creditors. The SASB standards include metrics and technical protocols that allow companies to integrate sustainability disclosure into their existing financial management and reporting processes, including the internal control framework.

What is an example of a sustainability accounting metric?

There are many different sustainability metrics, which are industry specific. The SASB website allows a user to input a ticker symbol to reference a particular industry and download the relevant sustainability standard for that industry. For example, if you use the lookup tool at https://www.sasb.org/approach/sics/, and input "sam," the ticker symbol for Boston Beer Company, you can see that the standard that applies is the Consumption I Sector, further broken down into alcoholic beverages. Examples of sustainability metrics for Boston Beer Company are: total water withdrawn and total water consumed in regions with high baseline water stress, number of advertising impressions as a percentage made on individuals above the legal drinking age, total weight of packaging, and a description of efforts to promote responsible consumption of alcohol.

Will the United States adopt the International Financial Reporting Standards (IFRS)?

In 2002, the FASB and the IASB announced a memorandum, known as the Norwalk Agreement, indicating their commitment toward the convergence of U.S. GAAP with IFRS. To that end, the FASB has completed several joint projects with the IASB, including updating the conceptual framework. However, according to FASB chair Russ Golden in a meeting with the IMA's Financial Reporting Committee, as of September 2017, the FASB "realizes that constituents will spend most of their time in the next few years implementing the new standards for revenue recognition, leases, and financial instruments impairment, which means now isn't the time to introduce new projects." Accordingly, it does not appear that any major changes related to convergence with international standards are in store for the near future.

APPENDIX 1: JOURNAL ENTRIES

The following appendix provides examples of common journal entries prepared by businesses.

Forming a Sole Proprietorship by Investing Cash

Account:	Dr.	Cr.
Cash	XXXX	
Capital		XXXX

Example: On January 1, Christopher Thomas forms Spicy Pickle Company as a sole proprietorship and contributes $20,000 cash to the business.

Account:	Dr.	Cr.
Cash	20,000	
C. Thomas, Capital		20,000

Forming a Sole Proprietorship by Investing a Non-Cash Asset

Account:	Dr.	Cr.
Asset (specific)	XXXX	
Capital		XXXX

Example: On January 1, Christopher Thomas forms Spicy Pickle Company as a sole proprietorship and contributes a truck worth $25,000 to the business.

Account:	Dr.	Cr.
Vehicles	25,000	
C. Thomas, Capital		25,000

291

Recording Cash Withdrawals Made by the Owner of a Sole Proprietorship

Account:	Dr.	Cr.
Drawing	XXXX	
Cash		XXXX

Example: On January 31, Christopher Thomas withdraws $1,000 cash from Spicy Pickle Company for personal use.

Account:	Dr.	Cr.
C. Thomas, Drawing	1,000	
Cash		1,000

Forming a Corporation by Issuing Stock to Owners in Return for Cash

Account:	Dr.	Cr.
Cash	XXXX	
Common Stock		XXXX

Example: On January 1, Christopher Thomas incorporates Spicy Pickle Company and contributes $20,000 cash to the business in exchange for common stock.

Account:	Dr.	Cr.
Cash	20,000	
Common Stock		20,000

Forming a Corporation by Issuing Stock to Owners in Return for a Non-Cash Asset

Account:	Dr.	Cr.
Asset (specific)	XXXX	
Common Stock		XXXX

Example: On January 1, Christopher Thomas incorporates Spicy Pickle Company and contributes a truck worth $25,000 to the business in exchange for common stock.

Account:	Dr.	Cr.
Vehicles	25,000	
Common Stock		25,000

Recording Cash Dividends Paid to Stockholders of a Corporation

Account:	Dr.	Cr.
Dividends	XXXX	
Cash		XXXX

Example: On January 31, Spicy Pickle Company declared and paid $1,000 in dividends to stockholders.

Account:	Dr.	Cr.
Dividends	1,000	
Cash		1,000

Borrowing Money from the Bank

Account:	Dr.	Cr.
Cash	XXXX	
Notes Payable		XXXX

Example: On January 1, Spicy Pickle Company borrows $50,000 from the bank.

Account:	Dr.	Cr.
Cash	50,000	
Notes Payable		50,000

Repaying the Principal on Loans

Account:	Dr.	Cr.
Notes Payable	XXXX	
Cash		XXXX

Example: On February 1, Spicy Pickle Company repays $1,000 on the principal of its loan.

Account:	Dr.	Cr.
Notes Payable	1,000	
Cash		1,000

Paying Interest on Loans

Account:	Dr.	Cr.
Interest Expense	XXXX	
Cash		XXXX

Example: On February 1, Spicy Pickle Company pays $100 in interest on its loan.

Account:	Dr.	Cr.
Interest Expense	100	
Cash		100

Purchasing Equipment with Cash

Account:	Dr.	Cr.
Equipment	XXXX	
Cash		XXXX

Example: On February 15, Spicy Pickle Company purchases a new labeling machine for $5,000, paying cash.

Account:	Dr.	Cr.
Equipment	5,000	
Cash		5,000

Purchasing Equipment with a Loan

Account:	Dr.	Cr.
Equipment	XXXX	
Notes Payable		XXXX

Example: On February 15, Spicy Pickle Company purchases a new labeling machine for $5,000, signing a promissory note due in six months.

Account:	Dr.	Cr.
Equipment	5,000	
Notes Payable		5,000

Purchasing Supplies on Account Payable (invoice)

Account:	Dr.	Cr.
Supplies	XXXX	
Accounts Payable		XXXX

Example: On February 20, Spicy Pickle Company purchases supplies costing $250 and receives an invoice due in 30 days.

Account:	Dr.	Cr.
Supplies	250	
Accounts Payable		250

Paying for items purchased on Account Payable (invoice)

Account:	Dr.	Cr.
Accounts Payable	XXXX	
Cash		XXXX

Example: On March 20, Spicy Pickle Company pays $250 on the invoice for the supplies purchased on February 20.

Account:	Dr.	Cr.
Accounts Payable	250	
Cash		250

Selling Services for Cash

Account:	Dr.	Cr.
Cash	XXXX	
Service Revenue		XXXX

Example: On June 1, Loretta's Lawn Care mowed lawns, collecting $500 from customers.

Account:	Dr.	Cr.
Cash	500	
Service Revenue		500

Selling Services on Accounts Receivable (invoice)

Account:	Dr.	Cr.
Accounts Receivable	XXXX	
Service Revenue		XXXX

Example: On July 1, Loretta's Lawn Care mowed lawns, leaving invoices for $600 in customers' mailboxes, due in 15 days.

Account:	Dr.	Cr.
Accounts Receivable	600	
Service Revenue		600

Collecting on Accounts Receivable (invoice)

Account:	Dr.	Cr.
Cash	XXXX	
Accounts Receivable		XXXX

Example: On July 16, Loretta's Lawn Care collected $400 from the customers invoiced on July 1.

Account:	Dr.	Cr.
Cash	400	
Accounts Receivable		400

Collecting Cash in Advance

Account:	Dr.	Cr.
Cash	XXXX	
Unearned Revenue		XXXX

Example: On April 1, Loretta's Lawn Care collected $300 from a customer who pre-paid for the summer (April through September) lawn care services (six months at $50 per month).

Account:	Dr.	Cr.
Cash	300	
Unearned Revenue		300

Earning Revenue on a Prepaid Service

Account:	Dr.	Cr.
Unearned Revenue	XXXX	
Service Revenue		XXXX

Example: It is now April 30 and Loretta's Lawn Care has provided one month of services prepaid by the customer on April 1.

Account:	Dr.	Cr.
Unearned Revenue	50	
Service Revenue		50

Paying Cash for an Expense

Account:	Dr.	Cr.
Expense (specific)	XXXX	
Cash		XXXX

Example: On May 1, Loretta's Lawn Care paid $200 to repair a lawnmower.

Account:	Dr.	Cr.
Repairs Expense	200	
Cash		200

Paying Cash in Advance for Expenses

Account:	Dr.	Cr.
Prepaid Expense (specific)	XXXX	
Cash		XXXX

Example: On April 30, Loretta's Lawn Care paid $3,000 in advance for May, June, and July rent ($1,000 per month).

Account:	Dr.	Cr.
Prepaid Rent	3,000	
Cash		3,000

Incurring Expenses that were Prepaid

Account:	Dr.	Cr.
Expense (specific)	XXXX	
Prepaid Expense (specific)		XXXX

Example: At the end of the month of May, Loretta's Lawn Care had incurred one month of the rent expense that it prepaid in April.

Account:	Dr.	Cr.
Rent Expense	1,000	
Prepaid Rent		1,000

Incurring Expenses on Account Payable (invoice)

Account:	Dr.	Cr.
Expense (specific)	XXXX	
Accounts Payable		XXXX

Example: On March 1, Loretta's Lawn Care purchased $700 worth of advertising flyers, receiving an invoice due in 30 days.

Account:	Dr.	Cr.
Advertising Expense	700	
Accounts Payable		700

Paying for Expenses Purchased on Account Payable (invoice)

Account:	Dr.	Cr.
Accounts Payable	XXXX	
Cash		XXXX

Example: On April 1, Loretta's Lawn Care paid for the advertising flyers purchased on March 1.

Account:	Dr.	Cr.
Accounts Payable	700	
Cash		700

Closing Entries for a Sole Proprietorship

The year-end closing process was discussed in detail in the chapter entitled "Bookkeeping and the Accounting Cycle." However, the closing process discussed was for corporations. There are a few small changes to the closing process for sole proprietorships. First, revenue and expense accounts are closed to an account called "income summary" rather than "retained earnings." The income summary account is then closed to the owner's capital account. Finally, instead of closing the dividends account, the owner's drawing account is closed to the owner's capital account.

Example: Assume Loretta's Lawn Care is a sole proprietorship in this example. On December 31, Loretta's Lawn Care closes its revenue and expense accounts to the income summary account:

Account:	Dr.	Cr.
Service Revenue	264,000	
Wages Expense		83,000
Utilities & Fuel Expense		18,250
Rent Expense		5,000
Insurance Expense		1,100
Advertising Expense		2,000
Depreciation Expense		1,250
Income Summary		153,400

On December 31, Loretta's Lawn Care closes its income summary account to the owner's capital account:

Account:	Dr.	Cr.
Income Summary	153,400	
C. Thomas, Capital		153,400

On December 31, Loretta's Lawn Care closes the owner's drawing account:

Account:	Dr.	Cr.
C. Thomas, Capital	1,000	
C. Thomas, Drawing		1,000

Note that the closing entries for a sole proprietorship increase the owner's capital account by the amount of net income and decrease the owner's capital account for any withdrawals taken during the year.

APPENDIX 2: PARTNERSHIP ACCOUNTING

PARTNERSHIPS

Recall that a partnership requires an agreement between two or more people, which becomes a partnership contract. This partnership agreement should be in writing but can be merely a verbal agreement. Partnership agreements typically include the following information: the names of the partners and financial contributions to the partnership, the rights and duties of the partners, the ability to withdraw cash from the business, details on how income and losses will be shared among the partners, the procedures for settling disputes between the partners, admissions and withdrawals of partners, and the rights and duties in the event that a partner dies.

The accounting for partnerships is a bit more complicated than the accounting for sole proprietorships due to the multi-owner nature of partnerships. Additionally, it can be somewhat more complex than the accounting for corporations due to the stipulations in the partnership agreement regarding how to allocate income and losses among the partners, admit new partners, or allow a partner to withdraw. Partnership accounting uses a separate capital account for each partner, a separate withdrawal account for each partner, and allocates net income or net loss to each partner according to the partnership agreement. (Note that sole proprietorships also use a capital account and withdrawal account for the owner, although there is only one, so there is no need to allocate net income or net loss, etc.)

FORMING A PARTNERSHIP

When a partnership is formed, the partners can invest cash and/or non-cash assets in the business, as well as transfer liabilities to the business. Non-cash assets are recorded at an amount agreed upon by the partners, which is typically the market value of the asset.

Example: On January 1, 2020, Lucas Vega and Olivia Law form a partnership called The Clean Team that provides residential house cleaning services. Vega's initial invest- **299** ment consists of $5,000 cash. Law's initial investment consists of a truck that will be used as the primary vehicle for The Clean Team worth $40,000. Law also has the loan on the vehicle (a $30,000 balance) transferred to the business. The entries to record these investments are shown below:

Vega's Investment

Account:	Dr.	Cr.
Cash	5,000	
L. Vega, Capital		5,000

Law's Investment

Account:	Dr.	Cr.
Vehicles	40,000	
Notes Payable		30,000
O. Law, Capital		10,000

SHARING INCOME OR LOSS

Partners can choose to allocate income and losses in any way that they want as declared in the partnership agreement. As partners are entitled to the profits of the business, they are not paid a salary, but rather can choose to allocate a certain portion of profits to the partners as a "salary allowance." Some common methods of allocated income and losses are based on any of the following: specific ratios stated in the partnership agreement, the ratio of capital balances, or allocations based on salary and interest allowances. If the partnership agreement does not specifically address the income and loss allocations, income and losses will be allocated evenly to all partners. If the agreement only states how income is to be allocated, losses must be allocated the same way as income.

Example 1: Stated Ratios. Assume that The Clean Team had first-year income of $100,000. The partnership agreement states that income and losses will be split fifty/fifty between the partners. After closing the revenue and expense accounts, the income summary account would have a credit balance of $100,000, which must be closed to the partners' capital accounts. (Refer to Appendix 1 for the closing entries for a sole proprietorship for further review of closing accounts to the income summary account.) The entry to record the closing of the income summary account to the partners' capital accounts is shown below:

Account:	Dr.	Cr.
Income Summary	100,000	
L. Vega, Capital		50,000
O. Law, Capital		50,000

Note that each partners' capital account is increased by fifty percent of the net income for the year.

Example 2: Capital Balances. Assume that The Clean Team had first-year income of $100,000. The partnership agreement states that income and losses will be allocated according to the capital balances. After closing the revenue and expense accounts, the income summary account would have a credit balance of $100,000, which must be closed to the partners' capital accounts. Recall that Vega's capital balance is $5,000 and Law's capital balance is $10,000. That means that Vega will be allocated one third ($5,000/$15,000) of the income, and Law will be allocated two thirds of the income ($10,000/$15,000). The entry to record the closing of the income summary account to the partners' capital accounts is shown below (rounded):

Account:	Dr.	Cr.
Income Summary	100,000	
L. Vega, Capital		33,333
O. Law, Capital		66,667

Example 3: Salary Allowances, Capital Balances, and Stated Ratios. Assume that The Clean Team had first year income of $100,000. The partnership agreement states that income and losses should first be allocated by giving a salary allowance of $20,000 to each partner. Second, any remaining income after the salary allowances will be allocated by giving each partner an allowance of 25% of their beginning-of-the-year capital account balances. Any remaining income will be split fifty/fifty between the partners. After closing the revenue and expense accounts, the income summary account would have a credit balance of $100,000, which must be closed to the partners' capital accounts. The income allocation can be calculated as follows:

	Total	Vega	Law
Income:	$100,000		
Less Salary Allowance	$40,000	$20,000	$20,000
Income After Salary Allowance		$60,000	
Less Capital Interest Allowance	$3,750	$1,250*	$2,500**
Income After Salary & Interest	$56,250		
Less Stated Ratio Allowance	$56,250	$28,125***	$28,125***
Total Allocated to Partners		$49,375	$50,625

*25% of $5,000
** 25% of $10,000
*** 50% of $56,250

The entry to record the closing of the income summary account to the partners' capital accounts is shown below (rounded):

Account:	Dr.	Cr.
Income Summary	100,000	
L. Vega, Capital		49,375
O. Law, Capital		50,625

Example 4: Salary Allowances, Capital Balances, and Stated Ratios—Allowances Exceed Income. Assume that The Clean Team had first year income of $41,000. The part-

nership agreement states that income and losses first be allocated by giving a salary allowance of $20,000 to each partner. Second, any remaining income after the salary allowances will be allocated by giving each partner an allowance of 25% of their beginning-of-the-year capital account balances. Any remaining income will be split fifty/fifty between the partners. After closing the revenue and expense accounts, the income summary account would have a credit balance of $41,000, which must be closed to the partners' capital accounts.

The income allocation can be calculated as follows:

	Total	Vega	Law
Income:	$41,000		
Less Salary Allowance	$40,000	$20,000	$20,000
Income After Salary Allowance	$1,000		
Less Capital Interest Allowance	$3,750	$1,250*	$2,500**
Income After Salary & Interest	$(2,750)		
Less Stated Ratio Allowance	$(2,750)	$(1,375)***	$(1,375)***
Total Allocated to Partners		$19,875	$21,125

*25% of $5,000
** 25% of $10,000
*** 50% of $2,750

The entry to record the closing of the income summary account to the partners' capital accounts is shown below:

Account:	Dr.	Cr.
Income Summary	41,000	
L. Vega, Capital		19,875
O. Law, Capital		21,125

CASH WITHDRAWALS

Owner's can withdraw cash from the business, as agreed to in the partnership agreement. These cash withdrawals eventually end up reducing the partner's capital account, through the year-end closing process. (Note that this is similar to the sole proprietorship closing process, as shown in Appendix 1.)

Example: Assume that during the year, Lucas Vega withdrew $40,000 cash from the partnership and Olivia Law withdrew $50,000 cash from the partnership. The entries to record these cash withdrawals are shown below:

Vega's Cash Withdrawal

Account:	Dr.	Cr.
L. Vega, Drawing	40,000	
Cash		40,000

Law's Cash Withdrawal

Account:	Dr.	Cr.
O. Law, Drawing	50,000	
Cash		50,000

STATEMENT OF PARTNERS' EQUITY

A separate financial statement, called a statement of partners' equity, should be prepared with the financial statements. The statement of partners' equity shows a roll forward of the partners' capital balances during the year. The following example is provided using the income allocations from Example 3, above.

The Clean Team
Statement of Partners' Equity
For the Year Ended December 31, 2020

	Vega	Law	Total
Beginning Capital Balances	$ -	$ -	$ -
Investments by Owners	5,000	10,000	15,000
Income Allowances:			
Salary Allowances	20,000	20,000	40,000
Interest Allowances	1,250	2,500	3,750
Balance Allocated	28,125	28,125	56,250
Total Income Allowance	49,375	50,625	100,000
Partners' Withdrawals	(40,000)	(50,000)	(90,000)
Ending Capital Balances	14,375	10,625	25,000

ADMITTING A NEW PARTNER

The admission of a new partner or the withdrawal of an existing partner ends the partnership. The business can still continue to operate, but a new partnership is formed. A new partner can be admitted to a partnership by purchasing the partnership interest from an existing partner or by investing assets into the partnership.

Example 1: Purchase of Partnership Interest from an Existing Partner. Assume that at the end of The Clean Team's first year, Sydney Edgerton purchased one half of Olivia Law's partnership interest for $8,000 (assume this is allowed by the partnership agreement). Note that the $8,000 transferred from Edgerton to Law is not a transaction of the partnership but rather a personal transaction between two individuals. The partnership must simply record the reallocation of half of Law's partnership interest to Edgerton. Recall that at the end of the year, Law's partnership interest was $10,625. The entry to record the transfer of partnership interest is shown below:

Account:	Dr.	Cr.
O. Law, Capital	5,312.50	
S. Edgerton, Capital		5,312.50

Note that Vega's capital account is unaffected by this transaction. Also note that Law's capital account has been reduced by half, with that amount allocated to Edgerton.

Example 2: Purchase of Partnership Interest by Investing Assets. Assume that at the end of the year, The Clean Team decides to allow Sydney Edgerton to become a partner by investing $10,000 cash into the business. The entry to record the investment of the new partner is shown below:

Account:	Dr.	Cr.
Cash	10,000	
S. Edgerton, Capital		10,000

Note that in this case, Edgerton's payment of cash goes to the business, rather than to a specific partner. In that case, the cash received is the property of the business.

Admission of a new partner can get more complicated than this if the current value of the partnership is greater than the recorded equity on the books. For example, recall that the statement of partners' equity shows a total of $25,000 of equity at the end of 2020. However, assume that the business is doing really well, and Vega and Law want to charge Edgerton $10,000 for a 20% interest in the company. Edgerton's investment will result in total equity of $35,000, which Vega would be entitled to 20% of, which is $7,000. In this case, the partners must decide if the new partner will be credited with this extra $3,000 "bonus," or if it will be allocated to the old partners. A good introductory financial accounting textbook can provide further details on how to handle these situations.

WITHDRAWAL OF A PARTNER

If a partner wishes to leave the partnership, this is considered a withdrawal of the partner. This is not to be confused with a partner making a cash withdrawal of funds from the partnership. A partner can leave the partnership either by selling his/her partnership interest to another person or the partnership can "buy out" the partner.

Example 1: Sale of Partnership Interest. Assume that at the end of the first year of operations, Olivia Law decides to sell 100% of her partnership interest to Sydney Edgerton (rather than the 50% used in the previous example) for $20,000 cash. Recall that the cash exchanged between Edgerton and Law is not a transaction of the business. The business only needs to record the allocation of Law's partnership interest to Edgerton, as shown below:

Account:	Dr.	Cr.
O. Law, Capital	10,625	
S. Edgerton, Capital		10,625

Example 2: Partnership "Buy Out" of Partnership Interest. Assume that at the end of the first year of operations and after admitting Sydney Edgerton to the partnership, Olivia Law decides to leave the partnership and is paid for her remaining partnership interest of $5,312.50 by the partnership. The entry is recorded as follows:

Account:	Dr.	Cr.
O. Law, Capital	5,312.50	
Cash		5,312.50

The buyout of a partner can get more complicated than this if the partner who is withdrawing agrees to take less cash than their current capital account is valued at in order to get out of the partnership. In this case, the equity left behind by the partner is then allocated between the remaining partners. Likewise, if a withdrawing partner is able to get more cash from the business than their current capital account is valued at, the remaining partners must reduce their equity by the amount of extra cash that is paid to the withdrawing partner. Again, a good introductory financial accounting textbook can provide further details on how to handle these situations.

LIQUIDATION OF THE PARTNERSHIP

When the partners decide to end the partnership, they will need to first liquidate (sell) their assets. Any gains or losses arising from the sale of the assets will be allocated to the partners in the same way that net income or net losses are allocated. Second, they will need to pay off all liabilities owed. Finally, any remaining cash is allocated to the partners based on their capital balances.

Example: Assume that The Clean Team decides to close the business at the end of 2025. At that time, the accounts had the following balances:

Cash $90,000

Vehicles $70,000

Notes Payable $20,000

L. Vega, Capital $95,000

S. Edgerton, Capital $45,000

Assume that The Clean Team was able to sell their company vehicles for $80,000 cash, resulting in a $10,000 gain. The sale of the vehicles would be recorded as follows:

Account:	Dr.	Cr.
Cash	80,000	
Vehicles		70,000
Gain from Liquidation		10,000

The gain would then be split based on the income and loss allocations specified in the partnership agreement. Assume in this example that net income and net losses are split fifty/fifty between the partners. The entry to allocate the gain between the partners would be recorded as follows:

Account:	Dr.	Cr.
Gain from Liquidation	10,000	
L. Vega, Capital		5,000
S. Edgerton, Capital		5,000

Note that the partnership now has $170,000 cash ($90,000 beginning balance plus $80,000 from the sale of vehicles). Also note that the partners' capital balances have been affected and are now: L. Vega, Capital $100,000, and S. Edgerton, Capital $50,000.

The next thing The Clean Team must do is pay off any liabilities. The journal entry to pay off the $20,000 note payable is shown below:

Account:	Dr.	Cr.
Notes Payable	20,000	
Cash		20,000

Note that the partnership now has $150,000 cash ($90,000 beginning balance plus $80,000 from the sale of vehicles less $20,000 payment of notes payable).

The final step in the liquidation process is to distribute the remaining $150,000 cash to the partners according to their capital balances, as shown below:

Account:	Dr.	Cr.
L. Vega, Capital	100,000	
S. Edgerton, Capital	50,000	
Cash		150,000

After recording this entry, all accounts will have a zero balance and the partnership liquidation will be complete.

If there is a case in which a partner has a capital deficiency (negative balance) upon liquidation, the partner with the capital deficiency is obligated to pay the negative balance back to the partnership upon liquidation. If the partner is unwilling or unable to pay the deficiency back, the deficiency is split between the remaining partners according to the way they chose to split net income and net losses in the partnership agreement. The partner with the deficiency is not relieved of his/her liability and must repay the remaining partners in the future when that partner becomes able to. Again, a good introductory financial accounting textbook can provide further details on how to handle these situations.

APPENDIX 3: FINANCIAL STATEMENTS

OVERVIEW

Financial statements are not "cookie cutter" documents that look the same across all companies. The process of looking at financial statements can be quite confusing for non-accountants because the titles of financial statements can vary slightly, and the content and presentation vary, too. While Generally Accepted Accounting Principles (GAAP) gives very specific guidance on the methods of accounting and the presentation of the financial statements, there is still room for individuality in financial statement presentation. Financial statement presentation varies across industries, size of companies, and organizational preferences. In an attempt to point out some of these differences, this appendix is divided into three broad categories: service companies, merchandisers, and manufacturers. You will note many differences in the financial statements even within these categories.

SERVICE COMPANIES

Service companies are businesses that provide services, rather than goods, to the customer. Service businesses can be grouped into categories such as professional services, consumer services, business services, financial services, etc. Some service companies (with ticker symbol) that you may have heard of include:

- Accenture Plc. (ACN): management consulting, technology, and outsourcing services
- Paychex, Inc. (PAYX): payroll, human resources, retirement, and insurance services
- ManpowerGroup (MAN): recruitment, business services, outsourcing
- Western Union (WU): money transfers
- Capella Education Company (CPLA): higher education
- Navient Corporation (NAVI): student loans
- H&R Block, Inc. (HRB): tax preparation

307

- Nielsen N.V. (NLSN): data, research, and analytics

- Equifax, Inc. (EFX): data, research, and analytics

- LendingTree, Inc. (TREE): online loan marketplace

SERVICE COMPANY BALANCE SHEETS

The balance sheets for Accenture Plc., Paychex, Inc., and ManpowerGroup are provided in this section. Note that these are all professional services companies. While the content varies on each balance sheet, some general differences should be pointed out.

First, note that the headings of financial statements typically include the "who, what, and when" details; however, only the Accenture balance sheet includes the "when" in the heading of the examples provided. Also note that each company has a different year end. Accenture has an August 31 year end. Paychex has a May 31 year end. ManpowerGroup has a December 31 year end.

Second, all three companies round their financial statements, as indicated in the last line of the heading. However, note that Accenture rounds to thousands (which means they chopped off the last three digits), while the other two companies round to millions (which means they chopped off the last six digits). If you don't pay attention to the rounding, you may think a company is much larger or smaller than it actually is when compared to other companies.

Third, the overall look and feel of each balance sheet is slightly different. Accenture centered the large headings, while the other two companies kept everything left justified. ManpowerGroup included lines that run the entire width of the page, rather than just the standard underlines and double underlines under the amounts.

Fourth, the headings and subheadings vary slightly. Under the assets heading, Accenture has subheadings for current assets and non-current assets. Those two subheadings make up the total assets. Paychex does not include any subheadings under assets but totals current assets before funds held for clients, total current assets, and then total assets. Notice that there is no total for non-current assets, so if you wanted that amount to calculate a ratio, etc., you would have to add it up yourself (which would be every asset listed after the total current assets subtotal). ManpowerGroup uses many subheadings under the asset heading such as current assets, other assets, and property and equipment. The same differences in these three balance sheets follow through to the liabilities and stockholders' equity sections as well. Note that Accenture and ManpowerGroup refer to the last section as shareholders' equity, while Paychex refers to it as stockholders' equity. These represent the same thing.

These differences often confuse accounting students that are trying to calculate a ratio by looking for a precise wording. It is important to get comfortable with the differences in financial statements to better find what you are looking for. As a final note, remember that each individual line item may also differ because each company is unique and engages in different sorts of transactions.

ACCENTURE PLC

CONSOLIDATED BALANCE SHEETS

August 31, 2017 and 2016

(In thousands of U.S. dollars, except share and per share amounts)

	August 31, 2017	August 31, 2016
ASSETS		
CURRENT ASSETS:		
Cash and cash equivalents	$ 4,126,860	$ 4,905,609
Short-term investments	3,011	2,875
Receivables from clients, net	4,569,214	4,072,180
Unbilled services, net	2,316,043	2,150,219
Other current assets	1,082,161	845,339
Total current assets	12,097,289	11,976,222
NON-CURRENT ASSETS:		
Unbilled services, net	40,938	68,145
Investments	211,610	198,633
Property and equipment, net	1,140,598	956,542
Goodwill	5,002,352	3,609,437
Deferred contract costs	755,871	733,219
Deferred income taxes, net	2,214,901	2,077,312
Other non-current assets	1,226,331	989,494
Total non-current assets	10,592,601	8,632,782
TOTAL ASSETS	$ 22,689,890	$ 20,609,004
LIABILITIES AND SHAREHOLDERS' EQUITY		
CURRENT LIABILITIES:		
Current portion of long-term debt and bank borrowings	$ 2,907	$ 2,773
Accounts payable	1,525,065	1,280,821
Deferred revenues	2,669,520	2,364,728
Accrued payroll and related benefits	4,060,364	4,040,751
Accrued consumption taxes	383,391	358,359
Income taxes payable	708,485	362,963
Other accrued liabilities	474,547	468,529
Total current liabilities	9,824,279	8,878,924
NON-CURRENT LIABILITIES:		
Long-term debt	22,163	24,457
Deferred revenues	663,248	754,812
Retirement obligation	1,408,759	1,494,789
Deferred income taxes, net	137,098	111,020
Income taxes payable	574,780	850,709
Other non-current liabilities	349,363	304,917
Total non-current liabilities	3,155,411	3,540,704

309

COMMITMENTS AND CONTINGENCIES

SHAREHOLDERS' EQUITY:

Ordinary shares, par value 1.00 euros per share, 40,000 shares authorized and issued as of August 31, 2017 and August 31, 2016	57	57
Class A ordinary shares, par value $0.0000225 per share, 20,000,000,000 shares authorized, 638,965,789 and 654,202,813 shares issued as of August 31, 2017 and August 31, 2016, respectively	14	15
Class X ordinary shares, par value $0.0000225 per share, 1,000,000,000 shares authorized, 20,531,383 and 21,917,155 shares issued and outstanding as of August 31, 2017 and August 31, 2016, respectively	—	—
Restricted share units	1,095,026	1,004,128
Additional paid-in capital	3,516,399	2,924,729
Treasury shares, at cost: Ordinary, 40,000 shares as of August 31, 2017 and August 31, 2016; Class A ordinary, 23,408,811 and 33,529,739 shares as of August 31, 2017 and August 31, 2016, respectively	(1,649,090)	(2,591,907)
Retained earnings	7,081,855	7,879,960
Accumulated other comprehensive loss	(1,094,784)	(1,661,720)
Total Accenture plc shareholders' equity	8,949,477	7,555,262
Noncontrolling interests	760,723	634,114
Total shareholders' equity	9,710,200	8,189,376
TOTAL LIABILITIES AND SHAREHOLDERS' EQUITY	$ 22,689,890	$ 20,609,004

PAYCHEX, INC.
CONSOLIDATED BALANCE SHEETS
In millions, except per share amount

As of May 31,		2017		2016
Assets				
Cash and cash equivalents	$	184.6	$	131.5
Corporate investments		138.8		220.6
Interest receivable		35.9		36.1
Accounts receivable, net of allowance for doubtful accounts		507.5		408.6
Prepaid income taxes		45.0		10.5
Prepaid expenses and other current assets		58.3		58.8
Current assets before funds held for clients		**970.1**		**866.1**
Funds held for clients		4,301.9		3,997.5
Total current assets		**5,272.0**		**4,863.6**
Long-term corporate investments		454.0		441.1
Property and equipment, net of accumulated depreciation		337.2		353.0
Intangible assets, net of accumulated amortization		57.6		69.5
Goodwill		657.1		657.1
Prepaid income taxes		24.9		24.9
Other long-term assets		30.9		31.6
Total assets	**$**	**6,833.7**	**$**	**6,440.8**
Liabilities				
Accounts payable	$	57.2	$	56.7
Accrued compensation and related items		280.5		247.8
Deferred revenue		22.9		26.3
Other current liabilities		91.9		79.8
Current liabilities before client fund obligations		**452.5**		**410.6**

Client fund obligations	4,272.6	3,955.3
Total current liabilities	**4,725.1**	**4,365.9**
Accrued income taxes	45.6	72.8
Deferred income taxes	33.9	22.1
Other long-term liabilities	73.8	68.3
Total liabilities	**4,878.4**	**4,529.1**
Commitments and contingencies — Note O		
Stockholders' equity		
Common stock, $0.01 par value; Authorized: 600.0 shares;		
Issued and outstanding: 359.4 shares as of May 31, 2017	3.6	3.6
and 360.4 shares as of May 31, 2016, respectively.		
Additional paid-in capital	1,030.0	952.7
Retained earnings	901.7	926.2
Accumulated other comprehensive income	20.0	29.2
Total stockholders' equity	**1,955.3**	**1,911.7**
Total liabilities and stockholders' equity	**$ 6,833.7**	**$ 6,440.8**

MANPOWERGROUP, INC.
CONSOLIDATED BALANCE SHEETS
in millions, except share and per share data

31-Dec		2017	2016
ASSETS			
Current Assets			
Cash and cash equivalents	$	689.0	$ 598.5
Accounts receivable, less allowance for doubtful accounts of $110.8 and $98.2, respectively		5,370.5	4,413.1
Prepaid expenses and other assets		111.7	121.3
Total current assets		6,171.2	5,132.9
Other Assets			
Goodwill		1,343.0	1,239.9
Intangible assets, less accumulated amortization of $339.9 and $299.8, respectively		284.0	294.4
Other assets		927.7	759.7
Total other assets		2,554.7	2,294.0
Property and Equipment			
Land, buildings, leasehold improvements and equipment		633.4	567.0
Less: accumulated depreciation and amortization		475.7	419.7
Net property and equipment		157.7	147.3
Total assets	$	8,883.6	$ 7,574.2
LIABILITIES AND SHAREHOLDERS' EQUITY			
Current Liabilities			
Accounts payable	$	2,279.4	$ 1,914.4
Employee compensation payable		230.6	208.1
Accrued liabilities		490.9	398.6
Accrued payroll taxes and insurance		794.7	649.2
Value added taxes payable		545.4	448.7
Short-term borrowings and current maturities of long-term debt		469.4	39.8
Total current liabilities		4,810.4	3,658.8
Other liabilities			
Long-term debt		478.1	785.6
Other long-term liabilities		737.5	683.4
Total other liabilities		1,215.6	1,469.0

Shareholders' Equity			
Preferred stock, $.01 par value, authorized 25,000,000 shares, none issued		—	—
Common stock, $.01 par value, authorized 125,000,000 shares, issued 116,303,729 and 115,115,748 shares, respectively		1.2	1.2
Capital in excess of par value		3,302.6	3,227.2
Retained earnings		2,713.0	2,291.3
Accumulated other comprehensive loss		(288.2)	(426.1)
Treasury stock at cost, 50,226,525 and 48,146,658 shares, respectively		(2,953.7)	(2,731.7)
Total ManpowerGroup shareholders' equity		2,774.9	2,361.9
Noncontrolling interests		82.7	84.5
Total shareholders' equity		2,857.6	2,446.4
Total liabilities and shareholders' equity	$	8,883.6	7,574.2

SERVICE COMPANY INCOME STATEMENTS

The income statements for Accenture Plc., Paychex, Inc., and ManpowerGroup are provided in this section. While the content varies on each income statement, some general differences should be pointed out.

First, note that the titles of the income statements differ for all three companies. The Accenture income statement is titled "consolidated income statements." The Paychex income statement is titled "consolidated statements of income and comprehensive income." The ManpowerGroup income statement is titled "consolidated statement of operations." Even though the titles may differ, you will know you are looking at an income statement if it starts with revenues or sales and is followed by expenses, resulting in a calculation of net income or net earnings. Companies have a choice of preparing a single income statement that includes the comprehensive income at the bottom (as is the case for Paychex), or reporting the income statement separately from the statement of comprehensive income (as is the case for Accenture and ManpowerGroup). Note that all three companies present the calculations of earnings per share at the bottom of the income statement. Additionally, note again that only the Accenture income statement includes the "when" in the heading and that the year end dates are different for each company.

Second, all three companies round their income statements, as indicated in the last line of the heading. Again, note that Accenture rounds to thousands, while the other two companies rounded to millions.

Third, the overall look and feel of each income statement is slightly different. ManpowerGroup includes lines that run the entire width of the page, rather than just the standard underlines and double underlines under the amounts. There is differing use of bold font and all caps.

Fourth, the headings and subheadings vary quite a bit, as well as the level of detail provided under each. Note that Accenture provides the greatest level of detail, whereas ManpowerGroup provides the least. Of course, all three income statements start with revenues. It is common for service businesses to list their revenue as "service revenue," as is the case for Paychex and ManpowerGroup. Notice, however, that Accenture does not. Accenture and Paychex also list a second category of revenue, other than their primary revenue, and ManpowerGroup does not.

As for the expenses, Accenture provides a major category heading for operating expenses, and then further breaks out cost of services, sales and marketing, general and administrative, and pension settlement charges. Those four items total the operating expenses, which are subtracted from total revenues in arriving at operating income. Additionally, note that the term "cost of services" is used instead of "cost of goods sold," since service companies do not sell goods but rather sell services. Paychex follows the same general trend in listing expenses as Accenture but provides less detail. There are only two expense categories listed: operating expenses and selling, general, and administrative expenses. Note that Accenture includes selling, general and administrative expenses under the operating expenses heading, while Paychex does not. Like Accenture, Paycheck subtracts its two main expense lines from total revenue in arriving at operating income. ManpowerGroup takes a different approach. ManpowerGroup starts with total revenues and subtracts cost of services in arriving at the subtotal for gross profit, much like merchandisers and manufacturers do. ManpowerGroup then subtracts selling and administrative expenses in arriving at operating profit. All three companies then subtract non-operating expenses in arriving at net income or net earnings.

As noted with the balance sheets, these differences often confuse accounting students that are trying to calculate a ratio by looking for a precise wording, so it is important to get familiar with the differences in the income statements. Additionally, remember that each individual line item may also differ because each company is unique and engages in different sorts of transactions.

MERCHANDISERS

Merchandisers are business that buy goods from others and sell them to their customers. Some merchandisers (with ticker symbol) you may have heard of include:

- AutoZone, Inc. (AZO): automotive parts store
- Ulta Salon, Cosmetics & Fragrance, Inc. (ULTA): beauty products
- Barnes & Noble, Inc. (BKS): book store
- Foot Locker, Inc. (FL): footwear store
- The Gap, Inc. (GPS): clothing store
- Target Corporation (TGT): department store
- Dollar Tree, Inc. (DLTR): discount store
- Amazon.com, Inc. (AMZN): ecommerce
- The Home Depot, Inc. (HD): home improvement store
- Costco Wholesale Corporation (COST): membership warehouse

MERCHANDISER BALANCE SHEETS

The balance sheet for AutoZone, Inc., is provided in this section. While most of the same differences that exist between service company balance sheets are true for merchandisers, some general differences between a service company balance sheet and a merchandiser balance sheet should be pointed out.

First, note that, under the current assets heading, AutoZone has merchandise inventory. This is the primary difference on merchandiser balance sheet versus a service company balance sheet. Merchandisers purchase inventory for resale, so inventory is recorded as an asset on the balance sheet until they sell it to the customer.

Second, in general, merchandisers will most likely have more property and equipment relative to the remaining assets than service companies because merchandisers have store locations and warehousing facilities that service business would not usually have. As you can see, the listing of property and equipment for AutoZone includes much greater detail compared to any of the service companies provided in this appendix.

Finally, it should be pointed out that the AutoZone financials are rounded to thousands, although it does not say this directly in the heading. It is noted in small font on the left just before the financial data.

MERCHANDISER INCOME STATEMENTS

The income statement for AutoZone, Inc., is provided in this section. Again, most of the same differences that exist between service company income statements are true for merchandisers. You can see that the AutoZone, Inc., income statement layout is most similar to the ManpowerGroup layout in that there is not a lot of detail provided. Some general differences between a service company income statement and a merchandiser income statement are pointed out below.

AutoZone, Inc.
Consolidated Balance Sheets

(in thousands)	August 26, 2017	August 27, 2016
Assets		
Current assets:		
Cash and cash equivalents	$ 293,270	$ 189,734
Accounts receivable	280,733	287,680
Merchandise inventories	3,882,086	3,631,916
Other current assets	155,166	130,243
Total current assets	4,611,255	4,239,573
Property and equipment:		
Land	1,056,187	998,460
Buildings and improvements	3,423,056	3,169,575
Equipment	1,704,653	1,550,792
Leasehold improvements	470,998	434,615
Construction in progress	218,299	176,673
	6,873,193	6,330,115
Less: Accumulated depreciation and amortization	2,842,175	2,596,861
	4,031,018	3,733,254

Goodwill	391,887	391,887
Deferred income taxes	35,308	36,855
Other long-term assets	190,313	198,218
	617,508	626,960
	$ 9,259,781	$ 8,599,787
Liabilities and Stockholders' Deficit		
Current liabilities:		
Accounts payable	$ 4,168,940	$ 4,095,854
Accrued expenses and other	563,350	551,625
Income taxes payable	34,011	42,841
Total current liabilities	4,766,301	4,690,320
Long-term debt	5,081,238	4,924,119
Deferred income taxes	371,111	284,500
Other long-term liabilities	469,508	488,386
Commitments and contingencies	—	—
Stockholders' deficit:		
Preferred stock, authorized 1,000 shares; no shares issued	—	—
Common stock, par value $.01 per share, authorized 200,000 shares; 28,735 shares issued and 27,833 shares outstanding in 2017 and 30,329 shares issued and 29,118 shares outstanding in	287	303
Additional paid-in capital	1,086,671	1,054,647
Retained deficit	(1,642,387)	(1,602,186)
Accumulated other comprehensive loss	(254,557)	(307,529)
Treasury stock, at cost	(618,391)	(932,773)
Total stockholders' deficit	(1,428,377)	(1,787,538)
	$ 9,259,781	$ 8,599,787

First, you can see that the AutoZone, Inc., income statement starts with net sales. Merchandisers typically title the first line of the income statement as sales, rather than revenues. While they represent the same thing, merchandisers earn revenue when they *sell* a product, thus the wording "sales" is used.

Second, merchandisers will typically subtract the cost of sales from sales in arriving at the subtotal for gross profit. Recall that ManpowerGroup used the term cost of services because they were a service business, while merchandisers would use the term cost of sales or cost of goods sold.

Always keep in mind that each individual line item on merchandiser financial statements may differ since each company is unique and engages in different sorts of transactions.

AutoZone, Inc.
Consolidated Statements of Income

		Year Ended		
		August 26,	August 27,	August 29,
(in thousands, except per share data)		2017	2016	2015
		(52 weeks)	(52 weeks)	(52 weeks)
Net sales	$	10,888,676	$ 10,635,676	$ 10,187,340
Cost of sales, including warehouse and delivery expenses		5,149,056	5,026,940	4,860,309
Gross profit		5,739,620	5,608,736	5,327,031
Operating, selling, general and administrative expenses		3,659,551	3,548,341	3,373,980
Operating profit		2,080,069	2,060,395	1,953,051
Interest expense, net		154,580	147,681	150,439
Income before income taxes		1,925,489	1,912,714	1,802,612
Income tax expense		644,620	671,707	642,371
Net income	$	1,280,869	$ 1,241,007	$ 1,160,241
Weighted average shares for basic earnings per share		28,430	29,889	31,560
Effect of dilutive stock equivalents		635	599	646
Weighted average shares for diluted earnings per share		29,065	30,488	32,206
Basic earnings per share	$	45.05	$ 41.52	$ 36.76
Diluted earnings per share	$	44.07	$ 40.7	$ 36.03

MANUFACTURERS

Manufacturers are business that make the goods they sell. Some manufacturers (with ticker symbols) that you may have heard of include:

- The Boeing Company (BA): aircraft manufacturer
- General Dynamics Corporation (GC): national defense contractor
- 3M Company (MMM): industrial conglomerate
- General Electric Company (GE): industrial conglomerate
- Deere & Company (DE): construction equipment
- Johnson Controls (JCI): automotive supplier
- Generac Holdings Inc. (GNRC): generators and engines
- Briggs & Stratton Corporation (BGG): engines for outdoor power equipment
- Apple Inc. (AAPL): computer hardware
- Ford Motor Company (F): automobile and truck manufacturer

MANUFACTURER BALANCE SHEETS

The balance sheets for The Boeing Company, 3M Company, Briggs & Stratton Corporation, and Apple, Inc., are provided in this section. Again, most of the same differences that exist between service company and merchandiser balance sheets are true for manufacturers and will not be pointed out again in this section. However, some general differences between service company and merchandiser balance sheets and a manufacturer balance sheet should be pointed out. Additionally, there is somewhat greater variance between manufacturer balance sheets, which is why four examples are provided in this appendix.

First, note that Boeing uses the title Consolidated Statements of Financial Position, whereas the other three companies all use the title Consolidated Balance Sheets. These mean the same thing.

Second, note that among the current assets, you will see inventories on each of the four balance sheets provided. Recall that manufacturers make the products that they sell and thus have three categories of inventory: raw materials, work in process, and finished goods. Additionally, note that the balance sheets of 3M and Briggs & Stratton separately identify those three categories of inventory, while Boeing and Apple simply have one line item for inventories.

Third, as was noted with merchandisers, manufacturers will typically have an even greater amount of property, plant, and equipment relative to other assets, as compared to service companies because they have production facilities, machinery, and warehouses that service business do not have.

The individual line items on each balance sheet will vary due to the nature of the business and the transactions it engages in.

The Boeing Company and Subsidiaries
Consolidated Statements of Financial Position

(Dollars in millions, except per share data)

December 31,	2017	2016
Assets		
Cash and cash equivalents	$8,813	$8,801
Short-term and other investments	1,179	1,228
Accounts receivable, net	10,516	8,832
Current portion of customer financing, net	309	428
Inventories, net of advances and progress billings	44,344	43,199
Total current assets	65,161	62,488
Customer financing, net	2,740	3,773
Property, plant and equipment, net	12,672	12,807
Goodwill	5,559	5,324
Acquired intangible assets, net	2,573	2,540
Deferred income taxes	341	332
Investments	1,260	1,317
Other assets, net of accumulated amortization of $482 and $497	2,027	1,416
Total assets	$92,333	$89,997
Liabilities and equity		
Accounts payable	$12,202	$11,190
Accrued liabilities	15,292	14,691
Advances and billings in excess of related costs	27,440	23,869
Short-term debt and current portion of long-term debt	1,335	384
Total current liabilities	56,269	50,134

	1,839	1,338
Deferred income taxes	1,839	1,338
Accrued retiree health care	5,545	5,916
Accrued pension plan liability, net	16,471	19,943
Other long-term liabilities	2,015	2,221
Long-term debt	9,782	9,568
Shareholders' equity:		
Common stock, par value $5.00 – 1,200,000,000 shares authorized; 1,012,261,159 shares issued	5,061	5,061
Additional paid-in capital	6,804	4,762
Treasury stock, at cost	(43,454)	(36,097)
Retained earnings	45,320	40,714
Accumulated other comprehensive loss	(13,376)	(13,623)
Total shareholders' equity	355	817
Noncontrolling interests	57	60
Total equity	412	877
Total liabilities and equity	$92,333	$89,997

3M Company and Subsidiaries
Consolidated Balance Sheet
At December 31

(Dollars in millions, except per share amount)		December 31, 2017		December 31, 2016
Assets				
Current assets				
Cash and cash equivalents	$	3,053	$	2,398
Marketable securities — current		1,076		280
Accounts receivable — net of allowances of $103 and $88		4,911		4,392
Inventories				
Finished goods		1,915		1,629
Work in process		1,218		1,039
Raw materials and supplies		901		717
Total inventories		4,034		3,385
Prepaids		937		821
Other current assets		266		450
Total current assets		14,277		11,726
Property, plant and equipment		24,914		23,499
Less: Accumulated depreciation		-16,048		-14,983
Property, plant and equipment — net		8,866		8,516
Goodwill		10,513		9,166
Intangible assets — net		2,936		2,320
Other assets		1,395		1,178
Total assets	$	37,987	$	32,906

Liabilities

Current liabilities

Short-term borrowings and current portion of long-term debt	$	1,853	$	972
Accounts payable		1,945		1,798
Accrued payroll		870		678
Accrued income taxes		310		299
Other current liabilities		2,709		2,472
Total current liabilities		7,687		6,219
Long-term debt		12,096		10,678
Pension and postretirement benefits		3,620		4,018
Other liabilities		2,962		1,648
Total liabilities	$	26,365	$	22,563

Commitments and contingencies (Note 15)

Equity

3M Company shareholders' equity:

Common stock par value, $.01 par value	$	9	$	9
Shares outstanding - 2017: 594,884,237				
Shares outstanding - 2016: 596,726,278				
Additional paid-in capital		5,352		5,061
Retained earnings		39,115		37,907
Treasury stock		-25,887		-25,434
Accumulated other comprehensive income (loss)		-7,026		-7,245
Total 3M Company shareholders' equity		11,563		10,298
Noncontrolling interest		59		45
Total equity	$	11,622	$	10,343
Total liabilities and equity	$	37,987	$	32,906

BRIGGS & STRATTON CORPORATION
Consolidated Balance Sheets

AS OF JULY 2, 2017 AND JULY 3, 2016

(in thousands)

ASSETS		2017		2016
CURRENT ASSETS:				
Cash and Cash Equivalents	$	61,707	$	89,839
Receivables, Less Reserves of $2,645 and $2,806, Respectively		230,011		191,678
Inventories:				
Finished Products		265,720		271,718
Work in Process		102,187		104,468
Raw Materials		6,972		9,879
Total Inventories		374,879		386,065
Prepaid Expenses and Other Current Assets		22,844		28,419
Total Current Assets		689,441		696,001

GOODWILL		161,649		161,568
INVESTMENTS		51,677		52,757
OTHER INTANGIBLE ASSETS, Net		100,595		104,164
LONG-TERM DEFERRED INCOME TAX ASSET		64,412		98,203
OTHER LONG-TERM ASSETS, Net		18,325		17,701
PLANT AND EQUIPMENT:				
Land and Land Improvements		15,179		14,871
Buildings		135,226		128,218
Machinery and Equipment		867,445		862,312
Construction in Progress		86,733		51,492
		1,104,583		1,056,893
Less - Accumulated Depreciation		739,703		730,620
Total Plant and Equipment, Net		364,880		326,273
	$	1,450,979	$	1,456,667

LIABILITIES AND SHAREHOLDERS' INVESTMENT				
CURRENT LIABILITIES:				
Accounts Payable	$	193,677	$	181,152
Accrued Liabilities:				
Wages and Salaries		43,061		45,149
Warranty		28,640		26,313
Accrued Postretirement Health Care Obligation		9,755		9,394
Other		55,245		56,293
Total Accrued Liabilities		136,701		137,149
Total Current Liabilities		330,378		318,301
ACCRUED PENSION COST		242,908		310,378
ACCRUED EMPLOYEE BENEFITS		21,897		23,483
ACCRUED POSTRETIREMENT HEALTH CARE OBLIGATION		35,132		38,441
ACCRUED WARRANTY		14,468		18,054
OTHER LONG-TERM LIABILITIES		25,069		33,045
LONG-TERM DEBT		221,793		221,339
COMMITMENTS AND CONTINGENCIES (Note 13)				
SHAREHOLDERS' INVESTMENT:				
Common Stock -				
Authorized 120,000 Shares $.01 Par Value, Issued 57,854 Shares		579		579
Additional Paid-In Capital		73,562		72,020
Retained Earnings		1,107,033		1,074,437
Accumulated Other Comprehensive Loss		(300,026)		(338,450)
Treasury Stock at Cost, 15,074 and 14,675 Shares, Respectively		(321,814)		(314,960)
Total Shareholders' Investment		559,334		493,626
	$	1,450,979	$	1,456,667

320

Apple Inc.
CONSOLIDATED BALANCE SHEETS
(In millions, except number of shares which are reflected in thousands and par value)

	September 30, 2017	September 24, 2016
ASSETS:		
Current assets:		
Cash and cash equivalents	$ 20,289	$ 20,484
Short-term marketable securities	53,892	46,671
Accounts receivable, less allowances of $58 and $53, respectively	17,874	15,754
Inventories	4,855	2,132
Vendor non-trade receivables	17,799	13,545
Other current assets	13,936	8,283
Total current assets	128,645	106,869
Long-term marketable securities	194,714	170,430
Property, plant and equipment, net	33,783	27,010
Goodwill	5,717	5,414
Acquired intangible assets, net	2,298	3,206
Other non-current assets	10,162	8,757
Total assets	$ 375,319	$ 321,686
LIABILITIES AND SHAREHOLDERS' EQUITY:		
Current liabilities:		
Accounts payable	$ 49,049	$ 37,294
Accrued expenses	25,744	22,027
Deferred revenue	7,548	8,080
Commercial paper	11,977	8,105
Current portion of long-term debt	6,496	3,500
Total current liabilities	100,814	79,006
Deferred revenue, non-current	2,836	2,930
Long-term debt	97,207	75,427
Other non-current liabilities	40,415	36,074
Total liabilities	241,272	193,437
Commitments and contingencies		
Shareholders' equity:		
Common stock and additional paid-in capital, $0.00001 par value: 12,600,000 shares authorized; 5,126,201 and 5,336,166 shares issued and outstanding, respectively	35,867	31,251
Retained earnings	98,330	96,364
Accumulated other comprehensive income/(loss)	(150)	634
Total shareholders' equity	134,047	128,249
Total liabilities and shareholders' equity	$ 375,319	$ 321,686

MANUFACTURER INCOME STATEMENTS

The income statements for The Boeing Company, 3M Company, Briggs & Stratton Corporation, and Apple, Inc., are provided in this section. Again, most of the same differences that exist between service company and merchandiser income statements are true for manufacturers and will not be pointed out again in this section. However, some general differences between service company and merchandiser income statements and a manufacturer income statement should be pointed out.

First, notice that Boeing has two main types of revenue: sales of products and sales of services that are listed on the income statement. The other three companies just have one type of revenue listed as net sales.

Second, as Boeing has two main types of revenue listed on the income statement, they list two main costs after the revenue section: cost of products and cost of services. Both 3M and Apple use the term cost of sales following the net sales line on their income statements, while Briggs & Stratton uses the term cost of goods sold. They all mean the same thing.

Third, Boeing does not provide a subtotal calculation for gross profit. You would need to manually calculate that yourself if you needed it for a ratio. You could further break that out into the gross profit on products versus the gross profit on services if you wanted. 3M does not provide a subtotal calculation for gross profit, either. Briggs & Stratton subtracts both cost of goods sold and restructuring charges in arriving at the subtotal for gross profit. Apple uses the traditional approach in showing net sales minus cost of sales in arriving at gross profit; however, they refer to it as gross margin instead of gross profit, which is the same thing.

Fourth, Boeing, 3M, and Apple all list research and development costs on their income statements, which is common to manufacturers, because they need to research and develop the products that they make.

Again, recall that the individual line items on each income statement will vary because of the nature of the business and the transactions it engages in.

The Boeing Company and Subsidiaries
Consolidated Statements of Operations

(Dollars in millions, except per share data)

Years ended December 31,	2017	2016	2015
Sales of products	$83,204	$84,399	$85,255
Sales of services	10,188	10,172	10,859
Total revenues	93,392	94,571	96,114
Cost of products	(68,365)	(72,713)	(73,446)
Cost of services	(7,631)	(8,018)	(8,578)
Boeing Capital interest expense	(70)	(59)	(64)
Total costs and expenses	(76,066)	(80,790)	(82,088)
	17,326	13,781	14,026

Income from operating investments, net	**204**	303	274
General and administrative expense	**(4,094)**	(3,616)	(3,525)
Research and development expense, net	**(3,179)**	(4,627)	(3,331)
Gain/(loss) on dispositions, net	**21**	(7)	(1)
Earnings from operations	**10,278**	5,834	7,443
Other income/(loss), net	**129**	40	(13)
Interest and debt expense	**(360)**	(306)	(275)
Earnings before income taxes	**10,047**	5,568	7,155
Income tax expense	**(1,850)**	(673)	(1,979)
Net earnings	**$8,197**	$4,895	$5,176
Basic earnings per share	**$13.60**	$7.70	$7.52
Diluted earnings per share	**$13.43**	$7.61	$7.44

3M Company and Subsidiaries
Consolidated Statement of Income
Years ended December 31

(Millions, except per share amounts)		2017		2016		2015
Net sales	$	**31,657**	$	30,109	$	30,274
Operating expenses						
Cost of sales		**16,001**		15,040		15,383
Selling, general and administrative expenses		**6,572**		6,222		6,229
Research, development and related expenses		**1,850**		1,735		1,763
Gain on sale of businesses		**-586**		-111		-47
Total operating expenses		**23,837**		22,886		23,328
Operating income		**7,820**		7,223		6,946
Other expense (income), net		**272**		170		123
Income before income taxes		**7,548**		7,053		6,823
Provision for income taxes		**2,679**		1,995		1,982
Net income including noncontrolling interest	$	**4,869**	$	5,058	$	4,841
Less: Net income attributable to noncontrolling interest		**11**		8		8
Net income attributable to 3M	$	**4,858**	$	5,050	$	4,833
Weighted average 3M common shares outstanding — basic		**597.5**		604.7		625.6
Earnings per share attributable to 3M common shareholders — basic	$	**8.13**	$	8.35	$	7.72
Weighted average 3M common shares outstanding — diluted		**612.7**		618.7		637.2
Earnings per share attributable to 3M common shareholders — diluted	$	**7.93**	$	8.16	$	7.58
Cash dividends paid per 3M common share	$	**4.70**	$	4.44	$	4.10

BRIGGS & STRATTON CORPORATION
Consolidated Statements of Operations

FOR THE FISCAL YEARS ENDED JULY 2, 2017, JULY 3, 2016 AND JUNE 28, 2015
(in thousands, except per share data)

		2017		2016		2015
NET SALES	$	1,786,103	$	1,808,778	$	1,894,750
COST OF GOODS SOLD		1,402,274		1,438,166		1,511,363
RESTRUCTURING CHARGES		—		8,157		24,288
Gross Profit		383,829		362,455		359,099
ENGINEERING, SELLING, GENERAL AND ADMIN EXPENSES		297,538		305,482		289,916
RESTRUCTURING CHARGES		—		2,038		3,000
GOODWILL IMPAIRMENT		—		7,651		—
TRADENAME IMPAIRMENT		—		2,683		—
EQUITY IN EARNINGS OF UNCONSOLIDATED AFFILIATES		11,056		1,760		—
Income from Operations		97,347		46,361		66,183
INTEREST EXPENSE		(20,293)		(20,033)		(19,532)
OTHER INCOME, Net		2,607		9,028		10,307
Income Before Income Taxes		79,661		35,356		56,958
PROVISION FOR INCOME TAXES		23,011		8,795		11,271
NET INCOME	$	56,650	$	26,561	$	45,687
EARNINGS PER SHARE						
Basic	$	1.31	$	0.61	$	1
Diluted	$	1.31	$	0.6	$	1
WEIGHTED AVERAGE SHARES OUTSTANDING						
Basic		42,178		43,019		44,392
Diluted		42,263		43,200		44,442

Apple Inc.
CONSOLIDATED STATEMENTS OF OPERATIONS
(In millions, except number of shares which are reflected in thousands and per share amounts)

		Years ended				
		September 30, 2017		September 24, 2016		September 26, 2015
Net sales	$	229,234	$	215,639	$	233,715
Cost of sales		141,048		131,376		140,089
Gross margin		88,186		84,263		93,626
Operating expenses:						
Research and development		11,581		10,045		8,067
Selling, general and administrative		15,261		14,194		14,329
Total operating expenses		26,842		24,239		22,396
Operating income		61,344		60,024		71,230
Other income/(expense), net		2,745		1,348		1,285
Income before provision for income taxes		64,089		61,372		72,515

Provision for income taxes		15,738		15,685	19,121
Net income	$	48,351	$	45,687	$ 53,394
Earnings per share:					
Basic	$	9.27	$	8.35	$ 9.28
Diluted	$	9.21	$	8.31	$ 9.22
Shares used in computing earnings per share:					
Basic		5,217,242		5,470,820	5,753,421
Diluted		5,251,692		5,500,281	5,793,069
Cash dividends declared per share	$	2.4	$	2.18	$ 1.98

SUMMARY

Utilizing financial statement data and understanding the financial statements takes practice. It is important to remember that not all financial statements look alike or use the same wording. It is also important to look at the individual line items on the financial statements to determine what, exactly, is presented in subtotals and under headings. Additionally, the financial statements are not complete without reading the accompanying notes to the financial statements, which provide greater detail than what is on the financial statements themselves.

APPENDIX 4: ANNUAL REPORT EXAMPLE

ANNUAL REPORTS

A Form 10-K is an annual report filed with the U.S. Securities and Exchange Commission. The Securities and Exchange Commission requires a Form 10-K to be filed annually for all publicly traded companies other than foreign private issuers. The Form 10-K is organized into four main parts (I, II, III, and IV). Part I includes general business information. Part II includes financial information, such as presentations of selected financial data, management's discussion and analysis, and the audited financial statements. Part III includes disclosures of certain information, such as the directors, executive compensation, and accountants' fees. Part IV includes exhibits required by the SEC as well as the financial statements included in Part II. The Table of Contents for the Vera Bradley, Inc., 10-K for the period ended January 28, 2017 is shown below:

TABLE OF CONTENTS

PART I

Part I of the Form 10-K provides general information about that business and is divided into six parts: Item 1, Item 1A, Item 1B, Item 2, Item 3, and Item 4. Note (below) that Vera Bradley, Inc., starts Part I with a description of the fiscal year calendar of the business, since it does not use a straight calendar year:

PART I

In this Form 10-K, references to "Vera Bradley," "we," "our," "us" and the "Company" refer to Vera Bradley, Inc. and its subsidiaries, including Vera Bradley Designs, Inc. The Company utilizes a 52-53 week fiscal year ending on the Saturday closest to January 31. The fiscal years ended January 28, 2017 ("fiscal 2017"), January 30, 2016 ("fiscal 2016") and January 31, 2015 ("fiscal 2015") were each 52-week periods. The fiscal year ending February 3, 2018 ("fiscal 2018") will be a 53-week period.

ITEM 1

Item 1 describes the business in significant detail. This section can vary from business to business, but in general, it provides an in-depth description of the business and is a good place to start in gaining a basic understanding of how the company operates. Item 1 requires a description of the company's business, including its main products and services, what subsidiaries it owns, and what markets it operates in. Item 1 for Vera Bradley, Inc., includes headings such as Our Company Our History, Growth Strategies, Competitive Strengths, Our Product Release Strategy, Our Products, Product Development, Marketing, Seasonality, Channels of Distribution, Manufacturing and Supply Chain Model, Distribution Center, Management Information Systems, Competition, Copyrights and Trademarks, Employees, Government Regulation, and Executive Officers of the Company. Selected sections from Item 1 of the Vera Bradley, Inc., 10-K for the period ended January 28, 2017, are shown below as examples of the level of detail provided:

Our Company

Vera Bradley is a leading designer of women's handbags, luggage and travel items, fashion and home accessories, and unique gifts. Founded in 1982 by friends Barbara Bradley Baekgaard and Patricia R. Miller, the brand's innovative designs, iconic patterns, and brilliant colors continue to inspire and connect women.

Vera Bradley offers a unique, multi-channel sales model, as well as a focus on service and a high level of customer engagement. The Company sells its products through two reportable segments: Direct and Indirect. The Direct business consists of sales of Vera Bradley products through the Company's full-line and factory outlet stores in the United States, verabradley.com, direct-to-consumer eBay sales, and the Company's annual outlet sale in Fort Wayne, Indiana. As of January 28, 2017, the Company operated 113 full-line stores and 46 factory outlet stores. The Indirect business consists of sales of Vera Bradley products to approximately 2,600 specialty retail locations, substantially all of which are located in the United States, as well as department stores, national accounts, third party e-commerce sites, the Company's wholesale customer in Japan, and third-party inventory liquidators. For financial information about our reportable segments, refer to Note 16 of the Notes to Consolidated Financial Statements set forth in Part II, "Item 8. Financial Statements and Supplementary Data," of this report.

Our Products

The following chart presents net revenues generated by each of our four product categories and other revenues as a percentage of our total net revenues for fiscal 2017, 2016, and 2015.

	Fiscal Year Ended		
	January 28, 2017	January 30, 2016	January 31, 2015
Bags	42.8 %	42.9 %	45.4 %
Travel	24.5 %	24.9 %	21.4 %
Accessories	21.9 %	22.3 %	22.8 %
Home	5.7 %	4.5 %	3.5 %
Other [1]	5.1 %	5.4 %	6.9 %
Total	100 %	100 %	100 %

[1] Includes primarily apparel/footwear, stationery, merchandising, freight, licensing revenue, and gift card breakage revenue.

Bags. Bags are a core part of our product offerings and are the primary component of every seasonal assortment. The category consists of classic and new styles developed by our product development team to meet consumer demand. Our bag product category includes items such as totes, crossbodies, satchels, clutches, backpacks, baby bags, and lunch bags. Bags play a prominent role in our visual merchandising, and we focus on showcasing the different fabrications, patterns, colors, and features of each bag.

Accessories. Accessories include fashion accessories such as wallets, wristlets, eyeglass cases, jewelry, and scarves and various technology accessories. Our accessories are attractively priced and allow the consumer to include some color in her wardrobe, even if tucked into another bag. Our product development team consistently updates the accessories assortment based on consumer demand and fashion trends.

Travel. Our travel product category includes rolling luggage, cosmetics, travel and packing accessories, and travel bags which includes our iconic duffel and weekend bags. The first Vera Bradley product offering included duffel bags, which consistently have been a strong performer. We believe their popularity, as well as the appeal of our other travel items, results from our vibrant designs, functional styles, and lightweight fabrications.

Home. Our home category includes textiles, including throw blankets, beach towels, and comforters, wellness and beauty, as well as items such as mugs and tumblers.

Competition

We face strong competition in each of the product lines and markets in which we compete. We believe that all of our products are in similar competitive positions with respect to the number of competitors they face and the level of competition within each product line. Due to the number of different products we offer, it is not practicable for us to quantify the number of competitors we face. Our products compete with other branded products within their product categories and with private label products sold by retailers. In our Indirect business, we compete with numerous manufacturers, importers, and distributors of handbags, accessories, and other products for the limited space available for the display of such products to the consumer. Moreover, the general availability of contract manufacturing allows new entrants access to the markets in which we compete, which may increase the number of competitors and adversely affect our competitive position and our business. In our Direct business, we compete against other independent retailers, department stores, catalog retailers, gift retailers, and Internet businesses that engage in the retail sale of similar products.

The market for handbags, in particular, is highly competitive. Our competitors include not only established companies that are expanding their production and marketing of handbags, but also frequent new entrants to the market. We directly compete with wholesalers and direct sellers of branded handbags and accessories, such as Coach, Michael Kors, Nine West, Dooney & Bourke, Kate Spade, Fossil, Brahmin, and Tory Burch.

In varying degrees, depending on the product category involved, we compete on the basis of design (aesthetic appeal), quality (construction), function, price point, distribution, and brand positioning. We believe that our primary competitive advantages are consumer recognition of our brand, customer loyalty, product development expertise, and our widespread presence through our multi-channel distribution model. Some of our competitors have achieved significant recognition for their brand names or have substantially greater financial, distribution, marketing, and other resources than we do. Further, we may face new competitors and increased competition from existing competitors as we expand into new markets and increase our presence in existing markets.

Employees

As of January 28, 2017, we had approximately 3,100 employees. Of the total, approximately 2,450 were engaged in retail selling positions, approximately 315 were engaged in distribution, sourcing and quality functions, approximately 35 were engaged in product design, and approximately 300 were engaged in corporate support and administrative functions. None of our employees are represented by a union. We believe that our relations with our employees are good, and we have never encountered a significant work stoppage.

Government Regulation

Many of our imported products are subject to existing or potential duties, tariffs, or quotas that may limit the quantity of products that we may import into the United States and other countries or impact the cost of such products. To date, we have not been restricted by quotas in the operation of our business, and customs duties have not comprised a material portion of the total cost of a majority of our products. In addition, we are subject to foreign governmental regulation and trade restrictions, including U.S. retaliation against prohibited foreign practices, with respect to our product sourcing and international sales operations.

We are subject to federal, state, local, and foreign laws and regulations governing environmental matters, including the handling, transportation, and disposal of our products and our non-hazardous and hazardous substances and wastes, as well as emissions and discharges into the environment, including discharges to air, surface water, and groundwater. Failure to comply with such laws and regulations could result in costs for corrective action, penalties, or the imposition of other liabilities. Compliance with environmental laws and regulations has not had a material effect upon our earnings or financial position. If we violate any laws or regulations, however, it could have a material adverse effect on our business or financial performance.

Executive Officers of the Company

The following table sets forth certain information concerning each of our executive officers:

Name	Age	Position(s)
Robert Wallstrom	51	Chief Executive Officer, President and Director
Barbara Bradley Baekgaard	78	Co-Founder, Chief Creative Officer, and Director
Kevin J. Sierks	44	Executive Vice President – Chief Financial Officer
Sue Fuller	42	Executive Vice President – Chief Merchandising Officer
Kimberly F. Colby	55	Executive Vice President – Design
Theresa Palermo	41	Executive Vice President – Chief Marketing Officer
Mark C. Dely	41	Vice President – Chief Legal Officer and Corporate Secretary
John Enwright	44	Vice President – Financial, Planning and Analysis and Interim Chief Financial Officer

Robert Wallstrom has served as our Chief Executive Officer, President and Director since November 2013. Prior to joining Vera Bradley, Mr. Wallstrom served as President of Saks Fifth Avenue's OFF 5TH division from 2007 until November 2013. Previously, he was Group Senior Vice President and General Manager of Saks' flagship New York store from 2002 to 2007, where he articulated a vision to return the store to its luxury heritage and dramatically improve merchandising, service and the in-store experience.

Barbara Bradley Baekgaard co-founded Vera Bradley in 1982 and has served as a director since then. From 1982 through June 2010, she also served as Co-President. From the outset, Ms. Bradley Baekgaard has provided leadership and strategic direction in our brand's development by providing creative vision to areas such as marketing, product design, assortment planning, and the design and visual merchandising of our stores. In May 2010, she was appointed Chief Creative Officer. Ms. Bradley Baekgaard currently serves as a member of the Indiana University Simon Cancer Center Development Board and as a member of the board of directors of the Vera Bradley Foundation for Breast Cancer.

Kevin J. Sierks has served as our Executive Vice President – Chief Financial Officer since February 2014. Mr. Sierks joined the Company as the Vice President – Controller and Chief Accounting Officer in December 2011, and also served as the Interim Chief Financial Officer from January 2013 through January 2014. Prior to joining Vera Bradley, from 2007 to 2011 Mr. Sierks served as Vice President – Controller at Biomet, Inc., a large orthopedic medical device company. Mr. Sierks previously served as Director of Accounting and U.S. Shared Services at Boston Scientific Corporation from 2005 to 2007. From 2002 to 2005, Mr. Sierks served as Director of Financial Reporting and Business Development at Guidant Corporation, which was acquired by Boston Scientific Corporation in 2006. Mr. Sierks is a

Certified Public Accountant. Mr. Sierks will be leaving the Company effective March 31, 2017; at that time, John Enwright will assume the Interim CFO position.

Sue Fuller has served as our Executive Vice President – Chief Merchandising Officer since January 2014. Prior to joining Vera Bradley, Ms. Fuller served as Senior Vice President, General Merchandise Manager of Carhartt, Inc. from July 2010 through November 2013. Between 2005 and July 2010, she served in various roles of increasing responsibility with Kohl's Department Stores, including Director, Product Development for Juniors Private Label. Ms. Fuller gained prior experience with L.L. Bean, Lands' End and Polo Ralph Lauren.

Kimberly F. Colby has served as our Executive Vice President – Design since 2005. From 2003 through 2005, she served as our Vice President of Design. From 1989 to 2003, Ms. Colby served as our Design Director responsible for Marketing and Product Development. Ms. Colby's professional history includes retail advertising, public relations, direct mail creative direction and management, special event planning, and interior design.

Theresa Palermo has served as our Executive Vice President – Chief Marketing Officer since June 2015. Between 2013 and June 2015, Ms. Palermo served as Vice President, Global Marketing and Public Relations for Fossil Group, where she successfully created and executed innovative marketing strategies and campaigns for their extensive portfolio of luxury and fashion brands across North and Central America. Ms. Palermo joined Fossil in 2011 as Global Senior Director of Marketing. Prior to joining Fossil, Ms. Palermo held key marketing roles of increasing responsibility with several well-known retailers including global footwear company Collective Brands, The Timberland Company and the J. Jill Group.

Mark C. Dely joined the Company in August 2016 as our Vice President, Chief Legal Officer and Corporate Secretary. Between January 2013 and August 2016, Mr. Dely served as Senior Vice President, Chief Legal Officer, General Counsel and Secretary of Fred's, Inc., a publicly-traded retailer and pharmacy with over 650 locations throughout the Southeast. From July 2007 to December 2012, Mr. Dely was Vice President and Divisional General Counsel of the Franchise Services Group for The Service-Master Company, where he managed the legal function for the Company's global franchise businesses. Mr. Dely's additional experience includes being the first in-house counsel for NYSE-listed seed and agricultural-biotech company, Delta and Pine Land Company. Mr. Dely began his legal career at New York law firm Fried Frank, LLP. He earned his law degree from the New York University School of Law.

John Enwright joined the Company in May 2014 as our Senior Director of Financial, Planning and Analysis and was soon promoted to his current post as Vice President, Financial, Planning and Analysis. In addition, Mr. Enwright has been named Interim Chief Financial Officer upon the departure of Mr. Sierks effective March 31, 2017. Prior to joining Vera Bradley, Mr. Enwright spent 15 years with Tiffany & Co. in various financial roles of increasing responsibility, including his most recent position of Director of Financial, Planning and Analysis.

ITEM 1A

Item 1A provides information related to risk factors that investors should consider prior to investing in the business, generally listed in order of importance. Certain risks may be true for the entire economy, while some may apply only to the company's industry or geographic area. Others may apply only to the company. The Vera Bradley, Inc. 10-K lists thirty-six risk factors and provides a detailed explanation of each one. A selection of the risks identified in the 10-K for the period ended January 28, 2017, are listed below (without the supporting detail):

If we are unable to successfully implement our long-term strategic plan and growth strategies, our future operating results could suffer.

Changes in general economic conditions, and their impact on consumer confidence and consumer spending, could adversely impact our results of operations.

We may continue to experience declines in comparable sales and there can be no guarantee that the strategic initiatives we are implementing to improve our results will be successful.

We may not be able to successfully open new stores and/or operate new and current stores as planned, which could adversely impact our results of operations.

Our business depends on a strong brand. If we are unable to execute our brand strategy, intended to enhance our brand, then revenues and our results of operations could be adversely impacted.

Our results of operations could suffer if we lose key management or design associates or are unable to attract and retain the talent required for our business.

A data security or privacy breach could damage our reputation and our relationships with our customers, expose us to litigation risk and adversely affect our business.

Our Company's ability to attract customers to our stores depends heavily on the success of the shopping centers in which many of our stores are located.

We rely on various suppliers to supply a significant majority of our raw materials. Disruption in the supply of raw materials could increase our cost of goods sold and if there are not sufficient raw materials available to meet product demand, our product revenue could decline.

We rely on a single distribution facility for all of the products we sell. Disruption to that facility could adversely impact our results of operations, and expansion of that facility could have unpredictable adverse effects.

We may be subject to unionization, work stoppages, slowdowns or increased labor costs.

We rely on independent transportation providers for substantially all of our product shipments.

We may suffer negative publicity and our business may be harmed if we need to recall any products we sell.

Our stock price may be volatile or may decline regardless of our operating performance, and you may not be able to resell shares at or above the price at which you purchase them.

ITEM 1B

Item 1B includes a description of any material unresolved comments from the SEC staff regarding the company's periodic and current reports that were received in the past 180 days. Note that the Vera Bradley, Inc. 10-K for the period ending January 28, 2017, does not include any, as shown below:

Item 1B. Unresolved Staff Comments
None.

ITEM 2

Item 2 provides detail relating to the entity's properties, both owned and leased. Item 2 is shown below in its entirety for the Vera Bradley, Inc. 10-K for the period ending January 28, 2017:

Item 2. Properties
The following table sets forth the location, use, and size of our distribution, corporate facilities, and showrooms as of January 28, 2017. The leases on the leased properties expire at various times through 2028, subject to renewal options.

Location	Primary Use	Approximate Square Footage	Leased /Owned
Roanoke, Indiana	Corporate headquarters, design center and showroom	188,000	Owned*
Roanoke, Indiana	Warehouse and distribution	428,500	Owned**
New York, New York	Office and showroom	3,700	Leased
Hong Kong	Asia sourcing office	5,100	Leased
Atlanta, Georgia	Showroom	5,200	Leased
Dallas, Texas	Showroom	1,800	Leased
Las Vegas, Nevada	Showroom	2,200	Leased

*The expansion of this property during fiscal 2015, added approximately 149,000 square feet to the existing building, which now serves as the Company's corporate headquarters.
**An additional 10,000 square feet of office space was added to this facility in fiscal 2015.

As of January 28, 2017, we also leased 165 store locations in the United States, including five store locations opened or to be opened in fiscal 2018 and one store to be opened in fiscal 2019. See below for more information regarding the locations of our open stores as of January 28, 2017.

We consider these properties to be in good condition generally and believe that our facilities are adequate for our operations and provide sufficient capacity to meet our anticipated requirements. The properties in the above table are used by both the Direct segment and Indirect segment, excluding the three showrooms which are used exclusively by the Indirect segment.

Store Locations

Our full-line stores are located primarily in high-traffic regional malls, lifestyle centers, and mixed-use shopping centers across the United States. The following table shows the number of full-line and factory outlet stores we operated in each state as of January 28, 2017:

State	Total Number of Full-Line Stores	Total Number of Factory Outlet Stores	State	Total Number of Full-Line Stores	Total Number of Factory Outlet Stores
Alabama	1	1	Minnesota	2	1
Arizona	3	—	Missouri	2	2
California	7	—	Nebraska	—	1
Colorado	3	1	Nevada	—	2
Connecticut	2	1	New Jersey	9	1
Delaware	1	1	New York	9	3
Florida	7	8	North Carolina	2	4
Georgia	2	2	Ohio	4	1
Hawaii	2	1	Oklahoma	2	1
Illinois	6	1	Pennsylvania	5	2
Indiana	2	1	Rhode Island	1	—
Iowa	1	—	Tennessee	3	2
Kansas	1	—	Texas	13	3
Kentucky	2	1	Virginia	3	2
Louisiana	2	—	Washington	1	—
Maryland	4	—	Wisconsin	2	—
Massachusetts	4	1	Totals	113	46
Michigan	5	2			

We lease all of our stores. Lease terms for our retail stores are generally ten years with options to renew for varying terms. The leases generally provide for a fixed minimum rental plus contingent rent, which is determined as a percentage of sales in excess of specified levels.

ITEM 3

Item 3 provides detail relating to any pending or threatened litigation that might have a materially adverse effect on the financial condition or results of operations of the business. Item 3 as presented in the Vera Bradley, Inc., 10-K for the period ending January 28, 2017, is shown below:

Item 3. Legal Proceedings

We may be involved from time to time, as a plaintiff or a defendant, in various routine legal proceedings incident to the ordinary course of our business. In the ordinary course, we are involved in the policing of our intellectual property rights. As part of our policing program, from time to time we file lawsuits in the United States and abroad, alleging acts of trademark counterfeiting, trademark infringement, trademark dilution, and ancillary and pendent state and foreign law claims. These actions often result in seizure of counterfeit merchandise and negotiated settlements with defendants. Defendants sometimes raise as affirmative defenses, or as counterclaims, the purported invalidity or unenforceability of our proprietary rights. We believe that the outcome of all pending legal proceedings in the aggregate will not have a material adverse effect on our business or financial condition.

ITEM 4

Item 4 is reserved for a discussion on mine safety violations or other regulatory matters as required by Section 1503(a) of the Dodd-Frank Act and Item 104 of Regulation S-K. Note that this is not applicable for the Vera Bradley, Inc., 10-K for the period ending January 28, 2017, as shown below:

Item 4. Mine Safety Disclosure

Not Applicable

PART II

Part II of the Form 10-K provides financial and supporting detail, including management's discussion and analysis and the audited financial statements. Part II is divided into eight parts: Item 5, Item 6, Item 7, Item 7A, Item 8, Item 9, Item 9A, and Item 9B.

ITEM 5

Item 5 provides detail about the company's common stock, including the trading market, historical high and low sales prices, the number of registered holders, the payment of cash dividends, unregistered sales of securities, and company repurchases of its common stock during the fourth fiscal quarter. Item 5 for the Vera Bradley, Inc., 10-K for the period ending January 28, 2017, includes a stock performance graph, as shown below:

Stock Performance Graph

The graph set forth below compares the cumulative shareholder return on our common stock between January 28, 2012, and January 28, 2017, to the cumulative return of (i) the S&P 500 Index and (ii) the S&P 500 Apparel, Accessories, and Luxury Goods Index over the same period. This graph assumes an initial investment of $100 on January 28, 2012, in our common stock, the S&P 500 Index, and the S&P 500 Apparel, Accessories, and Luxury Goods Index and assumes the reinvestment of dividends, if any.

The comparisons shown in the graph below are based on historical data. We caution that the stock price performance presented in the graph below is not necessarily indicative of, nor is it intended to forecast, the potential future performance of our common stock. Information used in the graph was obtained from The NASDAQ Stock Market website; we do not assume responsibility for any errors or omissions in such information.

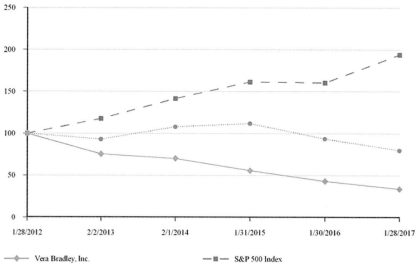

ITEM 6

Item 6 highlights selected financial data for the past five years, derived from the audited financial statements. Item 6 for the Vera Bradley, Inc., 10-K for the period ending January 28, 2017, includes both income statement and balance sheet data over a five-year period, as shown below:

Item 6. Selected Financial Data

The following tables present selected consolidated financial and other data as of and for the years indicated. The selected income statement data for the most recent three fiscal years presented and the selected balance sheet data as of January 28, 2017 and January 30, 2016 are derived from our audited consolidated financial statements included in Item 8 of this report. The selected income statement data for the fiscal years ended February 1, 2014, and February 2, 2013, and selected balance sheet data as of January 31, 2015, February 1, 2014, and February 2, 2013, are derived from our audited consolidated financial statements that are not included elsewhere in this report. These results include adjustments necessary for comparability, including discontinued operations which is discussed further in Note 14 to the Consolidated Financial Statements. The historical results presented below are not necessarily indicative of the results to be expected for any future period. You should read this selected consolidated financial and other data in conjunction with the consolidated financial statements and related notes and the information under "Management's Discussion and Analysis of Financial Condition and Results of Operations" appearing elsewhere in this report.

	Fiscal Year Ended [1]				
($ in thousands, except per share data and as otherwise indicated)	January 28, 2017	January 30, 2016	January 31, 2015	February 1, 2014	February 2, 2013
Consolidated Statement of Income Data [2]:					
Net revenues	$ 485,937	$ 502,598	$ 508,990	$ 530,896	$ 535,667
Cost of sales	209,891	221,409	239,981	238,684	231,135
Gross profit	276,046	281,189	269,009	292,212	304,532
Selling, general, and administrative expenses [2]	249,155	236,836	208,675	201,231	197,139
Other income	1,329	2,369	3,736	4,776	6,277
Operating income	28,220	46,722	64,070	95,757	113,670
Interest expense, net	178	263	407	571	679
Income from continuing operations before income taxes	28,042	46,459	63,663	95,186	112,991
Income tax expense	8,284	18,901	22,828	35,057	40,597
Income from continuing operations	19,758	27,558	40,835	60,129	72,394
Loss from discontinued operations, net of taxes	—	—	(2,386)	(1,317)	(3,524)
Net income	$ 19,758	$ 27,558	$ 38,449	$ 58,812	$ 68,870
Basic weighted-average shares outstanding	36,838	38,795	40,568	40,599	40,536
Diluted weighted-average shares outstanding	36,970	38,861	40,632	40,648	40,571
Net income (loss) per share - basic					
Continuing operations	$ 0.54	$ 0.71	$ 1.01	$ 1.48	$ 1.79
Discontinued operations	—	—	(0.06)	(0.03)	(0.09)
Net income	$ 0.54	$ 0.71	$ 0.95	$ 1.45	$ 1.70
Net income (loss) per share - diluted					
Continuing operations	$ 0.53	$ 0.71	$ 1.00	$ 1.48	$ 1.78
Discontinued operations	—	—	(0.06)	(0.03)	(0.09)
Net income	$ 0.53	$ 0.71	$ 0.95	$ 1.45	$ 1.70
Net Revenues by Segment [2]:					
Direct	$ 355,175	$ 351,286	$ 335,602	$ 321,092	$ 287,083
Indirect	130,762	151,312	173,388	209,804	248,584
Total	$ 485,937	$ 502,598	$ 508,990	$ 530,896	$ 535,667
Store Data [3]:					
Total stores open at end of year	159	150	125	99	76
Comparable sales (including e-commerce) (decrease) increase [4]	(7.0)%	(10.6)%	(7.6)%	(1.3)%	9.8 %
Total gross square footage at end of year	368,640	342,362	278,779	207,096	156,310
Average net revenues per gross square foot [3]	$ 642	$ 703	$ 760	$ 887	$ 1,083

	As of				
($ in thousands)	January 28, 2017	January 30, 2016	January 31, 2015	February 1, 2014	February 2, 2013
Consolidated Balance Sheet Data:					
Cash and cash equivalents	$ 86,375	$ 97,681	$ 112,292	$ 59,215	$ 9,603
Short-term investments	30,152	—	—	—	—
Working capital	193,070	187,090	204,648	193,511	151,107
Total assets	373,509	380,679	377,284	334,383	279,462
Long-term debt, including current portion	—	—	—	—	15,095
Shareholders' equity	283,786	285,255	284,471	255,147	194,225

(1) The Company utilizes a 52-53 week fiscal year. Fiscal years 2017, 2016, 2015 and 2014 consisted of 52 weeks. Fiscal year 2013 consisted of 53 weeks.

(2) Financial data recasts Japan results of operations as discontinued operations for all years presented. Japan was formerly included in the Direct segment results. Refer to Note 14 of the Notes to the Consolidated Financial Statements for additional information.

(3) Includes full-line and factory outlet stores. Our first full-line store opened in September 2007 and our first factory outlet store opened in November 2009.

(4) Comparable sales are calculated based upon our stores that have been open for at least 12 full fiscal months and net revenues from our e-commerce operations. Increase or decrease is reported as a percentage of the comparable sales for the same period in the prior fiscal year. Remodeled stores are included in comparable sales unless the store was closed for a portion of the current or comparable prior period or the remodel resulted in a significant change in square footage. Calculation excludes sales for the 53rd week in fiscal 2013.

(5) Dollars not in thousands. Average net revenues per gross square foot are calculated by dividing total net revenues for our stores that have been open at least 12 full fiscal months as of the end of the period by total gross square footage for those stores.

(6) Impairment charges, related to underperforming stores, recognized totaled $12.7 million, $2.8 million, $0.4 million, $1.2 million and $0.2 million during the fiscal years ended January 28, 2017, January 30, 2016, January 31, 2015, February 1, 2014, and February 2, 2013, respectively.

ITEM 7

Item 7 is reserved for management's discussion and analysis, otherwise known as MD&A. The layout of this section may vary by company but in general provides management's take on the past performance of the business. The MD&A provides a wealth of information about the business and is a good starting place for gaining an understanding of the financial performance of the business. The entire MD&A for the Vera Bradley, Inc., 10-K for the period ended January 28, 2017, is over fourteen pages long. Just the disclaimer and executive summary are shown below:

Item 7. Management's Discussion and Analysis of Financial Condition and Results of Operations

You should read the following discussion in conjunction with the consolidated financial statements and accompanying notes and the information contained in other sections of this report, particularly under the headings "Risk Factors," "Selected Financial Data" and "Business." This discussion and analysis is based on the beliefs of our management, as well as assumptions made by, and information currently available to, our management. The statements in this discussion and analysis concerning expectations regarding our future performance, liquidity, and capital resources, as well as other non-historical statements in this discussion and analysis, are forward-looking statements. See "Forward-Looking Statements." These forward-looking statements are subject to numerous risks and uncertainties, including those described under "Risk Factors." Our actual results could differ materially from those suggested or implied by any forward-looking statements.

Executive Summary

Fiscal 2017 was the third year of our multi-year turnaround, and we made significant progress against key elements of our long-term strategic plan, laid out in March 2014, focusing on the key planks of product, distribution, and marketing. Specifically:

Strategic Progress

• We made progress on our product strategies, including:

• Continuing to reinvigorate and modernize our cotton assortment with new patterns, styles, silhouettes, hardware, and functionality. We are also continuing to innovate and drive sales with the addition of non-cotton offerings to our assortment;

• Expanding our collegiate collection to represent over 70 schools; and

• Announcing six licensing agreements in the areas of bedding, hosiery, swim, tech, stationery, and publishing for products that will debut throughout fiscal 2018.

• We made progress on our distribution strategies, including:

• Opening four full-line stores, all in our new modern store design, including our first flagship store in New York, New York in the SoHo neighborhood, which features innovative design elements, limited edition items and a unique store experience;

• Opening six factory outlet stores;

- Implementing our store renovation strategy and completing refreshes of 14 of our higher-volume and traffic full-line stores by adding our new branding, including storefront facade, logo, and interior changes. We also completed facade updates at 15 of our newest full line stores to reflect our new logo and signage;

- Continuing to work on the redesign and conversion of verabradley.com to a new platform, creating a dynamic digital flagship which launched in February 2017. The new site offers a number of enhancements including, among others, the ability to strategically segment and personalize messaging, express check-out, and "order on-line, pickup in-store;" and

- Adding additional distribution to approximately 130 Macy's, Belk and Bon-Ton department stores.

- We drove customer engagement through our marketing programs by:

- Increasing brand visibility and igniting a social movement with our multi-faceted "It's Good to be a Girl" marketing campaign;

- An intensified emphasis on influencers, social, mobile, and video content than in years past; and

- Generating over 500 million impressions through:

- National ads, editorial content, and gift guides in publications such as *People StyleWatch*, *InStyle*, *Glamour*, and *Seventeen* and appearing in Oprah's Favorite Things Holiday Gift Guide;

- Online and digital ads on Hulu, Pandora, and the Conde Nast network; and

- Increased influencer and celebrity marketing.

Financial Summary

- Net revenues decreased 3.3% to $485.9 million in fiscal 2017 compared to $502.6 million in fiscal 2016.

- Direct segment sales increased 1.1% to $355.2 million in fiscal 2017 compared to $351.3 million in fiscal 2016. Comparable sales for fiscal 2017 decreased 7.0%.

- Indirect segment sales decreased 13.6% to $130.8 million in fiscal 2017 compared to $151.3 million in fiscal 2016.

- Gross profit was $276.0 million (56.8% of net revenue) in fiscal 2017 compared to $281.2 million (55.9% of net revenue) in fiscal 2016.

- Selling, general and administrative expenses were $249.2 million (51.3% of net revenue) in fiscal 2017 compared to $236.8 million (47.1% of net revenue) in fiscal 2016.

- Operating income was $28.2 million (5.8% of net revenue) in fiscal 2017 compared to $46.7 million (9.3% of net revenue) in fiscal 2016.

- Net income was $19.8 million in fiscal 2017 compared to $27.6 million in fiscal 2016.

- Diluted net income per share decreased 25.4% to $0.53 in fiscal 2017 from $0.71 in fiscal 2016.

- Store impairment charges were $12.7 million ($8.0 million after the associated tax benefit) in fiscal 2017 compared to $2.8 million ($1.8 million after the associated tax benefit) in fiscal 2016.

- Cash and cash equivalents and short-term investments were $116.5 million at January 28, 2017 compared to $97.7 million at January 30, 2016.

- Capital expenditures for fiscal 2017 totaled $20.8 million, which were funded from cash generated from operations of $65.2 million.

- Repurchases of common stock for fiscal 2017 totaled $24.5 million, or 1.6 million shares, compared to $31.2 million, or 2.5 million shares, in fiscal 2016.

ITEM 7A

Item 7A provides disclosures related to the company's exposure to market risk, such as interest rate risk and foreign currency exchange risk, Item 7A for the Vera Bradley, Inc. 10-K for the period ended January 28, 2017 is shown below:

Item 7A. Quantitative and Qualitative Disclosures About Market Risk

Interest Rate Risk

We are subject to interest rate risk in connection with borrowings under our second amended and restated credit agreement, which bear interest at variable rates. The second amended and restated credit agreement allows for a revolving credit commitment of $125.0 million, bearing interest at a variable rate, based on (A) the ABR plus the Applicable Margin, where the ABR is the highest of (i) the prime rate, (ii) the federal funds rate plus 0.5%, and (iii) Adjusted LIBOR for a one-month interest period plus 1%, and the Applicable Margin is a percentage ranging from 0.00% to 0.70% depending upon the Company's leverage ratio or (B) Adjusted LIBOR plus the Applicable Margin, where Adjusted LIBOR means LIBOR, as adjusted for statutory reserve requirements for eurocurrency liabilities, and Applicable Margin is a percentage ranging from 1.00% to 1.70% depending upon the Company's leverage ratio. Assuming borrowings available under the second amended and restated credit agreement are fully extended, each quarter point increase or decrease in the interest rate would change our annual interest expense by approximately $0.3 million.

Impact of Inflation

Our results of operations and financial condition are presented based on historical cost. Although it is difficult to accurately measure the impact of inflation due to the imprecise nature of the estimates required, we believe the effects of inflation, if any, on our results of operations and financial condition have been immaterial.

Foreign Exchange Rate Risk

We source a majority of our materials from various suppliers primarily in China and South Korea. Substantially all purchases and sales involving foreign persons are denominated in U.S. dollars, and therefore we do not hedge using any derivative instruments. Historically, we have not been impacted materially by changes in exchange rates.

ITEM 8

Item 8 is the "meat and potatoes" of the annual report. It includes the audit reports, the financial statements, and the notes to the financial statements. Item 8 for the Vera Bradley, Inc., 10-K for the period ending January 28, 2017, is provided below. Note that there are three audit reports for Vera Bradley, Inc., for this particular 10-K. Many 10-K's only have one audit report. The first audit report provides the audit opinion on the financial statements. The second audit report provides the audit opinion on the internal controls of the company, which is required for public companies. Auditors have the option to forego issuing two separate reports and issue just one integrated report on both the financial statements and internal control. The third audit report included in the Vera Bradley, Inc., 10-K for the period ending January 28, 2017, is for the audit of the period ending January 30, 2016. As the financial statements are comparative (two to three years are shown), the audit report needs to address all years included. Most auditors combine the years into one single report. However, you can see that the third audit report included in this 10-K is from a different audit firm. That means that Ernst & Young audited the two years ending January 30, 2016, while Deloitte & Touche audited the period ending January 28, 2017. Recall that an "unqualified opinion" is the desirable opinion.

The financial statements follow the audit reports. The balance sheet is presented first, followed by the income statement, and then the statement of comprehensive income. Note that companies can choose to combine the income statement with the other comprehensive income data, into one combined statement of comprehensive income rather than showing two separate statements. The statement of stockholders' equity comes next, followed by the statement of cash flows.

The notes to the financial statements are presented after the presentation of the financial statements. Recall that the notes to the financial statements provide a greater level of detail about items on the financial statements, as required by GAAP. The Vera Bradley, Inc., 10-K has seventeen notes to the financial statements, which include things such as a description of the company, significant accounting policies, inventories, property, plant & equipment, debt, related party transactions, earnings per share, discontinued operations, segment reporting, and quarterly financial information.

Item 8. Financial Statements and Supplementary Data

REPORT OF INDEPENDENT REGISTERED PUBLIC ACCOUNTING FIRM

To the Board of Directors and Shareholders of
Vera Bradley, Inc.
Roanoke, Indiana

We have audited the accompanying consolidated balance sheet of Vera Bradley, Inc. and subsidiaries (the "Company") as of January 28, 2017, and the related consolidated statements of income, comprehensive income, shareholders' equity, and cash flows for the year then ended. These financial statements are the responsibility of the Company's management. Our responsibility is to express an opinion on these financial statements based on our audit.

We conducted our audit in accordance with the standards of the Public Company Accounting Oversight Board (United States). Those standards require that we plan and perform the audit to obtain reasonable assurance about whether the financial statements are free of material misstatement. An audit includes examining, on a test basis, evidence supporting the amounts and disclosures in the financial statements. An audit also includes assessing the accounting principles used and significant estimates made by management, as well as evaluating the overall financial statement presentation. We believe that our audit provides a reasonable basis for our opinion.

In our opinion, such consolidated financial statements present fairly, in all material respects, the financial position of Vera Bradley, Inc. and subsidiaries as of January 28, 2017, and the results of their operations and their cash flows for the year ended January 28, 2017, in conformity with accounting principles generally accepted in the United States of America.

We have also audited, in accordance with the standards of the Public Company Accounting Oversight Board (United States), the Company's internal control over financial reporting as of January 28, 2017, based on the criteria established in *Internal Control - Integrated Framework (2013)* issued by the Committee of Sponsoring Organizations of the Treadway Commission and our report dated March 28, 2017 expressed an unqualified opinion on the Company's internal control over financial reporting.

/s/ Deloitte & Touche LLP
Indianapolis, Indiana
March 28, 2017

REPORT OF INDEPENDENT REGISTERED PUBLIC ACCOUNTING FIRM

To the Board of Directors and Shareholders of
Vera Bradley, Inc.
Roanoke, Indiana

We have audited the internal control over financial reporting of Vera Bradley, Inc. and subsidiaries (the "Company") as of January 28, 2017, based on criteria established in *Internal Control - Integrated Framework (2013)* issued by the Committee of Sponsoring Organizations of the Treadway Commission. The Company's management is responsible for maintaining effective internal control over financial reporting and for its assessment of the effectiveness of internal control over financial reporting, included in the accompanying Management's Report on Internal Control over Financial Reporting. Our responsibility is to express an opinion on the Company's internal control over financial reporting based on our audit.

We conducted our audit in accordance with the standards of the Public Company Accounting Oversight Board (United States). Those standards require that we plan and perform the audit to obtain reasonable assurance about whether effective internal control over financial reporting was maintained in all material respects. Our audit included obtaining an understanding of internal control over financial reporting, assessing the risk that a material weakness exists, testing and evaluating the design and operating effectiveness of internal control based on the assessed risk, and performing such other procedures as we considered necessary in the circumstances. We believe that our audit provides a reasonable basis for our opinion.

A company's internal control over financial reporting is a process designed by, or under the supervision of, the company's principal executive and principal financial officers, or persons performing similar functions, and effected by the company's board of directors, management, and other personnel to provide reasonable assurance regarding the reliability of financial reporting and the preparation of financial statements for external purposes in accordance with generally accepted accounting principles. A company's internal control over financial reporting includes those policies and procedures that (1) pertain to the maintenance of records that, in reasonable detail, accurately and fairly reflect the transactions and dispositions of the assets of the company; (2) provide reasonable assurance that transactions are recorded as necessary to permit preparation of financial statements in accordance with generally accepted accounting principles, and that receipts and expenditures of the company are being made only in accordance with authorizations of management and directors of the company; and (3) provide reasonable assurance regarding prevention or timely detection of unauthorized acquisition, use, or disposition of the company's assets that could have a material effect on the financial statements.

Because of the inherent limitations of internal control over financial reporting, including the possibility of collusion or improper management override of controls, material misstatements due to error or fraud may not be prevented or detected on a timely basis. Also, projections of any evaluation of the effectiveness of the internal control over financial reporting to future periods are subject to the risk that the controls may become inadequate because of changes in conditions, or that the degree of compliance with the policies or procedures may deteriorate.

In our opinion, the Company maintained, in all material respects, effective internal control over financial reporting as of January 28,2017, based on the criteria established in *Internal Control - Integrated Framework (2013)* issued by the Committee of Sponsoring Organizations of the Treadway Commission.

We have also audited, in accordance with the standards of the Public Company Accounting Oversight Board (United States), the consolidated balance sheet as of January 28, 2017, and the related consolidated statements of income, comprehensive income, shareholders' equity, and cash flows for the year then ended of the Company and our report dated March 28, 2017 expressed an unqualified opinion on those financial statements.

/s/ Deloitte & Touche LLP
Indianapolis, Indiana
March 28, 2017

REPORT OF INDEPENDENT REGISTERED PUBLIC ACCOUNTING FIRM

To the Board of Directors and Shareholders of
Vera Bradley, Inc.

We have audited the accompanying consolidated balance sheet of Vera Bradley, Inc. and subsidiaries as of January 30, 2016, and the related consolidated statements of income, comprehensive income, shareholders' equity and cash flows for each of the two years in the period ended January 30, 2016. These financial statements are the responsibility of the Company's management. Our responsibility is to express an opinion on these financial statements based on our audits.

We conducted our audits in accordance with the standards of the Public Company Accounting Oversight Board (United States). Those standards require that we plan and perform the audit to obtain reasonable assurance about whether the financial statements are free of material misstatement. An audit includes examining, on a test basis, evidence supporting the amounts and disclosures in the financial statements. An audit also includes assessing the accounting principles used and significant estimates made by management, as well as evaluating the overall financial statement presentation. We believe that our audits provide a reasonable basis for our opinion.

In our opinion, the financial statements referred to above present fairly, in all material respects, the consolidated financial position of Vera Bradley, Inc. and subsidiaries at January 30, 2016, and the consolidated results of their operations and their cash flows for each of the two years in the period ended January 30, 2016, in conformity with U.S. generally accepted accounting principles.

/s/ Ernst & Young LLP
Indianapolis, Indiana
March 29, 2016

Vera Bradley, Inc.
Consolidated Balance Sheets
(in thousands)

	January 28, 2017	January 30, 2016
Assets		
Current assets:		
Cash and cash equivalents	$ 86,375	$ 97,681
Short-term investments	30,152	—
Accounts receivable, net	23,313	31,294
Inventories	102,283	113,590
Income taxes receivable	3,217	785
Prepaid expenses and other current assets	10,237	10,292
Total current assets	255,577	253,642
Property, plant, and equipment, net	101,577	113,711
Deferred income taxes	13,539	11,363
Other assets	2,816	1,963
Total assets	$ 373,509	$ 380,679
Liabilities and Shareholders' Equity		
Current liabilities:		
Accounts payable	$ 32,619	$ 24,606
Accrued employment costs	12,474	14,937
Other accrued liabilities	16,906	16,924
Income taxes payable	508	10,085
Total current liabilities	62,507	66,552

Long-term liabilities		27,216	28,872
Total liabilities		89,723	95,424
Commitments and contingencies			
Shareholders' equity:			
Preferred stock; 5,000 shares authorized, no shares issued or outstanding		—	—
Common stock, without par value; 200,000 shares authorized, 40,927 and 40,804 shares issued and 36,218 and 37,701 outstanding, respectively		—	—
Additional paid-in capital		88,739	85,436
Retained earnings		263,767	244,009
Accumulated other comprehensive loss		(50)	(43)
Treasury stock		(68,670)	(44,147)
Total shareholders' equity		283,786	285,255
Total liabilities and shareholders' equity	$	373,509	$ 380,679

The accompanying notes are an integral part of these consolidated financial statements.

Vera Bradley, Inc.
Consolidated Statements of Income
(in thousands, except per share data)

		Fiscal Year Ended					
		January 28, 2017		January 30, 2016		January 31, 2015	
Net revenues	$	485,937	$	502,598	$	508,990	
Cost of sales		209,891		221,409		239,981	
Gross profit		276,046		281,189		269,009	
Selling, general, and administrative expenses		249,155		236,836		208,675	
Other income		1,329		2,369		3,736	
Operating income		28,220		46,722		64,070	
Interest expense, net		178		263		407	
Income from continuing operations before income taxes		28,042		46,459		63,663	
Income tax expense		8,284		18,901		22,828	
Income from continuing operations		19,758		27,558		40,835	
Loss from discontinued operations, net of taxes		—		—		(2,386)	
Net income	$	19,758	$	27,558	$	38,449	
Basic weighted-average shares outstanding		36,838		38,795		40,568	
Diluted weighted-average shares outstanding		36,970		38,861		40,632	
Net income (loss) per share - basic							
Continuing operations	$	0.54	$	0.71	$	1.01	
Discontinued operations		—		—		(0.06)	
Net income	$	0.54	$	0.71	$	0.95	
Net income (loss) per share - diluted							
Continuing operations	$	0.53	$	0.71	$	1.00	
Discontinued operations		—		—		(0.06)	
Net income	$	0.53	$	0.71	$	0.95	

The accompanying notes are an integral part of these consolidated financial statements.

Vera Bradley, Inc.
Consolidated Statements of Comprehensive Income
(in thousands)

	Fiscal Year Ended		
	January 28, 2017	January 30, 2016	January 31, 2015
Net income	$ 19,758	$ 27,558	$ 38,449
Cumulative translation adjustment	(7)	(28)	(3)
Comprehensive income	$ 19,751	$ 27,530	$ 38,446

The accompanying notes are an integral part of these consolidated financial statements.

Vera Bradley, Inc.
Consolidated Statements of Shareholders' Equity
($ in thousands, except share data)

	Number of Shares		Additional Paid-in Capital	Retained Earnings	Accumulated Other Comprehensive (Loss) Income	Treasury Stock	Total Equity
	Common Stock	Treasury Stock					
Balance at February 1, 2014	40,606,731	—	$ 78,153	$ 178,002	$ (1,008)	$ —	$ 255,147
Net income	—	—	—	38,449	—	—	38,449
Translation adjustments	—	—	—	—	993	—	993
Restricted shares vested, net of repurchase for taxes	88,564	—	(674)	—	—	—	(674)
Stock-based compensation	—	—	3,513	—	—	—	3,513
Treasury stock purchased	(620,985)	620,985	—	$ —	$ —	(12,957)	(12,957)
Balance at January 31, 2015	40,074,310	620,985	$ 80,992	$ 216,451	$ (15)	$ (12,957)	$ 284,471
Net income	—	—	—	27,558	—	—	27,558
Translation adjustments	—	—	—	—	(28)	—	(28)
Restricted shares vested, net of repurchase for taxes	108,228	—	(583)	—	—	—	(583)
Stock-based compensation	—	—	5,027	—	—	—	5,027
Treasury stock purchased	(2,481,367)	2,481,367	—	—	—	(31,190)	(31,190)
Balance at January 30, 2016	37,701,171	3,102,352	$ 85,436	$ 244,009	$ (43)	$ (44,147)	$ 285,255
Net income	—	—	—	19,758	—	—	19,758
Translation adjustments	—	—	—	—	(7)	—	(7)
Stock-based compensation	—	—	4,032	—	—	—	4,032
Restricted shares vested, net of repurchase for taxes	123,002	—	(729)	—	—	—	(729)
Treasury stock purchased	(1,606,102)	1,606,102	—	—	—	(24,523)	(24,523)
Balance at January 28, 2017	36,218,071	4,708,454	$ 88,739	$ 263,767	$ (50)	$ (68,670)	$ 283,786

The accompanying notes are an integral part of these consolidated financial statements.

Vera Bradley, Inc.
Consolidated Statements of Cash Flows
(in thousands)

	Fiscal Year Ended		
	January 28, 2017	January 30, 2016	January 31, 2015
Cash flows from operating activities			
Net income	$ 19,758	$ 27,558	$ 38,449
Adjustments to reconcile net income to net cash provided by operating activities:			
Depreciation of property, plant, and equipment	19,516	19,418	14,802
Impairment charges	12,706	2,755	414
Provision for doubtful accounts	439	515	(148)
Loss on disposal of property, plant, and equipment	14	141	21
Stock-based compensation	4,032	5,027	3,513
Deferred income taxes	(2,176)	(3,340)	428
Discontinued operations	—	—	996
Gain on short-term investment	(152)	—	—

Changes in assets and liabilities:			
Accounts receivable	7,542	(435)	(2,052)
Inventories	11,307	(15,187)	38,520
Prepaid expenses and other assets	(798)	(2,571)	1,353
Accounts payable	9,001	(8,665)	2,873
Income taxes	(12,009)	12,508	(4,833)
Accrued and other liabilities	(3,994)	5,546	9,476
Net cash provided by operating activities	65,186	43,270	103,812
Cash flows from investing activities			
Purchases of property, plant, and equipment	(20,778)	(26,322)	(37,128)
Purchase of short-term investment	(30,000)	—	—
Proceeds from disposal of property, plant, and equipment	8	—	—
Net cash used in investing activities	(50,770)	(26,322)	(37,128)
Cash flows from financing activities			
Tax withholdings for equity compensation	(729)	(583)	(674)
Repurchase of common stock	(24,959)	(30,870)	(12,841)
Other financing activities, net	(27)	(78)	(89)
Net cash used in financing activities	(25,715)	(31,531)	(13,604)
Effect of exchange rate changes on cash and cash equivalents	(7)	(28)	(3)
Net (decrease) increase in cash and cash equivalents	(11,306)	(14,611)	53,077
Cash and cash equivalents, beginning of period	97,681	112,292	59,215
Cash and cash equivalents, end of period	$ 86,375	$ 97,681	$ 112,292
Supplemental disclosure of cash-flow information			
Cash paid for income taxes, net	$ 24,824	$ 9,302	$ 25,957
Cash paid for interest	$ 248	$ 259	$ 275
Supplemental disclosure of non-cash activity			
Non-cash operating, investing, and financing activities			
Repurchase of common stock incurred but not yet paid			
As of January 28, 2017, January 30, 2016 and January 31, 2015	$ —	$ 436	$ 116
As of January 30, 2016, January 31, 2015 and February 1, 2014	$ 436	$ 116	$ —
Purchases of property, plant, and equipment incurred but not yet paid			
As of January 28, 2017, January 30, 2016 and January 31, 2015	$ 2,204	$ 2,872	$ 2,172
As of January 30, 2016, January 31, 2015 and February 1, 2014	$ 2,872	$ 2,172	$ —

The accompanying notes are an integral part of these consolidated financial statements.

Vera Bradley, Inc.
Notes to Consolidated Financial Statements

1
Description of the Company

Vera Bradley, Inc. ("Vera Bradley" or the "Company") is a leading designer of women's handbags, luggage and travel items, fashion and home accessories, and unique gifts. Founded in 1982 by friends Barbara Bradley Baekgaard and Patricia R. Miller, the brand's innovative designs, iconic patterns, and brilliant colors continue to inspire and connect women.

Vera Bradley offers a unique, multi-channel sales model, as well as a focus on service and a high level of customer engagement. The Company sells its products through two reportable segments: Direct and Indirect. The Direct business consists of sales of Vera Bradley products through the Company's full-line and factory outlet stores in the United States, verabradley.com, direct-to-consumer eBay sales, and the Company's annual outlet sale in Fort Wayne, Indiana. As of January 28, 2017, the Company operated 113 full-line stores and 46 factory outlet stores. The Indirect business consists of sales of Vera Bradley products to approximately 2,600 specialty retail locations, substantially all of which are located in the United States, as well as department stores, national accounts, third party e-commerce sites, the Company's wholesale customer in Japan, and third party inventory liquidators.

Principles of Consolidation

The consolidated financial statements include the accounts of the Company and its wholly owned subsidiaries. The Company has eliminated intercompany balances and transactions in consolidation.

Fiscal Periods

The Company utilizes a 52-53 week fiscal year ended on the Saturday closest to January 31. As such, fiscal year 2017, 2016 and 2015 ending on January 28, 2017, January 30, 2016 and January 31, 2015, respectively, each reflected a 52-week period.

2.
Summary of Significant Accounting Policies
Use of Significant Estimates

The preparation of financial statements in conformity with accounting principles generally accepted in the United States of America ("GAAP") requires management to make estimates and assumptions that affect the reported amounts of the Company's assets, liabilities, revenues, and expenses, as well as the disclosures relating to contingent assets and liabilities at the date of the consolidated financial statements. Significant areas requiring the use of management estimates include the valuation of inventories, accounts receivable valuation allowances, sales return allowances, and the useful lives of assets for depreciation or amortization. Actual results could differ from these estimates. The Company revises its estimates and assumptions as new information becomes available.

Prior period amounts related to impairment charges in the Consolidated Statements of Cash Flows have been reclassified to conform to the current year presentation.

Cash and Cash Equivalents

Cash and cash equivalents represent cash on hand, deposits with financial institutions, and investments with an original maturity of three months or less.

Concentration of Credit Risk

The Company maintains nearly all of its cash and cash equivalents with one financial institution. The Company monitors the credit standing of this financial institution on a regular basis.

Short-Term Investments

Short-term investments consist of a certificate of deposit with an original maturity of one year and a one-time option to accelerate maturity to 31 days without penalty. Interest income from the investment is included in interest expense, net, in the Company's Consolidated Financial Statements. The Company's objective with respect to this investment is to earn a higher rate of return, relative to deposit accounts, on funds that are otherwise not anticipated to be required to meet liquidity needs in the near term while maintaining a low level of investment risk. The Company has the intent and ability to hold this investment to maturity. As of January 28, 2017, the Company held $30.2 million in short-term investments, which included $0.2 million in interest income recognized in interest expense, net in the Company's Consolidated Financial Statements. The Company did not have short-term investments as of January 30, 2016.

Inventories

Inventories are stated at the lower of cost or market. Cost is determined using the first-in, first-out ("FIFO") method. Market is determined based on net realizable value, which includes costs to dispose. Appropriate consideration is given to obsolescence, excess quantities, and other factors, including the popularity of a pattern or product, in evaluating net realizable value.

Property, Plant, and Equipment

Property, plant, and equipment are carried at cost and depreciated or amortized over the following estimated useful lives using the straight-line method:

Buildings and building improvements	39.5 years
Land improvements	5 – 15 years
Furniture and fixtures, and leasehold improvements	3 – 10 years
Equipment	7 years
Vehicles	5 years
Computer equipment and software	3 – 5 years

Leasehold improvements are amortized over the shorter of the life of the asset or the lease term. Lease terms typically range from three to ten years.

When a decision is made to abandon property, plant, and equipment prior to the end of the previously estimated useful life, depreciation or amortization estimates are revised to reflect the use of the asset over the shortened estimated useful life. At the time of disposal, the cost of assets sold or retired and the related accumulated depreciation or amortization are removed from the accounts and any resulting loss is included in the Consolidated Statements of Income.

Property, plant, and equipment are reviewed for impairment whenever events or changes in circumstances indicate that the carrying amount of the assets may not be recoverable. The reviews are conducted at the lowest identifiable level of cash flows. If the estimated undiscounted future cash flows related to the property, plant, and equipment are less than the carrying value, the Company recognizes a loss equal to the difference between the carrying value and the fair value, as further defined below in "Fair Value of Financial Instruments."

Routine maintenance and repair costs are expensed as incurred.

The Company capitalizes certain costs incurred in connection with acquiring, modifying, and installing internal-use software. Capitalized costs are included in property, plant, and equipment and are amortized over three to five years. Software costs that do not meet capitalization criteria are expensed as incurred.

Revenue Recognition and Accounts Receivable

Revenue from the sale of the Company's products is recognized upon customer receipt of the product when collection of the associated receivables is reasonably assured, persuasive evidence of an arrangement exists, the sales price is fixed and determinable, and ownership and risk of loss have been transferred to the customer, which, for e-commerce and most Indirect sales, reflects an adjustment for shipments that customers have not yet received. The adjustment of these shipments is based on actual delivery dates to the customer.

Included in net revenues are product sales to Direct and Indirect customers, including amounts billed to customers for shipping fees. Costs related to shipping of product are classified in cost of sales in the Consolidated Statements of Income. Net revenues exclude sales taxes collected from customers and remitted to governmental authorities.

Historical experience provides the Company the ability to reasonably estimate the amount of product sales that customers will return. Product returns are often resalable through the Company's annual outlet sale or other channels. Additionally, the Company reserves for other potential product credits granted to Indirect retailers. The returns and credits reserve and the related activity for each fiscal year presented were as follows (in thousands):

	Balance at Beginning of Year		Provision Charged to Net Revenues		Allowances Taken		Balance at End of Year
Fiscal year ended January 28, 2017	$	2,317	$	32,905	$	(29,862)	$	5,360
Fiscal year ended January 30, 2016		2,173		25,707		(25,563)		2,317
Fiscal year ended January 31, 2015		1,424		30,140		(29,391)		2,173

The Company establishes an allowance for doubtful accounts based on historical experience and customer-specific identification and believes that collections of receivables, net of the allowance for doubtful accounts, are reasonably assured. The allowance for doubtful accounts was approximately $0.6 million and $0.5 million as of January 28, 2017, and January 30, 2016, respectively.

The Company sells gift cards with no expiration dates to customers and does not charge administrative fees on unused gift cards. Gift cards issued by the Company are recorded as a liability until they are redeemed, at which point revenue is recognized. In addition, the Company recognizes revenue on unredeemed gift cards when the likelihood of the gift card being redeemed is remote and there is no legal obligation to remit the value of unredeemed gift cards to the relevant jurisdictions. The Company determines the gift card breakage rate based on historical redemption patterns. During the fiscal years ended January 28, 2017, January 30, 2016 and January 31, 2015, the Company recorded $0.3 million, $0.3 million and $1.4 million of revenue related to gift card breakage, respectively. Gift card breakage is included in net sales in the Consolidated Statements of Income, as well as Direct segment sales.

Cost of Sales

Cost of sales includes material and labor costs, freight, inventory shrinkage, operating lease costs, duty, and other operating expenses, including depreciation of the Company's distribution center and equipment. Costs and related expenses to purchase and distribute the products are recorded as cost of sales when the related revenues are recognized.

Operating Leases and Tenant-Improvement Allowances

The Company has leases that contain rent holidays and predetermined, fixed escalations of minimum rentals. For each of these leases, the Company recognizes the related rent expense on a straight-line basis commencing on the date of initial possession of the leased property. The Company records the difference between the recognized rent expense and the amount payable under the lease as a deferred rent liability. As of January 28, 2017 and January 30, 2016, deferred rent liability was $12.7 million and $11.5 million, respectively, and is included within long-term liabilities on the Consolidated Balance Sheets.

The Company receives tenant-improvement allowances from some of the landlords of its leased properties. These allowances generally are in the form of cash received by the Company from its landlords as part of the negotiated lease terms. The Company records each tenant-improvement allowance as a deferred credit and amortizes the allowance on a straight-line basis as a reduction to rent expense over the term of the lease, commencing on the possession date. As of January 28, 2017 and January 30, 2016, the deferred lease credit liability was $15.8 million and $16.2 million, respectively. Of this, $2.4 million and $2.3 million is included within other accrued liabilities and $13.4 million and $13.9 million is included within long-term liabilities on the Consolidated Balance Sheets as of January 28, 2017 and January 30, 2016, respectively.

Store Pre-Opening, Occupancy, and Operating Costs

The Company charges costs associated with the opening of new stores to selling, general, and administrative expenses as incurred. Selling, general, and administrative expenses also include store operating costs, store employee compensation, and store occupancy and supply costs.

Stock-Based Compensation

The Company accounts for stock-based compensation using the fair-value recognition provisions of Accounting Standards Codification 718, *Stock Compensation*. Under these provisions, for its awards of restricted stock and restricted-stock units, the Company recognizes stock-based compensation expense in an amount equal to the fair market value of the underlying stock on the grant date of the respective award. The Company recognizes this expense, net of estimated forfeitures, on a straight-line basis over the requisite service period.

Other Income and Advertising Costs

The Company expenses advertising costs at the time the promotion first appears in media, in stores, or on the website, and includes those costs in selling, general, and administrative expenses in the Consolidated Statements of Income. The Company classifies the related recovery of a portion of such costs from Indirect retailers as other income in the Consolidated Statements of Income.

Total advertising expense was as follows (in thousands):

	January 28, 2017	January 30, 2016
Raw materials	$ —	$ 151
Finished goods	102,283	113,439
Total inventories	$ 102,283	$ 113,590

Debt-Issuance Costs

During the fiscal year ended January 30, 2016, in connection with the second amendment and restatement of the credit agreement (see Note 5), the Company incurred additional debt-issuance costs of $0.5 million. The Company is amortizing the remaining debt-issuance costs to interest expense over the five-year term of the second amended and restated credit agreement. Debt-issuance costs, net of accumulated amortization, totaled $0.6 million at January 28, 2017, and $0.8 million at January 30, 2016, and are included in other assets on the Consolidated Balance Sheets. Amortization expense of $0.2 million is included in interest expense in the Consolidated Statements of Income for each of the fiscal years ended January 28, 2017, January 30, 2016, and January 31, 2015.

Fair Value of Financial Instruments

Fair value is defined as the price that would be received to sell an asset or paid to transfer a liability in an orderly transaction between market participants at the measurement date. Assets and liabilities measured at fair value are classified using the following hierarchy, which is based upon the transparency of inputs to the valuation as of the measurement date:

- Level 1 – Quoted prices in active markets for identical assets or liabilities;

- Level 2 – Inputs, other than the quoted prices in active markets, that are observable either directly or indirectly;

- Level 3 – Unobservable inputs based on the Company's own assumptions.

The classification of fair value measurements within the hierarchy is based upon the lowest level of input that is significant to the measurement.

The carrying amounts reflected on the Consolidated Balance Sheets for cash and cash equivalents, accounts receivable, other current assets, and accounts payable as of January 28, 2017 and January 30, 2016, approximated their fair values.

Short-term investments consist of a certificate of deposit with an original maturity of one year and a one-time option to accelerate maturity to 31 days without penalty. The initial investment was $30.0 million, and the Company has the positive intent and ability to hold the certificate of deposit to maturity. The accrued interest on the certificate of deposit is recognized in interest expense, net, in the Company's Consolidated Financial Statements. Due to the observable inputs, the certificate of deposit approximated its fair value as of January 28, 2017, and is classified within Level 2 of the fair value hierarchy.

The Company has certain assets that are measured under circumstances and events described in Note 4. The categorization of the framework to price these assets are level 3 due to subjective nature of unobservable inputs.

Income Taxes

The Company accrues income taxes payable or refundable and recognizes deferred tax assets and liabilities based on differences between the book and tax bases of assets and liabilities. The Company measures deferred tax assets and liabilities using enacted rates in effect for the years in which the differences are expected to reverse, and recognizes the effect of a change in enacted rates in the period of enactment.

The Company establishes liabilities for uncertain positions taken or expected to be taken in income tax returns, using a more-likely-than-not recognition threshold. The Company includes in income tax expense any interest and penalties related to uncertain tax positions.

Recently Issued Accounting Pronouncements

Recently Adopted Accounting Pronouncements

In March 2016, the Financial Accounting Standards Board ("FASB") issued Accounting Standards Update ("ASU") 2016-09, *Compensation - Stock Compensation (Topic 718): Improvements to Employee Share-Based Payment Accounting*. The updated guidance changes how companies account for certain aspects of share-based payment awards to employees, including the accounting for income taxes, forfeitures, and statutory tax withholding requirements, as well as the classification of related matters in the statement of cash flows. The standard is effective for public entities for annual periods beginning after December 15, 2016, and interim periods within those annual periods. Early adoption is permitted.

The Company early adopted this standard beginning with the quarter ended April 30, 2016. The impact of the adoption of this standard was as follows:

- excess tax benefits were combined with other income tax cash flows within operating cash flows adopted on a prospective basis;

- excess tax benefits were recorded to income tax expense as a discrete item adopted on a prospective basis; and

- cash paid by the Company when directly withholding shares to satisfy an employee's statutory tax obligations continued to be classified as a financing activity.

- The Company has elected to continue its current policy of estimating forfeitures rather than recognizing forfeitures when they occur.

Recently Issued Accounting Pronouncements Not Yet Adopted

In May 2014, the FASB issued ASU 2014-09, *Revenue from Contracts with Customers*. This guidance requires companies to recognize revenue in a manner that depicts the transfer of promised goods or services to customers in amounts that reflect the consideration to which a company expects to be entitled in exchange for those goods or services. The new standard also will result in enhanced disclosures about the nature, amount, timing and uncertainty of revenue and cash flows arising from contracts with customers. The standard allows for either a full retrospective or a modified retrospective transition method. In August 2015, the FASB issued ASU 2015-14 to defer the effective date of ASU 2014-09 for all entities by one year to annual periods beginning after December 15, 2017, including interim periods within that reporting period, which for the Company is fiscal 2019. Earlier application is permitted as of the original effective date, annual reporting periods beginning after December 2016, including interim periods within that reporting period.

In its preliminary assessment, the provisions of the standard the Company believes to be most significant is the determination of when a customer receives control of the product upon a sale, as this could result in earlier recognition of revenue as compared to the Company's current practice of adjusting for shipments not yet received. The Company is still evaluating the final impact on its consolidated results of operations, financial position and cash flows, as well as additional provisions that may impact the Company's recognition of revenue. The Company will adopt the standard in the first quarter of fiscal 2019 and is continuing to evaluate the transition method upon adoption.

In July 2015, the FASB issued ASU 2015-11, *Inventory*, which requires entities to measure inventory at the lower of cost and net realizable value. This guidance is effective for interim and annual periods beginning on or after December 15, 2016 which for the Company is fiscal 2018. The application of this standard will not have a material impact on the Company's Consolidated Financial Statements upon adoption.

In February 2016, the FASB issued ASU 2016-02, *Leases*, which increases transparency and comparability among organizations by requiring lessees to recognize assets and liabilities on the balance sheet for the rights and obligations created by leases and disclosing key information about leasing arrangements. This guidance is effective for interim and annual periods beginning on or after December 15, 2018. The Company has operating leases at all of its retail stores; therefore, the adoption of this standard will result a material increase of assets and liabilities on the Company's Consolidated Balance Sheets. The Company is continuing evaluate the impact on its consolidated results of operations and cash flows.

3
Inventories

The components of inventories were as follows (in thousands):

	January 28,		January 30,	
	2017		2016	
Raw materials	$	—	$	151
Finished goods		102,283		113,439
Total inventories	$	102,283	$	113,590

4

Property, Plant, and Equipment

Property, plant, and equipment consisted of the following (in thousands):

	January 28,		January 30,	
	2017		2016	
Land and land improvements	$	5,981	$	5,981
Building and building improvements		46,233		46,145
Furniture, fixtures, leasehold improvements, computer equipment and software		127,791		127,913
Equipment and vehicles		20,329		19,931
Construction in progress		7,885		8,034
		208,219		208,004
Less: Accumulated depreciation and amortization		(106,642)		(94,293
Property, plant, and equipment, net	$	101,577	$	113,711

Property, plant, and equipment are reviewed for impairment whenever events or changes in circumstances indicate that the carrying amount of the assets may not be recoverable. The reviews are conducted at the lowest identifiable level of cash flows. If the estimated undiscounted future cash flows related to the property, plant, and equipment are less than the carrying value, the Company recognizes a loss equal to the difference between the carrying value and the fair value, as further defined in Note 2. An impairment charge of $12.7 million, $2.8 million and $0.4 million was recognized, using level 3 inputs, in the fiscal years ended January 28, 2017, January 30, 2016 and January 31, 2015, respectively, for assets related to underperforming stores and is included in selling, general, and administrative expenses in the Consolidated Statements of Income and in impairment charges in the Consolidated Statements of Cash Flows. The impairment charges are included in the Direct segment.

Depreciation and amortization expense associated with property, plant, and equipment, excluding impairment charges and discontinued operations (in thousands):

Fiscal year ended January 28, 2017	$	19,516
Fiscal year ended January 30, 2016		19,418
Fiscal year ended January 31, 2015		14,425

5

Debt

As of January 28, 2017 and January 30, 2016, the Company had no borrowings outstanding and availability of $125.0 million under the amended and restated credit agreement.

Second Amended and Restated Credit Agreement

On July 15, 2015, Vera Bradley Designs, Inc. ("VBD"), a wholly-owned subsidiary of the Company, entered into a Second Amended and Restated Credit Agreement among VBD, the lenders from time to time party thereto, JPMorgan Chase Bank, National Association, as administrative agent, Wells Fargo Bank, National Association, as syndication agent, and KeyBank National Association, as documentation agent (the "Credit Agreement"), which amended and restated the Company's prior credit agreement. The Credit Agreement provides for certain credit facilities to VBD in an aggregate principal amount not to initially exceed $125.0 million, the proceeds of which will be used for general corporate purposes of VBD and its subsidiaries, including but not limited to Vera Bradley International, LLC and Vera Bradley Sales, LLC (collectively, the "Named Subsidiaries").

Amounts outstanding under the Credit Agreement bear interest, at VBD's option, at a per annum rate equal to either (A) the Alternate Base Rate ("ABR") plus the Applicable Margin, where the ABR is the highest of (i) the prime rate, (ii) the federal funds rate plus 0.5%, and (iii) Adjusted LIBOR for a one-month interest period plus 1%, and the Applicable Margin is a percentage ranging from 0.00% to 0.70% depending upon the Company's leverage ratio or (B) Adjusted LIBOR plus the Applicable Margin, where Adjusted LIBOR means LIBOR, as adjusted for statutory reserve requirements for eurocurrency liabilities, and Applicable Margin is a percentage ranging from 1.00% to 1.70% depending upon the Company's leverage ratio. Any loans made, or letters of credit issued, pursuant to the Credit Agreement mature on July 15, 2020.

VBD's obligations under the Credit Agreement are guaranteed by the Company and the Named Subsidiaries. The obligations of VBD under the Credit Agreement are secured by first priority security interests in all of the respective assets of VBD, the Company, and the Named Subsidiaries and a pledge of the equity interests of VBD and the Named Subsidiaries.

The Credit Agreement contains various restrictive covenants, including restrictions on the Company's ability to dispose of assets, make acquisitions or investments, incur debt or liens, make distributions to stockholders or repurchase outstanding stock, enter into related party transactions and make capital expenditures, other than upon satisfaction of the conditions set forth in the Credit Agreement. The Company is also required to comply with certain financial and non-financial covenants, including maintaining a maximum leverage ratio, a minimum ratio of EBITDAR to the sum of interest expense plus rentals (as defined in the Credit Agreement), and a limit on capital expenditures. Upon an event of default, which includes certain customary events such as, among other things, a failure to make required payments when due, a failure to comply with covenants, certain bankruptcy and insolvency events, a material adverse change (as defined in the Credit Agreement), defaults under other material indebtedness, and a change in control, the lenders may accelerate amounts outstanding, terminate the agreement and foreclose on all collateral.

6
Income Taxes

The components of income tax expense were as follows (in thousands):

	January 28, 2017	January 30, 2016	January 31, 2015
Current:			
Federal	$ 8,810	$ 19,823	$ 20,715
Foreign	526	18	54
State	1,124	2,400	1,631
	10,460	22,241	22,400
Deferred:			
Federal	(1,623)	(2,813)	(19)
State	(553)	(527)	447
	(2,176)	(3,340)	428
Total income tax expense	$ 8,284	$ 18,901	$ 22,828

A breakdown of the Company's income from continuing operations before income taxes is as follows (in thousands):

	January 28, 2017	January 30, 2016	January 31, 2015
Domestic	$ 24,891	$ 46,386	$ 63,445
Foreign	3,151	73	218
Total income from continuing operations before income taxes	$ 28,042	$ 46,459	$ 63,663

A reconciliation of income tax expense to the amount computed at the federal statutory rate is as follows (in thousands):

	January 28, 2017		January 30, 2016		January 31, 2015	
Federal taxes at statutory rate	$ 9,815	35 %	$ 16,261	35 %	$ 22,282	35 %
State and local income taxes, net of federal benefit	371	1.3	1,217	2.6	1,350	2.2
Impact of foreign rate differential	(413)	(1.5)	—	—	—	—
Change in uncertain tax positions	(1,426)	(5.1)	—	—	—	—
Other	(63)	(0.2)	1,423	3.1	(804)	(1.3)
Total income tax expense	$ 8,284	29.5 %	$ 18,901	40.7 %	$ 22,828	35.9 %

The decrease in the Company's effective income tax rate from the federal statutory rate was primarily due to the release of certain federal and state income tax reserves resulting from the conclusion of an IRS audit in fiscal 2017. Additionally, in April 2016, the Company opened an office in Hong Kong to lead the global supply chain in Asia, including the oversight of sourcing and procurement. As a result, the Company began recognizing a small benefit in the current year.

During the third quarter of fiscal 2015, the Company discontinued retail operations in Japan. The above information consists of continuing operations only. At the beginning of fiscal 2015, the Company made an election for tax purposes to treat the Japan operations as a branch thereby causing the Japan activity to be taxed in the United States. The final tax accounting regarding Japan was recognized upon the sale of all Japan inventory in fiscal 2016.

Deferred income taxes reflect the net tax effects of temporary differences between the book and tax bases of assets and liabilities. Significant components of deferred tax assets and liabilities were as follows (in thousands):

	January 28, 2017	January 30, 2016
Deferred tax assets:		
Compensation and benefits	$ 5,420	$ 5,761
Inventories	2,718	4,855
Deferred credits from landlords	11,722	11,056
Other	4,913	5,162
Subtotal deferred tax assets	24,773	26,834
Less: valuation allowances	—	(194
Total deferred tax assets	24,773	26,640

Deferred tax liabilities:

Property, plant, and equipment	(8,505)	(12,970
Other	(2,729)	(2,307
Total deferred tax liabilities	(11,234)	(15,277
Net deferred tax assets	$ 13,539	$ 11,363

As of January 28, 2017, a provision for U.S. income tax has not been recorded on the temporary difference of approximately $1.9 million related to the Company's foreign subsidiary. The Company has determined that this temporary difference is indefinitely reinvested outside of the U.S. The amount of unrecognized deferred tax liability related to this temporary difference is estimated to be $0.4 million.

Uncertain Tax Positions

A reconciliation of the beginning and ending gross amount of unrecognized tax benefits (excluding interest and penalties) is as follows (in thousands):

	January 28, 2017	January 30, 2016	January 31, 2015
Beginning balance	$ 3,099	$ 3,018	$ 3,115
Net increases (decreases) in unrecognized tax benefits as a result of current year activity	15	81	(97
Reductions for tax positions of prior years	(1,695)	—	—
Settlements	(214)	—	—
Lapse of statute of limitations	(328)	—	—
Ending balance	$ 877	$ 3,099	$ 3,018

As of January 28, 2017, of the $0.9 million of total unrecognized tax benefits, $0.6 million, which is net of federal benefit, would, if recognized, favorably affect the effective tax rate in future periods. Total unrecognized tax benefits are currently not expected to decrease by a significant amount in the next twelve months. The Company recognized an immaterial amount of interest only, no penalties, related to unrecognized tax benefits in the fiscal years ended January 28, 2017, January 30, 2016 and January 31, 2015. Unrecognized tax benefits are included within long-term liabilities in the Company's Consolidated Balance Sheets.

The current year decrease is primarily related to the release of federal and state income tax reserves resulting from the conclusion of an IRS audit.

The Company files income tax returns in the U.S. federal jurisdiction and various U.S. state and foreign jurisdictions. The Company is subject to U.S. federal income tax examinations for fiscal years 2015 and forward. With a few exceptions, the Company is subject to audit by various state and foreign taxing authorities for fiscal 2013 through the current fiscal year.

7
Leases

The Company is party to non-cancellable operating leases. Future minimum lease payments under the non-cancellable operating leases through expiration are as follows (in thousands and by fiscal year):

Fiscal Year	Amount	
2018	$	32,681
2019		31,456
2020		30,642
2021		29,908
2022		27,408
Thereafter		70,055
	$	222,150

Rental expense for all leases, excluding discontinued operations, was as follows (in thousands):

Fiscal year ended January 28, 2017	$	33,925
Fiscal year ended January 30, 2016		32,456
Fiscal year ended January 31, 2015		25,198

Lease terms generally range from three to ten years, generally ten years in the case of the Company's retail stores, with options to renew for varying terms. Future minimum lease payments relate primarily to the lease of retail space. Additionally, several lease agreements contain a provision for payments based on a percentage of sales in addition to the stated lease payments. Percentage rent expense was $2.8 million, $2.4 million and $1.9 million for fiscal years ended January 28, 2017, January 30, 2016, and January 31, 2015, respectively.

During fiscal 2015, the Company leased one of its facilities from leasing companies owned by certain shareholders and directors. Lease expense related to this arrangement was $0.1 million for fiscal year ended January 31, 2015.

8
Stock-Based Compensation

The Company's stock-based compensation consists of awards of restricted stock and restricted stock units. The Company recognized stock-based compensation expense of $4.0 million, $5.0 million and $3.5 million in the fiscal years ended January 28, 2017, January 30, 2016, and January 31, 2015, respectively.

Awards of Restricted-Stock Units

The Company reserved 6,076,001 shares of common stock for issuance or transfer under the 2010 Equity and Incentive Plan, which allows for grants of restricted stock units, as well as other equity awards. As of January 28, 2017, there were 4,961,706 of shares remaining in that program.

During the fiscal year ended January 28, 2017, the Company granted a total of 413,457 time-based and performance-based restricted stock units to certain employees and non-employee directors under the 2010 Equity and Incentive Plan with an aggregate fair value of $7.6 million. The Company determined the fair value of the units based on the closing price of the Company's common stock on the grant date.

The majority of time-based restricted stock units vest and settle in shares of the Company's common stock, on a one-for-one basis, in equal installments on each of the first three anniversaries of the grant date. Restricted stock awards issued to non-employee directors vest after a one-year period from grant date. The Company is recognizing the expense relating to these awards, net of estimated forfeitures, on a straight-line basis over the vesting period.

The majority of performance-based restricted stock units vest upon the completion of a three-year period of time (cliff vesting), subject to the employee's continuing employment throughout the three-year performance period and the Company's achievement of annual earnings per share targets, or other Company performance targets, during the three-year performance period. The Company is recognizing the expense relating to these units, net of estimated forfeitures and based on the probable outcome of achievement of the financial targets, on a straight-line basis over the vesting period.

The following table summarizes information about restricted-stock units as of and for the year ended January 28, 2017 (units in thousands):

	Time-based Restricted Stock Units		Performance-based Restricted Stock Units	
	Number of Units	Weighted-Average Grant Date Fair Value (per unit)	Number of Units	Weighted-Average Grant Date Fair Value (per unit)
Nonvested units outstanding at January 30, 2016	463	$ 18.05	303	$ 20.95
Granted	234	18.41	180	18.30
Vested	(164)	18.87	—	—
Forfeited	(46)	17.08	(108)	22.99
Nonvested units outstanding at January 28, 2017	487	$ 18.04	375	$ 19.10

As of January 28, 2017, there was $6.0 million of total unrecognized compensation cost, net of estimated forfeitures, related to nonvested restricted stock units. That cost is expected to be recognized over a weighted-average period of 1.5 years. The total fair value of restricted stock units for which restrictions lapsed (vested) during fiscal 2017 was $3.0 million. No restricted-stock awards were granted, vested, or forfeited for the year ended January 28, 2017.

9
Commitments and Contingencies

Payment Card Incident

Description of Event

On September 15, 2016, the Company received information from law enforcement regarding a potential data security issue related to our retail store network. Findings from the investigation show unauthorized access to the Company's payment processing system and the installation of a program that looked for payment card data. The program was specifically designed to find track data in the magnetic stripe of a payment card that may contain the card number, cardholder name, expiration date, and internal verification code as the data was being routed through the affected payment system. There is no indication that other customer information was at risk. Payment cards used at Vera Bradley store locations between July 25, 2016 and September 23, 2016 may have been affected. Not all cards used in stores during this time frame were affected. Cards used on verabradley.com were not affected.

The Company has resolved this incident and continues to work with the computer security firm to further strengthen the security of its systems to help prevent this from happening in the future. The Company continues to support law enforcement's investigation and also promptly notified the payment card networks so that the banks that issue payment cards could initiate heightened monitoring on the affected cards.

Expenses Incurred and Amounts Accrued

During fiscal 2017, the Company recorded an immaterial amount of expense relating to the Payment Card Incident. Expenses included costs to investigate the Payment Card Incident and obtain legal and other professional services.

Future Costs

The Company expects to incur additional legal and professional services, as well as expenses and capital investments for remediation activities associated with the Payment Card Incident and will recognize the expenses as incurred. In addition, payment card companies and associations may require the Company to reimburse them for unauthorized card charges and costs to replace cards and may also impose fines or penalties in connection with the Payment Card Incident, and enforcement authorities may also impose fines or other remedies against the Company. At this time, the Company cannot reasonably estimate the potential loss or range of loss related to any fines or penalties that may be assessed. The Payment Card Incident, including customer response and any possible third-party claims or assessments from payment card companies, could materially adversely affect the Company's financial condition and operating results. The Company expects its insurance coverage will offset most of the expenses for the investigation and other non-remediation legal and professional services associated with the incident, possible third-party claims, as well as fines, penalties, or other expenses, if any, imposed by payment card companies, as discussed above.

Insurance Coverage

The Company maintains $15.0 million of cyber security insurance coverage above a $0.1 million deductible.

Other Commitments and Contingencies

The Company is also subject to various claims and contingencies arising in the normal course of business, including those relating to product liability, legal claims, employee benefits, environmental, and other matters. Management believes that at this time it is not probable that any of these claims will have a material adverse effect on the Company's financial condition, results of operations, or cash flows. However, the outcomes of legal proceedings and claims brought against the Company are subject to uncertainty and future developments could cause these actions or claims, individually or in aggregate, to have a material adverse effect on the Company's financial condition, results of operations or cash flows of a particular reporting period.

10.
401(k) Profit Sharing Plan and Trust

The Company has a 401(k) profit-sharing plan and trust for all qualified employees and provides a 100% match for the first 3% of employee contributions and a 50% match for the next 2% of employee contributions, for a maximum Company match of 4% of employee contributions, limited to the annual legal allowable limit. Additionally, the Company has the option of making discretionary profit-sharing payments to the plan as approved by the board of directors. As of January 28, 2017, January 30, 2016 and January 31, 2015, no discretionary profit-sharing payments had been approved. Total Company contributions to the plan, excluding discontinued operations, were as follows (in thousands):

Fiscal year ended January 28, 2017	$	1,624
Fiscal year ended January 30, 2016		1,965
Fiscal year ended January 31, 2015		2,394

11.
Related-Party Transactions

The Company leased its former corporate headquarters in fiscal 2015 from leasing companies owned by certain shareholders and directors, as described further in Note 7.

During the fiscal year ended January 28, 2017 and January 31, 2015, the Company made charitable contributions of approximately $0.1 million and $0.8 million, respectively, to the Vera Bradley Foundation for Breast Cancer (the "Foundation"). The Company did not make charitable contributions during the fiscal year ended January 30, 2016. The Foundation was founded by two of the Company's directors, who are also on the board of directors of the Foundation. The liability associated with commitments to the Foundation was approximately $0.4 million as of January 28, 2017 and January 30, 2016. The liability consisted of pass-through donations from customers and is included in other accrued liabilities in the Consolidated Balance Sheets.

The associated expense for contributions to the Foundation, which is included in selling, general, and administrative expenses, was as follows (in thousands):

Fiscal year ended January 28, 2017	$	53
Fiscal year ended January 30, 2016		—
Fiscal year ended January 31, 2015		750

12.
Earnings Per Share

Basic net income per share is computed based on the weighted-average number of common shares outstanding during the period. Diluted net income per share is computed based on the weighted-average number of shares of common stock plus the effect of dilutive potential common shares outstanding during the period using the treasury stock method. Dilutive potential common shares include outstanding restricted stock and restricted-stock units. The components of basic and diluted net income per share are as follows (in thousands, except per share data):

	Fiscal Year Ended		
	January 28, 2017	January 30, 2016	January 31, 2015
Numerator:			
Income from continuing operations	$ 19,758	$ 27,558	$ 40,835
Loss from discontinued operations, net of taxes	—	—	(2,386)
Net income	$ 19,758	$ 27,558	$ 38,449
Denominator:			
Weighted-average number of common shares (basic)	36,838	38,795	40,568
Dilutive effect of stock-based awards	132	66	64
Weighted-average number of common shares (diluted)	36,970	38,861	40,632
Earnings per share - basic:			
Continuing operations	$ 0.54	$ 0.71	$ 1.01
Discontinued operations	—	—	(0.06)
Net income	$ 0.54	$ 0.71	$ 0.95
Earnings per share - diluted:			
Continuing operations	$ 0.53	$ 0.71	$ 1
Discontinued operations	—	—	(0.06)
Net income	$ 0.53	$ 0.71	$ 0.95

As of January 28, 2017, January 30, 2016 and January 31, 2015, there were an immaterial number of additional shares issuable upon the vesting of restricted stock units that were excluded from the diluted share calculations because they were anti-dilutive. The diluted share calculations include performance-based restricted stock units to the extent of the completed performance periods.

13.
Common Stock

On December 8, 2015, the Company's board of directors approved a share repurchase program (the "2015 Share Repurchase Program") authorizing up to $50.0 million of repurchases of shares of the Company's common stock. The 2015 Share Repurchase Program expires in December 2017. The prior share repurchase program (the "2014 Share Repurchase Program") was approved by the board of directors on September 9, 2014, and authorized share repurchases up to $40.0 million. The 2014 Share Repurchase Program was completed in fiscal 2016.

During the fiscal year ended January 28, 2017, the Company purchased and held 1,606,102 shares at an average price of $15.27 per share, excluding commissions, for an aggregate amount of $24.5 million, under the 2015 Share Repurchase Program.

During the fiscal year ended January 30, 2016, the Company purchased and held 2,481,367 shares at an average price of $12.57 per share, excluding commissions, for an aggregate amount of $31.2 million. Of these purchases, 283,354 shares at an average price of $14.64 per share, for an aggregate amount of $4.1 million, were purchased under the 2015 Share Repurchase Plan.

As of January 28, 2017, there was $21.3 million remaining available to repurchase shares of the Company's common stock under the 2015 Share Repurchase Program.

As of January 28, 2017, the Company held as treasury shares 4,708,454 shares of its common stock at an average price of $14.58 per share, excluding commissions, for an aggregate carrying amount of $68.7 million. The Company's treasury shares may be issued under the 2010 Equity and Incentive Plan or for other corporate purposes.

14.
Discontinued Operations

On June 4, 2014, the Company entered into a five-year agreement with Mitsubishi Corporation Fashion Company and Look Inc. to import and distribute Vera Bradley products in Japan. As a result of moving to this wholesale business model, the Company exited its direct business in Japan during the third quarter of fiscal 2015 and the results of operations are reported as discontinued operations. Japan results were previously reported in the Direct segment, which has been restated to exclude the results of the discontinued operations for the periods presented. Following are the Japan results of operations (in thousands):

	Fiscal Year Ended January 31, 2015
Net revenues	$ 2,963
Cost of sales	1,470
Gross profit	1,493
Selling, general, and administrative expenses	2,985
Operating loss	(1,492)
Loss on disposal from discontinued operations[1]	(1,769)
Loss before income taxes	(3,261)
Income tax benefit	(875)
Loss from discontinued operations	$ (2,386)

(1) Loss on disposal from discontinued operations primarily relates to cumulative foreign currency translation adjustments.

The fiscal years ended January 28, 2017 and January 30, 2016, did not have activity related to discontinued operations.

15.
Restructuring and Other Charges

Fifty-Two Weeks Ended January 28, 2017

Refer to Note 4, herein, regarding the recognition of store impairment charges reflected in selling, general, and administrative expenses and Note 6, herein, regarding the release of certain income tax reserves related to uncertain tax positions reflected in income tax expense.

Fifty-Two Weeks Ended January 30, 2016

In the first quarter of fiscal 2016, the Company closed its manufacturing facility located in New Haven, Indiana. The Company incurred restructuring and other charges during the first quarter of fiscal 2016 of approximately $3.4 million ($2.1 million after the associated tax benefit), related to the facility closing. These charges included:

- Severance and benefit costs of approximately $1.7 million;

- Lease termination costs of approximately $0.7 million;

- Inventory-related charges of approximately $0.6 million; and

- Other associated net costs, which include accelerated depreciation related to fixed assets, of approximately $0.4 million.

These charges are reflected in cost of sales in the Company's Consolidated Financial Statements. All production from the facility was absorbed by the Company's third-party manufacturing suppliers. There are no remaining liabilities associated with the facility closure.

Additional charges, incurred in the first quarter of fiscal 2016, affecting comparability of the financial results totaled approximately $1.8 million ($1.3 million after the associated tax benefit). These charges included:

- $1.2 million due to a retail store early lease termination agreement (reflected in selling, general, and administrative expenses) and

- $0.6 million related to an increase in income tax reserves for uncertain federal and state tax positions related to research and development tax credits (reflected in income tax expense).

Also refer to Note 4, herein, regarding the recognition of store impairment charges reflected in selling, general, and administrative expenses.

16.
Segment Reporting

The Company has two operating segments, which are also its reportable segments: Direct and Indirect. These operating segments are components of the Company for which separate financial information is available and for which operating results are evaluated on a regular basis by the chief operating decision maker in deciding how to allocate resources and in assessing the performance of the segments.

The Direct segment includes the Company's full-line and factory outlet stores, the Company's website, verabradley.com, direct-to-consumer eBay sales, and the annual outlet sale. Revenues generated through this segment are driven through the sale of Company-branded products from Vera Bradley to end consumers. The Company exited its direct Japan operations in the third quarter of fiscal 2015. Direct segment results for the current and prior periods presented are reported on a continuing operations basis unless otherwise stated. Discontinued operations are described further in Note 14.

The Indirect segment represents revenues generated through the distribution of Company-branded products to specialty retailers representing approximately 2,600 locations, substantially all of which are located in the United States, as well as select department stores, national accounts, third party e-commerce sites, the Company's wholesale customer in Japan, and third-party inventory liquidators. No customer accounted for 10% or more of the Company's net revenues during fiscal years 2017, 2016 and 2015.

Corporate costs represent the Company's administrative expenses, which include, but are not limited to: human resources, legal, finance, information technology, and various other corporate-level-activity-related expenses. All intercompany-related activities are eliminated in consolidation and are excluded from the segment reporting.

Company management evaluates segment operating results based on several indicators. The primary or key performance indicators for each segment are net revenues and operating income. The table below represents key financial information for each of the Company's operating and reportable segments, Direct and Indirect.

The accounting policies of the segments are the same as those described in Note 2. The Company does not report depreciation or amortization expense, total assets, or capital expenditures by segment as such information is neither used by management nor accounted for at the segment level.

Net revenues and operating income information for the Company's reportable segments consisted of the following (in thousands):

	Fiscal Year Ended		
	January 28, 2017	January 30, 2016	January 31, 2015
Segment net revenues:			
Direct	$ 355,175	$ 351,286	$ 335,602
Indirect	130,762	151,312	173,388
Total	$ 485,937	$ 502,598	$ 508,990
Segment operating income:			
Direct	$ 62,577	$ 74,114	$ 74,099
Indirect	50,955	60,409	66,213
Total	$ 113,532	$ 134,523	$ 140,312
Reconciliation:			
Segment operating income	$ 113,532	$ 134,523	$ 140,312
Less:			
Unallocated corporate expenses	(85,312)	(87,801)	(76,242)
Operating income	$ 28,220	$ 46,722	$ 64,070

Sales outside of the United States were excluded from the Direct segment, for all periods presented, due to the Japan operations being discontinued in the third quarter of fiscal 2015.

Revenues to external customers for Vera Bradley brand products are attributable to sales of bags, accessories, travel and home items. Other revenues to external customers primarily include revenues from our apparel/footwear, stationery, merchandising, freight, licensing, and gift card breakage.

Net revenues by product categories are as follows (in thousands):

	Fiscal Year Ended		
	January 28, 2017	January 30, 2016	January 31, 2015
Net revenues:			
Bags	$ 207,765	$ 215,835	$ 230,978
Travel	119,082	125,279	109,112
Accessories	106,223	112,066	116,031
Home	27,574	22,729	17,721
Other	25,293	26,689	35,148
Total	$ 485,937	$ 502,598	$ 508,990

As of January 28, 2017 and January 30, 2016, substantially all of the Company's long-lived assets were located in the United States.

17.
Quarterly Financial Information (Unaudited)

The table below sets forth selected quarterly financial data for each of the last two fiscal years (in thousands, except per share data). Each of the quarters presented was thirteen weeks in duration.

	Fiscal Year Ended January 28, 2017			
	First Quarter	Second Quarter[1]	Third Quarter[1]	Fourth Quarter[1]
	(unaudited)	(unaudited)	(unaudited)	(unaudited)
Net revenues	$ 105,181	$ 119,245	$ 126,662	$ 134,849
Gross profit	59,656	68,388	72,913	75,089
Operating income	3,857	8,303	11,402	4,658
Net income	2,418	5,109	8,780	3,451
Basic net income per share	0.06	0.14	0.24	0.1
Diluted net income per share	0.06	0.14	0.24	0.09

(1) Includes impairment charges related to underperforming stores of $1.6 million ($1.0 million after the associated tax benefit), $0.6 million ($0.4 million after the associated tax benefit) and $10.5 million ($6.6 million after the associated tax benefit) during the second, third and fourth quarter, respectively. See Note 4, herein, for additional information.

	Fiscal Year Ended January 30, 2016			
	First Quarter[1]	Second Quarter	Third Quarter	Fourth Quarter[1]
	(unaudited)	(unaudited)	(unaudited)	(unaudited)
Net revenues	$ 101,104	$ 120,724	$ 126,674	$ 154,096
Gross profit	51,694	66,554	73,298	89,643
Operating (loss) income	(4,971)	9,486	16,789	25,418
Net (loss) income	(4,136)	5,715	10,268	15,711
Basic net (loss) income per share	(0.10)	0.15	0.27	0.41
Diluted net (loss) income per share	(0.10)	0.15	0.27	0.41

(1) Includes restructuring and other charges described in Note 15, herein.

(2) Includes impairment charges related to underperforming stores of $2.8 million ($1.8 million after the associated tax benefit). See Note 4, herein, for additional information.

Information in any one Quarterly period should not be considered indicative of annual results due to the effect of seasonality of the business.

ITEM 9

If the audit firm has been changed during the period (which it was for Vera Bradley, Inc.), item 9 provides disclosures of any disagreements with the previous audit firm, which could indicate a red flag for users of financial statements. Item 9 for the Vera Bradley, Inc., 10-K for the period ending January 28, 2017, is shown below. As you can see, there were no disagreements with the previous audit firm that were required to be disclosed.

Item 9. Changes in and Disagreements With Accountants on Accounting and Financial Disclosure

None.

ITEM 9A

Item 9A provides the company's principal executive and financial officers conclusion regarding the effectiveness of the company's disclosure controls and procedure. It also provides a statement from management regarding management's assessment of the effectiveness of the company's internal control over financial reporting, including disclosure of any material weakness in its internal controls. Finally, any changes in the company's internal control over financial reporting that have materially affected, or are reasonably likely to materially affect, the internal controls must be discussed. Item 9A for the Vera Bradley, Inc., 10-K for the period ending January 28, 2017, is shown below.

Item 9A. Controls and Procedures

Disclosure Controls and Procedures

Based on the evaluation of the Company's disclosure controls and procedures, as that term is defined in Rule 13a-15(e) under the Securities Exchange Act of 1934, as amended (the "Exchange Act"), each of Robert Wallstrom, the Chief Executive Officer of the Company, and Kevin J. Sierks, the Executive Vice President – Chief Financial Officer of the Company, has concluded that the Company's disclosure controls and procedures are effective as of January 28, 2017.

Management's Report on Internal Control over Financial Reporting

The Company's management is responsible for establishing and maintaining adequate internal control over financial reporting, as defined in rules 13a-15(f) and 15d-15(f) under the Exchange Act. The Company's internal control over financial reporting is designed to provide reasonable assurance regarding the reliability of financial reporting and the preparation of financial statements for external reporting purposes in accordance with generally accepted accounting principles. Management, under the supervision and with the participation of the Company's Chief Executive Officer and Chief Financial Officer, has evaluated the effectiveness of the Company's internal control over financial reporting using the criteria set forth by the Committee of Sponsoring Organizations (COSO) of the Treadway Commission (2013 framework) in *Internal Control-Integrated Framework*. Based on the results of that evaluation, management has concluded that such internal control over financial reporting was effective as of January 28, 2017.

The effectiveness of the Company's internal control over financial reporting as of January 28, 2017, has been audited by Deloitte and Touche LLP, an independent registered public accounting firm, as stated in their report which appears in Item 8. of this Annual Report on Form 10-K.

Changes in Internal Control over Financial Reporting

There were no changes in internal control over financial reporting that occurred during the fourth fiscal quarter that have materially affected, or are reasonably likely to materially affect, the Company's internal control over financial reporting.

ITEM 9B

Item 9B is reserved for any other information that is required to be reported in a Form 8-K during the fourth quarter that was not reported. Item 9B for the Vera Bradley, Inc., 10-K for the period ending January 28, 2017, is shown below. As you can see, there was no other information to report.

Item 9B. Other Information

None.

PART III

Part III of the Form 10-K includes disclosures relating to directors, executive officers, corporate governance, executive compensation, the beneficial ownership of management and certain large shareholders, related person transactions, director independence, and accountant fees and services. It is divided into five parts: Item 10, Item 11, Item 12, Item 13, and Item 14. Note that these items may only be incorporated by reference if a proxy statement is filed within 120 days of the company's fiscal year end, which is the case for the Vera Bradley, Inc., 10-K for the period ending January 28, 2017. These proxy statements are provided to the shareholders in connection with annual meetings. The proxy statement is typically filed a month or two after the 10-K is filed.

ITEM 10

Item 10 provides information about the background and experience of the company's directors and executive officers, the company's code of ethics, and certain qualifications for directors and committees of the board of directors. Item 10 for the Vera Bradley, Inc., 10-K for the period ending January 28, 2017, is shown below. As you can see, the information is only incorporated by reference to the proxy statement.

Item 10. Directors, Executive Officers and Corporate Governance

The information set forth in the Proxy Statement for the 2017 Annual Meeting of Shareholders under the headings "Board of Directors Information," "Family Relationships," "Section 16(a) Beneficial Ownership Reporting Compliance," "Corporate Governance Guidelines, Committee Charters and Code of Ethics," and "Committees – Audit Committee" is incorporated herein by reference. The Proxy Statement will be filed with the Commission within 120 days after the end of the fiscal year covered by this Form 10-K pursuant to Regulation 14A under the Securities Exchange Act of 1934, as amended. In addition, the information set forth under the heading "Item 1: Business – Executive Officers of the Company" in this Form 10-K is incorporated herein by reference.

ITEM 11

Item 11 provides detail about the company's compensation policies and programs and the amount of compensation paid to the top executive officers of the company in the past year. Item 11 for the Vera Bradley, Inc., 10-K for the period ending January 28, 2017 is shown below. As you can see, the information is only incorporated by reference to the proxy statement.

Item 11. Executive Compensation

The information set forth in the Proxy Statement for the 2017 Annual Meeting of Shareholders under the headings "Executive Compensation Discussion and Analysis," "Compensation Committee Interlocks and Insider Participation" and "Compensation Committee Report" is incorporated herein by reference. The Proxy Statement will be filed with the Commission within 120 days after the end of the fiscal year covered by this Form 10-K pursuant to Regulation 14A under the Securities Exchange Act of 1934, as amended.

ITEM 12

Item 12 provides information about the shares owned by the company's directors, officers and certain large shareholders, and about shares covered by equity compensation plans. Item 12 for the Vera Bradley, Inc., 10-K for the period ending January 28, 2017, is shown below.

Item 12. Security Ownership of Certain Beneficial Owners and Management and Related Stockholder Matters

The information set forth in the Proxy Statement for the 2017 Annual Meeting of Shareholders under the heading "Share Ownership by Certain Beneficial Owners and Management" is incorporated herein by reference. The Proxy Statement will be filed with the Commission within 120 days after the end of the fiscal year covered by this Form 10-K pursuant to Regulation 14A under the Securities Exchange Act of 1934, as amended.

Securities Authorized for Issuance Under Equity Compensation Plans

The following table sets forth information regarding equity securities authorized for issuance under our equity compensation plans as of January 28, 2017:

Plan Category	Number of Securities to Be Issued upon Exercise of Outstanding Options, Warrants and Rights (a)⁽ᵃ⁾	Weighted-Average Exercise Price of Outstanding Options, Warrants and Rights (b) ($)	Number of Securities Remaining Available for Future Issuance Under the Equity Compensation Plans (Excluding Securities Reflected in Column (a)) (c)
Equity compensation plans approved by security holders [1]	1,114,295	—	4,961,706
Equity compensation plans not approved by security holders	—	—	—
Total	**1,114,295**	**—**	**4,961,706**

(1) Approved before our initial public offering

(2) Assumes that target performance requirements will be achieved for performance shares with incomplete performance periods.

ITEM 13

Item 13 provides information about relationships and transactions between the company and its directors, officers, and their family members, including information about whether each director of the company is independent. Item 13 for the Vera Bradley, Inc., 10-K for the period ending January 28, 2017, is shown below. As you can see, the information is only incorporated by reference to the proxy statement.

Item 13. Certain Relationships and Related Transactions, and Director Independence

The information set forth in the Proxy Statement for the 2017 Annual Meeting of Shareholders under the headings "Certain Relationships and Related Party Transactions" and "Board Independence" is incorporated herein by reference. The Proxy Statement will be filed with the Commission within 120 days after the end of the fiscal year covered by this Form 10-K pursuant to Regulation 14A under the Securities Exchange Act of 1934, as amended.

ITEM 14

Item 14 provides information regarding the fees the company paid to their accounting firm for various types of services during the year. Item 14 for the Vera Bradley, Inc., 10-K for the period ended January 28, 2017, is shown below. As you can see, the information is only incorporated by reference to the proxy statement.

Item 14. Principal Accounting Fees and Services

The information required by this item is incorporated herein by reference to our 2017 Proxy Statement under the caption "Principal Accounting Fees and Services." The Proxy Statement will be filed with the Commission within 120 days after the end of the fiscal year covered by this Form 10-K pursuant to Regulation 14A under the Securities Exchange Act of 1934, as amended.

PART IV

Part IV of the Form 10-K includes a list of the financial statements and exhibits included as part of the Form 10-K. Many exhibits are required, including documents such as the company's bylaws, copies of its material contracts, and a list of the company's subsidiaries. Many exhibits can be incorporated by reference to a previously filed document. As Part IV is generally a listing of exhibits and signatures, it has not been included as part of this appendix.

GLOSSARY

Account—used to track the increases and decreases in specific financial statement elements.

Accounting—a system of record keeping designed to analyze, record, and summarize the activities of the business and report the results to users.

Accounting Cycle—the process by which business transactions are recorded in the accounting information system and reported in financial statements.

Accounting Information System—a system that is designed to track the transactions of the business and report the results.

Accounts Payable—amounts the entity owes to its vendors.

Accounts Receivable—the account that is used to record amounts owed to the business by its customers.

Accounts Receivable Turnover—measures how quickly a company cycles through its accounts receivable, calculated as credit sales divided by average accounts receivable.

Accrual Basis Accounting—revenues are recorded when earned and expenses are recorded when incurred, regardless of when cash is received or paid.

Accrual Entries—adjusting entries for items where the cash transaction happens after the revenue is earned or the expense is incurred.

Accrued Expenses—amounts owed at the end of a reporting period that have not yet been recorded as an expense.

Accumulated Depreciation—the life to date depreciation expense recorded on an asset.

Acid Test Ratio—See "Quick Ratio."

Activity Rate—a rate used to allocate manufacturing overhead to activities in an activity-based costing system.

Activity-based Costing—a method of assigning costs to cost objects in companies that produce many different products or provide services, using multiple allocation bases.

Adjusted Trial Balance—a trial balance prepared after the adjusting entries are posted, showing the corrected amounts for each account, which is used to prepare the financial statements.

Adjusting Entries—journal entries posted at the end of the accounting period to report revenues and expenses in the proper period and assets and liabilities at their correct amounts.

Administrative Cost—the costs necessary to operate the business, with the exception of product costs and selling costs.

Aging of Accounts Receivable—an organized listing of all customers and their balances owed, with columns showing how old each amount is.

Allowance for Doubtful Accounts—a contra-asset account estimating the amount of accounts receivable that will ultimately result in bad debts.

Amortization—the allocation of the cost of the intangible asset over its useful life.

Asset Management Ratios—measure how efficient and effective a company is at managing their assets.

Assets—probable future economic benefits obtained or controlled by a particular entity as a result of past transactions.

Audit—an examination of a company's financial statements resulting in an opinion on the fair presentation of the financial statements.

Audit Report—a report describing the auditor's opinion on the financial statements.

Average Collection Period—a measure showing how quickly credit sales are turned into cash, calculated as 365 days divided by accounts receivable turnover.

Average Sale Period—a measure showing how quickly inventory is bought and sold calculated as 365 days divided by inventory turnover.

Avoidable Cost—a cost that can be avoided if one alternative is selected over another.

Bad Debt Expense—the expense recorded on the income statement associated with the value of invoices that will ultimately end up not being paid by customers.

Balance Scorecard—an approach to measuring a company's performance from both a financial and a non-financial standpoint. The balanced scorecard evaluates a company's performance based on four perspectives: financial, customer, internal business process, and learning and growth.

Balance Sheet—the financial statements that shows the financial position of the business.

Basic Accounting Equation—Assets = Liabilities + Stockholders' Equity

Basis—a tax concept, representing the cost of the property being recorded for tax purposes.

Bill of Lading—a source document that serves as evidence that the goods were shipped and represents a contractual agreement with the carrier of the goods.

Book Value per Share—measures what each share of stock would receive if all the company's assets were sold and all liabilities were paid, calculated as total stockholders' equity divided by the number of common shares outstanding.

Bottleneck—see "Constrained Resource."

Break-Even Point—the level of sales that provides $0 net income (no profit or loss).

Budget—a detailed plan for the financial transactions of the business for a specific time period.

Business Plan—a document that identifies the plan for the business. A business plan can take many forms (short, long, formal, informal), depending on the intended use and/or audience for the document.

Capital Budgeting—the process of planning for projects or investments that will have a long-term effect on the business.

Cash—funds in checking and savings accounts, petty cash on hand, or cash equivalents.

Cash Basis Accounting—not allowed under the generally accepted accounting principles, this basis of accounting records revenues when cash is received and expenses when cash is paid.

Cash Equivalents—investments the company holds that will mature, and thus be turned into cash, within the next three months.

Certified Public Accountant (CPA)—an individual who has been licensed by their state to provide accounting services to the public.

Chart of Accounts—a listing of accounts used in the business, showing the names of the accounts and assigning an account number to each account.

Classified Balance Sheet—a balance sheet that includes subtotals for current assets and current liabilities.

Closing Entries—journal entries prepared as part of the closing process that zero out the temporary accounts (revenues, expenses, dividends) and adjust the retained earnings balance.

Common Size Balance Sheet—a form of vertical analysis in which the balance sheet line items are shown as a percentage of total assets.

Common Size Income Statement—a form of vertical analysis where the income statement line items are shown as a percentage of revenue.

Comparability—enhances the usefulness of financial information by making financial information comparable across different companies and over time.

Comparative Balance Sheet—a balance sheet that lists the results of two or more time periods, side by side in columns.

Comparative Income Statement—an income statement that lists the results of two or more time periods, side by side in columns.

Comprehensive Income—the change in equity of a business enterprise during a period from transactions and other events and circumstances from non-owner sources. It includes all changes in equity during a period except those resulting from investments by owners and distributions to owners.

Conceptual Framework—the foundation that all accounting rules (GAAP) are based upon.

Conservativism—the idea that when in doubt, an accountant should err on the side of underestimating good news and overestimating bad news.

Constrained Resource—any resource in the business that limits the production output due to its capacity.

Contributed Capital—increases in equity of a particular business enterprise resulting from transfers to it from other entities of something valuable to obtain or increase ownership interests (or equity) in it.

Contribution Format Income Statement—an income statement that is presented with clear distinctions between fixed and variable costs.

Contribution Margin—the excess of sales over variable costs.

Contribution Margin Ratio—contribution margin as a percent of total sales. This can be done by taking contribution margin per unit divided by selling price per unit, or by taking the total contribution margin for the month divided by the sales revenue for the month.

Controlling—the regular and ongoing process of gathering information to ensure the plan is being achieved.

Conversion Cost—direct labor plus manufacturing overhead.

Copyright—the exclusive right to publish, use, and sell literary, musical, artistic, or dramatic work.

Corporation—a business that is a separate legal entity from its owners, from both an accounting and a legal standpoint.

Cost—a sacrifice of a business's resources.

Cost Center—any area of the business where the manager has control over costs but not the revenues or investments.

Cost Effectiveness Constraint—the overarching constraint of financial reporting that the benefits of the information outweigh the costs of providing that information.

Cost of Goods Manufactured—the accumulation of the three product costs (direct materials, direct labor, and overhead) that were used in the goods that were completed, or manufactured, during a particular period.

Cost of Goods Sold Expense—represents the cost of the goods that are sold to customers.

Cost-Volume-Profit Analysis (CVP)—a type of analysis that shows the relationships between cost (fixed and variable) and sales volume and how those two variables impact profit (net operating income).

Credit—The right side of an account.

Credit Memo—a source document that shows any reductions in the amount due from a customer.

Creditor—anyone to whom the business owes money.

Current Assets—those assets that will be used up in the business (i.e., inventory) or turned into cash (i.e., accounts receivable) within one year, or within the company's operating cycle, whichever is longer.

Current Liabilities—those liabilities that will be paid or fulfilled within one year, or within the company's operating cycle, whichever is longer.

Current Ratio—a measure of a company's short-term ability to pay its debts as they come due and is the result of current assets divided by current liabilities.

Days to Collect—see "Average Collection Period."

Days to Sell—see "Average Sale Period."

Debit—The left side of an account.

Debt-to-Assets Ratio—a measure the proportion of total assets that are financed with debt (as opposed to equity), calculated as total liabilities divided by total assets.

Debt-to-Equity Ratio—a solvency ratio that compares a company's debt balance to the equity balance, calculated as total liabilities divided by total owners' equity.

Deferral Entries—adjusting entries for items where the cash transaction happens before the revenue is earned or the expense is incurred.

Degree of Operating Leverage—a ratio that measures how sensitive net operating income is to changes in sales, calculated as contribution margin divided by net operating income.

Depreciation—the systematic and rational allocation of an asset's cost over its useful life.

Differential Cost—a cost that differs between two alternatives.

Differential Revenue—revenue that differs between two alternatives.

Direct Cost—a cost that is conveniently and easily traceable to a particular cost object.

Direct Labor—labor cost that is conveniently and easily traceable to the product.

Direct Material—a raw material that is conveniently and easily traceable to the product.

Disclosures—disclosures of information regarding the nature of the business and its activities, additional information to explain financial statement line items, and information that might affect future cash flows, shown as parenthetical amounts noted right on the face of the financial statements, in paragraph style notes following the financial statements, and/or supplemental schedules and tables.

Distributions to Owners—decreases in equity of a particular business enterprise resulting from transferring assets, rendering services, or incurring liabilities by the enterprise to owners.

Dividend Payout Ratio—measures the percentage of net income earned by the company that was returned to investors in the form of dividends paid, calculated as dividends per share divided by earnings per share.

Dividend Yield—measures the investors return on investment in stock through the payment of dividends, calculated as dividends per share divided by market price per share.

Dividends—see "Distributions to Owners."

Double Entry—refers to the system of accounting developed by Italian merchants and still in use as the form of modern accounting used today.

Earnings per Share (EPS)—measures the net income earned in the current year per share of common stock, calculated as net income divided by the average number of common shares outstanding.

Elements of Financial Statements—the building blocks that accountants use to construct the financial statements: assets, liabilities, equity, investments by owners, distributions to owners, revenues, expenses, gains, losses, and comprehensive income.

Enterprise Resource Planning System (ERP)—a type of information system that does more than the traditional accounting and financial packages. ERP systems integrate many aspects of the business processes into one system.

Equity—the residual interest in the assets of an entity that remains after deducting its liabilities.

Equivalent Unit—an estimation of a completed unit in a process costing system.

Expenses—outflows or other using up of assets or incurrences of liabilities (or a combination of both) from delivering or producing goods, rendering services, or carrying out other activities that constitute the entity's ongoing major or central operations.

External Users of Information—users that don't work for the company but rely on the financial information from the business, such as investors, creditors, directors, and the government.

Extraordinary Repairs—those expenditures that occur infrequently and typically involve a large dollar amount. These expenditures increase the asset's value, as they either enhance efficiency, increase the capacity, or increase the useful life of the asset. These items are capitalized (recorded as an increase to the asset value) rather than being recorded as an expense.

Faithful Representation—the user can rely on the information being presented as complete, neutral, and free from errors.

FICA—this stands for Federal Insurance Contributions Act, but in the case of accounting, it refers to how the Act requires taxes to be charged on employees and employers for Social Security and Medicare. On a paycheck, taxes taken out of a check for this are labeled "FICA."

Financial Accounting—a type of accounting directed towards preparing information for external users to evaluate the company, emphasizing precision and following generally accepted accounting principles.

Financial Accounting Standards Board (FASB)—The private organization responsible for setting generally accepted accounting principles.

Financial Reporting—the process of providing financial information that is useful to external users.

Financial Statements—reports that summarize the financial results of the business.

Financing Activities—those activities that involve getting the funds necessary to cover the operating and investing activities of the business.

Finished Goods Inventory—an inventory account that represents the completed product that is packaged and ready for sale.

First In, First Out (FIFO)—an inventory costing method that assumes that the first goods in are the first goods to be sold.

Fixed Asset Turnover—measures a company's ability to utilize its fixed assets to generate sales revenue, calculated as net revenue divided by average net fixed assets.

Fixed Assets—see "Long-Lived Tangible Assets"

Fixed Cost—a cost that does not change with changes in an activity.

Flexible Budget—a budget that estimates revenues and costs based on the actual quantity of goods sold.

Form 10-K—The annual report public companies file with the SEC.

Form 10-Q—The quarterly reports public companies file with the SEC.

Franchise—the right to use products and services, trademarks, or perform activities within a specified geographic location.

Fraud—an attempt to deceive others for personal or financial gain.

Fraud Triangle—a representation of the three factors that must be present for someone to commit fraud. The three factors are incentive, opportunity, and rationalization.

Full-Disclosure Principle—any information that is not included in the primary financial statements that would affect the decisions of the users should be disclosed to the users.

FUTA—the Federal Unemployment Tax Act requires taxes to be charged to employers to cover benefits workers may receive during periods of unemployment.

Gain—increases in equity from peripheral or incidental transactions of an entity and from all other transactions and other events and circumstances affecting the entity except those that result from revenues or investments by owners.

General Ledger—the listing of all transactions that have been posted for each individual account, showing the balance in each account.

Generally Accepted Accounting Principles (GAAP)—the rules that accountants must follow when recording and presenting accounting information.

Going-Concern Assumption—the assumption that the business will continue to operate into the foreseeable future.

Goodwill—an intangible asset that represents what the entity paid to acquire another business over the amount the other business was worth on paper (net assets).

Gross Margin—see "Gross Profit Percentage."

Gross Profit—an important subtotal on the income statement that calculates the difference between revenues earned and the costs of goods sold.

Gross Profit Percentage—the percentage of sales remaining after deducting cost of goods sold, calculated as gross profit divided by sales.

High-Low Method—a method of splitting a mixed cost into its fixed and variable components that uses only two data points, the high activity level and the low activity level.

Horizontal Analysis—refers to financial statement analysis that looks at performance over time.

Income Statement—The financial statement showing the operating results of the business.

Indirect Cost—a cost that is not conveniently or easily traceable to a particular cost object.

Indirect Labor—labor in the production facility that is not conveniently or easily traced to the product.

Indirect Material—raw materials that are not conveniently and easily traced to the product.

Intangible Assets—assets with long lives that lack a tangible substance, such as trademarks, patents, copyrights, software, licensing rights, franchises, and goodwill.

Internal Control—a process designed to promote the effectiveness and efficiency of operations, reliability of financial reporting, and compliance with laws and regulations.

Internal Rate of Return Method—a method of evaluating capital budgeting decisions that calculates the rate of return that sets the net present value equal to zero.

Internal Users of Information—users that are employees of the company and rely on the financial to make decisions for the company, such as managers and executives.

Inventory—property the entity owns that is being held to sell to customers, or that will be used to produce the goods to sell to customers.

Inventory Turnover—measures how quickly a company cycles through its inventory, calculated as cost of goods sold divided by average inventory.

Investing Activities—those activities that involve making an investment in your business or other business through the purchase of stock.

Investment Center—an area of the business where the manager has control over revenues, costs, and making investments in fixed assets for the business.

Job-Order Costing—a method of assigning costs to cost objects (jobs) in companies that produce many different products or provide services, usually to customer specifications.

Journal Entry—the standard form for recording a transaction, showing the accounts affected by the transaction, as well as the amounts increased or decreased. Journal entries use the debit/credit framework to record increases or decreases in an account.

Last In, First Out (LIFO)—an inventory costing method that assumes the last goods in are the first goods to be sold.

Liabilities—probable future sacrifices of economic benefits arising from present obligations of a particular entity to transfer assets or provide services to other entities in the future as a result of past transactions or events.

Licensing Right—a right to use a specified item for a specific purpose.

Liquidity Ratios—measure a company's ability to pay its short-term obligations as they come due.

Long-Lived Tangible Assets—assets that have a physical, or tangible, substance that the entity intends to use in the business for at least one or more years.

Loss—decreases in equity from peripheral or incidental transactions of an entity and from all other transactions and other events and circumstances affecting the entity except those that result from expenses or distributions to owners.

Lower of Cost or Market (LCM)—an inventory valuation method that recognizes losses when inventory market values drop below the cost of the inventory.

Managerial Accounting—a type of accounting directed towards preparing information for internal users to run the business, emphasizing timeliness and utilizing estimation.

Manufacturer—an entity that makes the goods that it sells.

Manufacturing Cost—a cost incurred to manufacture, or make, a product.

Manufacturing Overhead—represents the costs of manufacturing a product aside from direct materials and direct labor.

Margin of Safety—the amount of sales over the break-even sales, which can be computed in units or dollars, or as a percentage.

Market Performance Ratios—measure the overall financial performance of the company in the eyes of the stockholders.

Master Budget—the preparation of the budgeted balance sheet and income statement and all necessary supporting schedules.

Matching Principle—expenses should be recognized in the period in which they are incurred to generate revenues.

Materiality—the level at which an item's omission or misstatement would be significant enough to impact a user's decision.

Materials Requisition—a source document used to request materials that are needed for production that is typically approved by a supervisor to ensure the materials are requested for a legitimate purpose.

Merchandiser—an entity that purchases goods, called merchandise inventory, and sells those goods to their customers.

Mixed Cost—a cost that includes both a fixed and a variable component.

Monetary Unit Assumption—the assumption that the activities of the business should be reported according to a common unit of measure, which is the U.S. dollar in the United States.

Multiple Step Income Statement—an income statement presentation in which the revenues and expenses from the core operations of the business are listed separately from those that are non-operating and not part of the core business activities.

Net Accounts Receivable—accounts receivable are recorded at the amount owed, less an estimate for what won't be collected due to customer non-payment.

Net Book Value—the cost of a fixed asset less the accumulated depreciation.

Net Income—the result of revenues and gains less all expenses and losses; shown on the bottom line of the Income Statement.

Net Loss—occurs when the calculation of net income results in a negative number.

Net Margin—see "Net Profit Margin."

Net Present Value Method—a method of evaluating capital budgeting decisions that discounts the future cash inflows of a project to the present date and nets the result against the initial investment.

Net Profit Margin—shows what percentage of every dollar earned in revenue was kept (not spent on costs) by the business as net income, calculated as net income divided by sales.

Net Property, Plant, and Equipment—long-lived tangible assets shown on the financial statements at cost less depreciation.

Net Revenue—total revenues less any sales returns, sales allowances, and sales discounts.

Nominal Accounts—see "Temporary Accounts."

Non-Current Assets—those assets that will not be used up in the business or turned into cash within one year or the company's operating cycle.

Non-Current Liabilities—amounts owed that are due in over one year's timeframe.

Non-Manufacturing Cost—a cost incurred by a manufacturer that was not part of making the product.

Non-Operating Costs—other costs incurred by a business that are incidental to operating the business, such as interest expense and income tax expense.

Normal Account Balance—the side the account increases on and the side you would expect the balance to be on.

Notes Payable—formal, documented loans owed to lenders (called promissory notes).

Notes Receivable—formal, documented loans given to borrowers (called promissory notes).

Operating Activities—those activities that involve running the business.

Operating Costs—the costs necessary to operate the business. These costs include the costs of goods provided to customers, labor, selling, and administrative costs.

Operating Cycle—measures the number of days it takes to turn inventory into cash. It is the combination of the average collection period and the average sale period.

Operating Income—an important subtotal on the income statement that shows the income from operating the business before any non-operating costs (those that are incidental to operating the business), such as interest expense and income tax expense.

Opportunity Cost—the benefit given up by selecting one alternative over the other.

Ordinary Repairs and Maintenance—expenditures that are necessary for the general upkeep of fixed assets. Examples of ordinary repairs and maintenance include things like oil changes on vehicles, new paint on walls, and yearly cleaning of equipment. Ordinary repairs and maintenance are recorded as an expense when incurred.

Partnership—a business owned by two or more individuals.

Patent—an exclusive right to use, manufacture, or sell an item.

Payback Method—a method of evaluating capital budgeting decisions that compares the initial cash outflows to the net cash inflows per year to determine how many years it takes for the company to recoup its initial investment.

Per Diem—a flat ret set by the business to reimburse employees for travel and related expenses.

Period Cost—see "Non-Manufacturing Cost."

Periodic Inventory System—a system that tracks and records inventory transactions at the end of the accounting period (typically the end of the month). This is usually accomplished through taking a physical count of inventory and using a formula to calculate the cost of the goods that were sold.

Permanent Accounts—those accounts that record real balances at a point in time. The permanent accounts are those that show up on the balance sheet: assets, liabilities, and equity accounts. Permanent accounts are not closed in the closing process.

Perpetual Inventory System—a system that tracks and records inventory transactions in real time. It is typically accomplished by using a system of bar codes and scanning tools.

Ponzi Scheme—a form of fraud in which investors in an entity are fraudulently paid a return on their investment out of newer investors' investments, not actually out of a return generated by the entity.

Porter's Five Forces Analysis—a framework to analyze the level of competition within an industry and analyze the business strategy in relation to that competition.

Post-Closing Trial Balance—a trial balance prepared after the closing entries are posted, showing the temporary accounts with zero balances and the permanent accounts with their final year end balances.

Posting—a process that copies the information from the journal and puts it in the general ledger.

Predetermined Overhead Rate (POHR)—a rate used to allocate manufacturing overhead to jobs in a job-order costing system.

Prepaid Expenses—a resource that an entity has paid for in advance.

Price-Earnings Ratio (PE Ratio)—measures investor expectations about a given company, calculated as market price per share divided by earnings per share.

Prime Cost—direct materials plus direct labor.

Private Company—a company that issues stock privately, not on public stock exchanges.

Process Costing—a method of assigning costs to products in companies that produce uniform products, usually on an assembly line basis.

Product Cost—see "Manufacturing Cost."

Profit Center—an area of the business where the manager has control over both the revenues and costs, but not investments.

Profitability Ratios—measure a company's ability to generate income during a specific time period.

Property, Plant, and Equipment (PP&E)—see "Long-Lived Tangible Assets"

Public Company—a company that has stock listed on public stock exchanges for purchase and sale.

Public Company Accounting Oversight Board (PCAOB)—an entity created by the Sarbanes–Oxley Act of 2002 to develop standards for the audits of public companies.

Purchase Order—a source document initiated by the customer that specifies what the customer wants to purchase.

Purchase Requisition—a source document used to request the purchase of goods that is typically approved by a supervisor to ensure the goods are requested for a legitimate purpose.

Quick Assets—those current assets that are cash or can be turned into cash quickly without having to rely on additional sales to customers, generally including only cash, marketable securities, accounts receivable, and short-term notes receivable.

Quick Ratio—a tougher version of the current ratio, measuring a company's ability to pay its short-term debts without having to rely on the sale of inventory to do so. Calculated as quick assets divided by current liabilities.

Ratio Analysis—a form of financial statement analysis that looks at the relationships between different financial statement items.

Raw Materials Inventory—an inventory account that represents the materials used as inputs to the final product.

Receiving Report—a source document recording the quantity and type of goods received.

Relevant Benefits—see "Differential Revenue."

Relevant Cost—see "Differential Cost."

Relevant Information—information that makes a difference in the decision process of the user.

Responsibility Accounting—a system of tracking financial performance that holds managers accountable for their decisions.

Responsibility Center—any part of an organization where a manager has control over the cost, profit, or investment.

Retailer—a merchandiser that buys goods from a wholesaler and sells those goods to the end consumer.

Retained Earnings—represents the profits earned by the business that have been kept in the business and not paid out to the owners as dividends or distributions.

Return on Assets (ROA)—measures a company's ability to utilize its total assets to generate net income, calculated as net income divided by average total assets.

Return on Equity (ROE)—compares the profits earned by a company to the dollar amount of owner's equity, calculated as net income divided by average stockholders' equity.

Return on Investment (ROI)—a method of evaluating the success of an investment, calculated as net operating income divided by average operating assets.

Revenue Recognition Principle—revenue should be recognized when goods or services are transferred to customers for the amount the company expects to be entitled to receive in exchange for those goods or services.

Revenue Variances—variances that are caused by charging a different price for goods or services than what was budgeted.

Revenues—inflows or other enhancements of assets of an entity or settlements of its liabilities (or a combination of both) from delivering or producing goods, rendering services, or other activities that constitute the entity's ongoing major or central operations.

Sales Invoice—a source document that shows the quantity and price of goods sent to customers, along with payment terms and total amount due.

Sales Order—a source document that takes the basic information from the customer purchase order and relays that information to various departments for approval.

Securities and Exchange Commission (SEC)—the government agency responsible for determining financial reporting requirements for public companies.

Self-Imposed Budget—a budget that is calculated and prepared by all levels of management.

Selling Cost—the costs of obtaining sales and delivering the finished product to the customer.

Selling, General, and Administrative Expenses (SG&A)—include expenses incurred to operate the business, not including the cost of the product.

Separate Entity Assumption—the assumption that the activities of the business are separate from the activities of the owner.

Service Company—an entity that provides services, rather than goods, to the customer.

Shipping Document—a source document indicating the quantity of goods being shipped.

Shrinkage—a merchandising industry term for missing inventory.

Simple Rate of Return Method—a method of evaluating capital budgeting decisions that compares the incremental net operating income of the project to the initial investment in the project to compute a return on investment.

Single Step Income Statement—a simple income statement presentation in which all revenues are listed first, followed by all expenses (usually listed from largest to smallest), and then net income is calculated at the bottom.

Sole Proprietorship—a business owned by one individual.

Solvency Ratios—measure a company's ability to pay its long-term obligations as they come due.

Source Document—provide evidence of the transaction and provide supporting details, such as invoices, purchase orders, and credit memos.

Specific Identification—an inventory costing method that tracks items by an individual identifier.

Spending Variances—variances that are caused by incurring expenses that are greater than or less than anticipated on the flexible budget.

Standard Cost—represents the benchmark for manufacturing costs per unit of product. Companies typically compute standard costs for direct materials, direct labor, and variable manufacturing overhead.

Statement of Cash Flows—the financial statement showing changes in cash over a given period of time.

Statement of Retained Earnings—the financial statement showing the roll-forward of the net income that is kept in the business over time, and not paid out as distributions.

Step Cost—a cost that increases in step increments.

Straight Line Depreciation—a method of calculating depreciation that records the same amount of depreciation each period.

Sub-Ledger—a detailed listing of items in a general ledger.

Sunk Cost—a cost that has already been incurred. Sunk costs are never differential costs and, therefore, never relevant in a decision.

Sustainability Accounting—a complement to financial accounting that helps provide a more complete view of a corporation's performance and its ability to create long-term value by defining qualitative and quantitative non-financial metrics on industry-specific sustainability topics likely to be of interest to investors and creditors.

SWOT Analysis—an analysis of a business in terms of its strengths, weaknesses, opportunities, and threats. It is usually shown in a matrix form.

T-Account—a simplified form of the general ledger.

Temporary Accounts—those accounts that track activity over a certain period of time. Temporary accounts must be "reset" or "zeroed out" at the end of each year to start tracking activity for the following year. The temporary accounts are revenues, expenses, and dividends/distributions.

Time Period Assumption—the assumption that the long life of a business can be divided up and measured in shorter periods, such as a month, a quarter, or a year.

Time Value of Money—the basic concept recognizing that a dollar today is worth more than a dollar in the future.

Timeliness—users have the financial information in enough time to use it in their decision-making process.

Times Interest Earned Ratio—a measure of a company's ability to pay interest payments on loans, calculated as (Net Income + Interest Expense + Income Tax Expense) / Interest Expense.

Top-Down Budget—a budget that originates from upper management and is then pushed down to levels of lower management and supervision.

Trademark—a name, slogan, or image that can be used to identify a company. Trademarks provide value to companies in the form of instant brand recognition and reputation.

Transaction—an exchange or event that affects the assets, liabilities, or equity of the business.

Trend Analysis—see "Horizontal Analysis."

Trial Balance—a listing of all accounts in financial statement order showing the debit or credit balances.

Understandability—when a reasonably informed user can comprehend the information provided.

Variable Cost—a cost that changes in direct proportion to changes in an activity.

Verifiability—financial information should be able to be independently verified or audited.

Vertical Analysis—typically displayed as a common size financial statement, refers to financial statement analysis that looks the relationships among financial statement amounts for a specific point in time.

Weighted–Average Cost—an inventory costing method that smooths the price changes by taking an average cost of inventory and using that to compute cost of goods sold and ending inventory.

Wholesaler—a merchandiser that buys goods from the manufacturer and sells them to a retailer.

Withholdings—amounts withheld from employees' gross pay to cover the costs of the employee share of any benefits, taxes, and other voluntary reductions.

Working Capital—the difference between current assets and current liabilities.

Work-in-Process Inventory—an inventory account that represents a partially completed product.

Further Reading

Accounting-Degree.Org. n.d. *The 10 Worst Corporate Accounting Scandals of All Time.* Accessed January 12, 2018. http://www.accounting-degree.org/scandals/.

accountingWEB. 2006. *Honoring the Patron Saint of Accountants on All Saints' Day.* November 1. Accessed January 12, 2018. https://www.accountingweb.com/aa/standards/honoring-the-patron-saint-of-accountants-on-all-saints-day.

AICPA. n.d. *About the AICPA.* Accessed January 12, 2018. https://www.aicpa.org/about.html.

———. 2017. *CPA Examination Passing Rates.* Accessed January 11, 2018. https://www.aicpa.org/content/dam/aicpa/becomeacpa/cpaexam/psychometricsandscoring/passingrates/downloadabledocuments/pass-rates-2017.pdf.

Block, Stanley B., Geoffrey A. Hirt, and Bartley R. Danielsen. 2014. *Foundations of Financial Management 15th Edition.* New York: McGraw-Hill Education.

Bloomberg Tax. n.d. "Impact of 2017 Tax Act on Business." Accessed March 8, 2018. https://www.lbmc.com/webfiles/TAX_RPT_Impact_of_2017_Tax_Act_on_Businesses_011118.pdf.

Brewer, Peter C., Ray H. Garrison, and Eric W. Noreen. *Introduction to Managerial Accounting.* 7th edition. New York: McGraw-Hill Education, 2016.

CCH Incorporated. *2014 U.S. Master Payroll Guide.* Chicago: Wolters Kluwer, 2014.

CPA Canada. *Eight Famous People Who Are Accountants.* October 20. 2017. Accessed January 12, 2018. https://www.cpacanada.ca/en/connecting-and-news/blogs/cpa-stories/eight-famous-people-who-are-accountants.

———. *The 10 Worst Corporate Accounting Scandals of All Time.* June 12, 2015. Accessed January 12, 2018. https://www.cpacanada.ca/en/connecting-and-news/news/professional-news/2015/june/the-10-worst-corporate-accounting-scandals.

Darby, Mary. "In Ponzi We Trust." *Smithsonian Magazine*, December. Accessed January 12, 2018. https://www.smithsonianmag.com/history/in-ponzi-we-trust-64016168/.

Devonish-Mills, Linda. "IMA's FRC Meets with the FASB." *Strategic Finance*, December 2017.

Elkins, Jenna. *10 Total Random but Interesting Facts about Accounting.* May 2017. Accessed January 12, 2018. https://nasba.org/blog/2017/05/22/10-totally-random-but-interesting-facts-about-accounting/.

FASB. *Convergence with the International Accounting Standards Board (IASB).* Accessed January 12, 2018. http://www.fasb.org/jsp/FASB/Page/SectionPage&cid=1218220079490.

———. *FASB About Us.* Accessed January 1, 2018. http://www.fasb.org/jsp/FASB/Page/LandingPage&cid=1175805317407.

Flesher, Dale L., Gary J. Previts, and Tonya K. Flesher. "Profiling the New Industrial Professionals: The First CPAs of 1896-97." *Business and Economic History,* Fall 1996, 252–266.

Gleeson-White. *Double Entry: How the Merchants of Venice Created Modern Finance.* New York: W. W. Norton & Company, Inc., 2011.

Henry, Byron, and Margaret Hicks. "A Survey of Perspectives on the Future of the Accounting Profession." *The CPA Journal,* 85, no. 8, 2015, pp. 10–12.

IFRS. *Who We Are.* Accessed January 12, 2018. http://www.ifrs.org/about-us/who-we-are/.

IIA North America. *About the IIA.* Accessed January 12, 2018. https://na.theiia.org/about-us/Pages/About-The-Institute-of-Internal-Auditors.aspx.

IMA. *About IMA.* Accessed January 12, 2018. https://www.imanet.org/about-ima?ssopc=1.

King, Thomas A. *More than a Numbers Game: A Brief History of Accounting.* Hoboken: John Wiley & Sons, Inc., 2006.

Kohler, Mark J. *The Tax and Legal Playbook.* Entrepreneur Press, 2015.

Lanen, William, Shannon W. Anderson, and Michael W. Maher. *Fundamentals of Cost Accounting.* New York: McGraw-Hill/Irwin, 2014.

London School of Business & Finance. *7 Famous People You Didn't Know Were Accountants.* March 13, 2014. Accessed January 12, 2018. https://www.lsbf.org.uk/blog/opinion-features/7-famous-people-didnt-know-accountants/950.

Mandell, Andrea. "Academy Will Keep Accounting Firm PwC for Next Oscars Show, Despite Flub." *USA Today*, March 29, 2017.

Marr, Bernard. *Machine Learning, Artificial Intelligency - And the Future of Accounting.* July 7, 2017. Accessed January 12, 2018. https://www.forbes.com/sites/bernardmarr/2017/07/07/machine-learning-artificial-intelligence-and-the-future-of-accounting/#7bfe19052dd1.

NASBA. *NASBA: About Us.* Accessed January 12, 2018. https://nasba.org/about/.

Phillips, Fred, Robert Libby, and Patricia A. Libby. *Fundamentals of Financial Accounting,* 5th edition. New York: McGraw-Hill Education, 2016.

Previts, Gary J., and Mer. *A History of Accountancy in the United States.* Columbus: Ohio State University Press, 1998.

Robert Half. *2018 Salary Guide for Accounting and Finance Professionals.* Salary Guide, Menlo Park: Robert Half, 2018.

Rogers, Jean. "The Future Is Here: What to Know about Sustainability Accounting." *California CPA,* 85 (3), 2016, pp. 17–19.

SEC. *EDGAR: Company Filings Search.* Accessed December 13, 2017. https://www.sec.gov/edgar/searchedgar/companysearch.html.

———. "How to Read a 10-K." Accessed February 15, 2018. https://www.sec.gov/fast-answers/answersreada10khtm.html.

Soll, Jacob. *The Reckoning: Financial Accountability and the Rise and Fall of Nations.* New York: Basic Books, 2015.

Spiceland, David J., James F. Sepe, Mark W. Nelson, and Wayne B. Thomas. *Intermediate Accounting,* 8th edition. New York: McGraw-Hill Education, 2016.

Sustainability Accounting Standards Board. *Alcoholic Beverages Sustainability Accounting Standard.* June, 2015.

Weltman, Barbara. *Small Business Taxes 2008.* Hoboken: John Wiley & Sons, 2008.

Whittington, O. Ray, and Kurt Pany. *Principles of Auditing & Other Assurance Services.* New York: McGraw-Hill Education, 2016.

Wild, John J., Ken W. Shaw, and Barbara Chiappetta. *Fundamental Accounting Principles.* New York: McGraw-Hill/Irwin, 2013.

Index

Note: (ill.) indicates photos and illustrations.

current portion of long-term debt, 28–29
debt, 29
definition, 27
noncurrent, 28
notes payable, 27
"other liabilities," 28
types of accounts, 27
licensing right, 152
Liddell, Chuck, 284
limited liability company (LLC), 264
limited liability partnership (LLP), 263
liquidity ratios. *See also* asset management ratios; market performance ratios; profitability ratios; solvency ratios
  acid test ratio, 74
  current ratio, 73
  measurement of, 71
  quick ratio, 73–74
  short term creditors, use of, 71
  solvency ratios vs., 74–75
  working capital, 72
long-lived tangible asset, 24–25
long-term creditors, 75
losses, 32. *See also* assets; comprehensive income; equity; gains; liabilities; revenues
Lotus 1-2-3, 9
lower of cost or market rule for inventory, 139–40, 140 (ill.)

M

machine learning, 289
Madoff, Bernie, 287
make-or-buy decision, 247 (ill.), 247–49, 248 (ill.)
management team, 265
managerial accounting
  avoidable cost, 242
  break-even point, 234, 238, 240 (ill.), 240–41
  business performance, 256
  capital budgeting, 256, 260
  cash inflows, 257–58
  cash outflows, 257
  constrained resource, 251
  constrained resource decision, 251–54, 252 (ill.), 253 (ill.), 254 (ill.)
  contribution format income statement, 231–32, 232 (ill.), 233
  contribution margin, 232–33
  contribution margin per unit, 232–33
  contribution margin ratio, 233
  cost center, 255
  cost structure, 236–38, 237 (ill.)

cost-volume-profit analysis, 233
cost-volume-profit equation, 233–34
cost-volume-profit graph, 234–35, 235 (ill.)
decentralized organization, 254–55
decision making, 241
degree of operating leverage, 236, 236 (ill.)
differential cost, 241–42
differential revenue, 242
drop or retain a segment decision, 243–47, 244 (ill.), 245 (ill.), 246 (ill.)
financial accounting vs., 3–4
internal rate of return, 260
investment center, 255–56
make-or-buy decision, 247 (ill.), 247–49, 248 (ill.)
margin of safety, 239
margin of safety in units, 239
margin of safety percentage, 240
net operating income, 233
net present value method, 259–60
opportunity cost, 243, 248 (ill.), 248–49
payback method, 258
preference decision, 257
profit center, 255
relevant costs and relevant benefits, 241, 242, 243
responsibility accounting, 254
responsibility center, 255
return on investment, 256
screening decision, 257
shared fixed costs, 246 (ill.), 246–47
simple rate of return method, 259
special order decision, 249 (ill.), 249–50, 250 (ill.)
sunk cost, 242
target profit, 238–39
time value of money, 258–59
manufacturer, 158, 160 (ill.)
manufacturing cost, 162
manufacturing overhead, 163, 176, 178, 184–86, 185 (ill.), 188–89, 189 (ill.), 196
manufacturing overhead budget, 210–11, 211 (ill.)
margin of safety, 239
margin of safety in units, 239
margin of safety percentage, 240
market performance ratios. *See also* asset management ratios; liquidity ratios; profitability ratios; solvency ratios
  book value per share, 89
  dividend payout ratio, 88
  dividend yield ratio, 88

earnings per share, 86–87
  investors' use of, 86
  measurement of, 86
  price-earnings ratio, 87–88
marketing strategy, 267
Marr, Bernard, 288–89
master budget, 203
materiality, 13
materials requisition, 116–17
Matthew, Saint, 285
meal and entertainment expenses, 276–77
measurement, 18
measurement attributes, 20
merchandiser
  customer payment, 132–33, 132–33 (ill.)
  definition, 126, 158
  free on board (FOB) destination mean, 128
  free on board (FOB) shipping point, 128, 128 (ill.)
  inventory purchaser, 127–28, 128 (ill.)
  periodic inventory system, 126
  perpetual inventory system, 126–27
  purchase allowances, 129, 129 (ill.)
  purchase discount, 129, 130 (ill.)
  purchase payments, 129–30, 130 (ill.)
  purchase returns, 129, 129 (ill.)
  sales allowances, 131, 132, 132 (ill.)
  sales discount, 132, 132 (ill.)
  sales of inventory, 130–31, 131 (ill.)
  sales returns, 131, 131 (ill.), 132
  service company vs., 126
  shrinkage, 127
  2/10, n/30, 128
Mesopotamia, 4–5, 5 (ill.)
metrics, 267–68
Microsoft Excel, 269, 269 (ill.)
mileage rate, 277
minimum wage, 272
mixed costs, 169, 169 (ill.), 170, 171–72
modern accounting, 5–6
monetary unit assumption, 18
monitoring, 121
Morgan, John Pierpont, 284
multiple-step income statement, 42 (ill.), 42–43

N

National Association of State Boards of Accountancy (NASBA), 282–83
net accounts receivable, 23